encyclopedia of
SCIENCE FICTION

encyclopedia of
SCIENCE

consultant editor robert holdstock

FICTION
Foreword by isaac asimov

First published 1978 by
Octopus Books Limited
59 Grosvenor Street
London W1

© 1978 Octopus Books

ISBN 0 7064 0756 3

Produced by Mandarin Publishers Limited
22a Westlands Road
Quarry Bay, Hong Kong

Printed in Italy by New Interlitho SpA.

contents

I suppose it is a measure of the richness of the field of science fiction that no two of its practitioners are liable to agree on even something as fundamental as its definition – or on the boundaries that encompass it, and on where one draws the dividing line between itself and realistic fiction, or between itself and fantasy.

With eleven contributors to this encyclopedia, each making his own assumptions and expressing his own views, the reader may well grow confused on such matters. I hasten, therefore, to seize upon the invitation to write this introduction, in order to place my own view at the very beginning.

Realistic fiction, as I see it, deals with events played against social backgrounds not significantly different from those that are thought to exist now, or to have existed at some time in the past. There is no reason to suppose that the events in realistic fiction could not, conceivably, have taken place exactly as described.

Science fiction and fantasy (which we may lump together as 'surrealistic fiction' if we wish) deal, on the other hand, with events played against social backgrounds that do not exist today, and have not existed in the past. Examples would include the social satire of *Gulliver's Travels*, the talking animals of *The Jungle Book* or *The Voyages of Dr. Dolittle*, the supernatural influences of *Paradise Lost* or *The Lord of the Rings*, and the scientific extrapolation of *War of the Worlds* or *Rendezvous with Rama*.

To distinguish between the two major varieties of surrealistic fiction, I would say that the surreal background of the story in science fiction could, conceivably, be derived from our own by appropriate changes in the level of science and technology. The change could represent an advance, as in the development of colonies on Mars, or in the successful interpretations of signals from extraterrestrial life-forms. It could represent a retreat, as in a study of the destruction of our technological civilization by nuclear or ecological disaster. By a liberal interpretation of what scientific advances we can make, we could include such not-likely items as time-travel, faster-than-light velocities and so on.

Fantasy, on the other hand, portrays surreal backgrounds that cannot reasonably be supposed to be derived from our own by any change in the level of science and technology. (Or if they can be so derived, given enough ingenuity, the author does not bother to do so – as Tolkien scorns to try to fit Middle-Earth anywhere into human history). Given this definition of science fiction, we can see that the field can scarcely have existed in its true sense until the time came when the concept of social change through alterations in the level of science and technology had been evolved in the first place.

Through all of history, science and technology did advance and did, in so doing, alter society. However, those changes progressed so slowly in time and spread so slowly in space that, within an individual's own lifetime, no change was visible. Hence, human history – barring trivial changes through war and dynastic succession, or fantasy changes through supernatural intervention –

was viewed as essentially static.

The advance of science and technology, however, is cumulative, and each advance tends to encourage a more rapid further advance. Eventually, the rate of change, and the extent of the effect of that change on society, becomes great enough to be detected in the space of an individual lifetime. The future is then, for the first time, discovered.

This took place, clearly, with the development of the Industrial Revolution. It makes sense, then, to suppose that science fiction had to be born some time after 1800 and most likely in Great Britain, and that its birth came about as the literary response to this discovery. Brian Aldiss considers *Frankenstein*, published in Great Britain in 1818, to be the first true science fiction story and I tend to agree with him.

In supplying a society that is technologically changed from that of the present, there is no need to produce one that will, in actual fact, some day come to exist. One which is not at all likely to come into being in any way can still be just as entertaining and have the necessary values to be successful.

In the search, however, for a society which, although different, will carry conviction, and which will be consistent with the science and society of today, a writer does sometimes deal with matters which, eventually come to pass. Atomic bombs and trips to the Moon are classic examples.

To suppose that this predictive aspect of science fiction, this foreseeing of details, is the truly impressive thing about science fiction, serves, however, only to trivialize the field. What is important about science fiction, even crucial, is the very thing that gave it birth – the perception of change through technology. It is not that science fiction predicts this particular change or that that makes it important; it is that it predicts *change*.

Since the Industrial Revolution first made the perception of change through technology clear, the rate has continued to increase, until now the wind of change has risen from a zephyr to a hurricane. It is change, continuing change, inevitable change, that is the dominant factor in society today. No sensible decision can be made any longer without taking into account not only the world as it is, but the world as it will be – and naturally this means that there must be an accurate perception of the world as it will be. This, in turn, means that our statesmen, our businessmen, our everyman must take on a science fictional way of thinking, whether he likes it or not, or even whether he knows it or not. Only so can the deadly problems of today be solved.

Individual science fiction stories may seem as trivial as ever to the blinder critics and philosophers of today – but the core of science fiction, its essence, the concept about which it revolves, has become crucial to our salvation, if we are to be saved at all.

And for that reason, a wide-ranging, broad-stroked view of the field, as in this 'Encyclopedia', is as important a literary work as can well be imagined.

locations

Robert Holdstock

The importance of science lingers in science fiction, but increasingly tempered with an emphasis on the human condition. At its core sf is no different from any other fiction, but to the sf writer there is a fundamental crisis of importance; to concentrate on fiction is to deny space to the fascinating but superficial features that make sf different.

This is a book about the ingredients of science fiction: the symbols, the themes, the ideas, the settings, the novels and the writers, the magazines and the social motivations.

There are 11 contributors, each with his own idea of what science fiction is or – in some cases – what it is not. As Isaac Asimov has said, there are many definitions of science fiction around (perhaps not one for every writer) and the direction sf takes at any one time is the direction its practitioners choose to take it. It is as hard, and as pointless, to pin sf down to a convenient nutshell definition as it is to define the content of children's fiction, or historical fiction. On the whole, however, an sf novel has its basis in an imaginary future; the bulk of the exceptions are novels set in imaginary earths – the parallel world – or upon imaginary worlds, or in the historical past where a single ingredient, usually a time traveller, has come from an imaginary future. If science fiction is to be distinguished from any other fiction, then, it is in the chosen setting, the location. This book is about locations. But the symbolic or literary use of those locations is ultimately concerned with that same human condition that is the concern of all fiction. Our book deals with that as well. If individual feelings about science fiction emerge from these articles then perhaps that adds an extra dimension to the volume, which in one sense stands as the longest definition of sf in print.

Whatever sf is, and wherever it came from, two things are clear: these questions will remain endlessly fascinating and endlessly irrelevant; and there will never be agreement upon whether or not that word 'science' is important. Not for years has sf been consciously used to fictionalize science. Infrequently is sf a fiction of extrapolated science in the sense that Hugo Gernsback thought of 'science' when he wrote, in a 1932 issue of *Wonder Stories*:

> If an author [in past years] made a statement as to certain future instrumentalities, he usually found it advisable to adhere closely to the possibilities of science as it was then known.
>
> Many modern science fiction authors have no such scruples. They do not hesitate to throw scientific plausibility overboard, and embark upon a policy of what I might call scientific magic, in other words, science that is neither plausible nor possible. Indeed it overlaps the fairy tale, and often goes the fairy tale one better.

In the last 20 years, however, the word science has become so loose, so wide, that quite suddenly sf has undergone a perspective change – human sciences, social sciences, and even para-sciences, these have always been the hardcore of science fiction; but then, the human and social sciences have always been the hardcore of *all* fiction. Redefined, and more intellectually considered, the Gernsback approach to sf still stands strong among many sf writers, but perhaps David Gerrold, one of America's most active young writers, has come closest to illustrating the much modified thinking of what the true value of science fiction is when he wrote in two different anthologies in the early 1970s:

> Science fiction is theology for the Modern Man. It is a theology that is based upon the scientific method, a method that is central to the growth of our present day technology and (you should pardon the expression) civilization. *Protostars 1971.*
>
> As the field has grown it has matured and each succeeding generation of writers has become more and more involved with what it is to be human. *Generation 1972.*

So the importance of science lingers in science fiction, but increasingly tempered with an emphasis on the human condition. And yet, even to relate sf to the 'scientific method' is to impose a false scientific value upon it. At its core sf is no different from any other fiction – to the literate writer there is a fundamental crisis of importance: to concentrate on *fiction* is to deny space to the fascinating but superficial features that make sf different. To concentrate on the imaginative metaphors – the gimmicks and gadgets – is to deny the fictional core, the central importance of sf as fiction as entertaining and didactic as any fiction, as much a part of the greater framework of literature as an historical novel or a novel set firmly and squarely in the 1970s.

This was very much the thinking in the early 1960s as, on both sides of the Atlantic, anarchy spread in sf, to the horror of the sf 'technicians', and to the delight of readers tired of the 'idea-as-hero' philosophy that seemed to be offered as the perennial excuse for the awfulness of so much science fiction. The 'New Wave' started quietly, almost self-consciously, often manifesting as a strong double standard in editorials, or yearly reviews. Judith Merril who, with Michael Moorcock, Samuel Delany and Brian Aldiss, was part of the core of literate thinking on which the change to a more speculative, less scientific fiction was based, drew attention in *The Years Best SF (9)*, in 1962, to a survey among writers on what they believed set sf apart from other literary forms:

> the overwhelming majority gave as their main answer . . . the freedom offered in sf, as compared with other contemporary forms: freedom to express any and all opinions, to explore unconventional and unpopular ideas, to examine human problems and relationships and to experiment with style and technique.

Science fiction, then, had the potential to be 'dangerous', to criticize and satirize the contemporary environment in ways that, in many countries, were difficult because of popular opposition to such criticism. It didn't work out.

Harlan Ellison's *Dangerous Visions*, a collection of stories which he hoped would reflect the title, appeared in 1967; alas, the stories, though excellent, were not even mildly threatening. *New Worlds*, around which 'speculative fiction' was centred, was in trouble for 'obscenity' by 1968, having alienated a large amount of its audience who gave, as their reasons, what became a fashionable word in science fiction in the late sixties: obscurity.

Samuel Delany and Marilyn Hacker's editorial in *Quark/3 1971*, has an undertone of disappointment:

> One's only objection to science fiction 'of value as social criticism' is precisely that it *failed* to be dangerous, because of an aesthetic choice by the authors deferring to 'popular entertainment'.

Written about the science fiction of an earlier decade the words, in part at least, are nonetheless appropriate to several of the commendable but unrealized ideals of speculative fiction. But not all. When Dave Kyle wrote, in his *Pictorial History of Science Fiction 1976* that 'Without [*New Worlds* magazine] the New Wave proponents lost their crusade', he could hardly have been more wrong. The science fiction of the 1970s shows a heightened literary awareness among new writers that surely is due entirely to the efforts of the 'New Wave proponents'. Writers today are far more concerned with the use of the ingredients of science fiction as literary metaphor, rather than *only* as imaginative ideas for imaginative adventures. And few such writers would claim that science and technology were anything but two of many 'tools' that they can draw upon for their work. It is the nature of humanness that increasingly fascinates the sf writer, and science fiction's unique ability to explore that nature from a position of imaginary retrospect. The future, the alien world, the parallel world, these are the locations of sf, the settings of the fantastic, that allow the writer an almost irresistable imaginative freedom, a unique vantage point for intellectualizing and entertainment. What motivates the sf writer, in general, is an extreme case of what motivates all artists – John Fowles put it best during a recent television interview when he said that art,

concerned with the unknown, strives towards the unknowable; mystery has *energy*.

Sf is centrally concerned with the relationship between man and those mysterious shores of the unknown, and the energy generated – the imaginative energy, the intellectual energy – is so great that it increasingly shapes culture as well as continuing to reflect it.

For example, the symbol of the alien was, for many years, more a reflection of the writer's naïvity and cultural conditioning than it was good entertainment – one 'hard core' sf editor, during the pulp years, did not object to alien beings featuring in his magazine, provided that by the end of the story they were proved inferior to human beings. Now the theme of alienness has a new importance to the sf writer for, though it can be used to illustrate the distance between worlds, more importantly it can be used to explore the distance between men, and also of the uncertainty of our present reality, and of time, and of belief.

We need very urgently to know that we are not strangers and aliens in the physical Universe . . . We did not arrive like birds on barren branches: we grew out of this world, like leaves and fruit. Our Universe 'humans' just as a rosebush 'flowers'. We are living in a world . . . where science has made us theoretically aware of our

Two views of the future – the optimism of star flight counterpointed against the pessimism of a decayed future earth in this striking picture by Tony Roberts

interdependence with the entire domain of organic and inorganic nature.

Alan Watts, in *LSD: The Consciousness Expanding Drug 1964.*

Labelling

Twenty-five years ago Theodore Sturgeon bemoaned the fact that sf was continually judged on the basis of its worst examples. He was right, and things have not changed. But in the 1970s there is a new source of discontent among many of the writers of science fiction. Why is a novel judged as science fiction at all? Why is it not just judged as a novel? The question may seem as irrelevant as all the questions asked of science fiction – what are you, where do you come from, what will you write about now that man has reached Mars? – but the question of the *label* is a touchy one.

And that is what 'sf' is, of course – a commercial label, an easy means of packaging the vast quantity of literature that is not set in the present or the past.

It ought not to matter, but the invention of the label (by Hugo Gernsback, we are told, who called it 'scientifiction', or 'stf', a label recently picked up again by Ted White at *Amazing Stories*, though probably for reasons of irony) has had two effects. First it has created a false sense of continuity and influence between science fiction of all decades, from the 1880s to the present. Thus, when you finally accept the 'arguments' that Mary Shelley's *Frankenstein* was an early sf novel, instantly she is placed at the beginning of a line or progression that ends, say, with Ursula Le Guin and Doris Piserchia, which is nonsensical. There really isn't any link, emotionally, conceptually, or even evolutionally, between a modern novel using the symbols of the fantastic, and, for example, a pulp space adventure of 40 years ago. It is a body of readership that links the decades, not writers or genres. A genre grows out of a reader-population's demand for 'more of the same', and there are always writers – usually bad writers – ready to supply the cheap cuts of the body literate, to fulfil the popular demand; watch out for the effect of *Star Wars* on the written market! Meanwhile the true novelists continue to write with their own ideas, for themselves, for the expression of self, writing with their own voices, producing their own unique vision. Willis McNeilly, speaking at the 1976 Dublin SF Writers Conference:

> The artist is a fabulous artificer who moulds reality and his own vision until they combine almost mystically. The only thing a writer has to offer is his own interpretation of the Universe – he must not write what the *editor* wants. The ability to fantasize is necessary for survival. Fantasy is advanced imagination used in the process of a redefinition of reality.

To be labelled science fiction doesn't alter the words of a novel, but don't be misled into believing you are necessarily reading words in common with, or influenced by, words of 40 years ago. Nor, for that matter, words and ideas in common with the other sf books on the same shelf. This is the second irksome affect of the sf label, the sense of unity and interdependence it creates among all modern novels

labelled sf; there really is as much distance between Robert Silverberg and Perry Rhodan as there is between John Fowles and Timothy Lea. It would be completely pointless to compare books by those two writers, and yet in science fiction such comparison, such lumping together, is never questioned. How many times have you heard someone say they can't stand science fiction because they once tried to read an sf book and it was awful? If you hate one it makes sense, of course, to hate them all. And if you think that attitude is naïve, then keep watching the book review programmes on TV, and count the number of literate and intelligent people who patronize an sf selection as 'good for a science fiction book,' or having 'typical sf cardboard characters'.

The roots of this attitude again can be seen in the pulp magazines, wonderful in so many ways, and yet such mixed blessings. They were a market set up specifically to exploit future fiction, and ultimately they caused the exclusion of this certain form of fiction from more general areas – if the story features the future, or an alien world, then it's science fiction, and there are sf magazines for that sort of thing. Thus adventure and literary vision become lumped together, and inevitably the latter suffers. Orwell, Huxley, Stapledon, Kingsley Amis, are just a few who escaped the pernicious influence of the 'genre' for the obvious reason of their existing literary standing. The tradition, and inevitably the clichés, continue; how many potentially major writers have become major *science fiction* writers, not particularly proud of, but totally dominated by, the false image of a false literary classification?

This, at least, is the argument, and it is not universally felt among writers of science fiction. Quite obviously there are those who stand apart from the rest, who are read because their individual work is valued, and not because it is part of a genre. Others are only too happy to be writing in a field with a guaranteed audience. And in France young political novelists have rapidly realized that to write within the framework of the future, and thus to be labelled 'sf', means they will reach a much wider audience, for science fiction sells far better than straight political fiction, at least in some publishing houses.

In the final analysis, however, it is the enormous potential of science fiction, its versatility, its boundlessness, its creative energy that is important, and which all writers value.

S.F. Art

There is no question but that so-called sf art is great fun, and though it is totally irrelevant to science fiction *literature*, sf markets have always worked very hard on their visual interpretation. Throughout the

Painting by Melvyn illustrating Flash Gordon, science fiction's ever popular pulp mainstay. The pulp influence in sf is still a major part of the field, but science fiction has now grown big enough to comfortably accommodate all extremes

13

decades when pulp sf magazines were freely available, the cover pictures showed what sf never was – a continual sequence of improbable aliens, sex-crazed robots, Hollywood femininity and Buck Rogers masculinity – rarely did a cover relate to the content and this fact must have been well known to those who bought the magazines. But their imaginations were anticipating the content and this is all that mattered. Galactic Empires *were* falling in the pages, pirates *were* walking space gang-planks, strange creatures *were* living in utopias on Pluto – there might not have been quite the sexy or garish encounter featured on the cover, but perhaps the covers were visual prompts to the reader, allowing him to flesh out the action and the characters (which, certainly, often needed something along these lines). *Astounding Science Fiction* stands out during the pulp era, and after, as never succumbing to these cheap and effective artistic clichés. Its covers were usually inspired by content, and those that weren't were often those wonderful astronomical scenes, usually by Chesley Bonestell.

The clichés continue to feature, better drawn, many of them exquisite – there is a freedom of form available to the commercial artist today that has been hard won. The rocket ships still thunder through ninety degree turns, the weird and the wonderful still catch the eye, the more naturalistic looking women still glance coyly – but more often arrogantly – from below the overprinting, the Statue of Liberty still stands, crumbling and corroded above the wastelands of man's domain – but now the range of vision is as wide as the increased range of expectation. To assay contemporary sf art is to assay a field of visual metaphor as extensive, as searching, as that attempted by the novelist – art reflects energy and the imaginative energy of artist and sf writer have never been closer – when they meet, when the

Where would sf be without the Statue of Liberty? For decades it has towered or crumbled above the wasteland of deserted earth – giants have uprooted it, aliens have found it curious, Charlton Heston has gazed up at it and realized which planet his new ape-infested homeland really is. How strange that the symbol of Liberty, of optimism, has become a symbol of science fiction's pessimistic view of the future

The striking painting by J. Burns draws together the several unconscious moods of science fiction – the imaginative vision of the star, the outward striving of man's intellect, coupled with the crumbling of that which is artificial – the natural order of decay – Pegasus, the symbol of man's conquering of the heavens, fading into dusk's oblivion

position is reversed, how quickly many of the modern pictures in this book will seem as feeble, as devoid of dynamism as those early pulp covers with their very limited aspirations.

Wild Talents

Teaching science fiction is big business in the 1970s. The imaginative symbols of sf are as relevant to children in this decade as any historical symbol ever was, and science fiction is particularly well suited to the task of education since learning and imaginative expression are very closely linked. In higher education sf is gradually slipping into English Literature courses everywhere, nudging aside, if not Shakespeare, at least the drier narratives of the last century.

Teaching sf *writing* is something else that has grown big in the 1970s, taking off from the Milford writer's circle organized by Damon Knight. This is a professional meeting for discussions of the state of the art by reference to participant's own submitted work, stories that are very thoroughly dissected in a critical way. James and Judy Blish brought the concept to England and after a shaky start Milford UK and Milford USA run a popular and very stimulating meeting of professionals every year. Semi-professional critical groups have sprung up all over the USA, Australia and the United Kingdom (where Oxford University runs an excellent circle). In France, the occasional gatherings of writers for such mutual criticism usually ends – I am reliably told – close to bloodshed.

In no way can these be considered writing *schools*, but yes, there are those too.

The big three are (were) Clarion, Tulane and Washington. Schools frequently spring up and die down. There are workshops in Australia and very soon there will be writing workshops in France, Germany and Sweden. A brief course at Reading

This remarkable series of flying cities, landing on an arid world, is by Angus McKie

disciplines of authorship. Whether they have learned to *write* they still have to discover.

Out of the early Clarion workshops, in the early 1970s, came three anthologies – stories by the trained, articles by the trainers. We have these three collections to judge the success of this sort of 'education', and we have the subsequent success or failure of the writers. The anthologies indicate one thing very clearly – that science fiction writing cannot be taught with complete success. They are depressing things, these collections, accumulations of images, half considered ideas, half finished stories – the voice is monotonously similar. On the basis of the collections, at least when considered from an English point of view, Clarion was only half successful. But Clarion and all the others were far more successful than that! The stories in the collections were much influenced by the teachers, by unlike minds. The ultimate lesson of any such informal education is that there is nothing more important than a writer's own voice or vision, and this is something inborn, instinctive, something that cannot be diminished or encouraged by anything but the writer's own experience. Whether they will admit it or not (after all, they had fun) those few writers who tried the writing-schools and have now become loud voices in the sf literary field have discovered this fact. They are the writers whose talent, whose originality, would have brought them to the forefront no matter what but perhaps the schools helped speed that rise: Ed Bryant, F. M. Busby, Geo. Alec Effinger, Robert Thurston, Lisa Tuttle, Alan Brennart, Vic Webb and others.

Perhaps the Australian workshops will similarly sharpen the vision of that country's young writers. Australian sf is neglected, appearing in the UK and the USA more by chance than design. But judging by *The Altered Eye*, a collection of fiction, articles, impressions and dialogues from the Booth Lodge, Melbourne, SF Writing Workshops, organized by Bruce Gillespie and run by Ursula Le Guin, there is as much potential talent in Australia as in America. Christopher Priest calls it a 'wild talent', an impression he gained when running the second such workshop with Vonda McIntyre in 1977. The book of that course has also just been published (by Norstrilia Press) and is called *The View from the Edge*. Both of these collections are strongly reminiscent of the Clarion anthologies; the stories have that raw edge of passion, and passionate concern with the written word – the writers are already distinct voices: David Grigg, Pip Maddern, Edward Mundie, Rob Gerrand, Randal Flynn and many others, and if they can find the outlets for their stories they can surely grow as fast as the young writers of the United States.

Are there outlets for the new writer? Perhaps more so in the 1970s than at any other time. David Gerrold put together three collections of 'rising stars': *Generation*, *Protostars*, *SF Emphasis* and drew attention to, among others, Pamela Sargant, andy offut, Stephen Goldin, Alice Laurance, Pg Wyal, and Chelsea Quinn Yarbro. No doubt he will put together more.

All the American magazines pay a great deal of attention to their unsolicited submissions (although

University in England, run by Ursula Le Guin, is Britain's only claim to a writing workshop to date.

The idea of a writer's workshop is simple, and draws much on the pattern of criticism started by Damon Knight. A large group of potential writers, unsold, substantially untried, are taught by professional writers of enormous experience – Samuel Delany, Frederik Pohl, Ursula Le Guin, Harlan Ellison, Christopher Priest, Damon Knight and many others – and by writers who have only recently brushed off the dust of their struggle for professional acceptance – Vonda McIntyre and Gene Wolfe are the names that spring to mind. The young writers *write* – on themes, gimmicks, words or images. The pieces they produce are read, criticized, hammered and torn asunder, rebuilt and reconsidered. The weaknesses of their writing are strengthened. The strengths are put into context. At the end of the course the amateurs know better the rules and

one charges for the privilege), Ben Bova's *Analog* perhaps most of all; no new sf magazine would dare begin without declaring that they will be hunting for new talent. Although Ken Bulmer's *New Writings in SF* is temporarily shelved, the standard hopefully will soon be picked up. Always interested in the new writer, this was the foremost testing ground for new talent in Britain and Australia. Peter Weston's *Andromeda* reflects and carries on this interest. Both major hardcover science fiction publishers in Britain have produced anthologies of new writers, and will presumably do so again. The first *Gollancz/Sunday Times SF Stories* and Faber's *Supernova 1* introduced, among others, Garry Kilworth, Chris Morgan, Robin Douglas, Don West and Cliff Lawther, writers whose names will become familiar over the next few years. Which brings me back to the *Octopus Encyclopedia of Science Fiction*, and its wide-angled look at many of the ingredients of science fiction as space has allowed.

Brian Stableford, a young critic and novelist, has nobly tackled the science fiction of the late Victorian and Edwardian eras, looking in particular at the great social and technological changes that were working through the imaginations of the writers of the time to produce many of the flights of fantasy we would now call 'classics'. Christopher Priest, a young novelist and critic who began his writing career during the heyday of *New Worlds Speculative Fiction*, takes a retrospective view of the 'New Wave' in the 1960s. Harry Harrison, well known for his fabulously outlandish fictional inventions, looks affectionately at all that hardware which science fiction has invoked, while Chris Morgan, a new writer and a very worthy one, does the same for the currently more popular 'software' of science fiction, the aliens, the modified men, the alien worlds. Mike Ashley, whose knowledge of sf magazines is legendary, surveys the pulps and the not-so-pulps and looks at the good and the bad that was printed within their pages; he has also written the short but excellent contribution on sf worldwide. Malcolm Edwards surveys the state of the art as it is today, and draws attention to the major names of the 1970s, and to the emerging names (look closely, now). Douglas Hill, a writer and critic, draws all these things together in his survey of the great themes of science fiction, and how these themes have changed through the decades in the hands of different writers. Patrick Moore discusses the science in science fiction, and speculates on the possibilities of some of the more exotic predictions coming true (how easily, for example, we accept faster than light travel!). Alan Frank, a film expert and sometime film extra (author of several enlightening books on science fiction film) looks at sf film, and Birmingham artist David Hardy takes a hard look at sf art around the world, a thorough selection of which can be found throughout this book. Finally there is a catalogue of information on science fiction compiled and edited by Roy Kettle, with the help of myself, Mike Ashley and Alan Frank.

marriage of

Brian Stableford

The concepts contained in the phrase science fiction did not exist until the late eighteenth century. One hundred years later, speculation about scientific and technological progress began to appear in prose fiction. They were not new ideas, but they were taken seriously for the first time in this period.

science and fiction

Historians trying to trace the prehistory of science fiction may go back as far as the whim takes them: to Cyrano de Bergerac, Lucian of Samosata or even Homer. But in those times the word science did not mean what we mean by it today, and nor did the word fiction. The concepts which lurk within the phrase science fiction did not exist until the late 18th century, and the various intrusions of science into fiction – the tentative meetings which became the foundations of an eventual marriage – did not happen until nearly a century after that. Indeed, the first writers who recognized the existence of science tended to react against it in horror. Mary Shelley's *Frankenstein 1818* is perhaps the perfect example of this allergic response.

In the second half of the 19th century certain possibilities inherent in scientific and technological progress began to appear in fiction. For the most part they were not new ideas, but they were taken seriously for the first time in this period. Prose fiction – especially stories set in the near future – was used as a means of exploring the implications of ideas and technological developments.

There were four particularly important stimuli to the imagination which generated speculative fictions of this kind. They were: the revolution in transportation; the theory of evolution; the socialist movement; and the anticipation of large-scale war. It was not so much the actual logical and social implications of these developments that were important, but the effect they made on the popular imagination. The four were initially quite separate, and produced quite distinct species of literature. Only gradually was it realized that the four types of fiction had something in common, and the notion that they constituted a whole which might be termed scientific romance or science fiction emerged slowly. However, once the genre had been established, argument never ceased as to what ought and what ought not to belong to it, and the matter of definition is still disputed. The conflict may be better understood by looking closer at the provocations to imaginative exploration which arose in the 19th century.

The impact of unlimited transport

The steam locomotive was the first major product of the industrial revolution to intrude itself into the world of the middle classes. In industry, it was the need to distribute mass-produced goods that brought about the transportation revolution but in the popular imagination the advent of railways and steamships meant the opening up of the world. For the first time, the not-so-rich were able to travel in comfort and style. The main literary response to the transportation revolution was the novel of imaginary tourism, and its most popular practitioner was Jules Verne.

Verne invented a host of marvellous vehicles to take his characters into every last corner of the world – and beyond. In 1863 he spent an imaginary *Five Weeks in a Balloon*. In 1864 he ventured on *A Journey to the Centre of the Earth*. In 1866 he was party to *The Adventures of Captain Hatteras* at the then-unexplored north pole. By 1870 he was ready for the ambitious trip *Round the Moon* and in the same year he published his account of Captain Nemo's submarine *Nautilus* and its adventures *Twenty Thousand Leagues Under the Sea*. There followed in 1871 a memoir of a real voyage on the early steamship *The Great Eastern* in *A Floating City*, and in 1873 he produced what is perhaps the ultimate tourist story when he sent Phileas Fogg *Around the World in Eighty Days*. By this time, Verne was internationally famous and extremely popular. After the first hectic decade, he slowed down, not in terms of his literary productivity but in the frenzied pace of his imaginary travellers, becalming himself for nearly a quarter of a million words on *The Mysterious Island* in 1875. He was never quite so fervent thereafter. He attempted a more ambitious trip into space in *Hector Servadae 1877* but could not make it convincing. The only significant fantastic vehicles he subsequently invented were the aëronef in *The Clipper of the Clouds 1886*, a popular and much illustrated piece of flying hardware, and the free-floating city in *Propellor Island 1895*.

Verne found a large audience among the young, and it was for juvenile readers that most of his imitators wrote. Prominent among his French disciples was André Laurie, who was noticeably less restrained in his inventions. In *The Conquest of the Moon 1887* the heroes decide that lunar travel is too difficult under present circumstances and undertake to make things easier by attracting the moon into

An unusual nineteenth century woodcutting, 1831, illustrating Mary Shelley's *Frankenstein*

Earth's atmosphere with giant magnets. His *New York to Brest in Seven Hours 1888*, featuring a sub-Atlantic oil pipeline, seems tame by comparison.

The English Vernians were not so ambitious, and most stuck to terrestrial adventures. The polar regions held a particular fascination for Gordon Stables, who wrote *Wild Adventures Round the Pole 1883* and *From Pole to Pole 1886* before his most ambitious novel, *The Cruise of the Crystal Boat 1891*. Harry Collingwood devised an all-purpose vehicle that was both submarine and airship for *The Log of the 'Flying Fish' 1887* and its sequels, while Max Pemberton designed a truly charismatic vessel with a phosphor-bronze hull and gas-powered engines in *The Iron Pirate 1893*. In the early 20th century, Vernian romances were still popular in Britain, a particularly prolific author being Herbert Strang. America was largely content to import material from Britain and France, although a notable domestic product was *The Great Stone of Sardis 1897* by Frank R. Stockton, which features the polar explorations of a submarine and discoveries made by means of a ray that probes the interior of the Earth.

The most ambitious of the novels of imaginary tourism were the interplanetary journeys. A notable early example is Percy Greg's *Across the Zodiac 1880*, while George Griffith's *A Honeymoon in Space 1901* features a package tour which takes in all the major planets. When the Russian space scientist Konstantin Tsiolkovski wanted to popularize his ideas regarding the possiblity of sending rockets into space he chose to do so in a Vernian novel aimed at juvenile readers – *Beyond the Planet Earth 1920*.

Assimilating the theory of Evolution

Darwin's theory of evolution made an impact on the imagination of the layman far greater than any other set of ideas in 19th century science. It challenged all man's cherished beliefs and called into question his self-image. Disraeli summed up the emotive issue when he described the argument as a debate on 'whether man is an ape or an angel'. No scientist would have put the matter like that, but it was the crucial question in the minds of most people.

Evolutionary philosophy was first popularized in France after the contribution made by Jean Baptiste de Lamarck, and it was in France that imaginative writers first explored the implications of the notion of evolution by adaptation. The astronomer Camille Flammarion applied it to the question of life on other worlds and designed the first alien beings in his *Récits de l'Infini 1872* – later revised as *Lumen* and published in Britain under that title. One writer who made evolutionary theory the imaginative springboard for the greater part of his work was J. H. Rosny the elder. He, too, imagined an alien evolutionary system in Les Xipéhuz' *1887* – translated by

Airborne Sanitarium, drawn by French artist A. Robida for his series 'Le 20ième Siècle'

The only significant fantastic vehicles that Verne invented after 1887 were the free floating city in *Propeller Island* and the aëronef (below) in *The Clipper of the Clouds*

A nineteenth century French view of life on Saturn, drawn by A. Robida for 'Voyages Très Extraordinaires'

Damon Knight as 'The Shapes', and then wrote a curious essay, 'La Légende Sceptique', which plots the evolutionary scheme of the whole cosmos. He wrote many novels about the prehistory of man, beginning in 1892 with *Vamireh*. The most famous is *La Guerre du Feu 1909* but the only one translated into English is *The Giant Cat 1918*.

Darwin's champion: H. G. Wells

In Britain, Samuel Butler, the author of several anti-Darwinian tracts, incorporated into his novel *Erewhon 1872* a satirical essay applying Darwinian logic to the evolution of machines, but the novel which most effectively dramatized the confrontation of the 'angel and the ape' was *Dr Jekyll and Mr Hyde 1886* by Robert Louis Stevenson. Darwin's most vociferous champion was Thomas Henry Huxley, who made a deep impression on a student he taught at the London School of Normal Science – H. G. Wells. Wells undertook the most comprehensive literary exploration of Darwinian theory, first in such speculative essays as 'The Chronic Argonauts' *1888* and the classic 'The Man of the Year Million' *1893*, and then in his early fiction. He turned 'The Chronic Argonauts' into *The Time Machine 1895*, which launched into the future to track the divergent evolution of two human species: the angelic Eloi and the bestial Morlocks. In *The Island of Dr Moreau 1896* he gave human form to wild beasts *via* the experiments of the scientist Moreau, and then followed developments after the creator is killed by one of his creations and the moral law he has imposed upon them loses its force. In *The War of the Worlds 1898* Wells submitted man to a Darwinian

'struggle for existence' against invading Martians – products of an alien evolution. In *The First Men in the Moon 1901* he designed a whole society to fit the criteria of efficiency implied by the theory of natural selection, and produced the image of the Selenite hive-society whose units are intelligent automata.

Like Rosny, Wells was impelled to investigate the prehistory of man in 'A Story of the Stone Age' *1897*, and a flourishing subgenre of prehistoric romances grew up in Europe and America. Notable examples include Austin Bierbower's *From Monkey to Man 1894*, Stanley Waterloo's *The Story of Ab 1897* and Jack London's *Before Adam 1906*. The classic of the species is part of *The Long Journey 1923* by the Nobel prize winner Johannes V. Jensen. The major preoccupation of these stories is the process by which man became human, and the essence of the change that raised him above the beasts. Wells saw the critical moment in the invention of weapons, while others nominated the discovery of fire. Not many were prepared to stress the importance of sociability and cooperation (though Darwin did in his own account of *The Descent of Man* in 1871).

Although man's evolutionary past was quite thoroughly explored by writers in the 1890s, there were very few contemporary attempts to explore his possible evolutionary future. Wells made a significant attempt in his earliest works, and Camille Flammarion also tracked the evolutionary future of Earth in his classic *La Fin du Monde 1893*, but they were virtually alone. However, in a later period, John Beresford wrote *The Hampdenshire Wonder 1911* about the freak birth of an 'evolved' human and Wells' fellow Fabian, George Bernard Shaw, took

THE LONDON SKETCH BOOK.

PROF. DARWIN.

This is the ape of form.
Love's Labor Lost, act 5, scene 2.
Some four or five descents since.
All's Well that Ends Well, act 3, sc. 7.

A contemporary satirical cartoon of Charles Darwin, from the London Sketch Book

human evolution to its limit in *Back to Methuselah 1921*. S. Fowler Wright imagined a world in which man has disappeared and given way to new sentient species in *The Amphibians 1924*, later incorporated into *The World Below*. Another evolutionary fantasia which shows a much-changed Earth is William Hope Hodgson's *The Night Land 1912*. Other ambitious novels dealing with the prospects for human evolution are *The Clockwork Man 1923* by E. V. Odle – the first novel which deals with artificial evolution *via* man/machine hybridization or 'cyborgization' – and *Emperor of the If 1926* by Guy Dent, stressing man's responsibility for his evolution.

The social revolution

The idea of social evolution – 'progress' in the wider sense of the word – became popular in the latter part of the 18th century. It influenced the ideology of the French and American revolutions and continued to be important in the social philosophy of both nations. In Britain it was somewhat less popular.

The first important literary work dramatizing the idea of social progress was L. S. Mercier's *Memoirs of the Year 2500 1772*. A notable early American example is Mary Griffith's *Three Hundred Years Hence 1836*. It was not until the late 19th century, however, that notions of the ideal society became inextricably linked with the idea of progress and utopia ceased to be a purely academic concept, becoming instead a social goal – a possible future. The most important historical factor in this change of emphasis was the growth of the various political movements which may be grouped under the heading of socialism.

The archetype of the late 19th century futuristic utopian novel was Edward Bellamy's *Looking Backward 1888*, which became a phenomenal best-seller in America. It presented a picture of the socialist world of the year 2000 where all men are equal, their work made easy by machines and their happiness assured by the wonders of piped music. The novel provoked considerable controversy, and many answers in kind, but it was itself only part of a trend. The previous year, W. H. Hudson had produced a vision of a human society reharmonized with nature in *A Crystal Age*, and the following year Theodore Hertzka produced an entirely independent version of a future reformed according to his own economic theories in *Freeland*.

The most significant of the many novels produced in the wake of *Looking Backward* were *Caesar's Column 1890* by Ignatius Donnelly, *News From Nowhere 1891* by William Morris and *A Traveller From Altruria 1894* by William Dean Howells. *Caesar's Column* was the first important anti-utopia: a vision of the future based on the assumption that things are getting worse rather than better, and that inequality will increase rather than vanish. *News From Nowhere* was a strong reaction against Bellamy's 'utopia of comfort', providing propaganda for a future in which machine production has been abandoned and the value of craftsmanship restored. *A Traveller From Altruria* reversed the traditional strategy of utopian literature by bringing a visitor from utopia into our world to comment upon it and criticize its failings. This 'reversed utopian' strategy was quickly imitated by Grant Allen in *The British Barbarians* and by H. G. Wells in *The Wonderful Visit*, both published the following year.

The novel which most effectively dramatized the confrontation of the 'angel' and the 'ape' was *Dr Jekyll and Mr Hyde*

'As Usual', a Pictorial Comedy by P. W. Read, illustrating Space Travel 1900. The caption reads, 'Let me know when we get to Mars'. 'We passed Mars ten planets ago, Ma'am'

Cover paintings by David Bergen for modern editions of H. G. Wells' *Men Like Gods* and *The Food of the Gods*

Ironically, the most prolific and determined of the futuristic utopians emerged in the country where reaction against progress was strongest. This utopian rebel was H. G. Wells. Although Wells was the most important British writer of evolutionary fantasies, in his early work there is a clear distinction between Wells the evolutionist and Wells the utopian socialist. His first investigation of social conditions in the future was the pessimistic 'A Story of the Days to Come' *1897*, and his creativity in designing utopias was always haunted by the fear that contemporary man was not really fitted for such a sublime residence. *When the Sleeper Wakes 1899*; revised as *The Sleeper Awakes* in 1910 has an unequal society destroyed by the messianic awakening of the sleeper, whose wealth has become vast while he lay for centuries in suspended animation. *A Modern Utopia 1905* is a painstaking piece of utopian design, but in *In the Days of the Comet 1906* it takes a miracle to bring about the necessary realignment of attitudes that would be the precursor of such a society. *The World Set Free 1914* and *Men Like Gods 1923* both presume that a large-scale disaster must destroy the old world before a new one might be built.

This pessimism was widespread. Jack London, in *The Iron Heel 1907* also foresaw things getting much worse before they could begin to get better, and Fritz Lang's classic film *Metropolis 1926* provided the definitive visual image of a society in which inequality has temporarily triumphed over social justice. A rather more ominous pessimism, however, was manifest in a series of works which questioned the assumption that a utopian society in the prominent contemporary mode would be worth having. In *The White Stone 1905* by Anatole France visitors to the utopian future find man much more comfortable but still unhappy, while E. M. Forster's 'The Machine Stops' *1912* is a direct attack on Wells, portraying the mechanized leisure-society as both intolerable and inviable. Victor Rousseau's *The Messiah of the Cylinder 1917* inverts Wells' *When the Sleeper Wakes* by having its sleeper wake into a socialist anti-utopia which he promptly sets out to subvert. The ultimate attack on the society whose goals are order and equality is *We 1924* by Yevgeny Zamyatin, written by a Russian socialist disenchanted by the trends he perceived in his post-revolutionary society.

The school of extreme optimism had firm roots only in America. Bellamy reiterated his views and answered his critics in *Equality 1897*, but the most determined optimism of all came from a man who had rather less interest in socialism and far more faith in the wonders of technology – Hugo Gernsback, author of *Ralph 124C41 + 1911*.

The threat of global war

Of the three nations where speculative fiction flourished in the late 19th century Britain was the most conservative and, in matters of progress, the most reactionary. One of the reasons why it was nevertheless prolific in the field was the fact that reformers had to work so much harder to capture the imagination of the people. This ideological endeavour was responsible for the growth of the fourth species of speculative fiction, the war-anticipation story.

The Victorian era was the period in which the mythology of the British Empire was at its height. Britannia was presumed to rule the waves and gunboat diplomacy was very much in vogue. Other powers, however, were making rapid progress – particularly the German Empire consolidated after the Franco-Prussian war of 1870. In 1871 there grew up in Britain a movement calling for the modernization, reorganization and rearmament of the armed forces. One of its leading members, Sir George Chesney, popularized the affair with a remarkable piece of propaganda fiction – an account of 'The Battle of Dorking', at which the British army is routed by a more efficient and better-armed force of German invaders. The story provoked a furore of debate, requiring Gladstone to make a speech against 'alarmism'. There were scores of replies in kind.

Short pamphlets rapidly gave way to full-length novels exploring all facets of this new anxiety. England was invaded again and again. M. P. Shiel widened the scope of the subgenre with *The Yellow Danger 1898*, the first of his many 'yellow peril' stories, and by 1907 Robert Hugh Benson had escalated the coming conflict into the Biblical Armageddon in *Lord of the World*, but the principal enemy throughout remained Germany.

The most impressive products of the species were Erskine Childers' thriller *The Riddle of the Sands 1902* and William le Queux's *The Invasion of 1910 1906*. Le Queux had made an earlier contribution in *The Great War in England in 1897 1894* and was commissioned to write *The Invasion of 1910* by Alfred Harmsworth (later Lord Northcliffe) of the *Daily Mail*. The *Mail* mounted massive publicity

Cover painting by A. C. Michael for the 1911 edition of H. G. Wells' *The War in the Air*

campaigns in various parts of the country as each became the focus of the action in the imaginary invasion. The whole subgenre was parodied by P. G. Wodehouse in his first novel, *The Swoop 1909*. How much this kind of literature contributed to anti-German feeling and to WWI itself is impossible to estimate, but it is notable that the propaganda novels about German atrocities which le Queux turned out during the war years are not noticeably different in content or tone from those he wrote in the 1900s.

Integrating the themes

These, then, are four distinct species of speculative literature, which emerged in response to separate historical stimuli. There are obvious affinities between the various categories, but it was not until the 1890s that anyone began to perceive them as aspects of a whole, and if we look at the processes by which bridges were built between them it is surprising how slow writers were to become truly eclectic in combining notions from different categories.

The most obvious affinity encouraging the transplantation of ideas from one category to another was that between the war-anticipation subgenre and the romance of transportation. And yet it seems odd looking back from today's vantage that so very many people utterly failed to foresee the extent to which transportation technology would remake war. Hardly anyone realized what a difference submarines, tanks and aeroplanes might make. Both the aeroplane and the tank were grossly underexploited when WWI actually began, and there is a certain irony in the fact that an anti-alarmist Admiralty spokesman reacting to Conan Doyle's 'Danger!' *1914* stated flatly that there was *no possibility whatever* of submarine attacks on shipping. This was mere weeks before the depredations of the U-boats

The first writer who arrived at an imaginative appreciation of what technology might mean to war was George Griffith, who wrote in *The Angel of the Revolution, 1893* about a world war fought with submarines, albeit unadvanced models, and armed airships. Griffith apparently took great delight in arranging carnage on a grand scale – his next novel, *Olga Romanoff 1894*, featured another great war followed by the destruction of the earth's surface by a passing comet. By 1911, when he wrote his last novel, *The Lord of Labour*, his version of the standard Anglo-German war was being fought with atomic missiles and disintegrator rays. Very few of his contemporaries, however, were prepared to let their speculations run so wild. Only Wells showed any real understanding of the destructive potential imminently available to the European nations for use in war. His 'The Land Ironclads' was the first fictional mention of tanks and *The War in the Air 1908* features a German airship invasion of America.

Another inter-category connection made (albeit tentatively) by Griffith and followed up by Wells was between the imminent war novel and socialism. The heroes of *The Angel of the Revolution* are socialists who name themselves the Terror, and their war is a great revolution. Other writers who contemplated such a possibility were by no means so enthusiastic. E. Douglas Fawcett's *Hartmann the Anarchist*,

published the same year (1893), exhibits rather different sympathies. William le Queux, a hard-line conservative, made his story of red revolution, *The Unknown Tomorrow 1910* a lurid horror story. Wells, of course, wrote a revolutionary novel in *When the Sleeper Wakes*, and later used international conflicts to 'soften up' the world for rebuilding along socialist lines – a theme particularly dominant in *The World Set Free 1914*, his nuclear war story.

Wells was a particularly important writer in the matter of cutting across categories. In his early work he moved from one species of speculative fiction to another with relative ease, but did not combine them. After 1900, however, he began to see social evolution and biological evolution as interrelated factors, and represented the former as an essential precursor to the latter in many works from the novel *The Food of the Gods 1904* to his last despairing essay 'Mind at the End of its Tether' *1945*.

The forces of the literary market place, which put continual pressure on a writer (especially one whose fame was built on speculative notions) to find something new to write about, were responsible for the fact that several authors wandered haphazardly from one category of speculative fiction to another in search of ideas. Even Verne had undertaken an adventure in social planning in *The Begum's Fortune, 1879*, designed a new kind of weapon in *For the Flag 1896* and toyed very tentatively with evolutionary theory in *The Village in the Treetops, 1901*. Verne made his living from writing, but he was essentially a hobbyist. The young Wells, however – and Griffith and le Queux even more so – was a thoroughly professional writer. He founded his reputation on a

Victorian illustration by Fred T. Jane in *English Illustrated Magazine*, c1902 for E. Douglas Fawcett's *Hartmann the Anarchist*

fertile imagination, and he was forced to keep using it to produce speculative articles and short stories long before he reached the kind of philosophical synthesis which bound his ideas into a whole.

Other writers who became hardened professionals also found it easy to flutter from one type of speculative fiction to another unconscious of any boundaries at all. A cardinal example is Arthur Conan Doyle, who was truly eclectic in his choice of materials and who had no initial affiliation to any of the categories created in response to historical stimuli. The Professor Challenger series (begun with *The Lost World* in 1912) are scientific romances without roots in any of the four categories. Ultimately, though, some of the ideas he had toyed with earlier became matters of serious concern to him when he became a spiritualist following the death of his son. The last Challenger novel, *The Land of Mist 1923* was openly didactic. Another writer who began by producing imaginative fiction in abundance, but who grew more serious in his speculations, was William Hope Hodgson. After dozens of short stories dealing with strange happenings at sea he let his imagination roam as far as it could in his cosmic vision story *The House on the Borderland 1908* and the bizarre far-future story *The Night Land 1912*.

These writers belonged to the first generation who were in a position to make a living out of the products of their imagination. The pressure which forced them to range through the categories of speculative fiction, ultimately generalizing them into the single unity of scientific romance, was essentially a commercial pressure. It was the demand of the readers which controlled it, and it was the readers who first perceived the common cause between such writers as Verne and Wells (who both insisted that their sources were very different).

Edgar Allan Poe

This is, however, not the whole story, and some mention must be made of work which lay outside the four species of 19th century speculative fiction.

An eclecticism that was not the product of market demand was exhibited by Edgar Allan Poe, who found scientific ideas awe-inspiring, but who usually represented them in his fiction with a calculated ironic tone which trivialized them. The best examples are the lunar voyage story 'Hans Pfaall', *1835* and 'The Thousand and Second Tale of Scheherezade', *1848*. 'The Balloon Hoax', *1844* is sober in tone, but the very sobriety was part of the irony, for this was a genuine hoax, published in a newspaper in the wake of a more spectacular hoax. This was Robert Donald Locke's account of lunar life observed *via* a giant telescope, which Poe thought to have been inspired by 'Hans Pfaall'. Only in the long poetic essay 'Eureka!' *1848* and the related short story 'A Mesmeric Revelation' *1844* is Poe's awed contemplation of the wonders of science manifest, and 'Eureka!' was a resounding failure. Only as satirical amusements were scientific ideas in literature acceptable to the public of the time. It had been so for some time. It is no coincidence that if we try to trace individual imaginative notions back to their literary origins we almost invariably find that they were first used satirically.

Cosmic voyages before Poe were more often than not satirical in intent, and Poe recognizes this tradition in 'Hans Pfaall', trying to stay within it while making uneasy claims to verisimilitude and plausibility. Butler's *Erewhon 1872* is similarly ambiguous – though primarily satirical it has hints of genuine utopianism and a not altogether frivolous interest in evolutionary theory.

The satirical impulse was by far the most powerful innovator of imaginative notions in literature before the growth of the four categories of speculative fiction identified earlier, and it continued to be an active force. F. T. Jane, who illustrated future war stories, satirized the novel of imaginary tourism in *To Venus in Five Seconds 1897*. The French illustrator Albert Robida was a prolific satirist of futuristic vehicles and future wars, and his countryman, dramatist Alfred Jarry, actually invented a whole mock science called 'pataphysics'. Utopian satires were common, culminating in the comprehensive *The Isles of Wisdom 1924* by Alexander Moszkowski, which debunks a whole series of utopian models one after the other. The American William Wallace Cook wrote several humorous works making fun of futuristic fantasies, including *A Round Trip to the Year 2000 1903* and *The Eighth Wonder 1906*. In England, G. K. Chesterton wrote a number of futuristic satires, beginning with *The Napoleon of Notting Hill 1904*.

Ideas broached in satirical work could occasionally work their way into serious fiction. Edwin Abbott's two-dimensional satire *Flatland 1884*, published under the pseudonym 'A Square' inspired Charles Howard Hinton to speculate about the multidimensional universe and the possibility of a four-dimensional God. Walter Besant's *The Revolt of Man 1882*, featuring a female-dominated society, began as a satire on the suffragette movement and ended up taking itself far *too* seriously. The eclecticism of satirists was undoubtedly of some importance in generalizing speculative fiction and generating ideas outside the major categories of thought.

The first man who produced a 'manifesto' for a generalised imaginative fiction based on ideas generated by science was a minor British poet and critic called William Wilson, who appealed in 1851 for fiction to be used as a means of popularising science. His proposal passed unnoticed and unheeded. A second prospectus was produced in 1895 by the American novelist Edgar Fawcett, who declared that imaginative fiction must discover new resources and new discipline in the imaginative territories opened up by scientific theory. Unlike Wilson, he practised what he preached in some of his novels. *Douglas Duane 1888* is an identity-exchange novel; *Solarion 1889* features a dog with artificially-augmented intelligence; *The New Nero 1893* is a study in abnormal psychology; and *The Ghost of Guy Thyrle 1895* is, in part, a cosmic voyage story. But Fawcett, too, passed largely unnoticed, though his prospectus was more timely. As a writer he was extremely

scornful of public demand, and it was public demand which would ultimately give form to the notion of the scientific romance while the literary elite had no use for it. He was addressing his prospectus to the wrong audience.

The fact that it was the popular magazines and the mass-market audience which actually evolved the concept of scientific romance – some time before Hugo Gernsback produced a new manifesto and a coherent ideology for his 'scientifiction' – has been seen by many commentators as the vulgarization of a great tradition that stretched from Homer through Jonathan Swift to Wells relatively unsullied by the crudities of mass-market publishing strategies. This is a misrepresentation, for it was in the minds of the mass audience and in the pressure which they put upon writers rather than in philosophical syntheses like that ultimately wrought by Wells that the concepts of scientific romance and science fiction actually originated. The 'tradition' of science fiction before 1900 is a wholly artificial construction which has meaning only in retrospect.

The situation is complicated by the fact that the demand for scientific romance really had little or no respect for science. The 'science' required was a mere jargon to enhance the pretence of plausibility, and the fact that writers were able to discover and use such a jargon as widely and as wildly as they did was largely due to the discovery by Röntgen in 1895 of the X-ray, and that of radioactivity which followed soon after. The possibilities of marvellous rays able to work all kinds of miracle gave a *carte blanche* to imaginative ambition, and it was not wasted.

Mechanical exotica of all kinds flooded from the pens of scientific romancers in the early decades of the 20th century, and they provided easy access to imaginary environments that could be as outlandish as anyone might wish to dream. One of the earliest of these bizarre odysseys was Edwin Lester Arnold's *Lt. Gulliver Jones – His Vacation 1905*, alias *Gulliver of Mars*, but it was not long before certain writers began to build careers based on exciting adventures in wonderful dream-worlds. All restraint ended when Edgar Rice Burroughs showed what might be done in *A Princess of Mars 1912*, and rapidly added to his fantasy-Mars other fabulous milieux such as Tarzan's fantasy-Africa and a Doylean Lost World within the hollow Earth, Pellucidar. The other-worldly romance became even more gaudy with the advent of A. Merritt and such stories as 'Through the Dragon Glass' *1917* and 'The Moon Pool' *1918*.

Thus, in the space of a few decades, a whole new fashion in imaginary fiction emerged from the syncretic synthesis of the various forms of the speculative imagination stimulated by events and processes in 19th century history. Hugo Gernsback brought all the threads together in his various pulp magazines, claiming as the fathers of scientifiction Poe, Verne, Wells and Bellamy and mingling with them the fantasies of Burroughs, Merritt and their kindred. On such a diet he nurtured a new gene-ration of science fiction writers, and following in his footsteps John W. Campbell Jr. nurtured yet another.

This was one marriage of science and fiction. Outside the genre there were a dozen marriages yet to come, each one made independently by individual writers such as John Beresford, Karel Capek and Olaf Stapledon. If we are to term their work 'science fiction' we must remember that it is our viewpoint which makes it so, not theirs, for the work is the product of an independent evolution. We will never understand the history of what we now call science fiction if we do not appreciate the complexity of the forces surrounding both the basic marriage of science and fiction and the many other unions which were made outside it.

En l'an 2000 – nineteenth century French view of life in the year 2000 – the earliest 'skyjack'?

major themes

The stamping ground of science fiction is the whole of all
imaginable futures, and the variety of its themes reflect this
vastness. From *Under the Treads of the Machine*, to the frontiers
of the mind, and of space, from the apparent idolatry of Utopia
to the hostile world of commerce – science fiction has
something to say about everything.

Because the stamping ground of science fiction is no less than the whole of all imaginable futures, an even cursory survey of the themes that have been engaged within those limitless tomorrows would demand not a few pages but a few books. So this essay has had to restrict itself. It will map out some of the broadest thematic *areas* to which authors have returned, again and again – though each by his chosen route.

'I have seen the future – and it works!' enthused the American journalist, essayist and radical, Lincoln Steffens, after a visit to post-revolutionary Russia.

But visions of an improved and workable tomorrow seen by literary optimists have more often emerged in *fictional* form – though usually no less rose-coloured and selective than Lincoln Steffens's. Such works of fiction, telling not how it is or was but how it ought to be, sprouted from the firm soil of Plato's example in the *Republic* and eventually took their generic name from Thomas More's *Utopia* of 1516. But it took the 19th century to bring these hopeful perceptions of perfectability to a peak.

Of course utopian fiction is not science fiction, not even a direct ancestor: it is more a distant evolutionary relative, of a similar genus. Still, it injected into literature the essential shape and nature of what was to become science fiction – the imaginatively plausible speculation and extrapolation that comes into a literary mind with the question 'what would happen if . . . ?'

And, like the utopias, science fiction at its best has always kept its social and moral awarenesses close at hand when it looked through its windows on the future (though it has always been more aware of its responsibilities as a form of entertainment than ever was the heavy-footed and didactic utopia). While the glass in those windows allows glimpses of tomorrow, that glass also reflects an image of the today in which writer and reader live. Shelley once cast poets, rather grandly, in the role of 'unacknowledged legislators'

of mankind, and a century later Ezra Pound updated the image by terming poets 'the antennae of the race'. Science fiction, at its speculative best, can be said to have inherited at least a share of that role.

But the messages that have come through the sf antennae, this century, have been a far cry from utopian enthusiasm or early socialist optimism. H. G. Wells's hopes of a workable world order, in *A Modern Utopia 1905*, *Men Like Gods 1925* and elsewhere, foundered eventually into the lost disillusion of 'A Mind at the Edge of its Tether', *1944*; and by then the heyday of the utopia was over. It had been wrecked by events, but also from within by the basic catch-22 of utopias, rarely so painfully visible as in Edward Bellamy's *Looking Backward 1888*: that the glories of a perfected social order would bring about all the positive transformations of human nature – but, regrettably, human nature would need to be transformed, to create the ideal social order.

So early sf writers like C. S. Lewis, still feeling a utopian urge, sadly transplanted their dreams off-world: it is the alien beings of *Out of the Silent Planet 1938* who demonstrate how things ought to be. And it is the Martians of Robert Heinlein's *Stranger in a Strange Land 1961* whose way of life shows up human inadequacies.

Heinlein's view of the Martian way, though patched with sheer fantasy where the plausibility wears thin, gave rise to something of a cult among the love-peace-and-revolution flower children of America's 1960s. And that short-lived ethos created another area where the utopian urge could flourish – the 'alternative society', encysted within the world of the 'straights', not too different from the Coleridge-inspired ideal society, called 'Pantisocracy', of the early 1800s or the communes of Robert Owen. Such separate and always idealized islands can be found in science fiction in, say, Mack Reynolds's *Commune 2000 AD, 1974* or among the hippie communards of the inferno city in Samuel Delany's *Dhalgren 1974*.

Dystopia

Otherwise, the utopian vision declined into wishful or wistful dreaming – except in some backwaters, as when Ivan Yefremov of the Soviet Union imagined a heroic Leninist utopia in *The Andromeda Nebula, 1957*. In this century, science fiction writers on the genre's higher levels have reworded Steffens's exclamation: they have seen the future, and it stinks. They have become the purveyors of pessimism, of the anti-utopia, for which the name is 'dystopia'.

That mode, too, has a considerable pedigree – reaching back, perhaps, to the prophet Jeremiah. And in the dystopian tradition belong also the satirists, above all Jonathan Swift with *Gulliver's Travels 1826*, and also Samuel Butler, who mocked the utopian fashion itself in *Erewhon 1872*. Out of this respectable literary tradition grew two books in particular that form an unalterable part of modern science fiction's claim to credibility among thoughtful readers. But both Aldous Huxley's *Brave New World 1932* and George Orwell's *Nineteen Eighty-four, 1949* set out to do what modern sf has rarely attempted – to use, as their predecessors did, the whole social and moral order of human life as

Glass towers rising above the city – the artistic vision of the future reflects more optimism than the literature ever does. Both these illustrations show the contemporary obsession for the towering and the big – the ship juxtaposes with the city – the outward urge and the inward urge perfectly balanced in an imaginative and technically precise vision of an ultra-bright future

The subtle interaction of future architecture and the recognizable signs of increasing entropy make Chris Foss's illustration for *A torrent of Faces* a remarkably symbolic vision

Programming the human mind, and human behaviour, is a familiar and inexhaustable theme of much sf, but all too often shows up the narrow focus of the writer who concentrates on political dystopia. Cover by Emsh

their canvases. One must look long and hard in sf for novels of comparable range and scope.

Yet they exist. Indeed, for scope, few writers of any sort have attempted what Olaf Stapledon did in *The Last and First Men 1930*. It is a chronicle, hardly a novel, of 'future history', millions of years of it, progressing with inspired deliberation through the ages of man to come until the final dimming of the sun. Less overwhelming, but still worthy of comparison with the best in the direct literary utopian-dystopian tradition, is Ursula Le Guin's *The Dispossessed 1974*, which holds up two planets in opposition and examines every facet of their social orders. This novel can be as didactic and discursive as any utopia, but is unflaggingly thought-provoking – and, thankfully, the fictional elements are not just sugar coating on a socio-political treatise but integral and organic to the book's development.

The satiric side of the dystopia has not been a thematic area in itself, within science fiction, so much as an all-purpose weapon (as it always properly was) to be aimed at whatever target is chosen. Again, though, the Swiftian or Huxleyan breadth and scope seems hard to find in sf satire – approximated most closely, perhaps, in the free-wheeling, anarchic send-ups of modern life of Michael Moorcock's Jerry Cornelius tetralogy, which began with *The Final Programme 1966*.

So it must be admitted that, while sf writers at their best have clung tightly to their dystopian view, they have also tended to narrow the focus of their viewfinders, limiting to one or two the 'thematic areas' on which the central attention of their stories will rest. If a writer is feeling pessimistic about, say, the political future, he may produce a book in which all sorts of ideas and fancies and inventions are fizzing about; This will be a *political* dystopia.

A Totalitarian Future?

And, in the area of politics, an astonishing number of writers of every level of brow have been content to trail along in the directions indicated by Orwell, and before him by the Russian writer Yevgeny Zamyatin, author of *My 1920* and *We 1925*. Sf may follow so slavishly, of course, because that is in fact the way the world is going. But in any case sf assures us that the political future of the world will be totalitarian – on any part of the spectrum from absolute monarchy or outright dictatorship through ruling elites and oligarchies down to enlightened despotism, but always with democracy and liberty long extinct, and many sorts of Big Brothers watching.

The variations on this theme are innumerable, and of wildly varying quality as well. Oddly, though, not many of the authors engage directly or at length with the political processes they set up, being more concerned to show how sensationally awful life would be under them. There are some exceptions: C. M. Kornbluth, in his *The Syndic 1953*, shows a happy-go-lucky anarchy threatened by neighbouring totalitarianisms, and uses his narrative to make a strong commentary on just how much 'governing' a man or a society needs. And Christopher Priest, in his *Fugue for a Darkening Island 1972* paints a graphic picture of how Britain might stumble too easily into totalitarian shackles.

Then, too, Isaac Asimov's mighty *Foundation* trilogy from 1951–3 is at some pains to describe the formation of the benevolent oligarchy that tries to save an empire and the coming of a megalomaniac dictator who tries to take it over. But in both cases Asimov slides out of politics and into pseudo-science in his presentation – the 'psycho-history' of the

Foundation and the 'mutation' of the dictator.

But Robert Heinlein has no more doubt about how totalitarianism takes power than has any Nebraskan Rotarian worrying about creeping communism. Heinlein, whose right-wing conservative stance owes at least as much to John Wayne as to Ayn Rand, is a relentless exponent of the rugged-individualism, survival-of-the-fittest aspects of the American Dream. And he has written his share of polemics disguised as novels out of this position, of which *Farnham's Freehold 1964* is most explicit. By means of a time-slip, Farnham is transported from our sick and crumbling democracy (as he sees it) into a thriving future society, totalitarian and ruthless, through which Heinlein can expound on Middle America's favourite shibboleths regarding politics, economics, race and more. In the end Farnham escapes and achieves true freedom, in the manner of the pioneers of legend, on his own and safe from the corruptions of states and laws and social obligations

The Resistance

Farnham, perhaps thankfully, has fewer counterparts in sf's political futures than has Orwell's Winston Smith. But in all the visions of totalitarian repressions kept secure by secret police and civil control mechanisms, someone inevitably sets out to fight the system. He may be a one-man revolution (Vincent King's *Candy Man 1971*, or Michael Moorcock's *Fireclown 1965*); he may be part of an underground resistance movement (Heinlein, again, in *The Moon is a Harsh Mistress 1966*, or C. M. Kornbluth's *Christmas Eve 1955*). Often he will be a member of the ruling establishment who sees the light and opts out, joining and eventually, because he is the hero, leading the resistance (Henry Kuttner's *Fury 1947*).

Philip Dick, a consistently fine writer, wrote his

finest sf novel *The Man in the High Castle 1962*, within this theme, but chose to set his totalitarian state in what is known as an 'alternative past'. It is an attractive device, well used for imaginative fun and thoughtfulness by, notably, Harry Harrison, Keith Roberts and Ward Moore: it postulates that at some major crisis point in the past history turned a different way, thus altering the present. In Dick's book the 'Axis' won WWII, and America is an occupied nation. But of course there is a *maquis* in the making . . .

And finally, one of the most original treatments of what has now become a fairly hackneyed theme is Ray Bradbury's *Fahrenheit 451 1954*. In that totalitarian state the regime, aware of the dangers of a little learning, holds book burning of high importance among its forms of repression. And the hero is a 'fireman' who becomes attracted to reading, which marks him as a rebel. He escapes, as do so many other rebels in these books, and joins the revolution. But it ought to be added that neither Bradbury nor many other creators of such freedom-fighter heroes follow up the political truism taught especially by Latin America, that today's victorious revolutionary is too often tomorrow's Big Brother.

There are revolutions, however, whose effects and aftermaths fascinate the science fiction writer above all else. These are the scientific and technological revolutions of our age, which have continued the industrial revolution – one of whose side effects, in fact, was the birth of science fiction.

Now there have always been people who greeted these changes with optimistic delight, convinced that progress was in itself a positive good, that it would regenerate mankind and free him from many yokes. But there have also always been people who grumbled pessimistically that unregenerate mankind would use science and technology merely to fashion new yokes, as well as fostering old vices and corrupting or destroying much that was beautiful and valuable in the pre-industrial path.

Science fiction has had its share of writers taking one or the other of these simplistic extremist views. The pro-technology camp can be found plentifully among the authors of early sf's adolescent adventures (who could be said to have taken their leads from Jules Verne rather than H. G. Wells, though that is somewhat unkind to Verne). Even when, for these writers, technology was not much more than spaceships and ray guns, the implication was clear – that the well-armed spacemen were riding a wave of progress, and Mars help the grumblers (or the aliens) who got in the way.

That implication leaped out into the spaceways with the magazine stories of the 1920s and early 1930s, the (Hugo) Gernsback era. It rattled along with the adventure yarns of Edgar Rice Burroughs and E. E. 'Doc' Smith. It pushed into the 1940s with writers like A. E. van Vogt, whose cryptic and woolly *World of Null-A 1945* posits a form of advanced mind training that could lead to the scientific perfecting of mankind if only the villains will let it. And the implication infested nearly every page of

Pointing the way to the future! Picture for Lem's *Futurological Congress*

Machine or monster? Hal Clement's benevolent alien, in *Iceworld*, finds that scientific progress is less of a blessing as it struggles to survive in its machine armour on the coldest world imaginable – Earth!

John W. Campbell's enormously influential magazine of the 1940s, *Astounding*.

Out of the hothouse of ideas that was kept fertilized by Campbell as editor, the sf writer L. Ron Hubbard developed his own notions of mind training, which he called 'dianetics' and later rechristened Scientology, a name that reflects the roots of that odd movement in the belief that scientific progress holds most of humanity's hopes. And Campbell himself characterized this general approach in a note written in 1961 recalling the heady days of 1938 when he had taken over *Astounding* (and given it its name), when people had begun to think that 'the future could not only be different – but better'.

White-coated Heroes

So the scientist as hero and redeemer became something of a stock figure in sf. And many scientists themselves gratefully accepted the role. Astronomer Fred Hoyle, in his first venture into fiction, *The Black Cloud 1957*, puts these words into the mouth of his astronomer hero, chatting to a colleague:

> Has it ever occurred to you, Geoff, that in spite of all the changes wrought by science – by our control over inanimate energy, that is to say – we will preserve the same old social order of precedence? Politicians at the top, then the military, and the real brains at the bottom . . . We do the thinking for an archaic crowd of nitwits and allow ourselves to be pushed around by 'em into the bargain . . .

A great many sf writers might qualifiedly agree that a society of all-pervasive technology is perhaps not best governed by men trained as lawyers or peanut farmers. And a great many of sf's leading names went on asserting their faith in scientific progress as a blessing. Robert Heinlein manfully

defended the technocrats in a number of works, including a little gem of a story called 'The Roads Must Roll' *1940*, in which a heroic engineer fights to maintain the nationwide system of conveyor strips on which a vastly enhanced quality of American life depends. Arthur Clarke populated many of his novels with sincere and dedicated men adventuring among 'scientific and technical wonders' (*Sands of Mars 1951*), and retains to this day his innocent delight in having fictionally predicted the now factual communications satellites. And Isaac Asimov imagined a scientific revolution based on the virtuous and proper use of robots, bringing about a stabilized economy and 'what amounts to a Golden Age' (*I, Robot 1946*).

Machine or Monster

On the other hand, the anti-technology camp could be equally simplistic in its prophecies of the dire results of the machine age. The often nihilist C. M. Kornbluth, in 'With These Hands' *1951*, described an era when pseudo-art can be churned out by machines to satisfy the limited wants of the philistines, and there are no more artists. Fritz Leiber did much the same, though in fanciful satire, in *The Silver Eggheads 1961*, where machines have taken over the work of creative writers. But for the arch-poet of sf, Ray Bradbury, the effects of technology on spiritual and aesthetic values was nothing to laugh about. In his story 'The Exiles' *1950* he shows all the great creators of fantasy and horror as fugitives from technocracy, living on Mars, and whipping up their fearsome creations to baulk a spaceship from Earth – which is coming to finish off these leftover shades by burning the last of their books. They succeed – unlike the technocrats in a similar Bradbury story, 'Usher II' *1950*, where a rich eccentric sets up a living museum of macabre fiction

For the arch-poet of sf, Ray Bradbury, the effects of technology on spiritual and aesthetic values was nothing to laugh about. Illustration by Joe Petagno from Bradbury's *The Silver Locusts*

that does away with the representatives of 'reality' who come to close it down.

But if sf was divided on the subject of the blessing or the curse of the technological revolution, its wiser writers contained that conflict within themselves. Even Jules Verne, delighted inventor of delightful machines, could see in among the romance that 'if men go on inventing machinery they'll end by being swallowed up by their own machines' (*Five Weeks in a Balloon 1863*). His heirs in modern sf knew very well, as the 20th century provided ample evidence, that progress was a double-edged weapon, that technology, like magic, was in itself neither good nor evil, neither white nor black. Whatever their dreams of an ideal technology-based future, writers like Heinlein, Clarke, Asimov *et al.* did not need to be told that any advance from fire to microcircuitry can harm human prospects if the sorcerer's apprentices in the labs let things get out of control, or do the right things for the wrong reasons.

So the prevailing tone of more modern sf began to sound very like the anti-technology brigade. But it was not romantic idealism preferring fantasy to factories, nor was it crusty conservatism suffering from future shock. The tone came within salutary warnings, thoughtfully and entertainingly disturb-

ing, about what can and does happen when super-technology gets into the hands of all too flawed and inadequate humanity. No matter how blazingly objective and well-intentioned Dr Frankenstein may be, the writers would say, he tends to come up with a monster.

It is specifically the Frankenstein complex, as it has often been called, that imbues much of sf's nervousness about the effects of technology. Naturally the complex can be seen at its best in the sub-theme of 'robot fear'. The inventor of the term robot, the Czech writer Karel Capek in his *R.U.R. 1921*, also established the basic form of the fear — that the robots, invented as slaves, would rise up and eradicate their masters. Throughout early low-brow adventure sf, robots – either manmade or from other planets – vied with bug eyed monsters as the favoured blaster-fodder for the spacefaring heroes. (They also, oddly, posed a frequent threat to the virtue of partly clad maidens on early sf magazine covers.)

The beautiful people, and the humanoid machines, in Joe Petagno's illustration for *Lemmus 2*, stand before the ruins of a city, and a place of human ruin. Despite the pessimism of the message the art is optimistic – triumph by adversity, and can there be any doubt that they have struggled against the machine creations of their own technology?

Even in the quietly melancholy pages of Clifford Simak's classic *City 1952*, where robots are on the whole kindly and valued servants of men, they can get out of hand – and they eventually inherit the earth by a kind of default. And Isaac Asimov, whose 'three laws of robotics' to keep the metal men subservient are among his most famous contributions to sf, produced stories in the *I, Robot* series where those laws seem to be fearfully breakable.

Hand in hand with the robot fear went the computer fear. While ordinary people fretted that automation would put everyone (not just artists and writers) out of work, sf warned more chillingly that super-computers could render man obsolete, or corrupt him into mindless, spineless sloth, or enslave him. Evil or amok computers play the villain's role in Damon Knight's *Analogue Men 1955* and Alfred Bester's *Extro 1974* among many other treatments of the sub-theme. But nowhere is there a better sample of this anti-machine worry than in a short-short story by that master of the twist ending, Fredric Brown, entitled 'Answer' *1947*. Scientists, having built the ultimate in ultra-powerful computers, switch it on and ask the old question that has needed answering for centuries: is there a God? The mighty machine first uses its power to ensure that its switch can never again be turned off, then replies: 'There is now'.

In similar vein the satirists have harvested much from the computer fear. Kurt Vonnegut set the style in his *Player Piano 1952*, where man's destiny is in the dubious control of the monster EPICAC. John Sladek depicts machines with a built-in *Reproductive System 1968* which cannot be stopped from breeding more machines. And even a 'straight' satirist like Michael Frayn has dabbled in sf with his mockery of the computer complex in *The Tin Men 1965*.

But even while the writers might be picturing, or mocking, the atavistic fear with which laymen view the more sophisticated hardware, they did not often share it. For nearly every super-computer gone awry or power-mad, there will be one presented as benefactor, friend or at the least object of sympathetic approval. Many of these become memorable fictional characters in their own right – not only when they are friendly humanoid robots like Eric Frank Russell's 'Jay Score' *1955* or Asimov's 'Robbie' *1940* but even when they are immense computer complexes, with complexes, like the fully and poignantly realized 'human analogue' computer in David Gerrold's *When Harlie Was One 1972*.

Beyond the fear of machines with minds of their own, the dystopian view of the technological revolution has radiated out into a huge assortment of sub-themes, many of which have grown up into full thematic areas in their own right. For example the notion that technology is essentially anti-human finds a clear expression in sf's view of the future city, the metropolis where only machines really feel at home – where concrete, glass and steel have entirely replaced earth, grass and trees, and even the weather is computer-controlled. The literature of the inhuman city may show it underground, as in Isaac

Asimov's *The Caves of Steel 1954* or the more recent treatment by Vonda McIntrye in *The Exile Waiting 1975*. Or it may show mile-high tower blocks and all-engulfing urban sprawls, like the multi-levelled metropolis with slidewalks and aircars that Harlan Ellison's hero tries to disrupt in the gaudily titled story '"Repent, Harlequin!" Said the Ticktockman' *1965*. As for the pressures of living within these urban monstrosities, that is a related theme to be picked up later.

If ever there was a thematic area designed perfectly to exhibit technology's inhuman creations (as well as much diverting action-adventure), it is of course the area of human conflict. After all, 20th-century science fiction came into being in the aftermath of one world war and came of age in the aftermath of a second, with the ever-threatening likelihood of a third. In the process sf, like everyone else, learned more than it wanted to know about the misuse and abuse of technology for gruesome and perhaps genocidal ends.

These developments allowed a change of emphasis away from the generally anti-technology dystopian mood to a more congenial (to sf) anti-military stance. The more simplistic writers never tired of reminding us that while scientists may have invented the bomb, it was *soldiers* who dropped it. Certainly there have been occasions in sf when armies and generals have been held up as noble and glorious institutions (for instance, in Robert Heinlein's *Starship Troopers 1959*), but then they were usually pitted against some satisfactorily evil outsiders, like Russians or Martians. In terms of man's overall inhumanity to man, the Pentagon seems to have cornered much of the market in present or future sf villains, from the days of the cold-war nuclear terror.

Kelly Freas' illustration (above) for Everett B. Cole's *Final Weapon* says it all – words are more powerful than guns, and the 'ideas' in that folder will make nonsense of new weapons. Even the missiles become strangely beautiful in Bob Layzell's picture (opposite) a part of nature even while they retain their shape. But war can defy all of nature's frontiers, as the Emsh cover from *Galaxy* (below) shows an illustration for Frederik Pohl's *Slave Ship*

Often enough the sf view of the generals has spilled over into 'straight' fiction, in a host of near-future political thrillers like *Fail-Safe* by Eugene Burdick and Harvey Wheeler *1962* or its satiric film equivalent *Dr Strangelove*. And the nightmare of annihilation – man cutting off his world to spite his race – has produced apocalyptic novels that also inhabit the borders of sf, most notably Nevil Shute's famous *On the Beach 1957* where his characters gloomily await their death by fallout. Back in sf proper, Philip Wylie tackled the job of describing the Third World War itself, mushroom clouds in suburban America, in his grimly titled *Tomorrow! 1954*, as did Judith Merril in her *Shadow on the Hearth 1951*.

The Mad Militarist

More often, though, the writers tended to begin their novels in the post-holocaust era, usually with a prologue or flashback that vituperatively described how civilization had been destroyed. This living-in-the-rubble theme belongs in a later section, but something of the flavour of those angry introductions can be gained from a justly admired story by Ray Bradbury, 'The Million-Year Picnic' *1946*, in which Dad and his family have fled just in time to escape the bombs. He tells his children now on Mars:

Science ran too far ahead of us too quickly, and the people got lost in a mechanical wilderness, like

Whilst the mad militarist wages war, a more poignant and more searching culture conflict has featured in sf for many years – religious conflict – a God for all creatures? Or merely a God for man? In Harry Harrison's '*The Streets of Ashkelon*', here illustrated by Jim Burns, the aliens, converted to Christianity by the Space Missionaries, feel they must re-create the martyrdom of Christ – dogma rules once again, and the essential religious communication is lost in a sad reflection of contemporary human Christianity children making over pretty things, gadgets, helicopters, rockets; emphasizing the wrong items, emphasizing machines instead of how to run the machines. Wars got bigger and bigger and finally killed Earth . . . that way of life proved wrong and strangled itself with its own hands. . . .

Here of course is Bradbury the anti-technologist again, not restricting himself to a mere anti-military position. But even those writers who did concentrate their wrath on the generals would sometimes, if they were wise enough, pose the question of whether science did not retain some responsibility for the destructive uses made by the Pentagons of its discoveries. Are the scientists in chains to the generals, a metaphor made vivid in Aldous Huxley's *Ape and Essence 1949*? Are they murderous zealots or crackpots, willing accomplices of the bomb-droppers, like the inventor of an ultimate weapon getting his own back for memories of childhood bullying in 'Judgment Day' by L. Sprague de Camp *1955*? Or are they innocent dupes of the men who can seemingly twist any forward technological step into new weaponry, as Harry Harrison's scientist hero sees them in *In Our Hands, the Stars 1970*?

Harrison's hero goes into hiding to escape the weapon-hungry generals, and a similar crisis of conscience afflicts the scientist in Fredric Brown's story 'The Weapon' *1951*, who finally comes to the realization that 'only a madman would give a loaded revolver to an idiot child'. It seems to some extent a somewhat inflated, playing-God position for scientists to adopt, *vis-à-vis* humanity; and writers like Brown who sketch out the position seldom go on to ask whether scientists have the right to set themselves up as screens or censors, deciding when to give knowledge and when to withhold it. But at the same time the premise became a common theme in sf, out of an awareness that politico-military complexes were not excrescences on the body of an essentially peace-loving humanity, but grew from something innately violent within the human race – the aggressive drive built into the brain, the blood, the genes. It is a pessimistic thesis put forward cogently by writers of the stature of Arthur Koestler and Erich Fromm, and it suited the dystopian gloom of sf writers similarly to see the drooling face of Mr. Hyde in each of us, the psychopathic hominid always ready to draw a gun or drop a bomb.

A well-loved story by Henry Kuttner, entitled 'Or Else' *1953* neatly encapsulates the nature of man the mad militarist. A peace-loving alien lands his saucer between two Mexicans shooting it out over water rights. The alien, wanting to end the conflict, asks how it began. 'Because,' Miguel replies, 'Fernandez wishes to kill me and enslave my family.' The alien asks why he should wish to do that. ''Because he is evil,' Miguel said. 'How do you know he is evil?' 'Because,' Miguel pointed out logically, 'he wishes to kill me and enslave my family.'

There, sf might say, lie the roots of the old 'yellow peril' fear, McCarthyism, the Dulles 'domino' theory of communist takeover, and any other staging post along the mad militarist's road, which leads among other things to Vietnam.

It should be added that the Vietnam years, producing a violent reaction against war-making in

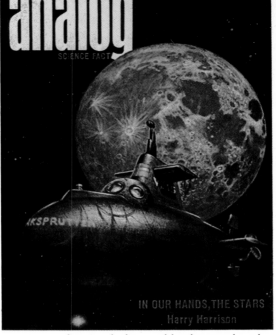

young people round the world, also produced a flurry of comparable anti-military sf ironies. The theme pervades all of Michael Moorcock's Jerry Cornelius writings, where surrealist future wars threaten the world daily, and in many acidically surrealist stories by Thomas Disch including his '1-A', *1968*.

But not all of these anti-war writings set their events on earth. For it is only a short goose-step from man the mad militarist visiting his inhumanity on man to the time when he leaps into spaceships and demonstrates it on non-men.

'It's moving,' he said curtly. 'Heading for us. Just what we'd do if a strange spaceship appeared in our hunting grounds! . . . Thank God for the blasters! . . .

'Blasters, sir? What for?'

The skipper grimaced at the empty visiplate.

'Because we don't know what they're like and can't take a chance!'

In fairness to Murray Leinster, from whose story 'First Contact' *1945* that exchange comes, the skipper and his blaster-toting crew *do* take a chance, and get adroitly out of an impasse that might have led to shooting. But in Leinster's time, when he and others were helping science fiction up out of the crudities of the pulp era, many sf writers and most of their readers would not have reached for their moral scruples or their brotherly love when faced with extraterrestrials. They would have reached for their ray guns.

Space adventure, also known as 'space opera', adapting the term from its coeval, the pulp western 'horse opera', usually involved exploration, boldly going where no man had gone before. But it rarely, in those days, involved serious or even half-serious speculation about the *effects* of visits to alien planets, on visitors and visited. Such planets existed as imagination-boggling locales for danger and excitement. And their denizens existed either as monstrous beasts, taxing man's ingenuity to find ways of killing them, or as sentient beings who fitted easily into the role of 'hostiles' filled by Indians in westerns.

A Danish submarine in space, powered by a revolutionary new drive, is hotly sought by the governments of many nations – Harry Harrison's book, *In Our Hands the Stars*, here illustrated by Kelly Freas, is a very fast-paced, and very sobering, look at the mis-use of technology

The Great Western Weapons Fanaticism springs out so often in both sf and sf art. Both illustrations by Kelly Freas

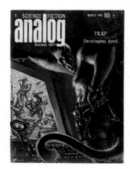

E. E. 'Doc' Smith's *Lensman* series would alone provide examples enough to turn any modern stomach, though for limited variety there is also A. E. van Vogt's much-loved *Voyage of the Space Beagle 1951*. Sadly, this sort of stuff became one of the main entry points into sf for youngsters who are now adults (as did the early comic strips like Flash Gordon), which explains why sf has taken so long to find widespread acceptance as legitimate adult reading. As an aside, anyone examining space opera out of historical interest must not overlook Harry Harrison's delicious parody, gung-ho dialogue and all, *Star Smashers of the Galaxy Rangers 1973*.

The Conquering Hero?

The accepted object of all this violent space exploration was what America once called 'manifest destiny' and Marxists now call 'imperialism'. Spacemen went looking for Earth-type planets to exploit and colonize in the same spirit as the covered wagons rolled into Texas, over the bodies of the Comanches. 'There was nothing, absolutely nothing, that could stop a human planetary survey party,' begins Clifford Simak's story 'Beachhead'; while Stanley Weinbaum's trader in 'The Parasite Planet' *1935* is one of those 'reckless daredevils pursuing danger' but pursuing no less the 'good, solid lure of wealth'.

The fun of it for the reader arose when the colonizers ran into beings who resented being colonized – often alien primitives, but equally often weird intelligences with unheard-of powers, like John Campbell's 'The Brain-Stealers of Mars' *1936*. But as sf began to grow up a little, the exploiting explorers began to meet some well-deserved setbacks: the cocky planetary survey party of Simak's story get their comeuppance when they find an entire planet aiming to stop them. And gradually a distaste for the blundering, blasting space exploiters came to dominate more modern treatments of the theme – as can be seen in Carol Emshwiller's story 'Pelt', a perfect transposition of the old fur trade on to an alien planet, where the trader doesn't know or care that the fur-bearing creatures he hunts are intelligent . . . until it's too late.

Even worse, the space colonizers sometimes *do* know that the aliens are not animals, but hunt them anyway, as in Poul Anderson's story of men slaughtering what they call 'owlies', 'Duel on Syrtis' *1951*. And Brian Aldiss coldly portrays men of equal callousness in *The Dark Light Years 1964* who meet aliens, deem them animals by human standards, kill them freely ('Our men surprised eight of those creatures, sir, and promptly shot six of them.') and take others home to be examined by vivisection.

Sometimes, obviously, the aliens whom the explorers meet turn out to be as advanced, aggressive and well-armed as the humans – and then a space war is declared. But here too sf has moved from the use of this theme for blood-and-blasters adventure to its use for often powerful anti-war statements, rarely finer than Joe Haldeman's award-winning *The Forever War 1975*: 'begun on false pretences and only continued because the two races were unable to communicate . . .'. Needless to say, the bitter narrator adds, the war was begun by humans: 'they

armed the colonizing vessels and the first time they met a Tauran ship, they blasted it'.

But if man the mad militarist is shown in his true colours in circumstances like those, he is wholly shown *up* when he comes across alien beings who are patently, and immensely, superior. There is often a touch of paranoia in stories on this sub-theme, as in A. E. van Vogt's 'Cooperate – or Else' *1942*, when an overwhelmingly powerful alien informs the hero that '. . . man is a frivolous, fragile, inconsequential *slave*. . . . Unfortunately, this monstrous, built-up weakling with his power lusts and murderous instincts is the greatest danger extant to the sane, healthy races of the Universe. He must be prevented from contaminating his betters.'

As it happens, the hero of this story turns out to have a thing or two to teach this arrogant super being. But the idea that man is generally unworthy of being out in space till he can curb those murderous instincts came to have wide currency. Advanced aliens keep a wary eye on him by means of a Moon-based device in Arthur Clarke's 'The Sentinel' *1954*; they even keep him thoroughly quarantined, as in 'Loophole', *1946* also by Clarke – or as Robert Sheckley's hero discovers, among the farcical surrealisms of *Dimension of Miracles 1968*, when he is told that 'Earth is a diseased place. I believe it is being phased out of the Galactic Master Plan on the basis of chronic cosmic incompatibility.'

Man the Imperialist arrives upon a new world in a blast of light (opposite – illustration by Bob Layzell); but it may not all go his way. The spear-carrying winged creature, dogfighting with a monoplane in Leo Summer's illustration (above) and the gun-toting, furry alien of George Martin's 'And Seven Times Never Kill a Man' (illustrated by John Schoenherr) share the human attribute of mistrust, and are letting it be known. Human insecurity manifesting itself in his most imaginative literature.

Within the sub-theme of alien encounter there are humbling stories where super-aliens volunteer altruistically to help man towards a civilised maturity. Such Close Encounters are common in sf writing, and probably never done better than in Arthur Clarke's *Childhood's End*. But what is man to make of Rama – in Clarke's *Rendezvous with Rama* – an enormous, deserted alien artificial world that drifts through the solar system? Alas, for the book, nothing at all. Illustration by Brian Boyle

Aliens of a totally different sort – benevolent and co-operative, one from Poul Anderson's Ensign Flandry novel, *A Knight of Ghosts and Shadows*, and the others the unforgettable aliens from Hal Clement's planet 'Mesklin', centipedal and the only creatures that can fully explore their own discus-shaped world with its extremes of gravity. Illustrations by Wendi Pini (top) and Kelly Freas (below)

Alternatively, aliens descend now and then to test mankind, to see if he is ready yet for 'galactic federation status' or the like, and this too affords much comedy, as in Theodore Sturgeon's slightly twee story 'The [Widget], the [Wadget] and Boff' *1955*. No humour, though, for once, exists in Fredric Brown's classic story 'Arena' *1944* where a super being finds humans and an alien race in a space war that may exterminate both sides. The being selects an individual from each side for single combat, and undertakes to eliminate the whole race of the loser so that one race at least – the fittest – will survive. It is of course old reliable human ingenuity and inspiration that allows the human champion to pass this test.

And still within this sub-theme there are humbling stories where super aliens volunteer altruistically to aid man towards a civilized maturity. The titles of two of the best-known treatments in this area are self-explanatory of the approach; Arthur Clarke's *Childhood's End 1953* and Clifford Simak's 'Kindergarten' *1953*. Equally humbling are the times when super aliens remain totally indifferent to man's existence, as we might be to ants beneath our feet – which is just what such a being calls us in Kurt Vonnegut's satiric masterpiece *The Sirens of Titan 1959*. Vonnegut also has some fun with the idea of super aliens popping humans into zoos, as part of the careering plot of *Slaughterhouse 5, 1969*.

Some of these stories may help to ease our paranoia by implying that even super aliens can be as ignorant, vicious and xenophobic towards us as we may be towards 'lesser breeds'. We can also be reassured by tales of the future when man has grown up and mingles freely with other species, perhaps as multiracial crews of spaceships (Eric Frank Russell's 'Symbiotica', *1955*) or as their passengers (Samuel Delany's *Empire Star, 1966*). But even when men rub shoulders with aliens all round the galaxy, in total familiarity, there are still chances for authors to amuse us by showing that old habits of xenophobia or plain bigotry die hard: it is one of the heaviest crosses to be borne by the patient Retief, hero of Keith Laumer's *Ambassador to Space* series from the mid-1960s.

Allegories of racism and xenophobia, not always satirical, dominate even more when the aliens set foot or tentacle on earth. Harry Harrison provides a model of the theme in 'Rescue Operation' *1962*, a first-contact story in which an alien crashlands on earth, is badly injured, and – in spite of one man's helpless attempts to be of use – dies in the face of human ignorance and superstition. Much the same sort of xenophobia hampers the growth of inter-species relations in Ian Watson's complex novel about communication failures, *The Embedding 1973*.

Earth Invasion

But aliens on earth bring an entirely new sub-theme, which usually gets us back to rayguns and the mad militarist. After H. G. Wells's pioneering *War of the Worlds, 1898* earth was threatened with invasion in pulp fiction as often as heroines were threatened with fates worse than death in melodrama. Now and then there may be a hint of allegory, as humans respond badly to alien arrivals, but more often paranoia and xenophobia rule supreme. Naturally the invaders have to be considerably advanced, in technology, to get here; also naturally, then, they have to be decidedly evil, to spare our egos. So xenophobia is permissible with beings like James H. Schmitz's *The Demon Breed 1968*. And it is even easier with aliens whose wrath could never be turned away by soft words, like the man-eating plants in John Wyndham's *Day of the Triffids 1951*, the monster wasps of Keith Roberts' *The Furies 1966* or the aquatic menaces of Brian Aldiss' 'The Saliva Tree' *1966*, not to mention a considerable series of invasion excitements from the indefatigable John Lymington.

Alien invaders seem even more incontrovertibly evil when they try to slip past the defences of our xenophobia with camouflage. Some like to take over and manipulate humans, like Fredric Brown's *The Mind Thing 1961* or the 'spores' from the stars that are John Christopher's *The Possessors 1965*. Sometimes they can change their own forms into human shape, as in Keith Laumer's *A Plague of Demons 1965* or Alan E. Nourse's story 'Counterfeit', also called 'The Counterfeit Man' *1952*. All this has become a stock favourite for children's television sf, probably because it saves on make-up and costumes.

Here it should be mentioned that some aliens do come this way with perfectly peaceable intentions, but even when they too resemble humans they must hide their alienness in the face of the xenophobic threat. At this point allegory is allowed to surface again, notably in Clifford Simak's *Way Station 1963*, where a chosen earthman keeps and maintains a transit point for interstellar travellers – who insist on secrecy because of Earth's known barbarity to the unfamiliar. Something of this crops up with the super-powered but cloyingly nice humanoids marooned on earth, and so hiding in the backwoods, in Zenna Henderson's *The People: No Different Flesh 1966* and her other works in that series. Another marooned alien, Walter Tevis' *The Man Who Fell to Earth 1963*, must also hide his identity, though he does so within the glare of extreme wealth. But even Superman, another extraterrestrial, has to disguise himself much of the time....

And the paranoias of the people bristle as much at the alienness of their own offspring, should they develop some evolutionary superiority, whether as mutations or scientific experiments. Philip Wylie's test-tube-induced superman in *Gladiator 1930*, runs into troubles that make Clark Kent's need to wear glasses seem paltry; it is the envy, hatred and fear inspired in ordinary men by his excessive strength, speed and, be it said, virility, that Wylie explores, in a Wellsian way. So, too, the humans who acquire superpowers – in Theodore Sturgeon's brilliant *More Than Human 1953*, Arthur Sellings's *The Silent Speakers 1962* and James Blish's *Jack of Eagles 1952* among many more – must come to terms with being *homo superior* in a world where everyone else is still merely *sapiens*, and not always even that.

The xenophobes keep their wary eye on time travel, too, fearing the monsters or superior beings who might come out of the future. Poul Anderson (*Guardians of Time 1961*) and Fritz Leiber (*The Big Time 1961*) both project a need for armed forces to guard the time-lanes against such terrors.

Finally, these fearful prejudices extend as well to the many modified creatures of sf. The pitiable creatures on *The Island of Dr Moreau 1896* by H. G. Wells were monsters even in their own eyes, while Olaf Stapledon's dog with a human intelligence, *Sirius 1944*, suffers equally from being neither one thing nor the other: 'Why did you make me without making me a world to live in?' he asks, perceptively at one point.

It is a question often asked by the 'androids' of sf, perfectly human in appearance and sharing human aspirations and urges, but not born of woman – so treated as inferiors and slaves in Philip Dick's *Do Androids Dream of Electric Sheep? 1968*, greeted everywhere with fear and suspicion in Isaac Asimov's *The Naked Sun 1957*. Some of their inner anguish also afflicts the half-human rebuilt beings to whom Martin Caidin, among others, gave the name *Cyborg 1972* – though it never seems to occur in the bionic bully who is both his, very successful, TV and cinema spinoffs.

In the end, it comes down to the provable fact that ordinary people tend to resent, hate and fear any being who is visibly different, especially if the difference is combined with visible superiority – whether a super alien who flits between galaxies or merely a man with an exalted IQ. It is a theme that science fiction has never ceased to examine – perhaps because in this society scientists and science-fiction readers, 'boffins' and 'eggheads' all, have themselves suffered a little from irrational prejudice.

This is the Way the World Ends

Obviously science fiction's overwhelmingly jaundiced view of the future is based on a sadly low opinion of mankind. There is nothing new in that: writers in any genre have always liked to take lofty positions from which to condescend and criticize, preach and instruct, or merely rail. Nor is there anything new in the progress from social criticism to clear jeremiad prophecies of disaster if things go on in this way. And so sf doom-mongers have been marching up and down for decades wearing signs saying 'The End is Nigh' and outlining in scarifying detail the precise nature of the bangs and whimpers.

Out of this end-of-the-world syndrome has come some of the finest work of sf's maturity. This may be because, since the 1950s at least, the prophets of doom are not mere peripheral ranters but skilled writers expressing a central preoccupying fear that exists among all thoughtful people. Mankind *can* destroy the world; we have, as the saying goes, the technology; we have already gone a good way towards accomplishing that end. It became the natural duty of the speculators and extrapolators of sf to describe our next steps along that way: it was the bang, not the whimper, that appealed most to sf some years ago. And writers who did not dwell on how we were leading up inexorably to dropping the bomb or the bacilli often made their points instead by showing what would remain, afterwards, for anyone who might be unlucky enough to survive.

Virgil Finlay's illustration for Cordwainer Smith's *Under Old Earth*, a story of the Under-people, creatures that are half-man, half animal

Magnificent artwork on the alien theme

Mutation, as the result of nuclear fall-out or bio-interfering, has been a common sf theme for decades. This illustration, by Peter Jones, illustrates a collection of stories on this theme, edited by Robert Silverberg

Hubert Rogers' cover for Isaac Asimov's classic story *Nightfall*, which tells of the first 'true' night on an alien world, and the religious upheaval it causes

New York City (opposite) buried under ice, is just one uncomfortable vision of the future that occurs in Robert Silverberg's story 'When we went to see the end of the World!'

Chris Achilleos' future city, inspired by Wells' *The Shape of Things to Come*, vividly counterpoints images of Utopia and Dystopia

The prospect seemed to be mainly fearful scavenging and cruel savagery – which led to many exciting but rather one-dimensional adventure novels, like Poul Anderson's *Twilight World 1961*. Television and films fell upon this notion with joy: no futuristic sets needed, just some manageable rubble or uninhabited wilderness. But at their best the sf writers developed some highly original variations, among them Richard Matheson's *I Am Legend 1954*, in which all the survivors of a worldwide plague have been transformed into vampires except for the narrator hero, the last real human being.

Another, even more unusual, variation occurs in Brian Aldiss' *Barefoot in the Head 1969*, depicting the chaotic aftermath of a European war fought with hallucinogens. The book is not merely a post-holocaust survival adventure, for Aldiss poses some potent questions about modern life and the spirit of the individual. But it shows the sort of opportunities that exist when the destruction of civilization forms a book's backcloth.

But even the more usual post-nuclear war setting has created outstanding work. Edgar Pangborn's *Davy 1964* shows a bomb-shattered world embedded deep in a new form of dark-age barbarism. And Walter M. Miller's classic *A Canticle for Leibowitz 1959* provides a uniquely imaginative and often blackly comic feast of a world centuries after nuclear destruction, where monasteries struggle to preserve half-understood fragments of the past amid harsh wasteland brutality. It also becomes a world where man still cannot learn from even his worst mistakes, for at the book's grim climax the bombs fall yet again.

Man cannot be cured apparently of xenophobia, either, which arises savagely in post-holocaust worlds where radiation has twisted everyone's chromosomes and mutants can emerge in any birth. John Wyndham's *Chrysalids 1955* represents this theme, but an even more established classic is Henry Kuttner's *Mutant 1949*, a sequence of stories about conflicts among normal people, good mutant telepaths, bad telepaths and assorted 'freaks'. In the end the good telepaths are only narrowly able to prevent the villains from launching another nuclear war. And there are mutant humans and monsters abundantly in Samuel Delany's *The Einstein Intersection 1967*, but Delany is another writer concerned to use the theme for his own literary purposes – to create a poetic and adventurous reworking of the Orpheus myth.

At other times sf writers abandon man the mad militarist and blame the ultimate calamity on man the thoughtless technologist. The fringes of sf have been full of near-future disaster stories recently, among them Michael Crichton's thriller about a deadly man-made virus, *The Andromeda Strain 1969*. But such books are pale shadows of works like George R. Stewart's *Earth Abides 1950* which begins with the destruction of civilization by another killer plague but which looks beyond, in a moving chronicle of how the survivors picked up the pieces over the next generation and reconstructed (as the title hints) some hope for the future.

Often enough in sf cataclysm novels the

characters are facing an act of God or nature, at which times the authors can leave aside moral lessons and indulge in plain thrills and suspense, in the manner of Max Ehrlich's planet on a collision course with Earth, *The Big Eye 1949* – though even this thriller has something of a social sting in its ending. More recent variations have larger intentions with regard to examining the human condition, as in John Christopher's *The Death of Grass 1956*, Brian Aldiss' world of soil depletion and famine in *Earthworks 1965* and Michael Coney's new ice age in *Winter's Children 1974*. But towering even above these is the remarkable originality of J. G. Ballard, preoccupied consistently with the 'inner landscapes' of the human being, and its transformation and renewal in the extremity of terminal chaos. His *The Wind from Nowhere 1962* was an early and weaker disaster tale (a world-rattling hurricane caused by a mad scientist). But three more catastrophe novels, using the other three of the four ancient elements – *The Drowned World 1963*, *The Drought 1965* and *The Crystal World 1966* – took this theme to heights that few others writers have surpassed.

Earth's Future

Other more recent writers have tended to turn away from dire visions of near-total annihilation, and instead consider the less abrupt (but accelerating) decline and breakdown of civilization, rooted firmly in what we are now doing to the world in the 1970s. Overpopulation has been a favourite standby (usually in terms of the theme of the future megalopolis), receiving fresh impetus from writers like Harry Harrison in *Make Room! Make Room! 1966*, Thomas Disch in the bleak humour of *334 1972* and John Brunner in *Stand on Zanzibar 1969*.

Brunner's title reminds us that whereas in the 1960s the population of the earth could have been accommodated, standing like upright sardines, on the Isle of Man, by the year 2000 we would all have to stand on Zanzibar. Through a variety of literary devices Brunner keeps many interwoven subplots moving simultaneously, which confers on its panoramic and pessimistic overview the status of a full dystopia.

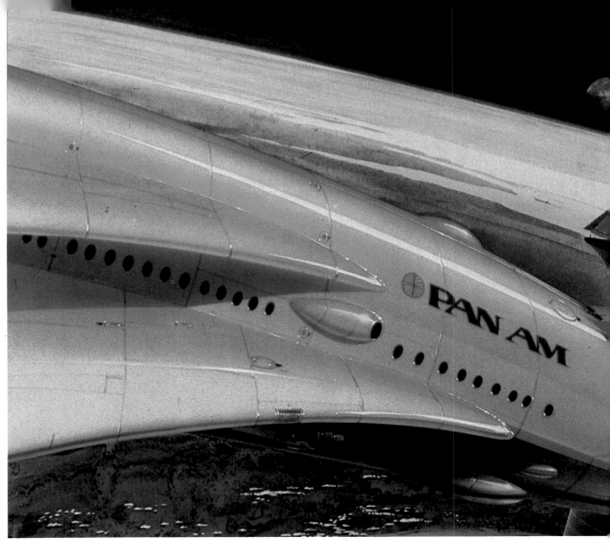

The optimistic vision underlying Chris Moore's *Pan Am* is perhaps more fashionable today than a few years ago. His near-future extrapolation of air transport is a striking and realistic image

But overpopulation is just one of the apocalyptic horsemen riding through our time, and neck and neck with it has been the comparatively new concern for eco-environmental collapse. James H. Schmitz was somewhat ahead of his time (even in the use of the term) with his neat story 'Balanced Ecology' *1965*, where greedy humans nearly upset the equilibrium of a controlled environment on another planet. On this world the ecological doom-criers have found John Brunner, again, at their head, in his follow-up to *Zanzibar, The Sheep Look Up 1974*.

A third related sub-theme (because they all intermingle in the good novels) grows out of the visible breakdown of 'law and order' and a return to the law of the jungle in urban streets. A distinguished 'straight' writer, Anthony Burgess,

once wrote a piece of unashamed science fiction about urban violence to come, *A Clockwork Orange 1962* – but he had to wait for our cities to become truly more violent, and for his book to become a film, before his prophecies received their due. And here too John Brunner has made a sizable contribution to doom-watching with his *Jagged Orbit 1969*, in which virtually every man runs his own arms race.

On the whole, then, our sick society is shown to be growing sicker, in each and all of its elements. Some of the specific ailments are fairly new to us, such as the nuclear madness, overpopulation and so on. But others arise more from present-day corruptions of age-old, innately human preoccupations, ob-

sessions, drives and urges.

Commerce can take pride of place – because it usually does – among the permanent human obsessions and drives which sf knows that man will carry into his future. Business is business, and is likely to remain so for however many centuries or decades we have left. But many modern writers are at pains to show the increasingly unpleasant face, as Edward Heath put it, of capitalism – as when in so many novels (*Zanzibar* among them) the multi-national corporations have stopped merely pulling governmental strings and have emerged as governments themselves. Often they have at the same time become multiplanetary, or multigalactic, like the 'trillion dollar empire' whose dictatress-president rules everything and everyone in Bob Shaw's *Orbitsville 1975*, or like the organization that remodels entire worlds in Michael Coney's *Brontomek! 1976*.

Other writers, though, especially Americans, inject a strong flavour of approval or at least willing acceptance into their pictures of the future of free enterprise. No Monopolies Commission troubles Isaac Asimov's *US Robots* (*I, Robot*) or Harry Harrison's Transmatter Ltd, makers of matter transmitters that dominate the economy in *One Step from Earth 1970*, or Robert Heinlein's Howard families with their tight grip on the secret of longevity (*Methuselah's Children*, and *Time Enough for Love 1973*).

Similarly, James Blish based a series of books, the best being *Earthman, Come Home 1956*, on the adventures of 'cities in flight' – whole urban conglomerates soaring off through space to make

generations, is everyone's economically patriotic duty, and a rich man is he with few possessions.

Medicine in all its forms comes into many sf visions, not always favourably: James White may take the Kildare notion out among the stars and alien beings on a heroic *Hospital Station 1962*, while writers like Heinlein and Blish can accept that medical advance (in, say, longevity) may transform society for the better, but usually sf writers make it clear that medical discoveries are as capable of disastrous side effects and abuses as any military hardware. Thomas Disch uses this theme brilliantly in *Camp Concentration 1968*, when drug experiments on humans prove that intelligence can be enhanced – but the drug infects the taker with an incurable venereal disease. The guinea pigs strike back when one escapes and infects as many people as she can, both with disease and high IQs.

Drugs in general feature large in sf: the writers do not like pharmaceutical companies, nor do they care for the development already visible in the 1970s – that the 'opiates of the people', to adapt Marx's term, are now mostly in fact opiates. Fritz Leiber sums it up in his story 'The Secret Songs' *1962*, in which a young couple are only truly alive in their ritualized, nightly hallucinations induced by drugs and television.

James Blish's 'Cities in Flight' series appeared as a sequence of stories and novels in *Astounding SF* in the 50s and early 60s. They were rarely more dramatically illustrated than here, by Timmins, showing one of these urban conglomerates touching down on a primitive colony world to trade

fortunes as contract labour, aided by anti-gravity and by longevity drugs which they mostly keep to themselves. But at least Blish made his city managers reasonably responsible men, unlike many of the interplanetary entrepreneurs keeping alive the spirit of free (i.e. cut-throat) competition. Poul Anderson made this theme his own in books like *Trader to the Stars 1964* and *The Trouble Twisters 1966* in which we are invited to applaud unscrupulous freebooters trading the equivalent of beads to the natives for their priceless alien treasures.

Happily we are *not* invited to admire big business in a wide-ranging satire that has become one of the all-time sf classics, *The Space Merchants 1953* by Frederik Pohl and C. M. Kornbluth. It is a poison-tipped look at the commercial uses of advertizing and the media for the profitable corruption and brainwashing of the populace. Kornbluth alone wrote what must be the most misanthropic view of the television audience in sf with his story 'The Marching Morons' *1951*, while the media also come in for calumny – over how far they will go to keep the ratings up – in Christopher Priest's unsettling story 'The Head and the Hand' *1972*. Equally, sf knows how the media can lend themselves to keeping the people quiet in totalitarian societies, to be seen in John Brunner's *The Squares of the City 1965*.

Finally, the inevitable result of commercial pressures and limitless economic growth results in the 'consumer society' writ large, in satires by Frederik Pohl 'The Midas Plague', *1951* and Robert Sheckley 'Cost of Living', *1955*, when the need to consume, to be in hire-purchase debt unto the next

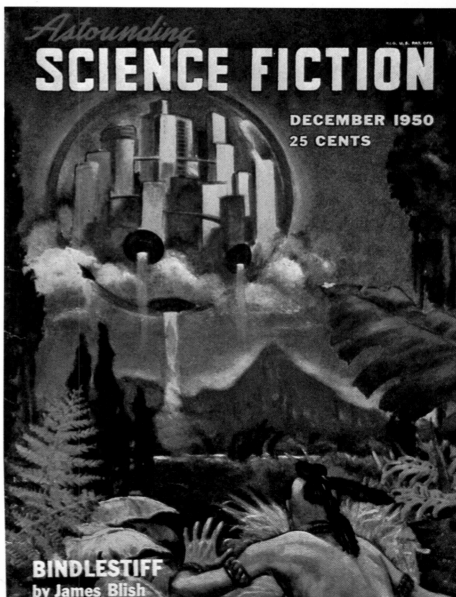

Astounding

SCIENCE FICTION

DECEMBER 1950
25 CENTS

BINDLESTIFF
by James Blish

'... death is now and has always been the driving-wheel of evolution ...' Naysmith, an explorer on the planet Chanda, discovers a religious ritual that involves genocide, in James Blish's 'Dusk of Idols,' here illustrated by Chris Foss, a classic short story that questions the nature of 'civilization'

A symbolism-saturated picture, an early cover by Kelly Freas, clearly links the sex-drive with the space-drive; but for the next twenty years only a handful of writers dared write about such things

Beyond drugs, the dire visions of future medicine include advanced spare-part surgery (especially in Bernard Wolfe's *Limbo '90 1952*). Transplants for the elite come to be a road to immortality in Norman Spinrad's *Bug Jack Barron 1969* and many other dystopian worlds, while sometimes it is the mind that is transferred into a new body, as in Michael Coney's *Friends Come in Boxes 1974*. At times the doctors can even reach back to beyond the grave, with often unfortunate results, as in Clifford Simak's *Why Call Them Back from Heaven? 1967* and Robert Silverberg's *Recalled to Life 1974*.

Rigid birth control by selective 'eugenic' breeding features in many images of totalitarianism, like Frank Herbert's world of the Optimen in *The Eyes of Heisenberg 1966* or among the elite of the female society in John Wyndham's *Consider Her Ways 1961*. Socially favoured, or demanded, euthanasia is another favourite theme, to be found in Vonnegut's 'Welcome to the Monkey House' *1968* and John Brunner's 'Wasted on the Young' *1965*. Elsewhere, genetic engineering ensures that not even chromosomes are free, and that birth in the normal way can be bypassed by methods such as 'cloning'· as in Richard Cowper's *Clone 1972*, and many others.

Engineers also take their spanners into the human psyche as well as the DNA, 'rehabilitating' people who might be criminal or insane but who might also merely be non-conforming, like voting for the wrong party. Damon Knight's 'The Country of the Kind' *1956* postulates such a well-adjusted society, with only one lonely misfit; Robert Silverberg's *The Second Trip 1971* presents a rehabilitated criminal with a whole new personality and set of memories – until his former identity begins to seep back and try to reassert itself. Sometimes, though, the psychic engineers do valuable service, as in the many versions of the telepathic therapist – John Brunner's *Telepathist 1965*, Roger Zelazny's *The Dream Master 1966*.

God among the Stars

Religion, the opiate that bothered Marx, retains that role in many dismal futures, including *The Space Merchants* and Vonnegut's satiric account of a cult that wrecks the world in *Cat's Cradle 1963*, while in Harry Harrison's *Planet of the Damned 1962* it is a totalitarian theocracy that must be overthrown by the hero. But nowhere is there a more thoroughly epic vision of theocracy, riddled with secret-society mystery and priests with strange powers, than in Frank Herbert's giant and imaginative trilogy that began with *Dune 1965*.

A few good writers have sought to interrogate Christianity itself, in an sf context, none better than James Blish in his classic *A Case of Conscience 1958*, in which a Jesuit travels to another planet and finds his faith shatteringly tested. The planet's intelligent beings are, in every social and moral way, faultless exemplars of the Christian ethic, of life as it must have been before the Fall of Man – yet they are wholly rational, lacking any religious faith or sense of a Divinity that might serve as underpinning to their perfection. The Jesuit painfully concludes that their entire, godless, ideal world is a complex trap set by man's demonic Adversary. Though Blish wisely leaves our options open as to whether it is God or cosmic accident that produces the staggering finale, he nonetheless proved for everyone that even the most abstract pillars of theological thought can be, like anything else, grist for sf's speculative mills.

Equally sprung from central, if more concrete, Christian realities are the actions of an interplanetary missionary – whose faith is not questioning but blinkered, with disastrous results for himself and his alien flock – in Harry Harrison's powerful story 'The Streets of Ashkelon' (also called 'An Alien Agony, *1962*). And the whole Christian structure totters a little when a time traveller takes on the title role, unavoidably on the road to Calvary, in Michael Moorcock's *Behold the Man 1969*.

Sex with Aliens can be fun

Sex, the oldest and most basic human drive, has been the last to find its way into science fiction. Certainly earlier utopians like Bellamy and Wells like to shock their readers with views of free love futures where inhibition and taboos are no more, but that was social criticism, not human relationship. At the other extreme, the adolescent space adventures of Edgar Rice Burroughs and others embraced a share of naked Martian princesses, but the reader's fevered pubescent imagination had to fill in what might have happened off-stage. That was where sexual activity had to be in sf – off-stage, or off-page, as much as it was in Hollywood films of the 1940s and 1950s.

The breakthrough began when Philip José Farmer stirred up a fury of controversy by blatantly taking sex as his central theme in his epoch-making story 'The Lovers' *1952*. And, at least as importantly, Theodore Sturgeon was embodying in sensitive and dramatic stories his belief that we must come to terms with our sexuality if we are ever to overcome our inner 'dissociated' psychological and social problems. One of his best pieces on this theme is 'The World Well Lost' *1953*, where after our sympathy has been engaged by the persecuted and literally star-crossed lovers we are allowed to learn that they are homosexual.

Because of pioneers like these (not to mention Aldiss, Vonnegut and a few others) sex came out of sf's bedroom closet and on to the page, in its normal role within the lives of people. In the writings today of Robert Silverberg, Harlan Ellison, Barry Malzberg and dozens more, human relationships will be sexual relationships when the plots and themes warrant it – and sexuality in the future can be just another useful theme in itself, as in Silverberg's excellent 'In the Group' *1973*. It also goes on being used in the one way that it did often crop up, before the breakthrough – in satire and comedy, from Brian Aldiss' *The Primal Urge 1961* through many tongue-in-cheek stories by Robert Sheckley, to newer mockeries like 'Planet of the Rapes' *1978* by Thomas Disch. One side effect of this newly permissive breeze, inevitably, has occurred in the so-called 'men's magazines', now sf-mad, with all yesterday's nude Martian princesses being dragged instantly into the soft-porn beds of mass-market erotica. On another level, though, writers like James Tiptree Jr now introduce the sexual dimension even into human-and-alien relationships ('And I Awoke and Found Me Here on the Cold Hill's Side', *1971*) though they must bow to Naomi Mitchison who was there much earlier, when her narrator in *Memoirs of a Spacewoman 1962* becomes pregnant by her attractive alien lover.

Space-age Woman

The role of women too has undergone its own liberating changes within sf, in part as a dividend of the new sexual freedom. There have of course always been women among the important writers of sf, many of whom have been mentioned in this essay. But in past years they were sometimes treated by male writers as a kind of auxiliary service, who were expected to write within the home-and-children, sensitive-emotional areas supposedly their own. This chauvinist attitude has taken something of a beating lately, when women have been proving what they at least knew all along – that there are no 'exclusively male' preserves in sf. Even as sheer full-blooded action entertainment, Anne McCaffrey's *Dragonflight* series (from 1968) outclasses most other available fantasy. And no one has taken readers so thoughtfully and comprehensively 'inside' an alien society, in all its elements, as Ursula Le Guin in *The Left Hand of Darkness 1969*.

Moreover, some women writers are making up for all those years when the female characters in an sf story were there either to be captured by monsters or to make the coffee (even when they were PhDs in astrophysics) while the heroes saved the world. Women are using the sf context and its devices to interrogate women's roles in society, present and future. Most prominent in this theme is Joanna Russ, especially in her novel *The Female Man 1975*. It is a powerful though complex condemnation, by means of a postulated society without men, of the relations between the sexes in this macho world of men.

In the treatments of that theme, perhaps above all others, can be seen how far science fiction has come in its maturity – and how far still it has to go.

The stunning illustration for Ursula LeGuin's *The Winds Twelve Quarters*, a collection of stories

pulps

Michael Ashley

The existence of science fiction magazines is vital to the field. Although basically an American phenomenon, such magazines first appeared in Sweden and are now published throughout the world. It is staggering to realise that there have been more than 200 sf magazines, totalling over 5000 separate issues.

and magazines

Since Hugo Gernsback founded the first all-sf magazine in the English language with *Amazing Stories* in April 1926 there have been more than 200 individual magazines published throughout the world totalling over 5000 separate issues. They have come in all manner of shapes and sizes. During the 1920s and 1930s the majority were called 'pulps', a name that has remained as a stigma on a brand of fiction. It originally referred to the paper used, cheap quality and low grade with untrimmed edges that showered the reader in faded confetti at the turn of a page. Gernsback's *Amazing* was not strictly a pulp at the outset. It was larger and printed on paper of heavier stock (with trimmed edges). Largest of them all were his *Quarterlies* which were over half-an-inch thick and threatened potential readers with a hernia if they dared lift more than one issue at a time.

After WWII most magazines changed to a more manageable digest-size (modelled on *Reader's Digest*), of which today's *Analog* was the sf prototype. Occasionally magazines appear in pocketbook format, as did Britain's *New Worlds* in the mid-1960s. More recently publishers have experimented with the standard glossy or 'slick' format, even though production costs have forced these magazines (notably *Cosmos* and formerly *Vertex*) to seek a higher circulation since they cannot rely on advertizing revenue.

Achieving any form of circulation is a constant life and death struggle for magazines, and it is important that a magazine gains as wide a distribution as possible. However, distributors are seldom interested in sf magazines, because of their low circulations, and inevitably dictate the policy. Distributors operate on a percentage of sales and thus are more interested in magazines with a guaranteed high market, like *Playboy*. It was through the decision of one leading American distributor in the mid-1950s to stop handling all pulp magazines that a whole empire of pulps, including most of the leading sf magazines, vanished overnight.

One way around this had been to treat the sf magazine as the specialist publication it is, and produce highly specialized semi-professional issues sold exclusively through the sf dealers. This area, once the domain of the fan and his amateur magazines (fanzines) has recently proved fairly lucrative, and semi-professional magazines like *Algol* and *Unearth* are surviving where big names like *Amazing* are suffering.

Sf magazines are basically an American phenomenon, although they first appeared in Sweden and exist today in many countries. Their continued existence is vital to the field. Not only do they allow authors more suited to short fiction to find a market for their work (and there are precious few markets for any kind of short fiction), but they also allow new writers to find their style and learn the trade, and give experienced writers an opportunity to experiment. They also act as a forum for writers and readers, and in their letter columns, book and film reviews and editorials offer far more of a service and reader/writer contact than any novel or anthology.

Even the hybrid 'original' anthologies, like Britain's *New Writings in SF*, which feature only new stories, are but a halfway house in this respect and are no replacement. Science fiction needs the magazines.

United States

While science fiction did not originate in the United States, and neither for that matter did the science fiction magazine, it was in that country that sf developed into its accepted form producing most of the world's leading writers, and this happened almost wholly through the magazines.

The first all-sf magazine was *Amazing Stories*, launched by a Luxembourg emigrant, Hugo Gernsback, 1884–1967, in April 1926. Before that sf was featured in general adventure fiction magazines, and arguably began with a series of juvenile paperbound novels in 1892 as the *Frank Reade Library*. It was in the general fiction pulps that sf became most popular, especially in the pages of *Argosy* (which had converted to pulp in 1896) and its companion *All-Story* (launched 1905). Both were published by Frank A. Munsey, 1854–1925, who created a major pulp empire. George Allan England, 1877–1936, best remembered for his *Darkness and Dawn* trilogy was probably the first writer of real talent to appear in these pulps. Momentum really gathered, though, with the advent of that master adventure writer Edgar Rice Burroughs, 1875–1950, who contributed two breathtaking series to *All-Story*: first his Martian adventures starring John Carter, beginning with *Under the Moons of Mars* (*1912*, book *A Princess of Mars*), and then with the immortal *Tarzan of the Apes 1912*. Burroughs's success naturally begat competition, and this opened the way to the pulps featuring more and more science fiction. By 1920 there was an active group of talented writers in the field, not least Abraham Merritt, 1884–1943, Ray Cummings, 1887–1957 and Murray Leinster, 1896–1975. Action and adventure were favoured in these stories, at the expense of scientific content. A near-miss sf pulp came with *The Thrill Book*, which appeared twice monthly during the summer of 1919, but it featured no more than the average quota of sf and fantasy.

A major step in the pre-*Amazing* days came in March 1923 when J. C. Henneberger, 1890–1969, issued *Weird Tales* from his Rural Publishing Company in Chicago. Henneberger was a fan of Edgar Allan Poe stories and had high hopes for a magazine of such fiction. Whilst it was never a financial success, the legacy of fiction from its 279 issues is legend. Here were regularly featured the seminal works of writers like H. P. Lovecraft, 1890–1937, Robert E. Howard, 1906–36, Ray Bradbury, born 1920 and Robert Bloch, born 1917. *Weird Tales* often carried science fiction, especially the work of Edmond Hamilton, 1904–77, who established the concept of an Interplanetary Patrol a whole decade before E. E. Smith, in stories published in *Weird Tales* in the late 1920s.

A secondary source of sf, outside the pulps, was in the technical magazines published by Hugo Gernsback. Gernsback had serialized his own invention-packed novel of the future, *Ralph*

Planet Stories was a magazine that began poorly, chiefly through lack of material. But editor Malcolm Reiss persisted and by the late 1940s *Planet* was publishing some of the most exciting space fiction around

STRANGE ADVENTURES ON OTHER WORLDS—

PLANET
stories

MAY
25¢

TRADE MARK REG.

A.N.C.

CAPTIVES *of the*
THIEVE-STAR
A Novelet of Rich and Lawless Galaxies
by JAMES H. SCHMITZ

Also H. B. FYFE

FRANK B. LONG

CHAN DAVIS

E. HOFFMAN PRICE

RICHARD WILSON

Between 1933 and 1936 *Wonder* (left) was an active rival to *Astounding*. Both magazines encourage originality in ideas and treatment

The January 1927 *Amazing Stories* (right) was important for more reasons than Frank R. Paul's cover and the story it illustrated, A. Hyatt Verill's 'The Man Who Could Vanish'. It was the first issue to carry a letter column 'Discussions', from which small seed the whole of science fiction sprang

124C41+, in *Modern Electrics*, *1911–2*, and the response was such that Gernsback continued to feature one or two such stories in subsequent issues. *Modern Electrics* became *The Electrical Experimenter* in 1914, and *Science & Invention* in 1920. In that guise, the August 1923 issue carried five sf stories, plus an episode of a Ray Cummings serial, and it is often cited as the first true sf issue of an English-language magazine.

The difference between Gernsback's sf and that in the pulps was only too clear. Gernsback's was only a cut above a technical narrative – a treatise of scientific extrapolation fitted into a flimsy fictional form. A few writers, notably Clement Fezandié and Ray Cummings, produced some memorable stories, but nothing comparable to the pulps. There the emphasis was on action, and any scientific theorizing took a back seat, often to the extent that the tales were more fantasy than sf.

Nevertheless these stories were popular, especially those by Merritt and Burroughs. Gernsback was only too conscious of this when he issued *Amazing Stories* in 1926. Although his ideal was that science could be taught through fiction, he nevertheless placed much emphasis on reprinting the works of Merritt and Burroughs, alongside Poe, Verne and Wells whom he cited as the founding fathers of sf. Only naturally the new writers showed the influence of all five of these progenitors.

Manuscripts poured into Gernsback's offices from aspiring authors like A. Hyatt Verrill, 1871–1954, Miles J. Breuer, 1889–1947, David H. Keller, 1880–1966, E. E. 'Doc' Smith, 1890–1965 and Jack Williamson, born 1908 and still actively writing. Of them all, perhaps the work of Keller, a Philadelphian psychiatrist, best epitomizes Gernsback's ideas, although the space opera extravaganzas of E. E. Smith, whose *Skylark of Space* was serialized in *Amazing* in 1928 and is now

more popular than ever, shows that readers will always prefer action to philosophy. Keller's approach was genuine however. He, more than most of his contemporaries, was responsible for considering the human angle rather than treating people as no more than cogs in a scientific framework. Keller would extrapolate trends to show their effects on mankind, and stories like 'The Revolt of the Pedestrians' *1928*, 'Stenographer's Hands' *1928* and 'The Threat of the Robot' *1929* were clear arguments that man should not put total reliance on technology.

The success of *Amazing* prompted Gernsback to issue an annual in 1927 featuring a new John Carter adventure by Burroughs. Despite its size and price it was a sell-out, and thereafter Gernsback issued a regular *Amazing Stories Quarterly*, carrying a complete novel per issue and a number of short stories.

In 1929 Gernsback's Experimenter Publishing Company was forced into bankruptcy and *Amazing Stories* and the *Quarterly* passed to a new publisher. Gernsback's assistant, T. O'Conor Sloane, 1851–1940, continued as editor. Although he was then 77 he stayed with the magazine for a further ten years. His many antiquated ideas, including the belief that space travel was impossible, robbed *Amazing* of any vitality, and whilst some good fiction appeared, as a rule it was dull and drab.

Gernsback soon established another company and issued a number of new magazines including *Air Wonder Stories*, *Science Wonder Stories* and *Science Wonder Quarterly*, much in the same mould as *Amazing*. The first two later merged as *Wonder Stories*, *Air Wonder* having only limited appeal. Gernsback brought with him artist Frank R. Paul, whose highly technical covers were the trademark of Gernsbackian sf. Paul, 1884–1963, noted for not using the same spaceship design twice, had a marvellous imagination for machines and landscapes, but was no good with people, who looked as cardboard as most of the writers portrayed them. Leo Morey, who took over from Paul as cover artist at *Amazing*, was at least more capable.

One important point here is that in the strict sense Gernsback's magazines were not pulps. They were of the larger, bedsheet, variety. The *Quarterlies* were even bigger, and so was *Scientific Detective Monthly*, another hybrid like *Air Wonder*, that satisfied neither market and soon exhausted its appeal.

The first *true* sf pulp appeared in 1929, from a regular pulp magazine publisher, William Clayton. January 1930 was the cover date on the first issue of *Astounding Stories of Super Science*, a magazine that was to change sf history, though not in its first incarnation. The editor was Harry Bates, born 1900, who later established himself as a writer with the classic short story 'Farewell to the Master' (*Astounding 1940*). He had the simple directive from Clayton to fill the magazine with action-packed adventures with a light smattering of pseudo-science. None of the cerebral scientific intellectualism of Gernsback.

Many of the new generation of writers flocked to Bates, including Ray Cummings and Murray Leinster (neither of whom had appeared with new material in *Amazing*), Jack Williamson, Edmond Hamilton and S. P. Meek, born 1894. Bates himself teamed pseudonymously with assistant editor Desmond Hall to provide a rip-roaring space opera series about Hawk Carse in direct imitation of E. E. Smith's *Skylark* series. The readers loved every word. Here was an entirely unpretentious, escapist magazine of scientific adventure.

What was especially good about *Astounding* from the writers' viewpoint, apart from there now being three clear markets for sf, was that Clayton paid two cents a word, whereas Gernsback seldom paid more than a begrudged half-cent a word. Even today some sf magazines pay only one cent a word, so Clayton's rate in the struggling days of the Depression, was fabulous money. Alas, it was as an indirect consequence of the Depression that Clayton suffered a financial blow and his company was dissolved in 1933. That year proved a major turning point in the sf world. The last Clayton *Astounding* was dated March, but the title was bought by the venerable firm of Street & Smith who reissued it in October, with new editor F. Orlin Tremaine, 1899–1956. That first issue, with a mixture of horror and sf stories left over from Clayton's stocks, was no indication of what was in store.

Both *Amazing* and *Wonder* staggered their issues, missing the monthly schedule, whilst the expensive *Quarterlies* faltered and folded. To capture a wider audience, and also cut costs, *Amazing* and *Wonder* abandoned their large format and went pulp, but at a time when every cent counted, discerning buyers noticed more than that. *Wonder* only offered 128 pages, whilst both *Amazing* and *Astounding* carried 144. In addition, *Wonder* and *Amazing* cost 25 cents, but *Astounding* was only 20 cents. Street & Smith were also a much respected firm with wide distribution facilities. These factors soon yielded a predictable result, and within months *Astounding* had the largest circulation of the sf magazines.

Later Gernsback slashed *Wonder*'s cover price to 15 cents, but circulation did not rise correspond-ingly, and this action was almost certainly the straw that broke the camel's back. By 1935 Gernsback's company was in financial trouble and an attempt to alleviate the situation by offering a subscription-only distribution failed dismally. In 1936 Gernsback sold *Wonder* to general pulp publisher Ned Pines.

Nevertheless between 1933 and 1936 *Wonder* had been an active rival to *Astounding*. Both magazines encouraged originality in ideas and treatment, *Wonder* with its 'new policy' and *Astounding* with its 'thought variants'. *Wonder* was being edited by 17-year-old Charles Hornig, who had captured Gernsback's interest in *The Fantasy Fan*.

In the end it was Tremaine's 'thought variants' that yielded the better crop of writers, although *Wonder* discovered one of sf's earliest major talents, Stanley Weinbaum, 1900–35. Today, after over 40 years, Weinbaum's first sale, 'The Martian Odyssey' (*Wonder 1934*) is still considered a classic. Instead of fearsome, mindless alien monsters, Weinbaum's creatures had a purpose for their existence, and a life and character all their own. Science fiction had a new lease of life but Weinbaum died of cancer 18 months after his first sale.

New Directions with Campbell

Astounding published most of Weinbaum's later fiction. Tremaine was building a stable of talented writers who were introducing some startlingly fresh idea to sf. Amongst them were Donald Wandrei, born 1908, Nathan Schachner, 1895–1955, John Russell Fearn, 1908–60, Jack Williamson, Murray Leinster, and above all Don A. Stuart. Stuart, it was later learned, was the pen-name of John W. Campbell, 1910–71, well known as a writer of super-science space epics on a par with E. E. Smith

After 1937 a rift occurred in sf as approaches to publishing changed. *Wonder Stories*, now retitled *Thrilling Wonder Stories* carried some good fiction, but also published much below-average material

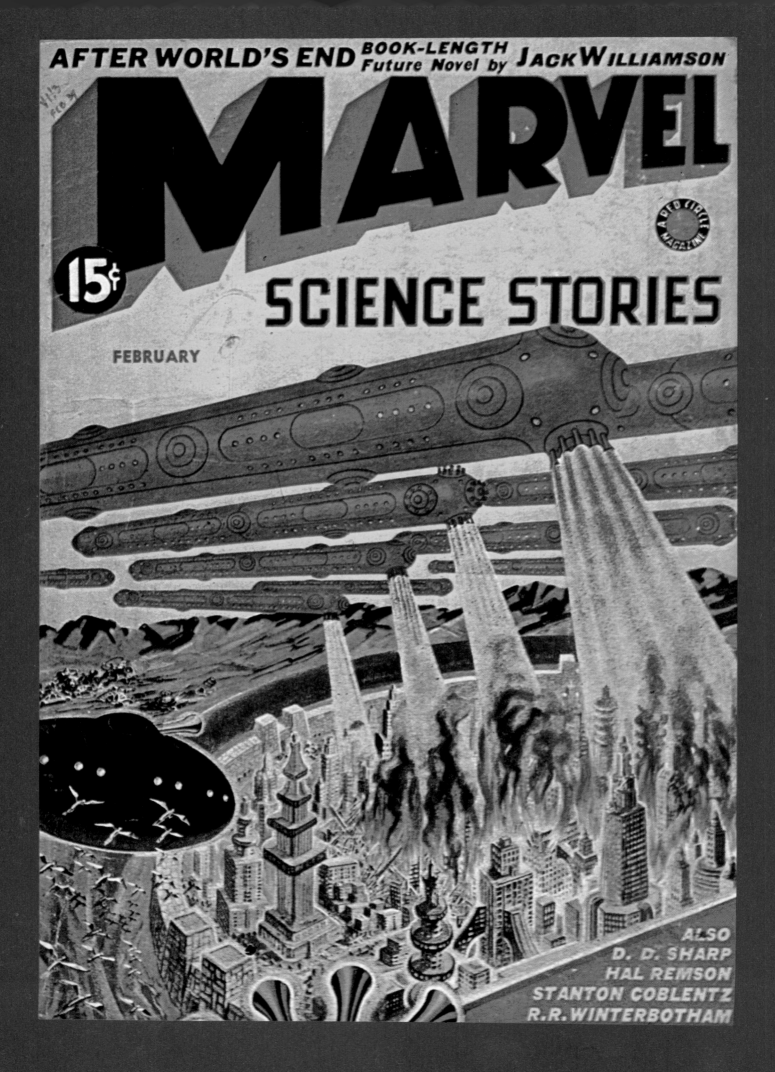

AFTER WORLD'S END BOOK-LENGTH Future Novel by JACK WILLIAMSON

MARVEL

A RED CIRCLE MAGAZINE

15¢

SCIENCE STORIES

FEBRUARY

ALSO
D. D. SHARP
HAL REMSON
STANTON COBLENTZ
R. R. WINTERBOTHAM

Incognito as Stuart however, Campbell created an entirely new mood in sf, bringing pathos and feeling to the genre. Stories like 'Twilight' *1934* and 'Night' *1935* depicting a dying, far future Earth inhabited solely by still-functioning machines long after man has passed away, gave sf an added dimension. Writers like Raymond Z. Gallun, born 1911 and Harl Vincent, 1893–1968, hitherto competent but not outstanding, adopted the Stuart style to produce classics of their own, such as 'Seeds of the Dusk' *1938* and 'Prowler of the Wastelands' *1935*.

Between them Campbell and Weinbaum altered the course of science fiction. Campbell was soon to become far more influential when in 1937 he stepped into the editorial chair at *Astounding*. At first Campbell alienated himself from many writers because of his strict attitude in casting aside the old pulp standards in a drive for quality and originality. He instructed writers to remember that people were as important in sf as the science and to think more about the social implications of scientific advance. Many of the old writers could not adapt to this policy, and as at this time the sf magazine market was expanding rapidly, why need they bother?

As a result a rift occurred in sf. *Astounding* was the field leader and a prestige publication to those who cared about sf. But most other magazines pandered to a less discerning, often more juvenile audience. *Wonder Stories*, now retitled *Thrilling Wonder Stories* in keeping with other magazines from its new publisher, carried some good fiction (notably that by Williamson and Campbell), but also published much below-average material.

The same happened to *Amazing*, though more drastically. In 1938 it was sold to Ziff-Davis Publications in Chicago. The new editor was Raymond A. Palmer, born 1910, one of the pioneers of sf fandom. He had an ever-open eye for gimmicks and sensational stunts. Physically handicapped as the result of a childhood accident, Palmer also showed signs of an inferiority complex that he was forever trying to master. His first action was to transform *Amazing* into a gaudy, juvenile pulp, with straight action adventure of the most elementary kind. Since Ziff-Davis' rates were equal to Street & Smith's and indeed, better for established writers, Palmer was able to attract most of the authors rejected by Campbell, as well as establish a stable of local Illinois writers, of whom the best known today, though not for their sf, are Robert Bloch and William McGivern.

1938 also brought a new magazine to the stalls. One of the many facets of pulp fiction was the terror story, filled with sex and sadism. Publisher Martin Goodman had started to expand into that field in 1937, and now added *Marvel Science Stories* to his titles. The first issue was surprisingly good, featuring 'Survival' by Arthur J. Burks, 1898–1974, which was highly thought of at the time. In keeping with Goodman's policy, the editor, Robert O. Erisman, instructed his writers to include sexy scenes in their fiction. Sf-purists objected, though no one else minded, and *Marvel*'s first issue had good sales.

But the promise given by *Marvel* as a competent rival to *Astounding* did not last. After a few issues the quality dropped, and for three issues, December 1939 to November 1940, with a title change to *Marvel Tales*, it used science fiction as a background only to pushing more sexy terror tales on an already satiated readership. Despite a return, as *Marvel Stories*, in April 1941, with a surprisingly good issue, the magazine had already dug its own grave, and Goodman suspended it whilst investigating the burgeoning comic-book field.

The Big Boom

The initial success of *Marvel*, coupled with the lucrative turnover of *Amazing*, heralded the beginning of a boom that lasted until the entry of the United States into WWII. Combined with a number of other factors, publishers decided that sf had sales potential, and companies began to add new titles to their chain. Sf fans were overwhelmed at first. In the 1930s scarcely any sf was available in book-form outside the standard classics (Verne, Wells, Stapledon, Burroughs), but even these were in hardback and too expensive for the reader to buy regularly. The magazines, at a very reasonable fifteen or twenty cents, offered as much, if not more, than a hardback, and readers were hungry for more.

And so they came. *Thrilling Wonder* acquired a companion *Startling Stories*, with a policy of carrying a complete novel per issue and a 'Hall of Fame' reprint. *Amazing* spawned *Fantastic Adventures*, and *Marvel* was twinned with *Dynamic Science Stories* which only saw two issues.

Fans who had grown up with sf over the last 12 years now found an opportunity to break into editing. Frederik Pohl, born 1919, became the editor of *Astonishing Stories* and *Super Science Stories*; Donald Wollheim, born 1914, began his own *Cosmic Stories* and *Stirring Science Stories*; and Robert Lowndes, born 1916, took over from Charles Hornig with *Future Fiction*, *Science Fiction* and *Science Fiction Quarterly*.

F. Orlin Tremaine returned to the scene with *Comet Stories*, but he split with the company over payment problems, and that magazine folded after just five issues.

Perhaps the most juvenile magazine was *Captain Future*, a companion to *Thrilling Wonder*, but then

One of the many facets of pulp fiction was the terror story, filled with sex and sadism. Publisher Martin Goodman expanded the field in 1937 and now added *Marvel Science Stories* to his titles

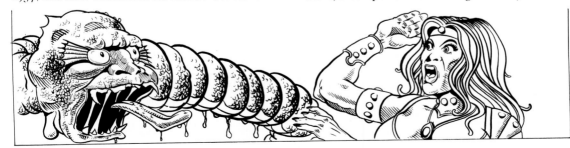

When Virgil Finlay went to War, Lawrence Stevens became the new cover artist at FFM, illustrating Augusta Groner's 1912 novel *City of the Dead* (opposite)

this was its aim. The lead adventure novels were written by Edmond Hamilton. *Planet Stories* was another poor magazine at first, chiefly through lack of material. But editor Malcolm Reiss persisted, and by the late 1940s *Planet* was publishing some of the most exciting space fiction around, especially work by Ray Bradbury, Leigh Brackett, Fredric Brown, and later Poul Anderson.

One of the most sought after items today is *Famous Fantastic Mysteries*, a reprint magazine from Munsey Publications. It unearthed many of the famous classics from the old pulps, especially the work of Merritt. The magazine's interior was further enhanced by the beautiful artwork of Virgil Finlay, 1914–71, and the imitative but equally spectacular art of Lawrence Stevens.

Astounding reigned supreme over this pulp turmoil. Campbell had retitled the magazine *Astounding Science-Fiction* in 1938 to squash some of the pulp stigma that the suffix *Stories* implied. He also introduced a regular scientific article per issue, adding respectability to the fiction. But for the sf fan, most important was his drive for a thoughtful and intelligent treatment of the development of science and society. A few writers adapted, veterans like Jack Williamson and Clifford Simak, born 1904, and Tremaine discoveries like Eric Frank Russell, born 1905, and L. Sprague de Camp, born 1907. Added to these came a torrent of new talent – A. E. van Vogt, born 1912, Theodore Sturgeon, born 1918, Lester del Rey, born 1915, Robert Heinlein, born 1907, Isaac Asimov, born 1920, L. Ron Hubbard, born 1911, Fritz Leiber, born 1910, and Cleve Cartmill, 1908–64, to name but a few.

A Golden Age?

The period 1940–42 has been called a Golden Age, not just of *Astounding* but of all science fiction. It was

Startling Stories, a companion magazine for *Thrilling Wonder,* grew out of the magazine boom immediately prior to WWII. It had a policy of carrying a complete novel per issue

at this time and shortly after that many of the classics of science fiction were first published. Not only novels like van Vogt's *Slan 1940,* E. E. Smith's 'Lensman' series, Asimov's *Foundation* stories, Simak's *City* series and Heinlein's *Methuselah's Children 1941,* but short fiction such as Asimov's immortal 'Nightfall' *1941,* Lewis Padgett's 'Mimsy Were the Borogoves' *1943,* Heinlein's 'The Roads Must Roll' *1940,* and numerous others.

This profusion of wonder should have been enough to satisfy any reader and editor, but Campbell produced equally remarkable results in *Astounding*'s shot-lived and now legendary fantasy companion *Unknown.*

WWII curbed much of this creativity, and the many forms of rationing killed a large number of the magazines. But after the war, when the atom bomb suddenly made the general public aware of science and its equal potential for good or evil purposes, sf began to emerge into the open. Novels and collections of stories from the sf pulps were published in hardback, first by specialist publishers like Gnome Press and Fantasy Press, and then by major general publishing companies, such as Doubleday. General magazines, most notably *The Saturday Evening Post,* regularly included sf in their pages. With this recognition publishers more readily accepted the idea of sf magazines, and events began to snowball.

Science fiction itself took a giant step to maturity. On the whole the days of space opera were past, even *Planet Stories* was moderately respectable. Only *Amazing,* subject to the cult antics of Ray Palmer then championing the Shaver Mystery, remained poor quality. Despite their titles *Thrilling Wonder* and *Startling Stories* became increasingly more adult, and it was in *Startling* in 1952 that a major breakthrough came with the publication of Philip José Farmer's 'The Lovers'. Its serious treatment of sexual themes as an essential part of the story heralded a sign that now was the time for an overhaul of the field. What Campbell had accomplished by 1942 as regards content and theme, other editors were now attempting with a view to quality and style.

Two of the most important editors were Horace L. Gold, born 1914, in charge of the new *Galaxy SF,* and Anthony Boucher, 1911–68, who, with J. Francis McComas, born 1910, coedited *The Magazine of Fantasy and Science Fiction* (or *F&SF* for convenience). Boucher was as well, if not better, known in the mystery fiction field, and both he and McComas had a specialist eye for quality above that of the general pulp editor. Gold, an old-time writer from the days of Tremaine, was in turn a harsh taskmaster who shoehorned his writers into treating science fiction with respect.

Throughout the 1950s *Astounding* was constantly challenged for field leadership by *Galaxy* and *F&SF,* collectively known as the 'Big Three'. Campbell had lost some of his respectability in 1950 when he had promoted the dianetic theories of L. Ron Hubbard in *Astounding.* Hubbard soon abandoned the sf field, and Campbell forsook Hubbard, but he still called for an emphasis in his fiction on the powers of the mind, and writers responded with a

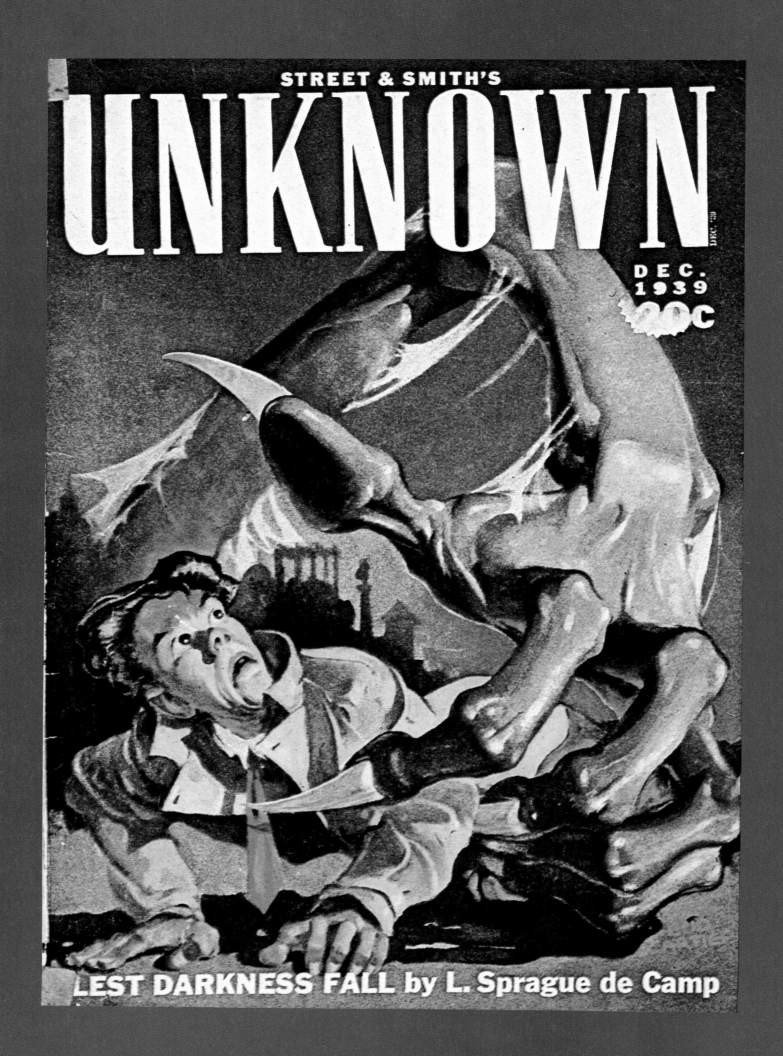

flood of 'psi' stories involving telepathy, telekinesis, precognition and similar talents. There were some good stories amongst them, but the trend alienated many readers who sought refuge in the fresher fields of *Galaxy* or the maturer pastures of *F&SF*.

To briefly distinguish between these three magazines, *Astounding* laid strong emphasis on the development of science, with fiction demonstrating the possibilities inherent in scientific expansion and its possible effects on Man. It's not enough to show a robot policeman at work. One must trace the full repercussions of that invention. *Galaxy*, which was edited by Gold in the 1950s and Frederik Pohl in the 1960s, put more emphasis on social rather than scientific trends. The fiction often carried an underlying message under Gold, but this was less evident with Pohl, when the fiction slanted more towards solid adventure often liberally sprinkled with humour as in, for example, Robert Sheckley's work. *F&SF* has always had the most open policy of all, since it publishes the entire range of fantasy from supernatural horror to solid 'hardware' sf. Its editors, including the current Edward Ferman, born 1937 – who has edited the magazine for longer than any of his predecessors – demand a high quality of fiction and a special brand of originality in theme and treatment.

The early 1950s saw the emergence of a talented new generation of writers, some of whom had dabbled briefly in the field in earlier years, but only now found their true direction: Damon Knight, Poul Anderson, James Blish, William Tenn, Philip Dick, Robert Sheckley, Katherine MacLean, Harry Harrison, Frank Herbert and H. Beam Piper.

The sf magazine world reached a publishing peak in 1953 when 34 different magazines were being issued in the United States alone. In many cases there was little to distinguish one from another, but rather than elaborate on them here, a brief guide will be found to every sf magazine in the catalog to this encyclopedia. Worth special mention however are *Space SF* edited by Lester del Rey, *If* edited by James Quinn, *Future SF* under Robert Lowndes, and *Fantastic Universe* from Leo Margulies. Even Ray Palmer, who had now left *Amazing* in less sensation-seeking hands, edited a moderately respectable *Other Worlds*, which whilst it still catered for the UFO devotee, carried some surprisingly good fiction by writers like Theodore Sturgeon and Eric Frank Russell.

Hard Times

By the mid-1950s however, the death-knell was sounding for many magazines, especially the pulps. A combination of causes such as television, the slick magazines and a blossoming paperback field, made the pulp magazine seem outdated, and, almost as one, they died. Just a few survived in the, by now, traditional digest format, *Amazing* successfully undergoing the change in 1953, but most of the old names in the field, including *Thrilling Wonder*, *Startling*, *Planet Stories*, *Famous Fantastic Mysteries* and the grandfather *Weird Tales*, passed into history.

These elements have continued to have a restrictive effect on the magazine field since the mid-

1950s, and while there have been sporadic eruptions of new, hopeful publications, the end result has always been the same.

One of the most popular magazines of the 1960s was *If*, or *Worlds of If* as it was temporarily titled. Also edited by Frederik Pohl, it expanded on *Galaxy*'s policy to include more fantastic stories and tales of epic adventure. It was hardly surprising to find that when E. E. Smith wrote the final novel in his *Skylark* series, *Skylark DuQuesne 1965*, it was first serialized in *If*. When A. E. van Vogt returned to writing sf after over a decade's absence, it was in *If* that his new stories first appeared. *If* also encouraged new writers by including at least one first sale each issue – the 'If-firsts'. Included amongst these budding hopefuls have been Joseph Green, Gary Wright, Larry Niven and Perry Chapdelaine, whilst Fred Saberhagen also made his first sale to Pohl. Harlan Ellison and Robert Silverberg, who had started writing in the mid-1950s but had left the field, returned with powerful results in *Galaxy* and *If* especially in the mid-1960s.

At the same time, *Amazing Stories* and *Fantastic*, now in the hands of the highly capable Cele Goldsmith, were also introducing much new talent,

61

In 1960 John Campbell had continued to strive for *Astounding*'s status, and had changed the magazine's name to *Analog*. *Analog* still leads the field of sf magazines with its circulation figures

including Keith Laumer, Piers Anthony, Roger Zelazny, Ursula LeGuin, Thomas Disch and Ben Bova.

It was Bova who succeeded Campbell when the inevitable, but what many thought impossible happened, Campbell died. In 1960 Campbell had continued to strive for *Astounding*'s status, and had changed the magazine's name to *Analog*, as it is still known today. When Campbell died in 1971 it was feared by some that perhaps there could be no successor, but Bova has admirably fulfilled his promise. *Analog* still leads the field of sf magazines with a circulation of 110,000 plus, more than double its closest companion. Both *F&SF* and *Galaxy* average 50,000 each, though *Galaxy* is rising. Its sister, *If*, was folded in 1974 even though its circulation was higher than *Galaxy*'s! The only other survivors are *Amazing*, and its companion *Fantastic*, both now in the hands of Ted White. Although they frequently carry some excellent sf, their circulations are only around the 20,000 mark, and their future is not bright. For a period from 1965 to 1972 their new publisher, Sol Cohen, instituted a policy of almost total reprint, including a number of all-reprint magazines like *Thrilling SF* and *Science Fiction Classics*. Since he did not intend paying for the reprints (because the previous publisher, Ziff-Davis, had acquired all rights), Sol Cohen was soon in trouble with the newly formed Science Fiction Writers of America. Nevertheless the reprint magazines made sufficient money to subsidize *Amazing* and *Fantastic*'s reversion to publishing new fiction, but since the last reprint title folded in 1975 that support has not been there.

A number of reprint and semi-reprint magazines has appeared in the last few years, none financially successful. The most attractive was *Forgotten Fantasy*, while at the other extreme was the recent *Sky Worlds*.

The Experimental 70s

Despite the gloomy prospect for magazines, there have been a number of experiments recently. One such was *Vertex*. A high-priced, glossy magazine, it attempted to throw itself directly at the mass market with the traditional slick magazine approach. It did well, but never recovered from the paper shortages of 1974, when the publisher adapted *Vertex* to a newspaper format, a tragic experiment. *Vertex* was not the first 'slick'. Gernsback had experimented with the form in 1953 with *Science Fiction Plus*, and Campbell converted *Analog* briefly in 1963–5. But production costs were too high to be supported by readership alone, and sufficient advertizing revenue was not forthcoming. However, since the *Vertex* experiment, there have been other attempts. *Odyssey* came and failed after two issues in 1976, and *Cosmos* saw four issues in 1977. *Galileo* however is less pretentious, and may possibly have struck the right chord. Rather than aim at the mass market, it has cut printing costs to the bone by publishing only a core run of initially some 8,000 copies for sale to a guaranteed readership. This also bypasses distribution problems since most of the sales are through specialists. The same method has been used success-

fully on *Unearth*, a magazine devoted to printing work by new writers, and *Algol*, formerly a fanzine, now turned professional. By slow development from this base, these magazines could well survive for many years.

Another ploy to escape the fate of other magazines has come with *Isaac Asimov's SF Magazine*. A digest edited by George Scithers, it relies on the selling power of Asimov's name, publishing the kind of fiction likely to appeal to his many readers. In many ways its contents resemble those of Campbell's early *Astounding*, and as such some readers are buying the magazine with renewed respect. Initially a quarterly, there are plans to advance it to a monthly schedule.

Every once in a while a prophet of doom announces the end of the sf magazines, but from an impossible nadir they always recover. If publishers are willing to experiment, especially the small-time semi-professionals, there will always be magazines. Without them the sf world would be considerably poorer, for where else can tomorrow's masters serve their apprenticeship?

United Kingdom

While in the United States it was the major publishers who investigated science fiction and ventured into its realms, in Britain it was through the efforts of the science fiction fans that sf was promoted and a professional magazine market eventually established.

Science fiction had appeared erratically in general fiction magazines in Britain before and after WWI, and from 1926 American magazines were irregularly imported, often being sold in cheap lots on Woolworth's counters. By the end of the 1920s Britain had its own subculture of fandom. The father of British science fiction in this respect was

Walter Gillings, who produced a high quality fanzine *Scientifiction*. He had for years tried to interest British publishers in an sf magazine. One of them, Pearson's, eventually issued a juvenile sf weekly tabloid of their own in 1934. It was called *Scoops*, and was edited by Haydn Dimmock, who knew very little about sf. The magazine was thus initially filled with very low-quality material, and by the time British fandom rallied it was too late to save it. *Scoops* folded after 20 issues.

By the late 1930s, Britain had an increasing number of talented writers who were selling regularly to the American market, amongst them John Beynon Harris, 1903–69, better known as John Wyndham, John Russell Fearn, J. M. Walsh, 1897–1952, William F. Temple, born 1914, Eric Frank Russell and Arthur Clarke, born 1917. Gillings knew these writers personally, and when he finally received the green light for his own magazine *Tales of Wonder* in 1937, he turned to them for material. Alas, WWII intervened just as *Tales of Wonder* was establishing itself as a major force. A rival firm, seeing the unoccupied green pastures, issued its own sf title, *Fantasy*, in 1938. That only saw three issues – all of a high quality – before the war killed it. *Tales of Wonder* struggled on valiantly until 1942, by which time Gillings was heavily reliant on American reprints.

Because of wartime restrictions American magazines were no longer imported, and consequently a number of British reprint editions appeared. The most important was that of *Astounding*, issued by the Atlas Publishing Co. in London. Starting in August 1939 it continued until August 1963, and for the wartime British was the only regular source of magazine sf.

After the war, Gillings established a new magazine, called confusingly *Fantasy*, but publishing problems brought that to a close after three important issues. (Gillings had bought the first sf from Arthur Clarke, but advised the aspiring author to send the stories to America rather than wait for the British publishing scene to return to normal.) The same fate befell *New Worlds*, started by Gillings's colleague Ted Carnell, 1912–72, in 1946. However, a core of British fans, who used to meet regularly in the White Horse Inn in London, established their own publishing company, Nova Publications, in 1948, and *New Worlds* was relaunched.

It found a highly responsive market, and after a few first tentative issues was able to increase its regularity until it became monthly in 1954. By then it had a companion title, *Science Fantasy*, initially edited by Gillings in 1950, but thereafter by Carnell. Under one roof therefore Carnell was in charge of the British equivalents of *Astounding* and *F&SF*, publishing mature, quality sf. Carnell encouraged a healthy number of new writers, like E. C. Tubb, born 1919, Brian Aldiss, born 1925, John Brunner, born 1934, James White, born 1928, and J. G. Ballard, born 1930.

New Worlds emphasized scientific development in its fiction, but always with that distinct British flavour. In the United States, sf was harsh and active in nature, infused with a frontier spirit. Not so British sf, which was far more restful and pastoral.

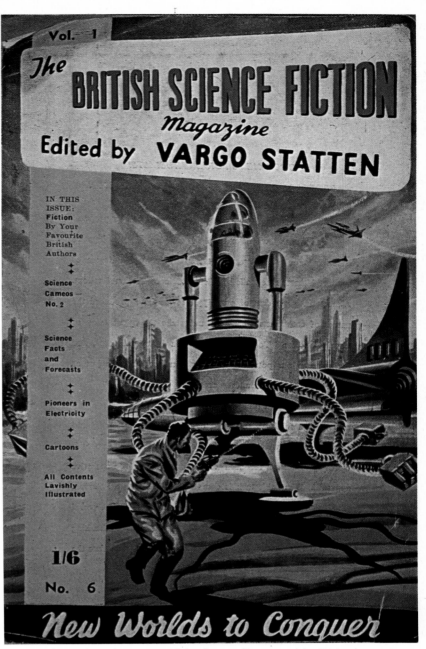

In American sf, explorers would land on a distant planet, and within a few pages would be up to their ears in conflict. British explorers on the other hand would let events take their course, and wait for trouble to come to them!

For most of the 1950s *New Worlds* had some healthy magazine rivalry. A number of cheap publications from the firm of John Spencer, namely *Futuristic Science Stories*, *Tales of Tomorrow*, *Worlds of Fantasy* and *Wonders of the Spaceways*, can be instantly passed over for the puerile rubbish that they were (even though they did carry early fiction by E. C. Tubb, Lan Wright and R. Lionel Fanthorpe). Despite the similarity of titles, *Vargo Statten's SF Magazine* was in fact a better product. After subsequent title changes, becoming finally the *British Space Fiction Magazine*, which went some way to raising its standard, editor John Russell Fearn opened the pages to fandom, which no other British magazine did, and encouraged new writers, of whom the best known today is Barrington Bayley.

John Richards was the regular cover artist on Vargo Statten's *British SF Magazine*. In order to cut costs the magazine often used the same cover more than once

New Worlds' biggest rival was *Nebula*, a one-man effort, edited and financed by Peter Hamilton of Glasgow. He paid the highest word rates of all British magazines, and thus often had first look at new sf, including that from America. Most of Britain's best writers, especially Aldiss, Russell, Temple, Tubb and Bulmer, were regulars in its pages, and Hamilton also bought the first fiction from Bob Shaw, and American Robert Silverberg.

The other major title was *Authentic*. It had started in 1951 as a fortnightly paperback novel, but as issues progressed and readers responded, so editor Gordon Landsborough began to include the occasional short story, non-fiction articles and letter columns. Finally it settled down as a regular magazine under the editorship of research chemist H. J. Campbell. Despite its popularity, *Authentic* sadly lacked originality. Its fiction was stereotyped and forced, frequently because Campbell had to rely on the same small band of regulars to supply the bulk of the fiction. The best came from the pens of E. C. Tubb, Kenneth Bulmer and John Brunner, who provided most of the lead novels. Tubb later edited *Authentic* in its last days. The publishers folded it in 1957 when they invested heavily in paperback books. *Nebula* lasted till 1959, but finally proved too costly for Hamilton to continue alone, and that died after 41 worthwhile issues.

That left Carnell in sole control of British magazine sf. He had added a third title to his brood. *Science Fiction Adventures* was originally a British edition of an American magazine edited by Larry Shaw. When that died in 1958, Carnell continued the offspring with new British material, concentrating on two short novels an issue, including some of the best fiction from Kenneth Bulmer, Lan Wright, John Brunner and Michael Moorcock. Between *New Worlds*, *Science Fantasy* and *SF Adventures*, Carnell catered for almost every taste in science fiction.

Beginning of the End

Alas, all good things come to an end, and by the early 1960s paperbacks were making their presence felt on the magazine market. *SF Adventures* folded, *New Worlds* passed to Michael Moorcock, and *Science Fantasy* to Kyril Bonfiglioli. Moorcock's manipulations with *New Worlds* over the next six years as the banner of the 'New Wave' is more fully recounted in that section. Bonfiglioli should be congratulated on his success with *Science Fantasy* which, in its new pocketbook format, he edited with remarkable astuteness. He encouraged several new writers, in particular Keith Roberts and Christopher Priest, and maintained a high and original quality. However a financial setback with the publisher, coupled with a none too successful title change to *Impulse* brought an abrupt end to the magazine in 1967.

Since *New Worlds* was no longer a true sf magazine, the British scene was a desert until 1969 when *Vision of Tomorrow* appeared. It was financed by Australian businessman Ronald E. Graham, and edited in Britain by Philip Harbottle, born 1941. Intended as a pocketbook, the distributors called for a slick-size magazine, in which format it remained for its brief life. Harbottle succeeded in bringing back into print many of the better writers from Carnell's *Nova* days, especially Tubb, Bulmer and Temple. Publishing restrictions disallowed any American material, which clearly harmed the magazine, and massive distribution troubles and behind-the-scenes wranglings led to a sudden ending of *Vision* after just 12 issues. Britain was again void of any sf magazine.

False Starts

When one was reborn it was in a bold new guise. *Science Fiction Monthly* was the result of its publisher's intentions to produce a poster magazine reproducing the popular covers from its sf paperback list. The fiction always took second place, and the magazine failed to acquire any good material from the leading names or sponsor new authors. When the glitter had faded from the original concept, circulation rapidly dwindled, and after just two years, 1974–76, *SF Monthly* also folded. An attempt to rationalize the magazine in *SF Digest* was killed by the publisher before the first and only issue was properly distributed.

A recent attempt to produce a new sf magazine met the same fate. *Vortex*, edited by aspiring young writer Keith Seddon, was a beautiful production in a slick format, with attractive Rodney Matthews' covers and coloured interior artwork. But Seddon did not capture Britain's leading authors (except Moorcock) until it was too late. When the publisher matched returns with production costs, he axed *Vortex* immediately.

At present Britain has no sf magazine. In comparison with America this might at first seem tragic, but not so when one discovers that the average sale of a science fiction paperback in Britain (30–40,000 copies) is about the same as America. America suffers from very patchy distribution, unlike Britain, and as a consequence British readers have a ready supply of paperbacks, sufficient in quantity to make up for the lack of magazines. But Britain will suffer in the future from the absence of a market for new writers. This is made more apparent by comparing Britain with the rest of the world.

Because of language barriers, the influence of non-English speaking countries on sf has been, until recently, negligible, even though we all bow in homage to the founding father from France, Jules Verne. Most countries have relied on translated reprint editions of United States magazines, chiefly *Galaxy* and *F&SF*, and only since the early 1960s have several countries started to develop an sf culture of their own.

Sweden can lay claim to the dubious honour of the very first all-sf magazine, *Hugin*. Conceived in 1916, it lasted for nearly four years, and was written almost single-handedly by its editor and publisher Otto Witt, 1875–1923, and had little, if any, influence in its own country, let alone the rest of the world. Much the same can be said of the German magazine *Kapitän Mors*, which had laid special emphasis on

One of the most unusual of the continental magazines is the French fantasy comic *Metal Hurlant*, which combines sf eroticism and exquisitely drawn figures

fantastic adventures in the pre-WWI years, and the Russian *Mirpriklusheniya*, which had regularly featured space fiction as early as 1903.

French fan Georges Gallet boldly tried to publish an sf magazine, *Conquêtes*, in 1939, but with fatal bad luck chose the week war broke out to launch his publication. France then had to wait until 1953 when publisher Maurice Renard issued *Fiction* as the French edition of *F&SF*. With Alain Doremieux as editor, it rapidly became the backbone of French sf,

regularly featuring new fiction by French and Belgian writers. Unfortunately the bankruptcy of its publishers in August 1977 suspended the magazine after 283 issues, though it was subsequently relaunched. *Fiction*'s companion, *Galaxie*, sadly has a bleaker outlook, but France can still be thankful for two other series: *Univers*, a quarterly pocketbook edited by Jacques Sadoul and Yves Fremion and specializing in new wave fiction from England and the United States as well as France, and *Piranha*, edited by sf writer Yann Menez, and featuring exclusively French material, including films and comic-strips.

Sweden succeeded in issuing a science fiction magazine during the War years, the reprint *Jules Verne Magasinet*. It initially featured adventures like Edmond Hamilton's *Captain Future* series, but later slanted away from sf towards westerns and general adventures. It was not until *Häpna!* that Sweden had its own *Astounding* (the title means *Be Astounded!*). Started in 1953 by two brothers, it survived against all financial odds until the illness of publisher Kurt Kindberg forced its closure in 1965, though it struggled on as a fanzine for a few more years. Its editor was Kjell Ekström who revolutionized Swedish sf and fandom, and his death from cancer in 1971 was a sad loss.

Italy – Field Leader?

The most active sf country in Europe is Italy, which since 1942 has had over 40 sf magazines. However a distinction must be drawn between magazines as such, and a regular, frequent series of paperback novels. Italy, as do Germany and Spain, specializes in such series, with novels occasionally being boosted with an additional story. This was based on the original successful format of Italy's *Urania*, which began life as *I Romanzi di Urania* in 1952 and has since seen over 700 issues. For a while in 1964 and 1965 it was appearing weekly, and still maintains a fortnightly schedule under editors Carlo Fruttero and Franco Lucentini.

These 'novel-magazines' aside, Italy can still boast some fourteen traditional sf magazines, including a number of experiments. *Au Dela du Ciel* for instance, which saw 40 issues from 1958 to 1961, was published in Rome, but printed in French. *Fantascienza Sovietica*, as the title suggests, was devoted to reprinting Russian sf. Few magazines were devoted to Italian fiction, although *Mondi Astrali* in 1955 and *Futuro* in 1963 were pioneers in this respect. Often Italians would use anglicized pseudonyms, thus *Altair* in 1977 carried fiction by 'Jack Azimov', whilst *Alpha Tau* as far back as 1957 had featured such writers as 'Peter Iota' and 'Jim Omega', a system that could survive through as many alphabets as necessary.

Today Italy has six active magazines, including *Urania*. These include *Galassia*, edited by Gianni Montanari, relying mostly on novels but also featuring many reviews and essays; *Nova* edited by Ugo Malaguti with a mixture of new and reprint sf; and the very attractive *Robot* edited by Vittorio Curtoni, that provides more of a magazine service with letter columns and reviews.

Behind the Iron Curtain

Science fiction is popular behind the Iron Curtain, although no Russian magazine is fully devoted to sf fiction. Closest comes *Teknika-Molodezhi*, which specializes in science and handiwork for young people and features one or two sf stories each issue. For many years Rumania produced *Colectia Povestiri Stiintifico-Fantastice* which was a supplement to the scientific magazine *Stiinta si Tehnica*. Edited by Rumania's leading sf writer, Adrian Rogoz, and publishing material from all over the world, it amassed 373 issues before folding in 1969. Rumania also produces the only Communist sf 'fanzine', *Solaris*, printed and edited by students at Bucharest University.

Hungarian sf owes its genesis to the formation of the Tudományos Fantasztikus Klub in 1968. Since then this fandom has helped support not only more clubs and organizations, but one of the world's most attractive sf magazines, *Galaktika*. This should not be confused with Yugoslavia's *Galaksija* which began in April 1972 and now has a thriving circulation of 50,000 or more. Vying with Hungary for the best European magazine is Spain's *Nueva Dimension*. Launched in 1968 it stalwartly survived the opposition of the Franco regime, even though at least one issue was seized by the State, and is now approaching its one hundredth issue, a fine example of what sf fans can achieve against all odds. In 1974 it won the Europa Award as the best sf magazine.

Outside Europe, most countries have been content with reprint editions of United States magazines, such as Mexico's *Ciencia y Fantasia* and Argentina's *Minotauro*. Nevertheless some of these, occasionally backed up by mature editorials and letter columns, have helped establish a firm sf culture within that country, as in the case of Argentina's *Mas Alla* in the mid-1950s.

Although Australia has produced a number of good writers, not least Lee Harding, John Baxter and Jack Wodhams, it has never yielded a satisfactory sf magazine. There was a spate of cheap reprint editions in the early 1950s, few of which are worth remembering. *Thrills Incorporated* included a number of new stories, but also printed many thinly disguised copies of American sf. As a result Australia's writers have had to make their names in the United States and British magazines. *Vision of Tomorrow* was backed by Australian money but edited in Britain and thus did not reflect a true antipodean flavour. Only now does Australia have a semi-professional magazine called *Void*, and even this carries some reprints. What's more the editor, Paul Collins, was born in England.

Yet in comparison Turkey has had two sf magazines, the short lived but important *Antares*, which engendered a strong Turkish fandom, and the current *X-Bilinmeyen*. And Japan has one of the most successful sf magazines of them all, called simply *S-F Magazine*. Started in 1960 as an edition of *F&SF*, its editor, Masami Fukushima, 1929–76, soon incorporated original Japanese material. Together with *Kiso-Tengai*, it has held several story contests, and now Japan has a very active sf scene.

Who knows, but the day may come when even the Eskimoes have their own sf magazine. Certainly the Amerindians have one in the shape of Craig Strete's semi-professional *Red Planet Earth*, a solid and exciting way of keeping a unique culture alive and looking to the future.

screen trips

Alan Frank

Visual science fiction can be assessed as a discreet form of science fiction as a whole. The cinema itself remains the nearest thing we have to Wells' *Time Machine* with its unique ability to make real our dreams and visions. The development of special effects has given rise to fantastic illusions recreating many of the writers' ideas.

Unlike its literary counterparts, the science fiction film has almost always been produced within the mainstream of the cinema. It has to be extracted from the corpus of the cinema as a whole. Films have always had to be constructed with a view to recouping their very large investment at the box office and so, by and large, they have tended to deal with the broader aspects of the genre: the themes and concepts that are dealt with in literature have been subordinated to the broad picture of a futuristic technology. The emphasis has been on the visual and the startling, employing all the tricks and devices of which only the film medium is capable. Special effects tend to dominate the philosophical content.

Science fiction has been part of the cinema from its inception. The Lumière Brothers' film *The Sausage Machine (Charcuterie Mechanique), 1895* postulated, albeit comically, the age of the futuristic machine with a device that converted live pigs into sausages and the British pioneer Robert W. Paul used the cinema itself as a kind of time machine, using film to project the illusion of a trip through time, inspired by H. G. Wells' 1895 novel. Indeed, it has even been suggested that Wells may have taken his inspiration for *The Time Machine* from the cinema. However, it was Georges Méliès' discovery that the camera could be made to lie that provided the genesis for science fiction film. Although he never developed from a creator of cinema tricks into

a sustained film maker, Méliès laid the basis for the major special effects employed by film makers subsequently – fast and slow motion, matte effects, multiple exposures, stop motion, dissolves and fades. Their execution has been refined over the decades but their basis remains unaltered.

Méliès' *A Trip To The Moon, 1902* brought space travel to the cinema although his intention was not to postulate what space travel was actually likely to be but rather to create a pantomime in which he could employ all his camera tricks. The film had a dramatic structure with the preparation, launching, flight and landing of its moon rocket, while its vision of the Moon with giant mushrooms evolving from the explorers' umbrellas and its exploding crustacean Selenites showed a filmic imagination the equal of its literary counterparts. Visions of the future became part of the cinema and the film medium was able believably (within its own terms) to extrapolate from current scientific thinking and prediction as well as to strike out in areas that were its own.

The First Twenty Years

The basic themes of the *genre* were established in the first two decades of this century. By 1916 Jules Verne's *20,000 Leagues Under The Sea* had already been filmed three times, the 1916 version being the first major film to feature scenes filmed under water,

The making of the robot Maria (Brigitte Helm) in Fritz Lang's masterly *Metropolis*

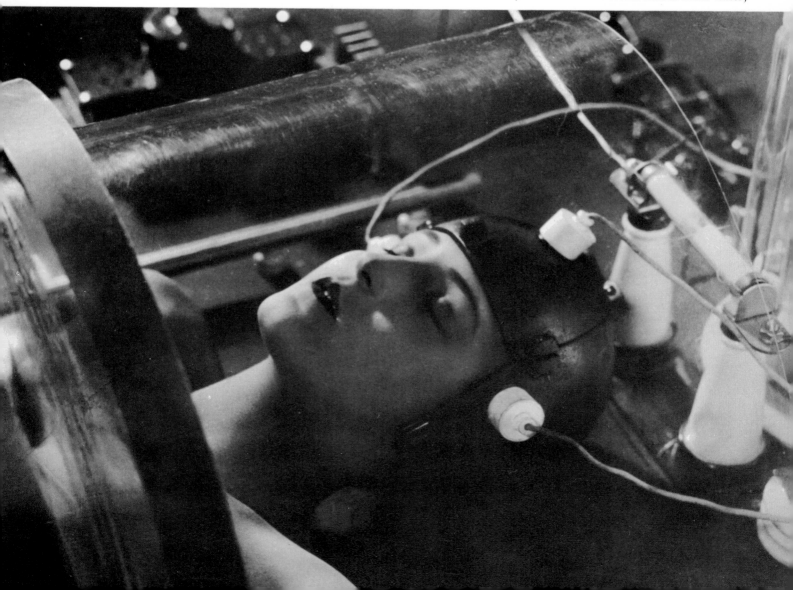

even to the extent of including an (artificial) octopus. Space travel was depicted in Edison's *A Trip To Mars* in 1910, the trip being made in the style of Wells by means of anti-gravity, in this case in the form of a powder accidentally spilled on the traveller's head. From Denmark came Forest Holger-Madsen's *Himmelskibet (Heaven Ship/A Trip to Mars) 1919* employing a space ship that owed its inspiration more to the aircraft than the rocket. The film showed Mars as a verdant garden planet and its message of international understanding and tolerance soon bogged the film down in philosophical dissertation.

Meanwhile, travel in the reverse direction was not ignored. E. Holman Clark came as a Martian to terrify Charles Hawtrey in the 1913 *A Message From Mars*, a film taken from the theatre, not normally a fecund field for science fiction. Germany, soon to become the home of the science fiction and horror cinema's first flowering, gave rise to yet another basic theme of the *genre*, the so-called mad scientist whose experiments inevitably, for whatever motives, lead to disaster. *Homunculus* was the most popular German film of the war years. Made in 1915 and owing something to Wegener's *Der Golem*, *Homunculus* was a six-part serial which featured an artificially created being, a superhuman in both intellect and moral nature: on discovering its true origin, the creature, like Mary Shelley's creation, went on a homicidal rampage through five episodes to be destroyed by that 'traditional' *deus ex machina*, a bolt of lighting.

With *Metropolis* in 1926, science fiction cinema achieved its first real masterpiece. Seen some 50 years later much of the film does seem muddle-headed and a rather naive excuse for staging some stunning visual effects and one can see how H. G. Wells came to call it 'quite the silliest film'. The plot *is* illogical, simplistic and filled with contradictions but, in terms of pure science fiction cinema, the plot is really only a vehicle for Fritz Lang's vision of the future, a vision that was to have a profound effect on the cinema for years to come. The story, set in the year 2000 had the son of the Master of Metropolis rebelling against the exploitation of the workers, sentenced to live perpetually underground and to keep the city's machines in operation. Only the persuasive powers of the heroine Maria keep the workers from revolution. When the son is chosen to mediate between workers and rulers, his father orders a robot double to be made of Maria and the double incites the workers to revolt and destroy the machines, flooding their own homes beneath. Only the intervention of the real Maria saves their children from drowning. The false Maria is unmasked, the Master is reunited and reconciled with his son and the last title of the film aptly sums up its utopian naivety: 'The heart must mediate between the brain and the hands'. What the film does succeed in portraying is a credible visual future metaphor, achieved by means of its powerful architecture and model work and by the use of the Schufftan process which enabled live action to be combined, by means of a mirror with some of its reflective surface removed, with models or paintings. *Metropolis* is, above all, an architectural film designed to show an all too credible future visually extrapolated from the

Germany and America of the 1920s, and in its visual aspects, including Lang's handling of the crowds, the film succeeds impressively. If the science fiction content seems dated now, the elements which have become clichés of the *genre* still retain their power. The machines are genuinely terrifying and the creation of the robot Maria, with its pseudo-scientific apparatus, flashing sparks and whirling generators, was to become the archetypal scene of creation for subsequent *genre* movies.

Lang then went on to the theme of interplanetary travel with his *Die Frau im Mond 1928*, which also was released under the titles *The Girl in The Moon* and *By Rocket to The Moon*. Leading members of the Rocket Society in Germany, Willy Ley and Hermann Oberth, provided technical advice, advice which when translated to the screen proved remarkably prophetic. Oberth was to go on and work for the Nazis on rocket propulsion while Ley emigrated to the United States to become a science fiction writer and expert on rocketry. Prints of the film were destroyed in Germany during the 1930s on the orders of Hitler because of the similarities between the space ships and the offensive rocket weapons then being developed for use in the bloody battles of WWII.

Developments in the 1930s

The film of H. G. Wells' *The Island of Dr Moreau*, made in 1932 by director Erle C. Kenton neglected the author's views on a corrupted science in favour of a firmly horrific treatment with a ripe performance by Charles Laughton as the eponymous Dr Moreau, while Wells' *The Invisible Man*, made the following year, was an excuse, brilliantly realized, for the fantastic special effects created by Universal's John P. Fulton, while its director, James Whale, used an uneasy mixture of straightforward horror and too much whimsy and quirky humour. The decade's key fantasy movie, *King Kong, 1933* was important to science fiction in that its special effects particularly Willis O'Brien's brilliant stop-motion photography of models used to animate Kong and his fellow monsters, paved the way for future, more controlled special effects work in science fiction films.

Britain's seminal *Things to Come* in 1936, based on Wells' 1933 book, *The Shape of Things To Come*, owed more in its final effect to the futuristic thinking (and spendthrift film making) of its producer Alexander Korda, than to Wells' writing. The picture shows the history of civilization from its destruction after a global holocaust to its rise as a science-based world. In its depiction of the futuristic city of Everytown, the film owed much to *Metropolis*, with the Schufftan process being employed in order to show the huge sets and actors within the same frame of film. Miniatures were made of the upper stories of the buildings while the lower portions were constructed full scale and combined photographically. Less successfully, in the climactic scenes set in 2036, Ned Mann's miniatures involved puppets moved along conveyor belts in miniature buildings to represent the crowds fighting their way towards the space gun.

Hollywood's major contribution during the 1930s was the serial. Science fiction by now had firmly established itself on the bookstands. The comic strip of *Buck Rogers in the 25th Century* had appeared on 7 January 1929 to be followed exactly five years later on 7 January 1934 by *Flash Gordon*. Soon the comic strip became a major medium for science fiction. *Buck Rogers* made his radio debut on 7 November 1932 and as coast-to-coast broadcasting became a reality in America, science fiction became a regular, if ephemeral, staple of the medium, forming a basis of such series as *I Love a Mystery* and certain elements of *Chandu The Magician. Flash Gordon* was, for its time, the most expensive cinema serial. It cost some $350,000 and had the advantages inherent in being made by a major studio, Universal: it was able to use (or rather, re-use) the sets from other Universal productions, notably the laboratory from *Bride of Frankenstein* and the giant statue from *The Mummy*, as well as long sections of music from other films, including Franz Waxman's score for *Bride of Frankenstein*. The serial was released in 13 parts in 1936 and based on the King Features Syndicate comic strip by Alex Raymond. With one-time Olympic swimmer, Buster Crabbe, the lead, it was the perfect screen incarnation of the comic strip hero. The film moves at a terrific pace which disguises much of its cut-price sets and costumes, medium-to-poor model work and special effects, and dialogue that would not have seemed out of place in the balloons of its comic strip ancestor. It was not only an immense popular success but it, and its serial successors, *Flash Gordon's Trip to Mars, Flash Gordon Conquers The Universe*, served to introduce science fiction to a much greater audience. For all their obvious budgetary limitations and serviceable rather than good action these serials form a key part of the *genre's* evolution.

The first of the post war films mirrored scientific advances – it was now conceivable that space flight would become a reality in the lifetime of people who had survived the war – as well as an acknowledgment that of something once confined to the province of speculative fiction – namely, the strategic value of control of the Moon. The film was *Destination Moon*, made in 1950, a film that painstakingly created a believable space flight and Moon landing, far in advance of the content and techniques of Fritz Lang's *Die Frau im Mond*. The film was almost documentary in its approach to the depiction of space flight and won for its makers the *genre's* first Academy Award for Special Effects, taken by George Pal and Lee Zavitz. The film was adapted from Robert Heinlein's book *Rocketship Galileo* and Heinlein himself was engaged as technical adviser on the film, along with the rocket expert Hermann Oberth who had worked 21 years previously on *Die Frau im Mond*. Astronomical artist Chesley Bonestell worked on the film in close consultation with art director Ernst Fegte and their recreation of the Moon's surface remains one of the finest effects in science fiction cinema. Immense care was taken with the special effects and cinematography, with 'floating' spacemen being suspended on piano wires to give the illusion of free fall, while their space suits were padded with lamb's wool to give the impression of pressurization. On the set of the Moon's surface, backed with an enormous blowup of Chesley Bonestell's artwork, the atmosphere was kept as clear as possible to simulate the vacuum of outer space. Smoking was prohibited on the sound stage and a battery of high speed blowers was used to keep the air clear of debris. The care lavished on the special effects, fully justified by the final appearance of the film, extended to almost total realism. To show the effects of the acceleration of the space ship on its occupants, a membrane was glued to each actor's face so that when levers were operated, their faces distorted as though under the effect of an increased gravitational pull. *Destination Moon* was immensely successful, despite a solemn air and near documentary technique that makes it somewhat dull when seen today in the light of real-life space travel and subsequent films, and it stands as a key achievement in the *genre*. Not surprisingly, not only did the film start off a new cycle of science fiction films but it also spawned cheap imitations, one of which, the silly *Rocketship X-M*, was made so quickly that it actually beat George Pal's film into the cinemas: it had cost only $95,000 to produce and grossed millions. Science fiction films had become a solid box office proposition.

George Pal's follow-up to *Destination Moon*, 1951's *When Worlds Collide*, showed the Earth destroyed by the impact of the wandering star Bellus, with only a chosen few making their escape to another world in a hastily constructed space ship.

If the *genre* films tended to indicate a world scared of its own destruction, they also showed a belief that man was not alone in the universe. John W. Campbell's story 'Who Goes There?' was transmuted into the first of a major visitors-from-another-world film cycle, emerging as *The Thing From Another World 1951*. The film, directed by Christian Nyby, created a tense and eerie effect as an American scientific expedition thaws out the alien creature from a block of ice after blasting it out of its flying saucer, with most of the creature's menacing actions being claustrophobically set in the half lit corridors and obscuring snows of an Arctic scientific base. *The Day The Earth Stood Still*, directed by Robert Wise in the same year, used Harry Bates' *Farewell To The Master* as the basis of an intelligent film which sought to bring the world to a realization that their playing with uncontrolled atomic fission could only lead to total devastation, summarized in Michael Rennie's choice to mankind: 'Join us and live in peace, or pursue your final course and face obliteration'. The message was neatly packaged in a film which had a 350-foot long flying saucer (constructed full size on the back lot of the Twentieth Century-Fox Studios) land on the lawns of the White House, from it emerging the extraterrestrial Klaatu and his nine-foot robot Gort to immobilize every electrical impulse on the planet when the world's leaders refuse to listen to his warning.

The prophetic American Moon landing (above), staged with near documentary realism for George Pal's *Destination Moon*

A typical scene from the Universal 'Flash Gordon' serials, featuring Larry 'Buster' Crabbe as the interplanetary hero

Classics from the mid-1950s

War of the Worlds, produced in 1953 by George Pal and directed in a fast, economical and anonymous style by Byron Haskin, transposed Wells' apocalyptic novel from England's Surrey in the 1900s to a post-atomic war America. The film managed to retain much of Wells' vision and the fleet of attacking Martian space ships fill the screen with some of its most opulent and beguiling images of science fiction destruction. In all this meticulously created savagery, the human performers, with Gene Barry and Ann Robinson in the lead became cardboard cyphers. The award winning special effects were the real stars.

In a much quieter vein, but just as effective in its evocation of an alien invasion was Jack Arnold's impressive 1953 film *It Came From Outer Space*, made in 3-D but equally effective when shown flat. The film uses Arizona desert locations to achieve alien atmosphere which sits uneasily on prosaic 1953 scenes. Although it was nominally from a story by Ray Bradbury, Arnold and screenwriter Harry Essex had to work on the original premise to quite an extent in order to make the film work. The theme of alien intelligences able to take over human bodies became the dominant thread of *The Invasion of The*

Body Snatchers three years later. Jack Finney's story of the imperceptible and terrifying take over of the minds and bodies of the inhabitants of a small American town was put over with an accumulative power and subtlety that made it one of the most pervasively frightening science fiction films ever made. Latterly it became something of a cult film, capable of such protean interpretations as Guy Draucourt's 'anti-fascist' and Erneste Laura's 'McCarthyite'.

Raymond F. Jones' novel *This Island Earth* was brought to the screen in 1954 as an exciting piece of space opera, containing the sort of cliff-hanging elements that characterized the best of the serials and remains uniquely one of the widest ranging – in visual content – films of the 1950s. Its special effects, in particular the war-torn surface of the planet Metaluna and its excellently created flying saucers stand out while Franklin Coen and Edward G. O'Callaghan's script stick to the spirit, if not the exact letter of Jones' book.

The Incredible Shrinking Man, based on *The Shrinking Man* by Richard Matheson and impeccably directed by Jack Arnold, had its unfortunate protagonist inexorably becoming smaller as the result of contamination by a radioactive mist combined with the effects of an insecticide. In the

After world-wide holocaust, Raymond Massey surveys the devastation in H. G. Wells' *Things To Come*

depiction of the horrors of the man's condition, rapidly becoming an alien in his own world, Matheson and Arnold never allowed sentiment to intrude and there was no easy solution. The film's ending was totally predestined and totally satisfying and the special effects – a combination of over-size props and some highly ingenious matte cinematography perfectly complemented the director's vision.

The 1950s then saw science fiction at its peak in terms of sheer output and diversity of theme and its diversification into various sub-genres, notably the monster picture, exemplified by films such as *The Creature From The Black Lagoon 1954*, *Godzilla (Gojira) 1955* and *Twenty Million Miles To Earth 1957*. The latter half of the decade saw the spread of *genre* films from America to Japan and Britain where *The Quatermass Experiment*, taken from Nigel Kneale's riveting television serial marked the post-war British advent into science fiction films. The film version was an intelligent compression of the television original, making up in terms of tension what it inevitably lost in its exposition of the anguish of a man slowly and inevitably mutating into a monster after contamination on a space trip.

Bomb Culture and the 1960s

The late 1950s/1960s also saw the incursion into the field of science fiction by film makers from the 'mainstream' cinema. This accorded with the end of the 'boom' in science fiction films, a *genre* that had burned itself almost to extinction in the 1950s with a constant stream of good, bad and quite terrible movies.

Stanley Kramer's 1959 *On The Beach*, taken from Neville Shute's novel was an apocalyptic prophecy of a world ending not with a bang but with a whimper as the results of the aftermath of an atomic war. It brought to the *genre* big name stars – Gregory Peck, Fred Astaire and Ava Gardner – along with the approach of a film maker whose background was that of general films.

In the 1960s and 1970s, science fiction was to become rarer in the cinema, although going through something of a renaissance on television. Joseph Losey's 1961 movie, *The Damned*, adapted by Evan Jones from H. L. Lawrence's ingenious and disturbing novel *The Children of Light* was an interesting failure as it showed the interrelationships of a group of children, raised from birth to be able to survive the radiation of a post-atomic war world and a couple fleeing from a group of hoodlums in a small British seaside town. Losey captured the chill of the children and their alien existence but allowed himself, as with most of his work, to overpower the film with would-be meaningful allusions that ended up by becoming just plain pompous.

In 1964 Stanley Kubrick made the first of his three forays into science fiction. The title of *Dr Strangelove; or, How I Learned to Stop Worrying and Love The Bomb* summed up Kubrick's ambivalent attitude towards science fiction. The film was black comedy as much as science fiction *per se* as a mad US general launched a nuclear attack on Russia and all attempts to abort it finally failed and the world reached Armageddon to the accompaniment of Vera

Lynn's ironic singing of the WWII song, *We'll Meet Again*. In the film's script, written by Kubrick, Terry Southern and Peter George from the latter's novel *Red Alert*, the basic premise gave way over and over again to a jejune approach that vitiated the film's more serious undertones. Although historically the film is important in the context of the international tensions of the Cold War in the 1960s it suffers from a dichotomous approach to its story. Neither the serious pieces nor the comic episodes really work, leaving instead an untidy narrative that works against the film's impact, an unimpressive ending – instead of irony, one gets the impression of an undergraduate sense of humour loose on the big screen, desperately needing a producer other than Kubrick to control it. In a director lesser than Kubrick, *Dr Strangelove* might have been acceptable as minor science fiction fare: as it is, the film does not stand the test of time.

The French Connection

French film makers had always looked to America as their spiritual home, often lauding incomprehensibly bad American directors whose sole achievement had been to make a large number of unimaginative and uninteresting films within the American system of film making. So it was not altogether surprising that the 1960s should see two key French makers essay their hands with science fiction films. In 1965, Jean-Luc Godard wrote, produced and directed *Alphaville* in which he uneasily married the conventions of the pulp private eye thriller with his own rather grandiose ideas of the science fiction film. Secret agent Lemmy Caution is sent into another galaxy where he finds a future society run by a central computer called Alpha 60 and where human love and emotion are rigorously banned. The theme of human domination by the and where human love and emotion are rigowrously banned. The theme of human domination by the computer, one that in the 1960s and 1970s seems set to rival the terror of the Bomb that dominated the 1950s, was better demonstrated in *The Forbin Project 1969* in which a computer designed to control the defences of the West, combines with its Russian counterpart in an uneasy alliance that first appeals to its human mentors but, as the computers gradually gain dominance, ultimately appalls. In *Demon Seed 1976* the computer attempts the ultimate in immortality seeking by impregnating a human subject who then gives birth 28 days later to a child in the image of her own dead daughter, a kind of science fiction reworking on the theme of *Rosemary's Baby* with the computer standing in for the Devil.

When French director François Truffaut came to make Ray Bradbury's novella *Fahrenheit 451* in 1966, it was not altogether surprising that the film should turn out to be less than satisfactory, given that Bradbury's works gain their effect from the page and lose most of it when translated to the screen. 1969's attempt to film *The Illustrated Man* as a three episode film proved the point and while it had its moments, in the end the film had to be seen as a (qualified) failure. *Fahrenheit 451* was marred by a script which was unable to translate Bradbury from

Meticulous special effects from *2001: A Space Odyssey* showing the space shuttle approaching the orbiting space station

page to screen so that what finally emerged was a down beat vision of a future set in a fascist state where books are burned because of their unsociable effect on people, and where the firemen are in charge of the destruction of books.

New directions in the late 1960s

Comic strips once more provided a new impetus in the late 1960s. The 'adult' strip that created *Barbarella 1967* gave rise to Roger Vadim's sexy space opera with Jane Fonda as the nubile female Flash Gordon loose in a 40th Century where angels and astronauts co-exist and where camp space opera skates over the surface of the *genre* with much soft core sex and little real depth. Of considerable impact was *Charly 1968* which deservedly won for Cliff

Robertson the Oscar for Best Actor for his portrayal of the mentally retarded young man who briefly is changed into a genius through the use of advanced surgical techniques, only to revert once more into his original state as the effects wore off. This was science fiction cinema at its most persuasive and moving, a future fantastic metaphor that came off perfectly, aided by Sterling Silliphant's neat script from Daniel Keyes' *Flowers For Algernon* and unobtrusively good direction from Ralph Nelson. *Charly* was that rare science fiction film, one whose philosophical content and concepts were never at variance with its visual presentation.

The late 1960s had seen the beginning of the 'Apes' films with *Planet of The Apes* in 1967, a series that was to continue into the 1970s with the law of diminishing returns (with the exception of Don

search of a plot. Arthur Clarke's short story *The Sentinel* had been taken by Kubrick as the starting point of his film which depicted the striving of mankind from the ape to the future scientist to discover his origins and place within the universe. The film was intended to work on two levels, one as an authentic prediction of the future of space travel and the second as a metaphysical speculation on the possibility of extraterrestrial life. In its 141 minutes running time, *2001* succeeded brilliantly on the first level, with masterly special effects that created utterly believable space craft, a surface of the Moon (that was not in any way made less believable by the photographs of the real thing that followed a year later with the first lunar landing), and a depiction of space travel that was far ahead of anything that had gone before.

In the 1970s, the cinema has essayed science fiction only occasionally, choosing individual themes not particularly related to the tensions of the time and remaining a relatively minor screen *genre*. Special effects are all there and available, having reached a level of immense sophistication and flexibility, but only *Star Wars* has stretched their capabilities to the fullest limits. Cornel Wilde's film version of John Christopher's apocalyptic novel *The Death of Grass*, entitled *No Blade of Grass* majored more on man's fight for survival against a Britain overtaken by anarchy rather than exploring, except at a rather superficial level, the deeper themes raised. What emerged was an undeniably exciting adventure – with a science fiction background – which concentrated on the rapid regression to savagery and self-interest of a people faced with starvation in an environment where law and order has totally broken

Cornel Wilde's apocalyptic view of an anarchic future: *No Blade of Grass*

Taylor's 1970 film *Escape From The Planet of The Apes*) rapidly setting in. But Franklin J. Schaffner's original film, with its astronauts caught in a time-warp which took them into the future of their own planet where humans were speechless and subservient to the intelligent apes that ruled the Earth, was solid science fiction, carefully thought out with a series of real and uncontrived shocks leading to one of the cinema's most effective surprise endings.

The 1970s

Undoubtedly, however, the major science fiction film of the 1960s was Stanley Kubrick's *2001: A Space Odyssey*, destined to be the ultimate in special effects movies until 1977's *Star Wars* exposed it for what it really was – a special effects masterpiece in

Malcolm McDowell and his gang in the milk bar from Stanley Kubrick's film of Anthony Burgess' *A Clockwork Orange*

Director Robert Fuest's experience and skill as a designer (opposite) is evident in this scene from his film of Michael Moorcock's *The Final Programme*

down. The film had more than a few affinities with Ray Milland's similar *Panic in The Year Zero, 1962* except that Milland's film, with a family having to fight for survival after a nuclear war was more maudlin, while Wilde's movie eschewed even the faintest trace of sentimentality – Wilde's world was one of total savagery where the order of the day was to kill first and forget the questions completely.

Four different themes from 1971 brought a quartet of interesting films in which the *genre* was explored in various ways with no common denominator save that the films were intended for a general audience for whom science fiction had no particular affinity. The theme of *Silent Running* was potentially capable of considerable development but, in the script by Deric Washburn, Michael Cimino and Steve Boccho, it emerged as slow and muddle-headed. Director Douglas Trumbull was far too concerned in ensuring that his film's message against the horrors of environmental despoilation would be appreciated fully to work out his story's development so that *Silent Running* was notable more for its impressive special effects and some good acting. Set, appropriately, in the year 2001, *Silent Running* had Bruce Dern, accompanied by fellow astronauts Cliff Potts and Jesse Vint, as a kind of celestial gardener, orbiting the earth in a space station and trying to grow new vegetation to replenish a world devastated by nuclear war. When the order goes out to Dern that he is to abandon his work, he kills his fellow astronauts instead and cruises the Solar System in his space station, aided only by robot helpers until he finally goes mad and kills himself. Dern acquitted himself impressively, suggesting a real concern with the survival of his mission and the work were of the very high order to be expected from Trumbull who had been responsible for much of the special effects in *2001: A Space Odyssey*. *Silent Running*, in many ways, is something of an aberrant film, not quite succeeding in putting across its serious intentions, while the special effects often seem to belong to another kind of film entirely.

Richard Matheson's *I Am Legend*, having been filmed back in 1964 as a more or less straight horror film, *The Last Man on Earth* with Vincent Price,

emerged again in 1971 as *The Omega Man*, competently if unimaginatively directed by Boris Sagal. The vampiristic overtones of the 1964 version gave way here to a 'rational' scientific explanation, with a mutated virus, the result of a germ war, turning most of the world's population into albino-like creatures only able to emerge at night. In the ruins of Los Angeles it is left to Charlton Heston to wage a one-man war against the plague carriers, spurred on by the knowledge he was one of the scientists whose work had been responsible for the virus-induced plague.

Anthony Burgess' novel *A Clockwork Orange*, with its pessimistic vision of a future both bleak and violent, was a superb example of prophetic science fiction and technically a *tour de force*. The relationship to Burgess' novel was in places tenuous, with much of the whimsy and sly humour lost in an adaptation that concentrated on an examination of a culture that both bred extreme violence and just as ruthlessly supressed it. Kubrick's film provided, in its exemplary handling and montage, a futuristic nightmare which at the time was taken to be overheated and over-stated but which, in the intervening years has come to be seen as horridly prophetic. The film's crux was centred in the Pavlovian conditioning of the violent gangster Alex by a State whose methods of persuasion were every bit as amoral as his own raping and murdering ethos, and this section remains one of the most powerful and persuasive in the *genre*. Unfortunately Kubrick's unflinching realism, particularly in the sequences of pure savagery deflected many critics and a large section of the public from fully comprehending the nihilistic but ultimately moral concept behind *A Clockwork Orange*, so that the film's contribution was obscured by a media furore over its content.

Robert Wise's *The Andromeda Strain*, taken from Michael Crichton's novel, retained much of the clinical approach of the novel but imbued the film with a sense of pace and urgency which, with the meticulous special effects from Douglas Trumbull and James Shourt and Boris Leven's convincingly antiscetic production design, combined to make the film one of the decade's best, a return to the near-documentary tradition of some of the key 1950 films.

More melancholy views of the future were supplied by *THX 1138*, a variation of the theme of *1984*, with its bleak vision of a soulless computerized world and sterile emotions: the film was impressive to look at with its bleached out visuals and is of interest as being the first movie to be directed by George Lucas, the maker of *Star Wars*. Less successful in its depiction of an alternate future was *ZPG*, also released in 1971, which dourly expounded a world where ZPG stood for Zero Population Growth and birth was outlawed.

The very real problems in attempting to transfer literary science fiction to the screen were underlined by George Roy Hill's 1972 *Slaughterhouse 5*. Kurt Vonnegut's humour and deeply ironic sense of justice lost out against a confused backtracking through time and space and the novel's essential qualities were lost with no meaningful screen insights being found to take their place.

Animation in science fiction had been mainly confined to television series and to special effects sequences such as the marauding Monster from the Id that attacked the crew of the space cruiser in *Forbidden Planet*. Something of an oddity, then, was the 1973 cartoon movie *Fantastic Planet*, a Franco-Czech co-production that marked the third collaboration of director René Laloux and artist Roland Topor. Based on Stefan Wul, the film makers claimed that they had 'portrayed intelligently' the author's intentions in showing the oppression of a race of humans, the Oms, by giant android masters, the Draags, on the planet Ygam.

John Boorman's *Zardoz 1973* which attempted to show a future in which the social classes were as viciously stratified as those in Huxley's *Brave New World* and Lang's *Metropolis*, succeeded only in

appearing facile, vitiated by Boorman's striving for a significance not to be found in his material. Set in the year 2293, *Zardoz* postulated a future in which the Exterminators of the Earth's outer world set about exterminating the Brutals, humans who still procreated in a basically sterile environment. What little dramatic structure the film possessed came from Sean Connery's performance as Zed, the educated exterminator.

The British film journal *Sight and Sound* found

Yul Brynner leads a survivor of world devastation through the deserted New York subway in *The Ultimate Warrior*

In an over-populated New York (right) the streets are cleared of people the hard way in Richard Fleischer's *Soylent Green*

Robert Fuest's 1973 film version of Michael Moorcock's *The Final Programme* to be 'clumsy and almost incomprehensible', a fair assessment of a film that succeeded in betraying almost all the intellectual content of Moorcock's work in favour of a surface gloss and an intellectual approach at total variance with its subject of the scientific coming of a new Messiah. Fuest's background as a production designer gave *The Final Programme* a spurious visual gloss but the film emerged as empty as a Klein Bottle. The presence of Charlton Heston in *Soylent Green*, directed by Richard Fleischer in 1974 wrongly shifted the emphasis of Harry Harrison's novel *Make Room! Make Room!* The exploration of an overcrowded world in which cannibalism, albeit disguised as a process of scientific recycling, had become the only solution to the problem of an adequate food supply, becomes a detective story in which hero Heston turned into a futuristic Philip Marlowe to discover a secret that was already obvious to the film's audience. The climax, even though it could be seen coming, still stunned but the film betrayed itself by skating over the surface of its theme in preference to elucidating Harrison's vision. Michael Crichton, who had written *The Andromeda Strain* turned his hand to direction with 1974's *Westworld*, an ingenious extrapolation of the Disneyland principle with a future entertainment complex in which people's every pleasure could be served by robots: human fear of automation was realized when Yul Brynner's android gunslinger went berserk and the pleasure seekers became the hunted. The concept was sufficiently interesting to provide the basis for a second re-working in 1976's *Futureworld*, with the anti-robot bias becoming even more pronounced.

Watching *Dark Star, 1974* is an experience that in many ways parallels what must be the actual tedium of long distance space travel. The film shows only too clearly its origins as a 45 minute student short, shot on 16 mm film and later transfered to 35 mm stock, with the addition of 38 minutes of extra footage to bring it up to feature length. The special effects and model work, by Dan O'Bannon and Ronald Cobb respectively, with additional animation by Bob Greenberg is impressive, especially considering its amateur origins (O'Bannon went on to work on the computer animation and graphic displays for *Star Wars*), but the content was jejune and its attempts to parody the *genre*, with its story of living bombs and conversations with the dead captain of the planet-eliminating space ship and its

Robot entertainment as Blythe Danner (left) takes on Peter Fonda vicariously in *Futureworld*

psychotic crew emerged as boring and sophomorish. *The Ultimate Warrior 1975* was somewhat bizarrely described by its publicists as 'the first Kung Fu sf movie'. Yul Brynner repeats his characterization of the avenging leader from the 1960 Western *The Magnificent Seven* as a super warrior hired to protect a group of frightened survivors in the ruins of 21st century New York after the world has been decimated by bacterial warfare. The film merely restates ideas that were common during the 1950s. Another 1950s theme, the alien visitor, was explored again by Nicolas Roeg in his 1976 film *The Man Who Fell To Earth* in which his training as a cinematographer became evident in some striking visual compositions which emphasized the otherwordly origins of David Bowie's visitor from another world.

Logan's Run 1976 was science fiction in the stream of *Flash Gordon* and the gadget obsessed visually orientated genre films: Glen Robinson's award-winning special effects creating the hedonistic, computer-run domed cities of the 23rd century where death was the fate of everyone reaching the age of 30, were the best part of a film which was simplistic in almost every other direction. The film retrogressed from a portrayal of a sterile future world not too far from that of Huxley into a straightforward chase movie as hero and heroine, fleeing the murderous Sandmen, search for the legendary 'Sanctuary' that lay beyond the domed cities, in a desolate and ruined outside world, and the film all too clearly betrayed the fact that it was aimed at the unsophisticated young who were by now the cinema's only regular audience. The search for themes led to a sober and well-made version – the second – of H. G. Wells' *The Island of Dr Moreau* in 1977, filmed in the lush locations of St Croix in the Virgin Islands. Burt Lancaster made a convincing Moreau and something of the fanatacism and tunnel vision of Wells' scientist emerged in his performance while John Chambers' designs for the 'Humanimals', the half-human, half-beast results of his experiments in evolution contributed to the film's impact, even if the final result, like the 1932 version, finally betrayed Wells' intentions by softening the centre with the romantic interest supplied by Michael York and Barbara Carrera.

Sf film from the eastern bloc

Science fiction on the screen is predominantly a Western *genre* which, given the pre-eminence of the cinema as a medium for entertainment rather than overt propaganda, is to be expected. As a *genre*, science fiction has been the exception in Eastern European countries, from which few films have emerged – for Western audiences, at any rate. *Aelita 1924* was one of the first Russian films to explore science fictional concepts, taken from Alexei Tolstoi's novel. Interestingly, this novel and Tolstoi's *The Hyperloid of Engineer Garin* appeared in the mid-1920s, before the establishment of the first major science fiction magazine, *Amazing Stories* in 1926. The East German/Polish co-production *First Spaceship on Venus 1959* with its multi-national cast was pure space opera as it showed an expedition to the second planet and its emphasis was on the

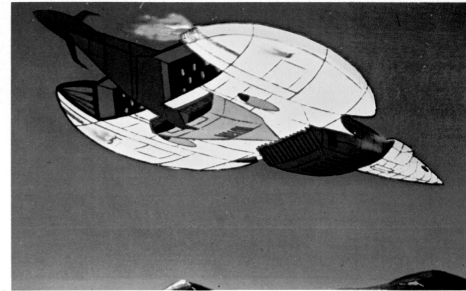

hardware of the *genre* with space ships and extraterrestrial landscapes that bore a striking similarity to the illustrations of Western science fiction magazines. The special effects were impressive but the intellectual content naive. Of considerably greater interest was *Ikarie XB 1*, filmed in Czechoslovakia in 1963 by Jindrich Polak and released in a badly truncated and dubbed version in the West as *Voyage to The End of The Universe*. In his film, Polak created a situation in which psychological and social problems could be explored and the film was the first to try and depict the interrelationships and emotional tensions of a group of space travellers, subordinating the gadgetry and special effects to the story's inherent dramatic content. The Russian *Solaris* was hailed by some on its 1972 release as the Eastern answer to *2001: A Space Odyssey* while for others it was seen as a slow and pretentious mixture of polemics and science fiction, deliberately obscurant in its exposition. Certainly it was impressive, if often difficult to follow; in content it was one of the few science fiction films concerned with an attempt to create for the cinema a metaphorical work equal in intellectual depth and exploration to literary science fiction.

Made in Japan

Japan had had a tradition of science fiction cinema that depended largely upon some skilled special effects work notably from Toho's Eiji Tsuburaya and Akira Watanabe, and the direction of the prolific Inoshiro Honda and Jun Fukuda. From *Godzilla (Gojia)* in 1956, Japanese science fiction had tended to concentrate upon variations of the monster theme and while many of their major and repetitive screen monsters came from outer space, the resolution of the films in which they were featured usually came with destructive battles which reduced the monsters, and usually Tokyo, to rubble. Films like *The Mysterians (Chikyu Boeigun)*, 1957 with Japan as the focus of an extraterrestrial invasion, the self-explanatory *Battle in Outer Space (Uchu Dai Senso)* in 1959 and the interplanetary vampire of *Goke – Body Snatcher From Hell (Kyuketsuki Gokemedoro)*

Animated space travel as seen in the Japanese *Space Cruiser/Space Cruiser Yamoto* (Academy 1977)

The attack on the Death Star from George Lucas' superb *Star Wars*

in 1963 demonstrated the Japanese preoccupation with the production of science fiction films with a totally visual and sensational content, the cinema equivalent of the pulp fiction and comic strip aspects of the *genre*. Of a quite different dimension was *Submersion of Japan 1973*, a film which, while using the convention of the disaster movie, was able to achieve some of the most startling and impressive special effects in the history of the *genre* while at the same time managing to bring out the human elements of a story whose scale was nothing less, as the title indicated, than the destruction of a complete country.

Star Wars: the ultimate sf entertainment

That science fiction is still, despite the doldrums of the last decade and a half, a viable screen *genre* has been triumphantly demonstrated by the runaway success of *Star Wars 1977*. As early as 1971, the film's writer-director George Lucas had wanted to make a space fantasy. His previous experience as a film maker hardly seems, in retrospect, heavyweight enough for him to have been given the $9.5 million needed to make Star Wars. His first film, *THX-1138*, had been an expansion of a short he had begun at the age of 23 while he was still a student. Although it had failed commercially, the film had impressed

executives of Universal Studios. When Lucas offered a 12-page outline of *Star Wars* to Universal, the studio felt unable to take the risk the film's making entailed. Two years later, after writing some four versions of the script, Lucas had his final screenplay and was ready to begin filming for Fox.

Synopsis of its plot conveys little about the impact of *Star Wars* apart from an indication of its basic scope. It follows a young man, Luke Skywalker from his small and arid planet of Tatooine in an intergalactic search for a kidnapped princess. Luke is joined in his odyssey by the last of the Jedi Knights, one-time guardians of peace and justice before the 'dark times' came to the galaxy. He and the knight Ben Kenobi are united with Han Solo, a cynical spaceship captain and his co-pilot, the alien Wookie Chewbacca and the film's comedy relief, the two robots See-Threepio (C–3PO) and Artoo-Detoo (R2–D2) in a sweeping battle against the powers of evil incarnated in the Princess' kidnapper, the Governor of the Imperial Outland Regions, Grand Moff Tarkin and Darth Vader, Dark Lord of The Sith who used his extrasensory powers in quelling the rebellion against the Galactic Empire. The story is one of heroism and villainy, romance and, above all, the power of good against evil.

Star Wars began filming in March 1976 and was released in mid-1977. Its locations had ranged from

Southern Tunisia where the small oasis town of Tozeur had stood in for the arid planet of Tatooine, and other Tunisian locations, including the cave dwelling town of Matmata were used for various scenes set on Luke Skywalker's home planet. Major studio filming was carried out in Britain's Elstree Studios where some 15 weeks of filming were devoted to the futuristic looking Imperial Death Star satellite sequences. Further locations included Death Valley and Guatemala and the post-production work and special effects were completed in Los Angeles. Where the technology available to the makers of *2001* meant recourse to the expensive and time consuming processes of multiple exposure to create their effects, and limited what they were able to show on the screen, Lucas and Dykstra had the advantage of another 15 years of progress in the field. They were able to link their camera to a sophisticated computer which memorized and recorded each shot. Access to the computer immeasurably speeded up the photographic process and resulted in shots of space craft and alien worlds which are totally new to the cinema in their complexity and realism. Where, it is claimed, Kubrick employed only about 35 different effects, *Star Wars* has 363. The same innovatory techniques

extended to the miniature work. The miniature crew cannibalized more than 300 model kits and used parts from WWII aircraft and old tanks, recasting in plastic to achieve realism. That realism was not the glossy unused realism of so many previous science fiction movies. The plastic models were worked on after casting to give the appearance of artifacts battered by daily usage.

In *Star Wars* one can see elements of *Flash Gordon* and *Buck Rogers*, *The Wizard of Oz*, *The Sword in The Stone*, just about every Errol Flynn swashbuckler, *Tarzan* and *Sir Gawain and The Green Knight*, while in the climactic attack on the Dark Star, Lucas, who employed footage from old war movies to plan the sequence, echoes of *The Bridge at Toko Ri* and *The Dambusters* can be detected. In his script and its execution there are references to most of science fiction's best writers – the planet Tatooine, for instance evokes much of the feeling of Frank Herbert's Dune trilogy – and there are echoes of Robert Sheckley.

On the planet Tatooine, Ben Kenobi (Alec Guinness) and Luke Skywalker (Mark Hamill) help See-Threepio (Anthony Daniels) while Artoo-Deetoo (Kenny Baker) looks on. *Star Wars*

Star Wars provides a proof that visual science fiction can be assessed as a discrete form of science fiction as a whole. Taking its analogies from literature, from the comic strips and from its own special effects armoury, from the earliest days of Méliès to the 1970s with Steven Speilberg's *Close Encounters of the Third Kind*, and Richard Donner's epic *Superman* still to come, the cinema itself remains the nearest thing we have to Wells' Time Machine with its unique ability to make 'real' dreams and visions, and to create and mould experience in an infinitely variable and repeatable manner. In the words of director Robert Wise: '... pure science fiction is much freer for it grows from a soaring imagination that need not be bound by what actually exists or is actually known.'

A truck driver comes under attack from alien visitors in Steven Spielberg's film about extraterrestrials landing on Earth, *Close Encounters of The Third Kind*

Radio and television

Radio remained very much a minor medium for science fiction as the cinema geared itself more and more to an enormous output which lasted until the post-war advent of television. Much of the science fiction programming was on the level of children's entertainment but on the evening of 30 October 1938, Orson Welles and his Mercury Players, with a script by Welles and Howard Koch, demonstrated the immense power of the medium with their famous broadcast of a dramatization of H. G. Wells' *The War of The Worlds*. By employing a documentary technique, interrupting apparently 'ordinary' programmes to give news, views and interviews about the Martians' invasion of America, Welles contrived to throw a nation into a total state of panic, with people believing that the Martians had really invaded the United States and that the east coast of the country was in the process of being destroyed. This was probably radio science fiction at its apogee: after that, a knowing cynicism set in and the medium became accepted as part of the furniture, a background for living.

Television has always had a steady output of science fiction although most of it has been aimed at younger viewers and as a result is usually fairly juvenile in theme, content and, to a certain degree, execution, certainly when measured against its cinema counterparts. There have been some popular and good programmes, notably *Twilight Zone* in America and *Out of The Unknown* in Britain. Also in Britain *The Time Machine* and, particularly, George Orwell's *1984* with Peter Cushing as Winston Smith had been accorded distinguished and successful television production.

The *Twilight Zone*, one of the best remembered series, did not rely on continuing characters or locations but instead used the short story as a means of creating some of the best science fiction ever made for television. Episodes – and there were 151 of them, filmed at MGM Studios and running from 1959 to 1964 – ranged through just about every major and minor, science fiction theme: space travel, robots, invasions from beyond the Earth, travel on other planets, as well as exploring ideas that strictly belonged in the realm of the kind of fantasy popularized in literature by writers such as Ray Bradbury and Fredric Brown. The series was created by Rod Serling who wrote many of the key episodes and won no less than three Emmys for his work.

However, television science fiction on the whole has produced more totally disposable material than programmes of a greater and (comparatively) longer lasting impact. Thus shows like *Atom Squad, Captain Video, Commando Cody, The Evil Touch, Fantastic Journey, Holmes and Yo-Yo, Men Into Space, My Favourite Martian, My Living Doll, Planet of The Apes, Science Fiction Theatre, Space Patrol, Tom Corbett, Space Cadet, Wonder Woman* and *World of Giants* from America, and *A For Andromeda, The Champions, Journey To The Unknown, Moonbase 3, Out of This World* (made on videotape and hosted by Boris Karloff), *UFO* from Britain, and a whole spectrum of cartoon series aimed strictly at children, ranging from the Japanese *Astro Boy* to *Fireball XL-5*, *The Lost Saucer*, *Do Do*, *The Kid From Outer Space* and *Space Angel*, have all vanished beyond recall as if they had been broadcast from a matter transmitter for which there was no receiving unit.

What, then, remains? Still being filmed and bringing in the ratings are such mediocre offerings as *The Six Million Dollar Man* and *The Bionic Woman* which, in their need to keep the material coming out on a conveyor belt basis have abandoned most of their science fiction content in favour of the adventure thriller format. *Man From Atlantis*, after a relatively promising pilot film which introduced the series' hero, a water-breathing alien apparently the last survivor of the legendary city of Atlantis, atrophied into a format in which the hero was no more than a superhuman (under water, at any rate) investigator in the mould of *The Six Million Dollar Man* whose ratings the show was obviously intended to attack. *Logan's Run*, ostensibly set in the 23rd century, and using not only some of the footage of the 1976 feature film from which it evolved but also the film's basic premise, soon became just another heroes-pursued-by-the-bad-guys series in which the futuristic hardware and not very good special effects were no more than extra gloss on pedestrian material. The chase motif running through *Logan's Run*, with the Runners in episodic peril from the pursuing Sandmen, clearly derived from one of the medium's more successful series, *The Invaders*, a series of 43 one hour episodes which ran from January 1967 to the end of the 1968 season.

The science fiction series produced by Irwin Allen, *Voyage To The Bottom of The Sea*, *Lost in Space*, *The Time Tunnel* and *Land of the Giants* all were more interesting for their special effects than for their plots and themes which by and large turned out to be stereotyped rather than innovative.

There was one series above all others which managed to touch a chord in a mass audience and succeeded in popularizing science fiction more effectively than any other television programme before or since. This series, which debuted in 1966 and ran to 78 episodes until 1969, has survived with almost continuous re-runs and has managed to increase its popularity with each repeat showing so that, in all probability, it will be revived in the near future, something almost unheard of in the medium. The series was, of course, *Star Trek*. The effect of *Star Trek* is hard to underrate. Isaac Asimov has been quoted as saying that it was the only television show he watched, the United States space shuttle was named *Enterprise* after the show's space craft and Trekkies continue to keep the show alive and running nearly a decade after its cancellation. The basic idea was an old one in science fiction terms, a theme that had served A. E. van Vogt well with *The Voyage of the Space Beagle* as well as seeing sterling service in dozens of other *genre* novels and short stories. But perhaps its most obvious roots can be traced to the magnificent 1956 film *Forbidden Planet* in which a space crew from the 23rd century visit the strange world of Altair IV. The theme of the quasi-military space exploration became the cornerstone of Star Trek, enshrined in the voice-over which began each show: 'Space, the final frontier. These are the

The Starship *Enterprise* from the television series *Star Trek* fires its phasers

voyages of the Starship *Enterprise*. It's five-year mission: to explore new worlds, to boldly go where no man has gone before.

Not surprisingly, *Star Trek* spawned imitators, the most considerable of which has been *Space 1999*, made in Britain but with American leads, Martin Landau and Barbara Bain, to give it appeal for the American networks. The series' premise was that Moonbase Alpha, under the command of Landau's Captain Koenig, is doomed to wander the universe after the Moon itself was torn out of Earth orbit because of a massive explosion of nuclear wastes dumped on the satellite. Once in space, however, the adventures of the 300 or so reluctant passengers of the wayward satellite soon turn out to be a poor imitation of the format of *Star Trek*. The series' failure was due to two main factors. The first was that the scripts themselves were banal and their science fiction content was soon subordinated to mediocre adventure themes. The second, and potentially more damaging factor was that the leading characters were dull and uninteresting, falling back on stock stereotypes and emotional clichés so that they never became alive in any sense or were able to transcend their material. Even the inclusion later in the series of a female alien, able to metamorphose into other life forms, never succeeded in being anything other than a not very good plot gimmick. Only the British children's series *Dr Who*, which began life in 1963 and follows the adventures of its hero, a 'Time Lord' able to travel through time and space, continues. Resolutely lowbrow and under-written, with a depressing tendency to use jargon in order to make plot points, the series has maintained its popularity with the children for whom the BBC has intended it and over the years it has explored, with variable success, most of science fiction's basic themes, as well as quite a few culled from the realms of horror and straight adventure. *Dr Who* has survived four changes of leading actor over the years and has also seen two cinema versions, both featuring its most popular monster, the robot Daleks, with Peter Cushing taking on the role – very well – of the Doctor. While *Dr Who*, like *Space 1999*, might serve to introduce science fiction to wider audiences, it remains resolutely rooted in a middle-class and under-developed ethos.

Harry Harrison

The machine in science fiction has been both hero and symbol.
From the gigantic space war-ships to the bronze space-brazieres,
sf's hardware has always been a vital ingredient of the *genre's*
sense of wonder. Hardware makes accessible the locations of
other worlds and other times; it also makes apparent man's
uneasy relationship with the inanimate.

Nineteenth century imagination took man into the skies in all manner of machines, but the balloon 'Cloud Clipper' was the most popular. Illustration by Gillot

Chris Foss set the cover market alight with his spectacularly detailed spaceships and buildings – craggy, ugly with the illusion of function (right)

Big is beautiful – Hubert Rogers (below) and other artists specialized in drawing every spaceship differently. The symbolism (bottom) in this Startling Stories cover was surely deliberate. Jane Russell in space, wearing the sort of evening gown that makes the future such an exciting prospect. The artist was Bergey

Flying machines

The hardware in science fiction is vital to its existence – surely sf is the only form of fiction that dares to have a gadget or an idea as hero. A quick look at antique sf art reveals that the earliest piece of hardware was the flying machine. It is pretty obvious that Leonardo's helicopter would never have gotten off the ground, no matter how hard the man flapped, but it is surely a more practical design than the pinwheels-on-masts that were supposed to propel Jules Verne's *The Clipper of the Clouds 1886*.

Undoubtedly the most unrealistic, yet most utterly charming, flying machines were those of the illustrator Harry Grant Dart. His preposterous planes have wings and propellors, and there is only the occasional glimpse of a dirigible. For a long time these were thought to be the aerial transportation of the future, as in Kipling's 'With the Night Mail'. This theme was amplified to exhaustion by H. G. Wells in *The War in the Air 1907*, where a fleet of these giant craft first bomb the United States, then launch an airborne invasion. The plot moves briskly along after that with Great Britain and France attacking Germany, being topped only by the Asians joining the fight with airships of their own. The crash of the *Von Hindenburg* and the *S-100* put paid to the dirigible menace, along with the accelerating growth of aeronautic science, though occasional deliberate anachronisms appear such as the coal-powered flying planes in Harry Harrison's *A Transatlantic Tunnel, Hurrah! 1972*.

Earliest credit for the more exotic forms of aerial transportation must be given to Phil Nowlan and Dick Calkins, the creators of *Buck Rogers*. Generations of preconceptions were shaped by this seminal comic strip. Professor Jamieson's anti-grav chute in A. E. van Vogt's 'Co-operate or Else' is nothing more than Buck's film-can, backpack, jumping belt writ large. Nor does it take an exceptionally keen eye to see the resemblance between his rocket belt and James Bond's modern equivalent. Equally seminal were the force field legs that supported the warships of the evil Red Mongols. Those legs are still stamping through the pages of sf.

In the 1930s, while real aeroplanes were still being made of bamboo and baling wire, the winged intellects of the sf writers were flying faster and further into the future. Unhampered by any aeronautical knowledge, Stanley Weinbaum's intercontinental jets blasted between continents in 'The Wheels of If', while the technocratic saviours in *Things to Come* flew in from Basra in gorgeously impractical flying palaces.

The master of the flying machine – as he was master of all sf machinery – was of course Frank R. Paul. This patient teutonic artist slave of the Luxembourg publishing fiend, Hugo Gernsback, gave graphic existence to the sf ideas of the 1930s. Not only did Paul's aircraft whiz from the pages of *Amazing*, they zipped their way across the covers of *Science and Mechanics*.

This brief period of aerial enthusiasm was interrupted by WWII when there was a geometric progression in plane design. (The wingspan of the B-

29 bomber was greater than the total distance first flown by the Wright brothers a few decades earlier.) With reality overtaking their imaginations, sf writers abandoned the competition and jumped directly into anti-gravity. The recent success of hovercraft, surface effect vessels that support themselves on a cushion of air, have brought these vehicles into sf, but this is obvious parasitism from reality since the sf authors didn't have the brains to invent the things themselves. (The 'floaters' that have floated through many a story have no connection with these later vehicles; they were powered by radium or magic or other unexplained sources of lifting energy.)

The ultimate in aerial transportation must be psi force where the person involved just wills himself to a new location, leaving and arriving apparently instantaneously. This does help to speed up the plot, and can produce masterpieces such as Alfred Bester's *Stars my Destination 1956* (published under the title of *Tiger! Tiger!* in England) where an entire civilization 'jaunts' in this manner.

Time Machines

Eternity was pierced for the first time in 1895 by H. G. Wells with *The Time Machine*, and this temporal activity has been going on ever since. The idea of moving in time was not a new one, but the act was usually accomplished by having the soul or mind of the traveller do the moving, as in Kipling's 'The Finest Story in the World'. Wells took the idea out of the realms of the fantastical or theological and put it firmly into the mechanical.

The time machine theme is inextricably entwined with the parallel world concept where there are many possible universes brought about by the changing possibilities of events in time. Jack Wil-

The detail in this picture by Bob Layzell is almost overwhelming – it is firmly in the modern tradition of giving an illusion of function, and an illusion of size

liamson blended the two in *The Legion of Time 1938* where the inhabitants of two 'possible' futures return to our time to attempt to alter history slightly, each in its own favour.

Once the concept of time travel is accepted there are no limits to the imagination. Van Vogt opened a 'Recruiting Station' to get volunteers for a future war. L. Sprague De Camp's hero lands in the declining days of the Roman Empire and works hard to prevent the slide into the night of the middle ages in *Lest Darkness Fall 1939*. Sightseeing in time was important in the earliest stories such as John W. Campbell's 'Night' or Pohl and Kornbluth's 'Trouble in Time', or those very special temporal sightseers in C. L. Moore's 'Vintage Season' who return from the future to the one safe spot where they can watch the atomic war begin.

Time paradoxes (what if I went back in time and

killed my grandfather before my mother was born?) hold endless fascination for writer and reader alike. Ross Rocklynne's 'Time Wants a Skeleton', which reveals modern artifacts in million-year-old rock, or Robert Heinlein's 'By His Bootstraps' are perhaps the best early examples of this variation. In 'Time's Arrow' Arthur Clarke reveals some interesting zigzag patterns in jurassic rock; dinosaur tracks meet these and it is discovered that they are Land Rover tracks – when the Land Rover is found with the remains of the archaeologist still in it.

The possibility that a character can return through time to meet himself – or more than one self – has confusing possibilities as in *The Technicolor Time Machine*, Harrison *1967*, or more fascinating sexual ones in Heinlein's 'All you Zombies' where every character is the same person so that, after a sex change, even the offspring turns out to have the same genes. This same theme was used again by David Gerrold in *The Man Who Folded Himself 1973*.

The disastrous possibilities of time travel are best displayed in van Vogt's *The Weapon Shops of Isher*, where the unhappy traveller oscillates through time, picking up 'temporal energy' all the while until he finally whips back to the distant past where he explodes – and makes the big bang that starts the universe. Van Vogt humbles the other sf writers with the grandness of his concepts.

To prevent this sort of temporal disaster police forces have been mobilized to prevent time accidents, giving rise to the Time Patrol theme, as in Poul Anderson's *Guardians of Time 1960*. (Anderson abandons the time machine gadgetry in *There Will Be Time 1972* where the hero uses brain-power alone to will himself into the past or future.) Since small changes in the past can produce major changes in the future – Ray Bradbury's time traveller kills a butterfly in 'The Sound of Thunder' which changes his own future world – we must be sure that these alterations are not made. In Fritz Leiber's *Big Time 1958* a time war is raging through eternity, with both sides fighting for the future they need the most.

The lure of this theme is so great that all of the writers are drawn to it sooner or later. Brian Aldiss with his chill theological world 'Danger, Religion!', Clifford Simak with *Time is the Simplest Thing 1961* and *Time and Again 1951*, Isaac Asimov and *The End of Eternity 1955*.

The theological possibilities are of course eternal, and while no one seems to have wanted to meet Mohammed as a small lad, all of our Judeo-Christian writers crave a look in on Christ. This thematic use was climaxed by Michael Moorcock's 'Behold the Man' where there is no Christ until the time traveller volunteers for the job.

Rockets and starships

The rocket ship is the classic sf symbol today, but it made a fairly late arrival on the scene. Francis Godwin got his traveller in *Man in the Moone 1638* to his destination being pulled by birds. Cyrano's flying chariot makes its *Voyage dans la Lune* in 1650 utilizing the power of the sun to 'suck up the dew'. Things weren't much better in 1865 when Verne got his travellers *From the Earth to the Moon* by firing them in a shell from a large gun. Slightly unrealistic (splatt . . .), though improved a bit by Well's barrels-within-barrels gun in the film *Things to Come*. Wells had learned a thing or two since 1901 with *The First Men in the Moon* when the ship reached its destination through the miraculous properties of a gravity-insulating material called Cavorite.

It wasn't until national rocket societies were formed in the late 1920s that the rocket propulsion idea entered fiction. The craft were usually built in the garden by gifted amateurs and the story ended when the thing took off. This period passed in a flash and rockets took their proper place as the accepted mode of transportation, a cliché each writer grabbed up as he came along. (Isaac Asimov's first published story in 1939 was 'Marooned off Vesta'.) Fictional rockets have been notoriously unreliable

artifacts, as the February 1939 cover of *Astounding* so graphically shows, and were notorious for their one-way-only trips as in Rex Gordon's *No Man Friday 1956*.

Nor were the larger generation ships much more reliable. (This is the simplest way of reaching the stars. A rocket large enough to contain an ecologically balanced, self-supporting world for many generations. The original crew dies but their descendents reach the destination.) Since a successful 200-year-long spaceship trip would make an exceedingly boring story, most of the generation ships suffer a breakdown of some kind, as in van Vogt's 'Far Centaurus'. The most dramatic possibilities are explored when the crew – and the reader – don't know that they are in a spaceship; Heinlein's *Universe 1941* and Brian Aldiss' *Non-Stop 1958*. One of the very few of these ships to make the hazardous voyage, without a disaster to crew or machinery, was in Harrison's *Captive Universe 1970*.

But the generation ships went the way of rockets and sail when the FTL craft burst through the ether. Faster Than Light. 'Impossible in our universe' Dr Einstein said, so the drive takes them through another universe. Jumpspace, warpspace, star drive – even the bloater drive – work their magic to get the heroes quickly to the stars. E. E. Smith used an intertialess drive in his *Lensman* novels, another cooking of the books of the laws of physics. No matter, these are just devices to get to the wonderful

Into the Black Hole, a fashionable alternative to FTL travel. Illustration by McKie for Duncan Lunan's excellent *Man and the Stars*

planets and meet and/or fight the aliens. Asimov's star drive in his *Foundation* series enables mankind to battle man, while Heinlein's *Starship Troopers 1959* travel to wipe out evil aliens. Joe Haldeman's troopers in *The Forever War 1974* are just as destructive though not as certain it is really a good thing to do. All of the interstellar drive stories are topped by Anderson's *Tau Zero 1970* which has his runaway ship banging and rattling through galaxy after galaxy.

Any mention of spaceships must make deep obeisance to that master of sf art, Frank R. Paul. While it was the writers who put us aboard the ships, it was Paul who showed us just what they looked like. Incredible! No flying-phalluses for him, but squadrons of blistered, portholed, convoluted and utterly fascinating vehicles – no two of them alike – that tore through space and right into the hearts of an entire generation of spotty little boys. This was *it*, the real stuff!

Transportation

All the world loves a good railway! In 'Mellonta Tauta' *1849* Poe has his transcontinental trains big enough to contain ballrooms for dancing, made possible by a highly illogical 50-foot track gauge. Nor was Wells a slouch. In *A Modern Utopia 1905* his trains have billiard rooms (untroubled by vibration?), bathrooms and libraries in addition to the usual fittings.

Monorails have always held a fascination for the sf author, although the only ones in operation today are in Disneyland, Seattle and Wuppertal, Germany. Never mind. Francis Stockton in *The Great Stone of Sardis 1897* has electric trains hanging from an overhead rail, while Wells's gyroscopically balanced

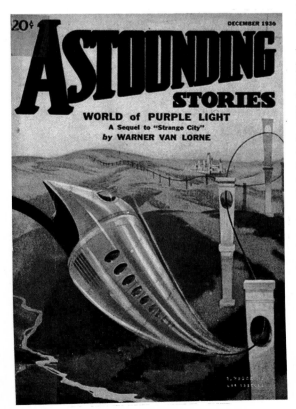

monorail trains in *The War in the Air 1908* zip along on cables right over the English Channel.

Once off the tracks anything goes. Verne gets plenty of mileage out of a steam-powered elephant that hauls a house across India titled, interestingly enough, *The Steam House 1880*. He also writes about electrically driven automobiles in *Floating Island 1876*, as does Percy Greg in *Across the Zodiac 1880*. His three-wheeled cars do a nineteenth century ton-up, going 'far faster than the swiftest mail coach'. That is between 15 and 30 miles an hour.

Wondrous are the power sources of these cars. In *Freeland 1891* Theodor Hertzka drives his with steel springs – which are wound up at steam-powered winding stations along the road. Wood, coal, charcoal, 'therms from a little petroleum lamp', are all utilized. And the faster they go, the better the roads they need. (Unless they are like the ur-James Bond cars in Von Hanstein's 'Utopia Island' that travel on either land or sea, propelled by a combination of compressed air and magnetism.) Rocket cars made their appearance in the 1930s – Buck Rogers always enjoyed driving one – giving way to automated highways, in *Methuselah's Children* by Heinlein *1941*, which are still being considered as a practical traffic solution today. Specially designed vehicles, such as Arthur Clarke's moonbuggy in *A Fall of Moondust 1961*, antedate and anticipate the reality of the real one that the astronauts drove.

Moving sidewalks, finally being put into use in airports today, were described fondly in Verne's *Floating Island*, as well as 'moving platforms' in Stockton's *The Great Stone of Sardis*. Once again Wells led the way in *When the Sleeper Wakes* with his 'moving ways'. These ways are separated into lanes each moving at a greater speed, so a passenger can work across from the local to the express lane. This design was lifted bodily by Heinlein for 'The Roads Must Roll' and improved with shops, restaurants, technology, police, strikers and the rest.

Once below the ground, transportation becomes very interesting. Buck Rogers ignores certain temperature problems and has a tube going right through the planet so that cars dropped in at one end shoot out of the other. Naturally, Buck's girlfriend gets suspended in no-gravity in the centre of the Earth. Deutsch's 'A Subway Named Möbius' presents certain unexpected topological problems to riders in the train; they vanish into another dimension for a couple of weeks. Earth technology is exported into space in Colin Kapp's 'The Subways of Tazoo' and its sequel, 'Railways up on Canis'.

The simplest form of transportation is undoubtedly MT, or matter transmission. Clarke had people broken down for transmission in 'Travel by Wire' *1937*, though later writers rolled up the wire and simply broadcast from transmitter to receiver. The history of MT, from invention to galactic use in the far future, is followed in Harrison's *One Step from Earth 1970*.

Among the more interesting and oddball forms of transportation invented are the giant war-tanks that go boring and grinding away deep underground in Carter's 'The Last Objective'. On Jack Vance's *Big Planet 1951* people roam the giant world in cars slung from ropes that loop from peak to peak.

Docking manœuvre in three dimensions (opposite) – Colin Hay has specialised in drawing craft arriving from outside the frame, and the illusion is exquisite

This cover for *Astounding SF*, shows a more chaotic docking manœuvre – a rocket-park in the middle of Manhatten

Rail transport of the future envisaged by Howard Brown in the 1930s

Vertical lift-off, tailored
for the individual.
Illustration by Peter Elson

War in the future

In 1871 *The Battle of Dorking* by Sir George
Chesney unleashed the rampaging Hun upon an
unprepared England in a remarkably successful
invasion. Chesney also unleashed ravening hordes of
invaders who are still stamping far into the future.
While his weapons were just improvements of
ordinary ones, Robert Grant's *The King's Men 1884*
starts the futuristic war inventions flowing with his
electrically charged bullets. It was then up to the
Master himself, Wells, to start the production lines
clanking with wartime hardware. In *The War of the
Worlds 1898* the Martian invaders land in spaceships
and march out in tripedal war machines. In 1893 in
'The Land Ironclads' he invented the armoured
tank, followed by the atomic bomb, dropped by
hand from planes, in *The World Set Free 1914*. By
1933 in *The Shape of Things to Come* he had outlined
the super-tanks, aerial bombardment, gas warfare
and all of the rest of the machines that have been
rattling through science fiction ever since.

Edgar Rice Burroughs took the battles of Earth
into space in 1914 with *A Princess of Mars*. The
Martians, both red and green, travelled in bathtub-
shaped aircraft propelled by rays, firing radium
bullets from radar-equipped guns. Warfare is warm-
ing up, and things really improved with the publication of *Amazing* in 1926. Soon there were stories
like Stanton Coblentz's *After 12,000 Years* where
warplanes of the future drop giant poisonous insects
on each other's territory. In *The Green Man of
Graypec 1935* Festus Pragnell invented desert tank
warfare, while in *The World Below 1924* S. Fowler
Wright depicts a worldwide war in the far future
where the flying craft are giant artificial insects, the
weapons sheets of energy.

It was those masters of the big-screen, star-
smashing story, E. E. Smith and John W. Campbell,
who really got war into space and moving on a

singularly imposing scale. Not just spaceships but
entire fleets – and fleets of fleets – blasted off, and
were often blasted out of existence. The armoured
spacesuit grew stronger and stronger, spaceaxes
clanked, blasters roared, screen after screen of
defensive force fields went down under the irresistable attack of ravening rays, and the universe has
never been the same since. Presser beams fought
against tractor beams, space torpedoes were knocked
out by disintegrator rays, while race after race of evil
aliens were blown into their component atoms. The
galactic war – impossible though it may seem – has
been a stock in trade ever since, as has been the
galactic empire.

Heinlein's *Starship Troopers 1959* vividly outlined the mechanics of this kind of warfare, his battle
armour so accurately described it could almost have
been built from the story. Joe Haldeman's *The
Forever War 1974* also has the forces of Earth
warring with terrible aliens right across the galaxy.
But there is major trouble caused by Einsteinian
time dilation; while only weeks pass for the troopers
on their mission, centuries have gone by at home. So
no matter how new the equipment is that they leave
with, it is terribly out of date by the time the battle
begins. This does not occur in Gordon Dickson's

Howard Brown's
spaceship on the cover of
Astounding (below) shows
his fascination for tiny
porthole details – the ship
is smooth and simpler
than his usual design, but
still seems futuristic.
Strange little green
invaders, as shown in this
Thrilling Wonder cover,
appeared time and time
again, always doing very
vicious things to helpless
humans – or even helpless
symbols of America!

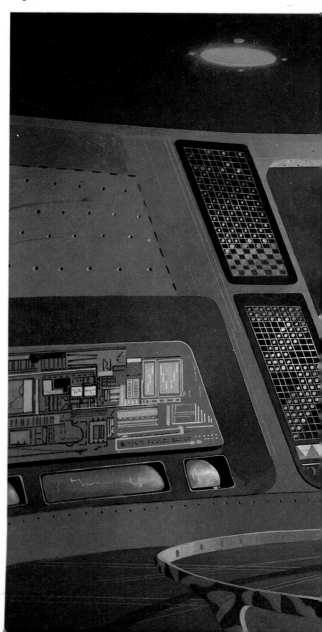

Dorsai series that chart the course of his planetful of professional space warriors, mercenaries of the future, nor does it in Harrison's *Bill the Galactic Hero 1965* which, tongue firmly jammed into cheek, attempts to blow up the concept of interstellar warfare and galactic empires once and for all.

That is a lost cause; the corpse will not lie down. The phasers and the lasers flash through *Star Trek* and aliens are still mostly baddies to be shot on sight. Now *Star Wars* has added light-swords to the already full armoury of weapons, and finally spreads out before us in eye-blasting colour, ear-destroying sound, space warfare just as we had always hoped to see it.

Submarines and underwater cities

Up until Verne's *20,000 Leagues Under the Sea 1870*, very little attention was paid to matters below the ocean's surface. He changed all that. Not only did he invent a big and comfortable submarine, complete with fish dinners and pipe organ, but he established once and for all the glamour of life in the deeps. Captain Nemo invented diving suits, and used electricity to drive, light and heat the sub, to manufacture oxygen and charge his electric bullets.

Perhaps the best realized submarine story is Frank Herbert's *Under Pressure 1956* where deep-diving subs use electric drives to maintain hull integrity, and advanced electronics and sonics to fight an undersea war. In this novel the author also invented the drogue, a reusable elastic envelope filled with petroleum and towed by a submarine, later actually developed, built and patented in England.

O'Donnell's *Fury 1950* depicted an underwater city within a giant pressure dome, but perhaps the most ingenious underwater device is Bass's *Godwhale 1974*, a sentient giant robot designed for harvesting plankton for undersea food processing plants.

Certainly the smallest, if not the most unusual underwater craft is the microscopic crawler in Blish's 'Surface Tension' that carries its contents overland – to the next pond. Perhaps the most impossible undersea artifact is Harrison's *A Transatlantic Tunnel, Hurrah! 1972* from London to New York, complete with a midocean underwater suspension bridge and a giant tunnel-laying machine.

L. Sprague de Camp did away with all the machinery in his story 'The Merman' where, after breathing the wrong kind of chemicals, the hero falls

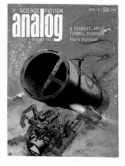

Underwater attack with mermen and beautiful girl; but written sf has always treated the undersea with great regard, recognising that the deep sea is as alien a place as the stars. Perhaps the most impossible undersea artefact (below) is Harrison's Transatlantic Tunnel, complete with mid-ocean suspension bridge

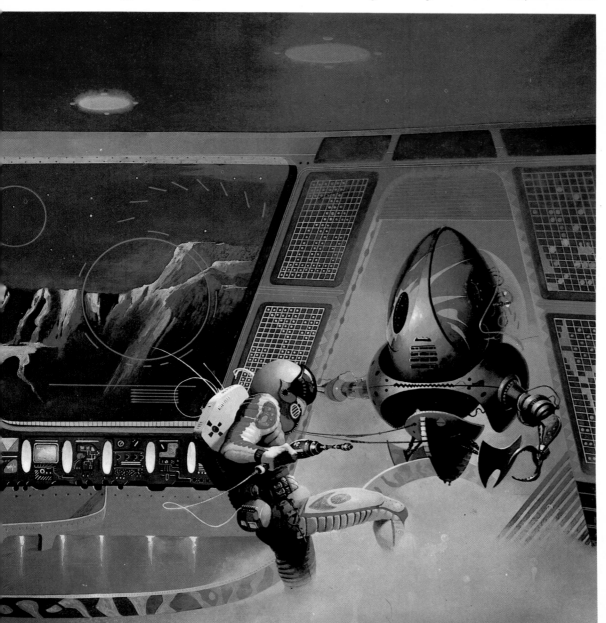

Familiar hardware confronts unfamiliar hardware in this illustration by Peter Jones

into a tank of water and discovers he can breathe this medium better than air. Mermen, and maids, have been swimming through sf ever since.

Spacesuits

When you have a spaceship you almost certainly must have a spacesuit to go with it. All of the historic space flights avoided this contingency by providing an atmosphere in space between Earth and the Moon, and even as keen a scientist as Wells was mistaken enough to supply the Moon with air, though at least he had the good sense to freeze it during the long lunar night. It wasn't until the pulp sf mags came into existence that spacesuits became the order of the day. While the authors were notoriously vague in their descriptions the artists, led as always by the incomparable Paul, had to pin down all of the details. The equipment they carried seems a little strange; hatchets, spades, boathooks; and the construction was invariably massive. Riveted solid steel, tractor treads on the boots, tiny windows in the helmets (the fishbowls were yet to come) and totally inadequate supplies of oxygen.

The major change in spacesuit design began with the space opera pulps, notably *Planet Stories*. Here we find the development and almost instantaneous acceptance of sexual dimorphism in space. While intensive research has never uncovered these facts in a story, it is more than obvious in the magazine illustrations and covers that men and women are togged out completely differently to face the rigours of total vacuum. The men, with good reason, wear heavy boots, suits made of thick and flexible fabric; cumbersome gloves cover their hands while a

transparent fishbowl with tiny air tank protects the head. Not so the women! They wear bikinis or skin-tight bathing suits, all of which can be clearly seen since their spacesuits are made of cellophane or some other transparent substance. Their light gloves would be worn to the opera and they sport the interesting novelty of highheeled space boots. The glass helm is all they share with the males. There is a mystery here, and it seems to be linked in with those brass breastplates that the girls of the future are forced to wear, metal brassieres turned out on a lathe from the look of them. Must be uncomfortable too, soggy in the summer, chill in the winter.

Pretty obviously this has more to do with sex than science. There is no physical reason for the different garb of the sexes. Now who would like to look at girls with very little clothes on? Why boys of course, and grown-up boys, even young men, the readers of the pulps where these exotic illustrations appeared. Maybe these readers were too young to touch girls, but you are never too young to look. There is also more than a whiff of fetishism in all those boots and gloves and hair, more than a soupçon of sadism in the whips and chains. And that means sex, good old sex, for that is what fetishism and sadism are all about. There was plenty of it around in the cleaner-than-clean pulps, in the illustrations and on the

covers. Nor was this completely by accident; girls on covers sell magazines. So while the authors simply wrote about spacesuits the artists had their jollies by turning them into sex objects.

It is interesting that when WWII began, two sf writer-engineers worked on the development of high altitude flying suits. (Heinlein and de Camp.) They took as their models for design artwork from science fiction magazines, artwork illustrating stories they had written. A complete feedback cycle.

Realism entered spacesuit design when men actually walked on the surface of the Moon. But reality can never catch up with sf which simply leaps thousands of years ahead to spacesuits that are self-contained spaceships and the story picks up and goes on from there.

Early scientific romances expressed a tender love of science and scientific progress – without going too much into the details. As early as More's *Utopia 1516* marvellous machines are mentioned, in this case an automatic horse-grooming and feeding machine. (Priorities were different in those days.) The pattern continued; machines and inventions were just *there*, how they were constructed or what discoveries lay behind them was never mentioned. Even in E. M. Forster's 'The Machine Stops' no attempt is made to explain how all the devices work that supply food, heat, entertainment, etc. to the solitary room dwellers. If any explanations were ever made, as in *20,000 Leagues Under the Sea*, they were lengthy descriptions of flora, fauna and scientific fact that read as though cribbed from an encyclopedia – and probably were. (Verne may have been the first, but certainly not the last to use this technique.)

But once again we have a lot to thank – or blame – Hugo Gernsback for. His *Ralph 124C41+ 1911* whips us right into the lab to demonstrate the wonders of the Hypnobiscope, Helio-Dynamophore, and Baccilatorium. Sf has never quite recovered from the detailed explanation by the man in the dentist's jacket ('Tell me, professor . . .'), or the crackling arcs, smoking flasks, dials and switches – not to mention the girl strapped on the operating table. The inventor is usually rich, has a full-breasted daughter, a well outfitted lab in a building in the garden, where everything from time machines to rocketships can be constructed as a hobby.

Sexual dimorphism in spacesuits – heavy, functional rubber for men, but transparent flimsies for women. Fashions designed by Kelly Freas

It reeled drunkenly from Outer Space! Chris Foss (opposite) took his passion for the unusually shaped hardware to an extreme in this illustration

The caterpillar-tread shoes shown on the cover of an earlier issue of *Astounding* (by H. W. Brown) were an artistic invention that vanished as fast, presumably, as the two intrepid explorers. The brass breast-plates (below), shown on *Startling Stories*, were one of the colder artistic cliches of the pulp era

A rare black and white
illustration by Chris Foss

Butler's *Erewhon 1872* destroy the mills and replace them with humming, out-of-sight factories that manufacture all of man's needs effortlessly. This quickly gives way to fear of unemployment, then absolute control of man by his machines. Science fiction finds no end of coming dangers to make us aware of.

Robots and androids

One of the dangers that haunts sf pages is the looming form of the threatening robot. The earliest of these were constructed of flesh and bone, what would now be called androids; Frankenstein's monster *1818* and Capek's *R.U.R.*, *1923*, Rossum's Universal Robots, the source of the term. The idea that if you built it it couldn't be good carries on through C. C. Campbell's 'The Avatar' *1935* where the perfect artificial man becomes dictator of the world and has to be destroyed.

It was only with the construction of metal robots – obedient machines – that mechanical men began operating on the side of justice. Frank Reade's Steam Man fought the indians for the good guys, and Eando Binder's robot, built for peace to prove its worth to mankind, was smart enough to choose sides against the Nazis in 'Adam Link fights a War'. Edmond Hamilton's Captain Future could count upon the faithful robot, Krag, to aid him at all times, as well as the faithful but not so nice android, Lothar.

A touch of order entered robotic circles in 1940 with Asimov's 'Robby' and 'Liar'. The mechanical men now began to clank about radiating security, since they had the Laws of Robotics stamped into their positronic brains. Asimov gets full credit for these laws, and countless are the writers who have utilized them:

One thing missing from these labs was any kind of computer. The equations were scribbled on sheets of paper with the occasional aid of the slide rule. It wasn't until the late 1930s, when computers were actually being used, that they crept into the science fiction scene. (And most of them were mechanical analog computers – just like the real ones in gunnery plotting rooms, bomb sights and aircraft power turrets.) It is indicative of this new trend that Robert Heinlein, a hard science sf writer, used a computer failure in his second published story, 'Misfit'. The computer still malfunctions in Anderson's 'A Logic Named Joe', and even when it works perfectly well in Clarke's 'Nine Billion Names of God', its final printout causes the end of the universe. Computers have not stopped growing, or failing, ever since. They are looked upon with unjustified suspicion and always seem too eager to take over and run the world as in D. F. Jones's *Colossus*, or even more. When the gigantic computer, the biggest ever, is constructed in Brown's 'Answer', it is designed to answer but one question. 'Is there a God?' It responds simply, 'There is now'. This hate-love fear that computers and machines are taking over in Vonnegut's *Player Piano 1952* causes mankind to rise up and destroy the machines they have created. And ends with a man tinkering with a machine to get it running.

These automated factories have taken over as hate objects from William Blake's dark satanic mills. All of the utopias, from More's original on through

Rocketships (below) that
truly look the part, and
alien with it. Illustration
by Hubert Rogers

1 A robot may not injure a human being, or, through inaction, allow a human being to come to harm.

2 A robot must obey the orders given it by human beings except where such orders would conflict with the First Law.

3 A robot must protect its own existence as long as such protection does not conflict with the First or Second Law.

Once the robotic threat had been removed the infinitely varied relationships of robot to man could be explored. Clifford Simak, in his *City* series, shows mankind evolving and leaving Earth to the robots and highly evolved dogs. Jack Williamson's *With Folded Hands . . . 1947* does discover a danger in robot control, but a benevolent one. To prevent men from being hurt the robots are stunting all development of the human race. With all the robotic goodness around it was a pleasure to see Alfred Bester's 'Fondly Fahrenheit' about a slightly insane, gentle robot.

Having once assigned man's attributes to a machine, we must consider the relationship of this intelligent machine to man's mystical nature. Boucher's 'The Quest for Saint Aquin' asks if it is possible to have a robot saint? Silverberg answered the question years later with 'Good News from the Vatican'. If you can have a robot Pope – then why not a saint?

Robots are seen as part and parcel of mankind's existence, even in the marketplace. Pohl's 'Tunnel Under the World' has unsuspecting little robots running a continuous market survey, which logically leads into his 'Midas Plague' where they solve a robot-created marketing problem.

Machines and inventions

The mind is tempted to reel at the excess of invention from the very earliest days. In *When the Sleeper Wakes* a tailor makes a few measurements, presses the right buttons – and a nifty suit is produced by the tailoring machine in a few minutes. The speech typewriter, that produces final copy when spoken into, goes back to 1931 in Von Hanstein's story 'Utopia Island'. Pneumatic tubes, still in use in department stores, were first mentioned in 1880 in Bellamy's *Looking Backward*, while weather control machines were cranking out the cold fronts as early as 1892 in William Bradshaw's *The Goddess of Atvatabar*. The brain-reading machine that reveals the subjects most innermost thoughts

dates to 1913 in Conan Doyle's *The Maracot Deep*.

With the advent of the pulps the fevered minds of the sf writers grew hotter and hotter. G. O. Smith's *Venus Equilateral* series beamed power to Earth from the sun, Henry Hasse's 'He Who Shrank' squeezed his hero into the depths of an atom, while William Tenn had a rather advanced toy in 'Child's Play', called a Build-a-man kit that did just that.

Rays could do anything. Paralyze, disintegrate, push, pull, heat-up, chill-down – you name it, they did it. Anything the mind could imagine a machine could accomplish. Walk through walls? Slip the right ring on your finger, as the hero does in Heinlein's *Methuselah's Children 1941* and your atoms slide between the others. What do you do if all the doctors in the world are morons? You give them 'The Little Black Bag' designed by C. M. Kornbluth that contains gadgets and potions that diagnose and work out a cure on their own. How do you talk to aliens who – unlike on TV and in the cinema – do not speak English? You use a translating machine like Katherine MacLean did in 'Unhuman Sacrifice'.

Unusual perils await the innovator in science fiction. 'And He Built a Crooked House' by Heinlein, really was so crooked that when jarred it folded upon itself right through the fourth dimension with resultant difficulties. The driver of Theodore Sturgeon's 'Killdozer', regretted that he had nudged a boulder and released an alien intelligence into his machine, supplying the classic battle between the possessed-bulldozer and a power shovel. Sturgeon also invented a complete and captive world of tiny beings in 'Microcosmic God'. In his story 'Waldo Inc.' Heinlein introduced a device that amplified the hand power of the individual using it. Waldo was the character's name, and devices like this – since invented and patented – are called 'waldoes' in honour of the achievement.

It would be hard to build a transparent spaceship if you did not have glass as strong as steel, or portholes in a ship without steel that is as transparent as glass. A different kind of substance is the slow glass of Bob Shaw's 'Light of Other Days' where the glass stores and releases the images falling upon it – many years even decades later.

Robert Heinlein first used the Waldo in an sf story – the machine that magnifies the movement of the human arm – and this *Astounding* cover picture by Rogers is a classic, though the alien machine (below) is less functional

Planetary survey with future realism. This illustration is by Tim White

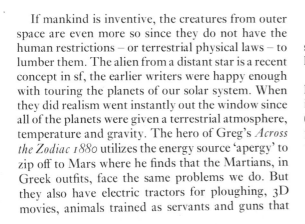

Letting your fingers do the walking is here taken to its ludicrous, but hilarious extreme by Patrick Woodroffe in his picture 'Waldo'

The lights in the sky are cars! This amazing domed city and its suburbs, and that row of enormous beacons, would probably drain the electrical power from North America in a week – but it's certainly effective. Illustration by Chris Foss

If mankind is inventive, the creatures from outer space are even more so since they do not have the human restrictions – or terrestrial physical laws – to lumber them. The alien from a distant star is a recent concept in sf, the earlier writers were happy enough with touring the planets of our solar system. When they did realism went instantly out the window since all of the planets were given a terrestrial atmosphere, temperature and gravity. The hero of Greg's *Across the Zodiac 1880* utilizes the energy source 'apergy' to zip off to Mars where he finds that the Martians, in Greek outfits, face the same problems we do. But they also have electric tractors for ploughing, 3D movies, animals trained as servants and guns that shoot out glass globes filled with poison gas. Just like home.

All of the other early planetary explorations found little evidence of alien science. The aliens were either insects (Wells's lunarians), prehistoric beasts (Astor's *A Journey in Other Worlds*), spirits or primitive races who could just as well have lived in the Amazon basin. Not until 1929 and O. A. Kline's *The Planet of Peril* do we get the aliens back into the factory and lab. His Venusians have gyroscopic air cars and machine-guns that fire poison-gas bullets. War is popular Out There, still. Keith Laumer's

A touch of order entered robotic circles in 1940 with Asimov's stories 'Robbie' and 'Liar'. The mechanical men now began to clank about radiating security, since they had the Laws of Robotics stamped into their positronic brains. Asimov gets full credit for these laws. His stories are collected in *I Robot*, and *The Rest of the Robots*, but he is still writing them, and the latest, *The Bicentennial Man* won both Hugo and Nebula Awards

long-buried fighting machine in 'The Last Command' is equalled in destructive ability only by Fred Saberhagen's Berserkers, giant alien constructs that roam space seeking only to destroy mankind. It takes nerve, in the face of all this destruction, to produce an alien artifact that projects love, not hate, but Sturgeon succeeds in 'Saucer of Loneliness'.

The aliens seem to enjoy keeping an eye on Earth – with good reason – as with Clarke's monolith, immortalized in the film *2001*, in the story 'The Sentinel'. When they hear the bad news they react strongly, as in Sturgeon's 'The Sky is Full of Ships'.

Perhaps the first serious attempt to describe alien life and artifacts was in Stanley Weinbaum's 'A Martian Odyssey'. We never quite understand what his creatures are doing, which is the name of the game. A. J. Budrys' *Rogue Moon 1960* uses the device of a matter transmitter to explore a totally alien artifact on the Moon, to walk inside it. On a still larger scale Clarke has a wandering planetoid in *Rendezvous with Rama 1973* bring an entire world of alien constructs whistling through our solar system. Easier to get to that than E. F. Russell's 'Mechanistria' where Earthmen had to travel far to find this planet inhabited totally by living machines. Another Russell space trip in 1947 takes the protagonist of 'Hobbyist' to a world and a museum built by a creature that might very well be God. Alien religion also does no good to the Earthmen in Heinlein's *Methuselah's Children*.

Ruins of alien civilizations are scattered thickly throughout the pages of sf, but never so precisely as in H. Beam Piper's 'Omnilingual' where the scientists learn to translate the records of a vanished alien race. Many times the machines still operate, doing no good at all, although in van Vogt's 'Enchanted Village' the machines are bent to the hero's will.

Alien time travellers have been keeping an eye on us from the far future for years, so much so that the alien artifact in Robert Holdstock's 'Travellers' turns out to be a quick glimpse of an alien whistling back to the distant past.

Communications

Modern and scientific means of communication were easy enough for Bacon to describe in *The New Atlantis* in 1627, but have been getting much more difficult ever since. He wrote 'We have all means to convey sounds in trunks and pipes, in strange lines and distances'. Fine for the 17th century, but readers demand more meat today. Electricity helps; Greg's Martians in *Across the Zodiac* dial in music carried over electric wires, while the inhabitants of *Erewhon* not only hear music but sermons, up to 150,000 at a time. Greg's Martians also used a facsimile transmitter to send messages.

But pictures that move are what are needed and as early as 1760 the natives in Tiphaigne de la Roche's *Giphantia* are sending pictures right around the world using mirrors. The mirrors are still flashing in *When the Sleeper Wakes* and in Harben's *Land of the Changing Sun 1894*, though aided by electricity for the first time. George Alan England's visualizer is plugged into telephone lines in *The Golden Blight*.

Then, again, along comes good old Hugo and

invents the term television which was instantly picked up by McLociard in the story 'Television Hill' who cannily sold it back to the inventor for publication in *Amazing* in 1932. From then on the visiscreen, the visiplate, scanner, viewplate and all the rest have been stock in trade for the writers. Until the first interstellar ships dashed out of our solar system.

The laws of physics state that radio waves propagate at the speed of light. So a radio signal sent to a star 75 light years away will take 75 years to get there. Not the quickest form of communication, and it plays havoc with a story plot. The FTL ships can of course carry the mails, but this does not permit the needed two-way conversations. The easiest way out is to have subspace radio that operates on the same imaginary wavelength as the subspace drive. Nice, but not elegant. Psi is a bit better since there is supposed to be no timelag in mental communication. A mechanical equivalent of this is seen in Blish's 'Bleep' where the sound of the title contains all of the instantaneous messages ever sent. Le Guin uses her communicating invention called ansible in all of her books.

Alien communication is envisaged in a speaking tree in Blish's *Case of Conscience 1953*, while aliens come to a watery end in a puddle in MacLean's 'Pictures Don't Lie' because of the fact that wavelengths don't vary – no matter what your size.

The first city in space, a satellite of the Earth, was launched in 1869 in Hale's 'The Brick Moon'. A moon is made of brick, 200 feet in diameter, and is to be hurled into space by flywheels as an aid to celestial navigation. It is accidentally flipped up too early and all of the bricklayers and their families, who are living aboard while the thing is being built, go along with it. At a height of 9,000 miles it goes into orbit where its inhabitants find life quite enjoyable.

Satellite design has been improved since then – it could hardly have gotten worse – and space around a thousand planets has been filled with populated

Eon Taylor robots really shine with metallic polish. This one seems almost functional, the illusion of meaningless mechanical detail

satellites of all kinds. Factories, power-generating satellites, spaceship stations, war satellites. All of them have to be built in space, with the exception of Blish's *Cities in Flight* series. Great anti-gravity machines called spindizzies are put into position around Manhattan Island – and lift the entire heart of New York City into space. A dazzling concept indeed; followed by other cities who leave the tired economies of Earth for the excitement of the stars.

Then, for many years, the biggest city in space was in Clifford Simak's 'Limiting Factor' where the spacemen discover an artificial metal world that is so big that, when they explore it, they can make no sense of it at all. But this world, and all of the others, are small time when compared with the concept of the physicist Freeman Dyson. He speculated that if all of the planets of the solar system are ground up

and melted down, there would be enough material available to form a thin sphere about the sun, a giant shell that could be inhabited on its inner surface. There would be no night or day, and the sphere could be placed at the correct distance from the sun to permit an endless balmy summer. This design was first used by Bob Shaw in *Orbitsville*, which though written earlier was not published until 1975. Here the Earth explorers zip into the sphere and must spend years getting back to the entrance they originally came in through. This Dyson design was also used later by Larry Niven in *Ringworld 1970*, though he limited himself to a single band in space rather than a sphere.

Satellite cities, small ones this time, appear in Fritz Leiber's *A Spectre is Haunting Texas 1969* and in John Boyd's *The Pollinators of Eden 1969*.

Illustration by Chris Foss for James Blish's 'Cities in Flight' series. Great antigravity machines called Spindizzies are put into position around Manhattan island – and lift the entire heart of New York city into space

103

alien encounter

Chris Morgan

Alienness is a question of viewpoint. The bizarre creatures and
ecologies of another world are alien enough, but man himself
can be alien, as can his world in the far future or the far past.
Even his mind, much modified, can become an alien thing.
When examined closely, the alien in science fiction is all of it.

Aliens are not only bug eyed monsters. Obviously, any non-human being – especially intelligent – is an alien, though alienness is very much dependent upon one's point of view. The Unicorn in Lewis Carroll's *Through the Looking Glass* considers all children to be fabulous monsters until it meets Alice, and vice versa. But not only are the creatures themselves alien; so are their planets – all extra-terrestrial planets. And there is more. L. P. Hartley, at the beginning of *The Go-Between*, says, 'The past is a foreign country: they do things differently there'. So, too, is the future a foreign country – an alien place. The human beings of the 21st century will be alien to us, because of their attitudes, language and ephemeral interests. As more time passes the degree of alienness will increase, physically and mentally as well as behaviourally. Their environment will change, too. Earth will become like one of those puzzle pictures that used to appear in children's comics, a familiar object seen from an unfamiliar angle, but the unfamiliar angle will be one of time rather than distance.

When examined closely, the alien in science fiction is most of it.

A novel which covers most types of sentient aliens is Olaf Stapledon's *The Star Maker 1937*. Roaming the galaxy as a disembodied observer, its narrator visits civilizations of humanoids (with dark red skin, green hair, and taste glands in their hands, feet and genitals), single-limbed men, flying men, six-limbed men, whale-like nautiloids, symbionts, composite beings (only the swarm is intelligent) and plant-men. Gradually the observer, joined on his mental journey by a mind of each of these races, comes to understand the existence of the Star Maker, that 'infinite spirit' which has created the cosmos.

Two current authors particularly noted for the creation of numerous convincing alien types are Larry Niven and James White. Niven's 'Known Space' stories – including the award-winning novel *Ringworld* – are populated by such species as the Pierson's puppeteer (tripedal, two-headed, more scientifically advanced than humans, but ruled by a racial instinct of extreme caution amounting to cowardice); the sedentary, telepathic Grog, which resembles a five-foot hairy cone; the fierce, orange-furred Kzinti, like an upright tiger; the Protector, related to humanity, but beaked, with knobbed joints and immense strength; the Outsiders, like 'black cat-o'-nine-tails with grossly swollen handles', who travel great distances between the stars, selling information. And in collaboration with Jerry Pournelle, Larry Niven wrote *The Mote in God's Eye*, about an astonishingly adaptable, fast-breeding and warlike alien race – the Moties.

James White is the creator of Sector General, a vast hospital in space, staffed by and catering for humans and many dozens of alien types. The hospital needs to be able to create an environment compatible with any sentient alien which requires treatment. Each type has a four-letter classification with, for example, warm-blooded oxygen-breathers being ELPH and furry, multipedal creatures being DBLF. This is one of the best examples of many alien types living and working in harmony. The Sector General books are *Hospital Station, Star Surgeon* and *Major Operation*.

Other writers good on aliens are the late E. E. 'Doc' Smith, who also invented a classification system, for the multitude of beings in his *Lensman* books; A. E. van Vogt, in novels like *Slan, The Voyage of the Space Beagle* and *The War Against the Rull*, and Keith Laumer, whose galactic diplomat, Retief, has encountered a multitude of aliens in dozens of stories about him.

Almost human

Before dealing with really unusual aliens, let us have a look at some which are almost human. The differences between them and us should not be just physical, such as the shape of the ears, but psychological and behavioural as well. Lord Lytton's *The Coming Race 1874* describes a species of supermen with great physical and mental powers who live in a light and airy world deep in the Earth's crust. Their society – without crime, war, government or change, but based on common consent – is so alien to ours that mutual understanding is difficult. Walter Tevis's *The Man Who Fell to Earth* (filmed starring David Bowie) shows the trials and tribulations of a near-human who comes to Earth and tries, without any sinister motive, to make sufficient money to pay for the construction of a spaceship. But he fails, being thwarted and crippled by his own alienness as much as anything. In Michael Bishop's *A Funeral for the Eyes of Fire*, the Tropemen are basically human except that they have no mouths and their eyes are crystalline. These differences have been crucial in shaping their whole society. For example, food is ingested through the palm of the hand, communication is by telepathy, and the eyes are greatly revered – many Tropemen carry the powdered eyes of an ancestor in a pouch hanging from a neck-chain. *Venus Plus X* by Theodore Sturgeon and the award-winning *The Left Hand of Darkness* by Ursula Le Guin deal in depth with races which are human but for the fact that the sexes are not differentiated. In Sturgeon's novel each member of the race has complete male and female organs, while in Le Guin's each has the potential to become either male or female during that part of the month when s/he is sexually active. Though the anatomical differences from the human norm are relatively small in both cases, the psychological and societal differences are very great.

Flying men have always been a challenge for the sf writer. Although many early stories in the pulp magazines featured types which could never, in fact, have got off the ground, more recent treatments have specified a low-gravity, high air pressure planet and

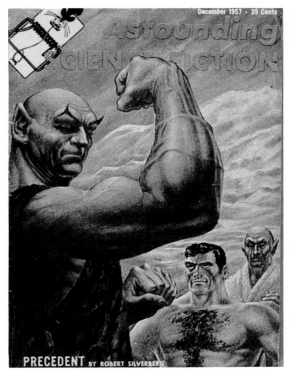

PRECEDENT BY ROBERT SILVERBERG

a very light creature with enormous wings. Poul Anderson has written two successful novels about such beings, *War of the Wing-Men* and *The People of the Wind*, with all planetary and anatomical details carefully calculated. A notable short story about flying men, which shows that aliens, too, may feel compassion, is 'Wings' by Vonda N. McIntyre (in *The Alien Condition* edited by Stephen Goldin).

Alien animals

Although the term 'sentient aliens' is taken to refer to creatures from other planets, it must be used also of Earth animals which somehow achieve intelligence. The earliest example is H. G. Wells' short story 'The Empire of the Ants' (in *The Time Machine and Other Stories*), where an army of ants is advancing across South America, killing all human beings in its path. 'About one in twenty was much larger than its fellows, and with an exceptionally large head'. They have 'things strapped about their bodies by bright white bands like white metal threads'. Although later examples abound, one of the most popular animals for achieving intelligence – either naturally or *via* surgery – is the dolphin. A particularly good story on these lines is Robert Silverberg's 'Ishmael in Love' (in *Earth's Other Shadow*), where a dolphin employed on a fish farm tells of his love for a human female.

A symbiotic relationship between two species of alien, or between human and alien, is occasionally met with. Perhaps the best known example is Hal Clement's *Needle*, in which a small, jelly-like alien –

Illustration (left) by Kelly Freas. *Astounding SF* in the 50s and early 60s ran many first-contact and confrontation stories – Robert Silverberg, Randall Garrett, Christopher Anvil and Eric Frank Russell wrote them with enormous energy. The aliens always seemed more advanced than us, but inevitably proved inferior to human cunning. And on the whole, as this illustration clearly shows, they were little more than modified men anyway, something that is in defiance of just about every evolutionary rationale there is. This is something that was discussed in Willy Ley's fact article 'How to build an extra-terrestrial' (below) illustrated by Emsh. John Schoenherr's drawing (bottom) of the creature from Joan Vinge's *Eyes of Amber* is far more acceptably alien

An echo of the bad old days of the pulp magazine alien is seen in this picture by Joe Petagno

The beings in Robert Silverberg's Award winning novel, *A Time of Changes* (below) are beautiful and human in every appearance, which focusses concern upon their society which is totally alien to the Earthman Schwartz who is visiting them. Cover by Szafran. Kelly Freas' terrified alien (bottom), from Poul Anderson's 'Wherever you are'

which must inhabit a more solid-bodied creature in order to survive – enters the body of a human youth (by sliding through the pores), conferring a number of biological advantages on its host. One of the most peculiar symbiotic relationships between human and alien is to be found in Cordwainer Smith's 'A Planet Named Shayol' (in *Galaxy, October 1961*). On Shayol the minute dromozoa 'infect' humans, bringing great pain but causing them to grow extra limbs and organs which can be removed and used for spare-part surgery. Shayol is used as a prison planet; its grotesque horror was well captured in Virgil Finlay's original *Galaxy* illustration. More recently, the award-winning novella 'A Song for Lya' by George R. R. Martin (in *A Song for Lya*), tells of an alien parasite which slowly consumes its humanoid host. But the humanoids are happy to 'die', for this enables them to join a union of minds of all past members of their species. Humans can join it, too.

Not so human

Although most intelligent aliens are roughly our size – and rarely larger than a half-grown elephant or smaller than a cat – there are notable exceptions. The largest is Fred Hoyle's intelligent hydrogen cloud in *The Black Cloud*, which has a mass as great as Jupiter's but a greater volume because of its lower density. The sentient ocean in Stanislaw Lem's

Solaris is small by comparison. At the other end of the scale, the smallest space-going race must be those in Katherine MacLean's 'Pictures Don't Lie' (in *Best SF* edited by Edmund Crispin), where an alien spaceship with a crew who have appeared human over a TV link lands at a US airfield and sinks in a shallow puddle. Obviously the aliens were microscopic, but the pictures gave no indication of relative size.

Aliens need not have solid bodies. They may be amorphous, with a facility for shape-changing. Robert Sheckley's delightful story 'Keep Your Shape' (in *Untouched by Human Hands*) tells of an alien advance party sent to prepare the way for their soldiers to invade Earth. They are able to change their shape at will, but have a moral code forbidding shapelessness or idle shape-changing. However, the exotic fixed shapes of Earth subvert them from their duty. They become a tree, a dog, a bird. The central section of Isaac Asimov's award-winning novel *The Gods Themselves* describes a society of amorphous creatures. They marry and procreate in triads (their sex practices are described in detail). They feed by direct absorption of solar energy. This may seem very alien indeed, but in fact their society is analogous to our own in so many respects that it is easily understood. This is a criticism which may be levelled at most of the works mentioned so far: the aliens are alien only in peripheral details (colour, limbs, feeding-habits) rather than in essence (ways of thinking, basic motivations, systems of logic). Perhaps an alien being should, by definition, be totally incomprehensible to us, but of course any writer must temper the alienness of his characters with the entertainment value of his story. This is why 'almost human' aliens tend to be more believable – they are easier to write and read about.

A major exception to this is an entertaining story about completely alien beings 'The Dance of the Changer and the Three' by Terry Carr (in his collection *The Light at the End of the Universe*). In it the aliens are 'almost wholly an energy life-form, their consciousness coalescing in each life cycle around a spatial center which they call a "life-mote", so that, if you could see the patterns of energy they form, . . . they'd look rather like a spiral nebula sometimes, or other times like iron filings gathering around a magnet, or maybe like a half-melted snowflake'. Between them and humans are no parallels, no equivalents, no reference points; that is the *raison d'être* of the story.

In pursuing the trend of ever more unusual aliens, we come to sentient plants. The best-known tale of these is *The Day of the Triffids* by John Wyndham. Developed by the Russians as a source of vegetable oil, triffids are about two metres tall. They are mobile, moving stiffly on three stumpy, root-like projections, and can strike at humans with their stems, distributing a potentially lethal poison. Their degree of intelligence is debatable, but they take

advantage of a planet-wide disaster to acquire control of large areas of Britain and (presumably) the rest of the world. A more recent novelette, Ursula Le Guin's 'Vaster Than Empires and More Slow' (in *New Dimensions 1* edited by Robert Silverberg) adopts a different approach, concerning itself with a planet whose land-mass is covered by various types of plants which constitute a single nervous system. This results in awareness rather than intelligence – an awareness which is manifested as fear when a human survey team arrives.

Invading aliens

The classic novel of alien invasion of Earth, often imitated but never bettered, is *The War of the Worlds* by H. G. Wells. The story of greyish, octopoid Martians landing in metal cylinders in Surrey, constructing war-machines with invincible heat-rays, terrorising much of southern England, and finally succumbing to the attack of terrestrial bacteria, is well known. When produced by Orson Welles as a radio play in the US in 1938 it was mistaken for a real invasion and caused panic.

Variations on this theme have been common. In Robert A. Heinlein's *The Puppet Masters*, slug-like aliens control humans by hag-riding them, perching between their shoulder-blades, while in Daniel F. Galouye's *Lords of the Psychon* Earth's inhabitants are killed or tortured in a variety of ways for no apparent reason by very convincingly alien invaders

Keith Laumer's Galactic Diplomat Retief has encountered a multitude of aliens in dozens of stories about him. Cover by Jack Gaughan

The classic novel of alien invasion is H.G. Wells' *The War of the Worlds*. The octopoid martians, riding tripodal war machines, have often been depicted in science fiction, but rarely better than in this illustration by David Hardy

Bob Layzell's illustration makes secret acknowledgement to the pulp era.

As *Planet Stories* (opposite) clearly shows, women altered and modified by bio-engineering inevitably grow to enormous sizes (in the pulp magazines at least), all proportions guaranteed of course. Gallons of lipstick and eye make-up form a perfect armour plating against the blaster wielded by our grim-faced male hero

Scantily clad women menaced by hideous aliens. Lawrence Steven's cover from *Super Science* or hilarious aliens, from *Astounding*, must nevertheless wait helplessly as male springs to defense, thus spoiling the fun of those who would like to know what the alien's intentions are

who are mostly invisible but build strange palaces of force at intervals across the world. How long will an alien invasion last? In *The Interpreter* by Brian Aldiss, Earth has been under the rule of the three-armed, three-legged nuls for 2,000 years, while in 'Idiot Stick' by Damon Knight (in *Far Out*) an alien invasion is thwarted in its early stages by turning the aliens' own tools against them.

The alien invaders need not always be sentient; unintelligent animals or plants may be just as deadly as intelligent ones. A typical example is Robert Sheckley's short story 'The Leech' (in *Notions Unlimited*), in which the invader is amoeboid and will eat anything or consume any form of energy, growing larger all the time.

A less obvious form of invasion is described in John Wyndham's *The Midwich Cuckoos* (filmed as *The Village of the Damned*). An English village is put to sleep by some unknown force for 36 hours, during which time every woman of child-bearing age there is artificially inseminated. The children appear normal enough at first, except for their golden eyes,

but soon it becomes clear that they have telepathic abilities and are not wholly human. Another form of alien possession occurs in 'Passengers', Robert Silverberg's award-winning short story (in *Nebula Award Stories 5* edited by James Blish). Here, anybody in the world is able to be taken over and controlled for a time by aliens of whom nothing is known. People 'ridden' in this fashion are made to perform all sorts of irrational or distasteful acts.

First contact and its consequences

Even when Earth is not invaded, first contact between man and alien inevitably brings surprises, misunderstandings and – all too frequently – strife. Often, such stories examine our own reactions rather than concentrating on the aliens. Man's instinct to 'kill first and ask questions later' is the point of Howard Fast's story 'The Large Ant' (in *Contact* edited by Noel Keyes). It seems likely that if a species of alien resembling a 40 cm ant tried to make contact with humanity its envoys would be slaugh-

photon storm, and its Pusher is killed. Without a Pusher the ship cannot hope to reach home before its constituents begin to die of old age. Because the Pusher had been of human appearance the ship lands on the nearest Pusher planet – Earth – and eventually a man consents to join the ship, so discovering the special human talent of pushing – a sort of telekinetic space drive.

Of course, first contact as such is not always possible. In Robert Silverberg's *The Man in the Maze*, the first human sent to contact the humanoid inhabitants of Beta Hydri IV is ignored, surely the most alien response possible. But when he becomes too much of a nuisance his mind is altered, making him repellant to other humans. Another aborted contact is described in Eric Frank Russell's 'The Waitabits' (in *Far Stars*), where the humanoid inhabitants of a planet move too slowly for any communication to be established. First contact may be frustrated by the lack of a common medium of communication and by different concepts of intelligence: in Ursula Le Guin's beautifully-told 'Mazes' (in *Epoch* edited by Roger Elwood and Robert Silverberg) the anguish of a sentient alien is shown as humans try to force it to perform tricks as a test of intelligence. It struggles to communicate in its normal manner – *via* intricate dances – but is not understood.

Woman consumed by amorphous alien. Fear fodder by Robert Gibson Jones

Josh Kirby's picture for Brian Aldis's *The Interpreter*. Earth has been under the rule of the three-legged, three-armed Nuls for 2000 years

tered out of hand by unthinking humans, regardless of its peaceful intentions. Simple misunderstandings seem to occur in every first contact situation. One such is in Fritz Leiber's 'What's He Doing in There?' (also in *Contact* edited by Noel Keyes). Earth's first Martian visitor is spending its first day here at the home of a cultural anthropologist. Indicating that it wants to visit the bathroom, it stays there all night, causing great consternation. The explanation is that Martians prefer to sleep in a tub of water. A subtle result of Martians visiting Earth is suggested in 'The Day After the Day the Martians Came' by Frederik Pohl (in *Dangerous Visions* edited by Harlan Ellison): perhaps all the jokes told against blacks and Jews will now be told against Martians.

First contact need not happen on Earth; it may occur in space or on the aliens' home world. Or it may even be 'staged' – set up by an all-powerful third party as a test of strength and intelligence between representatives of humanity and an alien species. The classic and frequently-reprinted story here is Fredric Brown's 'Arena' (in *Honeymoon in Hell*).

A highly original first contact story, which also stresses cooperation between different alien types, is Robert Sheckley's 'Specialist' (in the excellent critical anthology *The Mirror of Infinity* edited by Robert Silverberg). An organic spaceship, consisting of nine alien species, each with its own job (Engine, Wall, Talker, Eye, etc) is damaged in a

A Princess of Mars, in the tradition of Edgar Rice Burroughs. The low gravity of the planet Mars has meant a bio-genetic evolution of the thoraco-morphic area, without the need for extra pectoralis strengthening. Thus Mars, planet of war, was nonetheless planet of romance for the early sf adventurers, and Burrough's John Carter of Mars met many a Princess in the red shade of the dunes. Illustration by Boris Vallejo

The Vision of Wonder – an alien world painted by contemporary American artist Steve Fabian

Alien togetherness

A possible consequence of first contact between human and alien is sex. While this used to involve a many-tentacled green monster carrying off a nubile woman, as depicted on many pulp magazine covers, it has more recently come to be a believable form of sex between human and humanoid. In *The Lovers* by Philip José Farmer, an Earthman far from home establishes a sexual relationship with Jeanette, who is half human, half insectoid, though appearing human. She becomes pregnant and her offspring kill her as they develop: it is the natural way for her species. A more recent story, 'And I Awoke and Found Me Here On the Cold Hill's Side' by James Tiptree Jr (in *Ten Thousand Light Years From Home*), suggests that 'Man is exogamous – all our history is one long drive to find and impregnate the stranger. Or get impregnated by him, it works for women too'. So, for the humans living in or around a spaceship docking port, alien sex is a way of life – and death.

There is also the occasional marriage between human and alien, which is particularly complex when the human has undergone specialized treatment to make him into an amoeboid alien (for 12 hours a day) so that he could be a war-time spy, and when his bride is an amoeboid alien who has undergone similar treatment to make her human for about 18 hours a day. This situation occurs in Philip Dick's 'Oh, To Be a Blobel!' (in *The Preserving Machine*). A more serious treatment is in Robert Holdstock's *Eye Among the Blind*, where a human female takes an alien partner as much to immerse herself in his culture as for any physical reason.

Another consequence of first contact is the exposure of the alien to human religions – and vice versa. This is the basis of many stories, but perhaps the most interesting theme is whether it is possible for an alien race to be free from original sin. *A Case of Conscience* by James Blish deals with this problem. The alien inhabitants of the planet Lithia are reptiles as tall as elephants. They have no crime or sin of any sort, nor do they worship a god. A Jesuit priest who is part of a human survey party is disturbed by this Garden of Eden situation. He wonders how it can exist unless created by God, but why then do the Lithians not recognise God? The novel won a Hugo award.

Alien worlds

With the exception of future Earth the closest alien world is the moon. But after having entered all our sitting-rooms *via* live TV transmission and been trampled by numerous pairs of American boots, the moon is less alien than it used to be. Certainly it does not have the breathable atmosphere, the varied vegetation, the giant mooncalves or the intelligent bipedal Selenites of H. G. Wells' *The First Men in the Moon 1901*. Stories set on the moon have been popular ever since then, though the advance of science has considerably restricted plot possibilities. It may be that some alien artifact will still be discovered there, though, as in Arthur Clarke's short story 'The Sentinel' (in *Expedition to Earth*), which was the nucleus of *2001: A Space Odyssey*. But the most fruitful and interesting theme of more recent moon stories has been the different way of life which grows up over a number of years (or generations) in a hermetically sealed colony there. The best novel of this type is *The Moon is a Harsh Mistress*, an award-winner by Robert Heinlein which suggests that the first lunar colonists will be transported convicts, who will eventually rebel against Earth.

The Solar System

Mars has always seemed likely to support life. The 19th century observations of Schiaparelli, Lowell and other astronomers gave rise to the image of a habitable Mars criss-crossed by canals. Many authors seized upon this as a backcloth for adventure stories, and continue to do so, even now that the image has proved mythical. Not the earliest, but certainly the best known are Edgar Rice Burroughs' heroic tales of Barsoom (as his Martians called their world). His first, *Under the Moons of Mars* (later published as *A Princess of Mars*), appeared as a magazine serial in 1912. The exploits of his hero, John Carter, amongst various races of Martian 'men' and animals, fill 11 books and have achieved great popularity; they are still being reprinted. The best of his many imitators has been Leigh Brackett. Stories of a humanoid race existing on a Mars with breathable air continue to be written – such as Roger Zelazny's 'A Rose for Ecclesiastes' (in *Four for Tomorrow*) – perhaps just to prove that scientific progress cannot always kill off popular myth. Generally post-1945 sf has depicted Mars as the cold, almost airless planet it is, although most give it some

Duneworld, painted by John Schoenherr. Two of the most striking alien worlds in sf are Hal Clement's Mesklin and Frank Herbert's Arrakis, or Dune, an arid, almost barren world, whose main ecological danger are the gigantic sandworms, non-sentient, but ridden by man, and which can reach lengths of up to 200 metres

form of life – often lichen. One of the most recent examples is *The Martian Inca* by Ian Watson, in which a US expedition to Mars discovers a social slime mould and is infected by a mind-expanding micro-organism.

Venus, too, has been a popular setting for heroic adventure stories. The cloud-covered planet was long thought of as a young, perhaps more watery, version of Earth. Edgar Rice Burroughs set a series of books there, too, and C. S. Lewis used it for *Perelandra*, one of his metaphysical fantasies. Ray Bradbury, John Christopher, Robert Heinlein, Roger Zelazny and many others have written about the luxuriant swamps of Venus. When a Russian probe proved them all wrong in 1967, Brian Aldiss and Harry Harrison edited *Farewell Fantastic Venus!*, a nostalgic anthology of stories and articles about the fictional planet.

As for the rest of the solar system, every planet and moon has been the setting for a story at some time. Even the asteroid belt has not been neglected, with hordes of hopeful miners searching for asteroids of solid uranium, gold, and so on. But many of the settings are similar: if a colony exists beneath a dome, with artificial gravity, then life on a moon of Neptune (*Triton* by Samuel Delany) need not be very different to life in any other artificial environment, and the alienness is sociological and psychological rather than physical.

Beyond the Solar System

So many strange planets have been written of, orbiting factual or fictional stars, that even to classify them all would be a mammoth task. Every possible permutation of temperature, atmosphere and gravity seems to have been tried, with and without various strange forms of flora and fauna. If a surprisingly large number of these alien worlds possess conditions under which a human can survive, well, not only is that the sort of world for which all space scouts seem to be searching, but it makes a better story, too.

As in the case of alien beings, certain authors are noted particularly for the creation of original and highly-detailed alien worlds. Hal Clement deserves the first mention. His *Mission of Gravity* is set on Mesklin, a huge planet, very much flattened so that the equatorial diameter is many times the polar diameter. This has produced gravity varying between 3g at the equator and almost 700g at the poles. It is a cold world, with an atmosphere of hydrogen and seas of liquid methane. A valuable research rocket has been grounded close to one of the poles, where Earth's technology cannot reach it, and a local sea-captain and his crew are persuaded to travel to it and transmit the data to an orbiting ship. The Mesklinites resemble 45 cm centipedes; they are intelligent but have little knowledge of science. In

Cycle of Fire, Clement deals with a rather more Earth-like world – except that it is the planet of a binary system, in an eccentric orbit which makes it, for alternate 40 year periods, so hot that nothing Earth-like can survive. Both 'hot' and Earth-type life-forms have evolved there. And in *Close to Critical* a bathyscape with two children aboard (one human, one not) must be rescued from the surface of a high-temperature, high-gravity world. All three novels are problem stories set against extremely convincing alien backgrounds.

The most detailed alien ecology of all is by Frank Herbert, in *Dune* and its two sequels. The planet is Arrakis, sometimes known as Dune, an incredibly arid desert world with a large temperature range, the upper limit being higher than anything encountered on Earth. The most important endemic animal is the sandworm or *shai-hulud*, non-sentient but ridden by man, which regularly grows to a length of 200 metres and sometimes over twice that. It has great economic importance for its part in the production of melange, a priceless drug. These ecological factors, especially drought, make life on Arrakis the severe and intense business that it is.

Moving on to more specific alien worlds, the most peculiar of them all is Placet, in Fredric Brown's 'Placet is a Crazy Place' (in *Aliens and Spaceships*). It follows a figure-of-eight orbit around two dissimilar suns, passing through a very peculiarly distorted piece of space (Blakeslee Field) somewhere in between. And all three bodies are close together and moving very fast. Hence: 'Placet is the only known planet that can eclipse itself twice at the same time, run headlong into itself every forty hours and then chase itself out of sight.' Although Fredric Brown does a little pseudo-scientific explaining, he immediately throws in hallucinatory effects and troglodyte birds which fly through solid matter, just for laughs. More serious is 'Beachhead' by Clifford

Simak (in *Strangers in the Universe*). A large and well-equipped planetary survey party lands on a jungle world and begins to check it out. A native (humanoid, but just a naked savage) tells them, *via* a translation headset, that they will never go home. This is no defensive threat, for very soon their technology begins breaking down, as something on the planet destroys the metal on which that technology is based.

A very scientific story of alien ecology – first published back in 1955, when the word 'ecology' was known only to a few scientists – is 'Grandpa' by James H. Schmitz (in *Decade: the 1950s* edited by Aldiss and Harrison). It tells of the plants and animals on a world being surveyed by a human colonial team, a world where symbiosis, or parasitism at least, seems fairly common. When one of the large mobile lily-pads used as rafts by the humans (they can be started, stopped and steered by the touch of a heat-gun) stops responding to heat, attacks its passengers and moves out into deep water, it takes a while for the only uninjured person aboard to discover that another alien species – also non-sentient – is using the raft to reach its breeding-grounds.

Another detailed ecology, but one which seems dedicated to exterminating human settlers, is to be found in Harry Harrison's *Deathworld*. The planet is Pyrrus. 'Plants and animals on Pyrrus are *tough*. They fight the world and they fight each other . . . armour-plated, poisonous, claw-tipped and fang-mouthed. That describes everything that walks, flaps or just sits and grows. Ever see a plant with teeth – that bite?' The result is that those colonists who survive grow tougher – but so does the ecology. The explanation is that all animal and plant life on the planet is telepathic and fast to mutate, and has reacted to the 'shoot first' attitude of the original colonists. The solution is to think kindness at a Pyrran animal or plant; then it will not attack.

Man as alien

How much of a body must a man possess to remain human? In Frederik Pohl's recent award-winner *Man Plus*, a US astronaut bound for Mars is adapted to breathe the atmosphere and withstand the low temperatures, by the replacement (or augmentation) of his skin, nervous system, optical system, heart, lungs, etc. He resembles a monster, but his emotions remain human. In *Limbo 90* by Bernard Wolfe, artificial limbs have reached such a stage of perfection that they are preferred to the real thing, and it becomes fashionable to have one's arms and legs amputated and replaced by mechanical creations. The ultimate stage of this cybernetic process comes when only the brain remains, and is connected up directly to a factory or, perhaps, a spaceship (as in Anne McCaffrey's *The Ship Who Sang*) which it controls by electrical impulses. Or perhaps just a few cells are necessary – the essence of the person – for some semblance of consciousness to remain forever, as in John Barfoot's beautiful story 'House' (in *Orbit 17* edited by Damon Knight). And what if the question is asked in reverse: how much of a robot must be replaced by organic matter before it can

This beautiful and erotic illustration by Chris Achilleos is for Thomas Burnett Swan's *Will-o-the-Wisp*. A sensitive and evocative writer of fantasy, Swan has never received the full acclaim from the sf establishment that he deserves

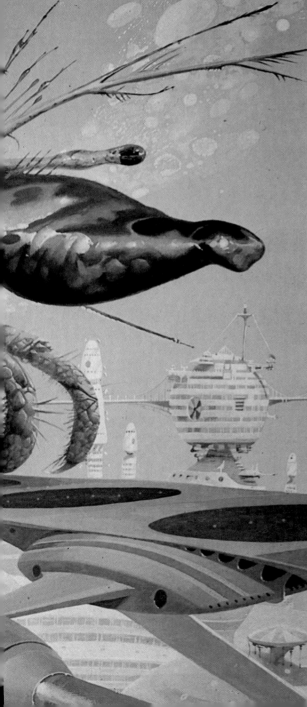

become a man? Perhaps it must die first. This is the situation in Isaac Asimov's award-winning novelette, 'The Bicentennial Man' (in *Stellar 2* edited by Judy-Lynn del Rey).

Modifying the human body

The biological adaptation of man seems to have endless possibilities. Kobo Abé and Hal Clement have suggested different approaches to aquatic life – gills and a heavily oxygenated liquid respectively, in *Inter Ice Age 4* and *Ocean On Top*. Body building for martial arts purposes can be carried to the most ridiculous lengths by embedding metallic rods in the bones, flexible plastic panels under the skin above vital organs and woven nylon patches over pressure points, as in *Sos the Rope* by Piers Anthony, while a number of fearsome appendages (sabre-teeth, claws, and barbed tail, for example) may be grafted onto the human body for little more than cosmetic reasons (Samuel Delany's *Babel-17*). And even immortality can be as close as a single shot from a hypodermic gun, according to Bob Shaw's *One Million Tomorrows*.

Creating 'life'

Ever since Mary Shelley's *Frankenstein 1818*, the idea of bringing dead bodies back to life has exercised the ingenuities of horror, fantasy and science fiction writers. Robert Silverberg's excellent novella 'Born With the Dead' describes the institutionalization of the idea, with many dead people being 'rekindled' to live again, but in a quieter, cooler, perhaps more civilized manner. It won an award and has been reprinted in *Nebula Award Stories 10* edited by James Gunn.

Cloning – the growing of new individuals from a single cell – has become a popular theme of recent years. That the 'offspring' will closely resemble their 'parent' is scientifically accepted, but telepathic links between cloned 'siblings' are often ascribed in fiction, bringing the clones closer but alienating them from normally-produced humans. Kate Wilhelm's recent award-winner, *Where Late the Sweet Birds Sang*, is a good example of this.

It is a short step from human clones to androids – artificially produced organic creatures which may be identical with humans. There seems always to be confusion between androids and robots (which are essentially mechanical constructions, without organic parts), probably because the first 'robots', in Karel Capek's *R.U.R. 1922*, were in fact androids. Robert Silverberg's *Tower of Glass*, with its details of android sex and android religion, is the best modern treatment of the subject.

Androids – which can often be made to reproduce themselves sexually – have brought us into the field of genetic engineering, the creation of 'different' human forms which will reproduce themselves. James Blish was one of the main contributors to this area of sf, with his scientifically-based novels *Titan's Daughter*, about the production of giant humans by means of doubling the number of chromosomes, and *The Seedling Stars*, about pantropy – the genetic alteration of many of man's body-systems to allow

Earth biology is used with effective and frightening results in this illustration of an alien commuting across the city. Slug and snail, a hint of insect and a little armadillo. A real nightmare

Man modified – Jack Gaughan's painting of Sos the Rope cannot show that Sos has been turned into a lethal bio-mechanical weapon by embedding metallic rods in his bones, and woven-nylon patches over his pressure points. The winged woman from *Thrilling Wonder* would never get off the ground, but winged men and aliens still feature in sf, on worlds where physical conditions would allow it

Cordwainer Smith wrote many stories about the 'Underpeople', intelligent humanoid creatures derived from cats, dogs, monkeys, bears etc., but treated as slaves by true humans; outstanding characters include C'Mell (Cat Mell) here illustrated by Virgil Finlay

Modified men and women, and of course to be good fear-fodder they must be giants – Guy McCord's giant Scot (drawn by Freas) lives on a world where a clan system has been established. Howard Brown painted the sea-creature

him to live and breed on alien planets. The end result, as might be expected, does not look human.

Manipulating evolution

Attempts to move in the opposite direction, by creating humans or near-humans from animals, originated with *The Island of Dr Moreau 1896* by H. G. Wells, though Wells contemplates only surgical techniques to alter the appearance and increase intelligence; he does not mention the possibilities of his beast folk reproducing themselves. Cordwainer Smith wrote much about the 'underpeople' – reasonably intelligent (sometimes very intelligent) humanoid creatures derived from cats, dogs, monkeys, cattle, bears, etc, but treated as slaves by true humans. Outstanding characters among the underpeople include C'mell, the beautiful red-haired cat-girl, in 'The Ballad of Lost C'mell' and *Norstrilia*, and the dog-girl D'joan, who teaches humans how to be a little more human, in 'The Dead Lady of Clown Town', a retelling of the Joan of Arc legend. (Both stories are in *The Best of Cordwainer Smith*.) The fusion of gene cells to create a hybrid man-lion figures in John Crowley's recent novel *Beasts*. The hybrids are sentient and bipedal, with fur and manes.

Freaks and mutations

Mutation as the result of nuclear fall-out has been a common sf theme ever since Hiroshima. A typical example, which details many human freaks, is Poul Anderson's *Twilight World*. Evolution is a slow form of mutation, of course, with changes spread over millions of years. The classic novel of future human evolution is *Last and First Men 1930* by Olaf Stapledon, describing 18 types of men over a period of 2000 million years. Most of these types would appear very alien to us (amphibians, flying men, quadrupeds), yet they form a direct evolutionary chain. In *Childhood's End*, Arthur Clarke writes of a sudden evolutionary change, from one generation to the next, as humans become superhumans who are fit to travel out into the galaxy, while in his award-winning *Hothouse*, Brian Aldiss shows in marvellous detail a far future Earth which teems with alien life including a much-mutated human form with a fascinating and complex life-cycle.

The effects of particularly high or low gravity upon the development of the human body are partly non-inherited physical changes and partly (through the survival of the fittest) genetic. At any rate, they can occur over just a few generations: Larry Niven's colonists on the high-gravity planet Jinx soon become very muscular and as broad as they are tall. They also become the butt of jokes. And Fritz Leiber's *A Spectre is Haunting Texas* portrays a human, raised on the Moon in one-sixth gravity, visiting Earth, his atrophied musculature aided by a titanium exo-skeleton.

Culture shock is another form of modification, as in the case of Valentine Michael Smith (in Robert

Heinlein's *Stranger in a Strange Land*) who is brought up by Martians for 24 years before meeting other humans. Indeed, the socialization process during upbringing is a crucial determinant of one's future behaviour. In Isaac Asimov's *The Caves of Steel* the inhabitants of Earth live in teeming underground cities: they all grow up agoraphobic. And in its sequel, *The Naked Sun*, is an opposite case where the few inhabitants of the planet Solaria, being conditioned from childhood to separate living, can scarcely bear to meet face to face.

Extraordinary mental powers

The most important way in which a man's mind can become alien to us is through the development of some form of extra-sensory perception (telepathy, precognition, telekinesis, etc). Though ESP figures in many sf stories, the creation of a believable ESP society has only been achieved rarely, and never better than in Alfred Bester's *The Demolished Man*. Only a tiny minority are telepaths – known as 'peepers'. Despite the constraints of distance (telepathy here is most effective with physical contact), the presence of mind-blocks and the strict rules of the Esper Guild, peepers are much sought after as security guards and in many specialised professions. Of course, premeditated crime has become almost extinct, but one man believes he can get away with murder. A more common theme is the suppression of ESP by society – often by the church in particular – as in *The Chrysalids* by John Wyndham. The multitude of possible ESP talents is covered most amusingly in Henry Kuttner's series of stories about the Hogben family, while the gestalt – a talented entity more powerful than the sum of the minds of which it is composed – is presented in Theodore Sturgeon's award-winning *More Than Human*.

The occasional appearance of mental supermen, born to normal parents, is the subject of Olaf Stapledon's *Odd John*, although there are also numerous stories of selective breeding for the development of ESP or super-intelligence. A marvellous story of an opposing trend – breeding to achieve the average, which is thereby reduced – is William Tenn's 'Null-P' (in *The Wooden Star*). Called 'abnegism' after George Abnego, the first completely 'average man', it results in man's gradual regression to idiocy. A colony of Newfoundland dogs eventually master the world.

There are many stories of man's mind becoming alien without the help of ESP. Progressive loss of memory is sufficient, as in 'Sketches Among the Ruins of My Mind' by Philip José Farmer (in *Nova 3* edited by Harry Harrison). The acquisition of other personalities, which are taped into one's mind, will create a more powerful individual but require the recipient to possess a strong personality if he is not to be taken over completely. This is the basis of Robert Silverberg's *To Live Again*.

Altering reality

Many drugs will alter the mind, affecting perception. Despite the recent rash of LSD-trip stories, the best novel of perception under drugs is *Ice* by Anna Kavan, herself a heroin addict. Christopher Priest's novel, *Inverted World*, also deals with altered perception, though the cause here is not a drug but a particular type of power generator, which makes the rest of the world seem alien to a relatively small group of people.

Akin to altered perception is the whole concept of the stability of reality. Here, the major contributor is Philip K. Dick, particularly in *The Three Stigmata of Palmer Eldritch*, *Ubik* and 'The Electric Ant' (from *The Best of Philip K. Dick*). In the last of these a 'man' discovers a slowly-unwinding roll of punched tape inside himself. By altering the tape he changes, and then destroys, reality. Also questioning existence and reality and seeking the boundaries of the mind are the 'inner space' stories of J. G. Ballard and novels such as Barry N. Malzberg's *Beyond Apollo*.

Man's behaviour is never far from being alien. The vast majority of us conform to the current norm because we are caught in the web of laws, families, government and the economic system. If some or all of these are removed, behaviour can very soon change, as in William Golding's *Lord of the Flies* and J. G. Ballard's *High Rise*.

In any case, the future is always closer than we think, bringing changes which may seem small at the time but when seen from, say, 10 or 20 years in the past, accumulate to massive proportions. In *The Continuous Katherine Mortenhoe* by D. G. Compton, which is set just a few years in the future, death from anything except old age is so rare that when a relatively young woman is known to be dying of an incurable disease she becomes an object of intense interest for the whole country – and has a TV camera

following her everywhere. Then there is Anthony Burgess's *A Clockwork Orange*, where the teenage sub-culture of the near future has its own argot with a vocabulary of hundreds of words, many of Russian origin. Thomas Disch's fine book *334* (set in the early 21st century) shows, among other things, an example of complete role reversal between marriage partners, with the husband staying at home and even breast-feeding their (bottle-grown) baby. Another example is *One* by David Karp, in which the behavioural norm has changed so much over a few years that a person can be brainwashed for thinking of his individual benefit ahead of the good of the state – yet this society is not, generally speaking, a repressive one.

Moving further ahead, we find future shock striking harder with every few decades that pass. This is well demonstrated in Joe Haldeman's award-winning *The Forever War*, where the time-dilation effect upon a soldier sent out to fight aliens in another star system means that the civilization of which he was a part has changed, by the time he returns, into something very alien. The only way out seems to be to sign on for another campaign – another few decades away from Earth. But another story provides another way. In 'The Graveyard Heart' by Roger Zelazny (in *Four for Tomorrow*), the Set skip across the years from party to party, sleeping frozen in between, carrying their past culture with them,

Beastman capturing helpless woman, hero about to spring into action – there is something about the human psyche that will not let an old cliché fade away. This dramatic picture is by Boris Vallejo.

This picture (opposite) by John Schoenherr illustrates Randall Garrett's intriguing novel *Too Many Magicians*, set in a parallel world where magic has never been rejected in favour of science. Lord D'Arcy is an aristocratic Sherlock Holmes figure, supported in his investigations of murder by a doctor Watson who is a Magician, a doctor of Thaumaturgy, well practiced in such arts as levitation and re-constituting clothing from the merest fragment

Urbanisation carried to an extreme is a popular contemporary theme-giant skyscrapers contain whole cities, often a different city on every level as in the classic novel *World Inside*, by Robert Silverberg. This illustration (*right*) is by Colin Hay

As a science fiction location, parallel worlds have not been very thoroughly exploited; most parallel worlds are seen as separating from our own at critical periods of history, such as the assassination of Elizabeth the First, or the defeat of the Normans by King Harold. This illustration seems to show a world where Tudor styles never went out of vogue

without doubt showing that wealth conquers all.

The further ahead one goes, the more chance social structure has had to change, and the more alien behaviour becomes. In 'Granny Won't Knit' by Theodore Sturgeon (in *Five Galaxy Short novels* edited by Horace L. Gold) there is a static society, unwavering patriarchal control of every household and clothing which totally covers the body, obscuring its shape – a naked hand, even, is an obscenity. W. H. Hudson's *A Crystal Age 1887* describes a far future with behavioural patterns which are most perplexing to its Victorian visitor, including punishments for being ill. And Frederik Pohl's 'Day Million' (in *Day Million*) gives a tantalizing glimpse of a very alien far future where human behaviour is almost inexplicable.

The alien earth

Many and varied are the future Earths in which sf has been set. Though a few are some form of utopia in which wondrous machines perform all labour while human beings (uniformly beautiful, healthy, intelligent and rich) amuse themselves with hobbies and sports, these are neither believable, nor do they leave much scope for a worthwhile plot. An example is Hugo Gernsback's *Ralph 124C 41 + 1911*. Much more common are dystopian futures. Apart from dire predictions of the end of everything there are many novels of futures even worse than our present. The trouble may stem from political dictatorship, as in *1984*, George Orwell's Stalinist nightmare, or from population pressure, as in Harry Harrison's *Make Room! Make Room!* Even where the situation is not uniformly bad for all, there is always somebody for whom the future is unpleasant. The poor, for example, are always present, but if the world's major problem is overproduction, which can only be combatted by non-stop consumption, then the 'poor' would be condemned to a life of grinding consumerism, with cripplingly huge rations of food, clothes and goods to use up; it would be the privilege of the rich to live simply. Crazy? Apparently so, but this is the situation in 'The Midas Plague' (in *The Case Against Tomorrow*), one of Frederik Pohl's delightful stories of economic inversion which he manages, in the end, to explain logically.

That a man of today would find it hard to survive were he suddenly thrust into the world of 100 years' time is a common theme, providing much scope for comparisons and for pointing out the alienness of the future. Edward Bellamy's *Looking Backward 1888* and H. G. Wells' *When the Sleeper Wakes 1899* are the archetypes here, but both are weighed down by philosophy. Better is Wells' 'A Story of the Days to Come' (in *Tales of Space and Time 1899*) in which he compares the typical businessman of the 19th and 22nd centuries, saying, 'it is doubtful which would have been the more shocked and pained to find himself in the clothing of the other'. His 22nd century world is one of pneumatically-shaped clothing, hypnotists as important as doctors, airships for long-distance travel and London inhabited by 30 million people while the countryside is almost deserted. A good modern treatment of the 'Sleeper Wakes' theme is Robert Sheckley's *Immortality Inc.*,

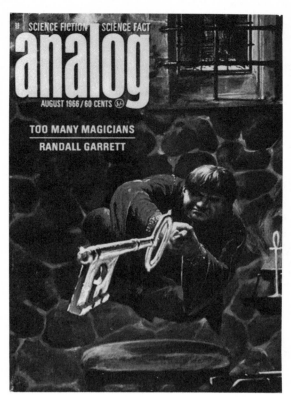

in which a man of 1958 wakes up in 2110. His biggest problem is finding a job, because none of his knowledge or training is relevant any longer.

There is no space here to mention more than a few of the bizarre future Earths which have appeared in sf. John Wyndham, in 'Consider Her Ways' (from *Consider Her Ways and Others*) sets out a future in which all men have died and women have organized themselves into a social structure resembling an ant's nest, with large Mothers who keep the race going through artificial insemination and multiple births, plus worker and technician classes. Edgar Pangborn, in most of his novels and stories (such as *Davy*), writes of a rural after-the-bomb future, with little technology. Other writers have predicted a future Earth as one huge artifact, building upon building, with no trace of countryside. Robert Heinlein's *The Day After Tomorrow* depicts an America under Asian rule. *Wolfbane* by Frederik Pohl and C. M. Kornbluth is set on an energy-starved Earth where the only 'sunlight' comes from the moon, reflected burning dimly. Diaspar, in Arthur Clarke's *The City and the Stars*, is the last great city on an old, dry, almost empty Earth.

Let us focus upon one aspect of this multiplicity of alien Earths: the weird and wonderful habitats of man. The most perfectly detailed example occurs in Robert Silverberg's *The World Inside*, where the tendency towards high-rise living has been extrapolated to the year 2381 when the whole of Earth's vast and burgeoning population lives in 1,000-storey skyscrapers called urban monads. Each block holds half a million people, and not just their apartments but all aspects of commercial and social life, too, for these are self-contained cities which their inhabitants almost never leave. Terry Carr, in 'They Live on Levels' (in *The Light at the End of the Universe*) portrays a crowded Earth where many societies occupy the same space by existing on different 'levels', which are separated only mentally. If, as William Tenn suggests, giant aliens take over the Earth, mankind may be reduced to living in burrows in the walls of alien houses, just like mice; this is the background to *Of Men and Monsters*. Also, men can live on anti-gravity rafts three miles up in the sky, as in *Shadow of Heaven* by Bob Shaw, or underground – because they have been tricked into hiding from a war which does not exist – as Philip Dick describes in *The Penultimate Truth*.

Parallel and alternative worlds

A method of creating an alien Earth without venturing into the future is for the author to accept the principle that every time a major decision is taken a branching-point has been reached and Earth effectively splits in two – a world where the decision was 'yes' and a world where it was 'no'. This means that over the centuries an almost infinite number of parallel Earth will have come into existence. Some remain similar whilst others diverge sharply.

In Randall Garrett's *Too Many Magicians* the divergence from our world came in the 12th century, producing a 20th century in which magic is practised as a science, though science itself had progressed more slowly, and Europe has retained all its monarchies, with Britain as an imperial power still. The critical occurrence in *Pavane* by Keith Roberts is the death of Elizabeth I in 1588, followed by Spain's conquest of England and the reestablishment of the Catholic Church, slowing down the advance of science. In a very descriptive novel, presented as six stories, this slowing-down is shown not to be a bad thing, allowing man more time to develop a sense of responsibility before the weapons of total war are discovered. Best known of all parallel worlds novels, and the only one to win a Hugo, is Philip Dick's *The Man in the High Castle*. Here, Germany and Japan won WWII and split the USA between them, the crucial event being the assassination of Franklin D. Roosevelt before the war.

The Ends of the Earth

What about the very end of the Earth itself? H. G. Wells, in *The Time Machine*, foresees the slowing down of Earth's rotation, the sun's growth into red giant-hood, and the disappearance of almost all life on the planet, save for green slime and a black, tentacled creature the size of a football, so that it is silent, cold, alien. Poul Anderson in his classic story 'Flight to Forever' has two time travellers, unable to reverse their machine; they travel endlessly forward through civilization after civilization, none of which can supply the raw power to help them back to their own time. Eventually, they come to the end of the universe, only to find that it is reborn again identically, and the travellers finally approach the point of their original departure. Many authors have written stories of a sudden finish, with the sun going nova. Or perhaps it could end – with a whimper or a bang – in any of the ways Robert Silverberg suggests in his savagely satirical story 'When We Went to See the End of the World'.

art and artists

David Hardy

The macabre, ominous, brilliant, futuristic and colourful
illustrations of the science fiction artists have dominated a
special area in art from the inception of sf. The artists have
always been a source of immense imagination and creativity —
from the gaudy early pulp covers with their impeccable women
to the incredible hardware and surrealistic figures.

Some people create by writing; others paint. Comparatively few do both. As soon as a new form of literature appears (or appeared: *can* there be any new forms? Surely nothing to possess the impact which science fiction has had over the last 50 years?), artists are hired to illustrate stories or to provide eye-catching covers to help sell the books. The artists must attempt to visualize, not always successfully it is true, the scenes or characters described in the books. There are those who would argue that by imposing his own ideas the artist deprives the reader of the chance to form his own personal impressions; the same applies, of course, to film and TV versions of stories and novels. Publishers, however, evidently believe in the efficacy of the 'artist's impression'; whatever degree of accuracy they achieve, they certainly sell the stock.

In recent years sf has appeared as an artform in its own right, without necessarily illustrating any author's ideas. It can be very tempting to apply the term sf art or fantasy art in retrospect to some of the strange images of 15th century artists such as Hieronymus Bosch or even to Leonardo da Vinci's sketches; to the macabre and ominous etchings of Giovanni Batista Piranesi in the 18th century; or to John Martin's smoking scenes of large-scale destruction, Odilon Redon's weird lithographs or Paul Gustave Doré's bizarre and grotesque illustrations in the 19th century. Nearer to our modern definition, perhaps, are the sometimes delightful but often horrific and prophetic fantasies of two Frenchmen: Isidore Grandville, originally Gérard 1803–1847, and Albert Robida 1848–1926. The latter's scenes of industry, pollution, ironclad ships, submarines and airships are particularly interesting to the student of the history of sf art. In more contemporary times, sf images may be found in the paintings of the Surrealists – epitomized by Salvador Dali – and in the work of René Magritte, M. C. Escher and others.

Early magazine art

However, the choice of these is largely a matter of personal taste, and it is in the field of illustration that most 'true' sf artists have made their appearance. In the 1880s and 1890s – years before the term science fiction appeared on the lurid covers of magazines in America – artists such as Warwick Goble, Paul Hardy, Stanley L. Wood and Dudley Hardy were illustrating futuristic stories (usually concerned with interplanetary flight) in *Cassell's Magazine* and *Pearson's Magazine*.

Many of these stories pre-date the better-known ones of H. G. Wells and Jules Verne, and contain such ideas as anti-gravity; usually ascribed to these 'fathers of science fiction'. 'Cavorite' was anticipated by George Parsons Lathrop in 1897, four years before Wells' *The First Men in the Moon*, in his story 'In the Deep of Time', illustrated by Dudley Hardy for the *English Illustrated Magazine*. Goble produced the memorable illustrations for Wells' *The War of the Worlds*, serialized in *Pearson's Magazine*.

It should not be thought that astronomical and astronautical themes were all that concerned science fiction in its early days, any more than they do today.

Certainly spacecraft and planets, in a bewildering variety of forms and colours, dominated the covers of the pulps, but there were also futuristic cities, fantastic machines (usually adorned with electrical discharges), strange alien creatures, 'bug eyed monsters' and huge metallic robots. The latter two seemed to have but one aim in life – to chase or carry off scantily-clad females; and it is perhaps this image more than any other which characterizes these magazine covers in the minds of most people who remember the period.

Frequently, to cut costs, these covers were printed in only three colours – red, blue and yellow, without the black plate normally used in four-colour printing. Sometimes, though by no means always, the result was remarkably good. The paintings themselves, it must be admitted when one strips away the rosy glow of memory, were often garish, totally inaccurate technically and artistically poor. It should be borne in mind that no-one claimed then (nor should they claim now) that this was Art with a capital 'A'; these usually poorly-paid illustrators were commercial artists, working to ridiculously close deadlines for editors whose main aim was to attract customers. Because of this low aesthetic level, the recent vogue for large-format books containing reproductions of sf magazine covers has been criticized. However, pulps from the 1930s can change hands for ten times their cover price today, and such

books at least offer a chance for those who are too young or for other reasons missed the era to make up their own minds on what they missed. Without the pulps there would perhaps *be* no field today; also, a look at the artwork of yesteryear makes an interesting standard of comparison with its often excellent counterpart of today.

The names of many of the cover and interior illustrators have deservedly faded into obscurity – if indeed they were ever credited; but a few have become almost legendary. Of these, the most famous is undoubtedly Frank R. Paul. He was highly prolific and certainly the major contributor to the first science fiction magazines, beginning with *Amazing Stories*, launched by Hugo Gernsback (as 'scientifiction') in 1926. Born in Austria, Paul trained originally as an architect: a fact which probably accounts for the obvious glee with which he demolishes the Woolworth and Municipal Buildings on the January 1929 cover of *Amazing Stories*, one of his more convincing efforts. However, he was working as a cartoonist for a New York newspaper when Gernsback engaged him in 1914, originally on his *Electrical Experimenter*, which published sf.

Paul certainly had a fertile imagination, elaborating on the often somewhat nebulous imaginings of

The Cellar of Invention (above) – an early vision of the fantastic by Piranesi

The Garden of Earthly delights (left) by Hieronymus Bosch

In 'The Moon Era' (below) Jack Williamson describes the ancient moon's sky as 'a deep, pure living blue'. Frank Paul preferred red. The attacking machines owe something to Wells' Martians

125

Wesso illustrated 'Something from Jupiter' (above) by Dow Elstar; the distant disc is over a mile in diameter, though its does not look it. As usual the two moons of Mars (centre) are much too large, but one can forgive a lot for this atmospheric city at dusk by Morey. Fuqua's figure work (below) is seen in his July 1939 *Amazing* cover. As often happened, the artist gave the spiders more humanoid characteristics than the author intended

Brown's astronomical cover for *Astounding* was quite successful. The details of Jupiter are good, but the shadow is impossible! Campbell later claimed that it was left in deliberately.

Kelly Freas, from a 1950's *Astounding* sf; this picture was recently used as a rock album cover.

the writers, who were strong on action but often weak on characterization or accurate, detailed description of background and mechanisms. Paul added character to buildings and depicted impressive-looking machines and gadgetry; however his figures were usually wooden and stiff-looking, whether human or alien. The latter were sometimes intentionally humorous, but often unconsciously comical when meant to be horrific. His figure-work did improve somewhat later in his career, however.

As one might expect in a completely new field in which artists had less scientific knowledge than the writers, other illustrators were quick to copy Paul's style. His covers often included a sky background painted in a completely flat, unlikely red, yellow or blue. While this could add an unreal quality to his scenes, it also sometimes made them unconvincing; it did, however, lend a distinctive character to Paul covers, first on *Amazing* and later, when Gernsback lost this in 1929, on his rival *Science Wonder Stories* (later to become simply *Wonder Stories*). Two artists in particular vied with Paul on the early covers: Howard V. Brown and Hans Wessolowski, who signed his artwork as 'Wesso'.

Wessolowski produced all the covers for *Astounding Stories of Super-Science* between 1930 and 1933, while it was published by William L. Clayton. Brown replaced him when the magazine was taken over, as *Astounding Stories*, by Street & Smith. Both began somewhat hesitantly but rapidly gained confidence, and their work gradually assumed greater authority and credibility. Brown later worked on *Startling Stories*, which featured some of his best covers. Both artists handled figures better and were capable of producing work with a more tasteful colour sense and subtler composition than Paul (not that this would necessarily be considered a good thing, since the main function of these covers was to catch the eye of the potential reader).

The March 1938 'Wesso' cover was the first to carry the now-famous words *Astounding Science Fiction*, John W. Campbell having taken over the editorship in September 1937. Previous to this Wessolowski had worked only on black-and-white interior illustrations for *Astounding*. This gave him a feeling for tone which proved to be of great benefit when he was allowed to turn to colour. However, Paul, Brown and Wessolowski did not have it all their own way. When T. O'Conor Sloane took the reins of *Amazing Stories* in 1929, his first cover artist was Leo Morey. With a few exceptions, Morey did not attempt to copy Paul's style, but introduced an accent on figures and the human element. This dichotomy between hardware and figure work on sf covers continues to the present day, and it is comparatively rare to see both combined really successfully in the same cover.

Magazine artists of the 1930s and 1940s

Another *Amazing Stories* artist was Robert Fuqua. His covers, from around 1938, showed a dramatic sense of lighting and often excellent human characterization. His gadgetry, like that of other artists of his time, was usually inspired by the technology which was then burgeoning all around: giant valves and transformers enlarged from radio sets, electrical generators and so forth. H. W. McCauley's work on magazines such as *Astounding Stories* and *Fantastic Adventures* was often in a similar mould, while as an interior illustrator Elliott Dold had a powerful style in which men were often dwarfed by the vast machines they apparently served.

Other artists of the late 1930s and 1940s worthy of mention are Norman Saunders for *Marvel Science Stories*; William Timmins, who worked on the *Astounding* covers during the 1940s, but often with a freer style than had been customary hitherto; Jack Binder, who did covers for *Astonishing Stories* as well as interiors for *Astounding Science Fiction*, often illustrating stories by his brothers Earl and Otto, who wrote together as Eando Binder; Charles Schneeman, who also drew interior illustrations and occasional covers for *Astounding*; Edd Cartier, whose beautiful figure-work adorned John W. Campbell's *Unknown* (strictly fantasy fiction); Stephen Lawrence, another figure specialist who did covers as well as interiors; and Hubert Rogers who, working in restrained colours, often achieved a fine sense of space and distance in his *Astounding* covers. He also introduced a semi-abstract, montage-like style which later became very popular on many American magazines, especially in the 1950s.

Another excellent interior and occasional cover artist, almost Rembrandtian in his use of light and shade, was A. Leydenfrost, who worked mainly on *Planet Stories*. In the late 1940s Paul Orban's pen, equally at home with alien planets and half-dressed females, introduced remarkably delicately-shaded illustrations and some superb draughtsmanship to sf readers, and continued in the 1950s in new magazines such as *Space Science Fiction*. However, the artists who achieved most fame in the field of superb interior illustrations were Hannes Bok and Virgil O. Finlay, the American artist.

While he did produce some colour covers, Bok's *forte* was black-and-white illustration. He excelled at figures – his women, as had become traditional, being usually semi-nude – and at alien creatures. Like Leydenfrost, his illumination was usually dramatic, giving his drawings great impact. Finlay worked very much in the same manner, but had an individual style, easily recognized by its stippled dots combined with delicate cross-hatching, time-consuming though these techniques are. Finlay died in 1971, but retains a large following among sf fans; books and folios of his work have been produced.

As happens today, covers were often uncredited (an unpardonable omission by publishers, considering the part covers play in selling their books), and it can be an interesting exercise for the student of sf art to try to identify a cover artist from his style.

British magazine artists

So far, we have discussed only American artists. In Britain, there was no such outlet for would-be cover artists (apart from juvenile magazines such as *Scoops*) until 1937, when Walter Gillings' *Tales of Wonder* hit the bookstalls. Published by World's Work of Tadworth, this included stories by American authors, but gave British artists such as John Nicholson and W. J. Roberts a chance to try out their brushes. Roberts' cover for No. 4 was especially fine, with dramatic low lighting. In 1939 Newnes published *Fantasy* (subtitled *Thrilling Science Fiction*) and introduced the work of S. R. Drigin, formerly an aeronautical artist. He too had a feel for *chiaroscuro*, though his figures mainly had a hollow-eyed look (strangely reminiscent of Alastair Sim!) and his covers lacked detail.

It was four years before Ted Carnell's *New Worlds* appeared and offered a chance for British artists to develop their own style. Hamilton's *Science Fiction Fortnightly* (a collection of novels) featured mainly nameless artists, but made way for *Authentic Science Fiction* in the 1950s under the editorship of H. J. Campbell. It featured a mixed bag of cover art, brightened by the appearances of Josh Kirby, an inventive artist who excels at fantastic figures and aliens, and is still very active today. *Authentic* also burst sporadically into a rash of astronomical covers featuring two of its art editors, John Richards and E. L. Blandford and artist Davis (who apparently had no Christian name). These were all remarkably similar in style, and owed a lot to American astronomical artist Chesley Bonestell; they included a 'tour of the Solar System' and 'the flight of the first starship', and were actually quite successful.

The Scottish-based magazine *Nebula Science Fiction*, which appeared between 1952 and 1959, also gave cover space to artists including Eddie Jones, Alan Hunter, James Stark and Gerard Quinn. Stark's covers were often just that; severe portrayals of technology against which men were mere ants. Quinn also produced many covers for *New Worlds*, and favoured astronomical scenes and space hardware. His work showed an excellent sense of colour and composition, though again it must be admitted that Bonestellian influences can often be seen. He later went into more lucrative commercial art, but

This remarkable painting of a ruined city perched precariously upon a wind-eroded pinnacle of rock is by Eddie Jones, a prolific English artist whose work has appeared on virtually every British magazine, and on hundreds of book covers

Astounding June 51 (below) shows Rogers' familiar montage style, incorporating various elements from the story. Typical swashbuckling figure work by Cartier (centre) for the *Hand of Zei*. Quinn produced many covers for *New Worlds* and favoured astronomical scenes and space hardware

On the British magazine *Authentic* artist Davis has given the space-craft legs and landed it on Mars' moon Phobos. An attractive cover, though the horizon is too distant for the tiny satellite – and the lighting is incorrect

This Bonestell illustration from *Across the Space Frontier* accurately forecast that the first trip to the Moon would be without landing – though the design of the space-ship is very different, and it was assumed that this would be built in Earth-orbit. Here it is 50 miles above the crater Aristillus

reappeared briefly on the short-lived *Vision of Tomorrow* in 1969/70 with a changed style and even signature.

Another *New Worlds* artist, who also worked on Gillings' new magazine *Science Fantasy* (later edited by Carnell), was Londoner Brian Lewis. His semi-abstract work, which often has the look of pendant 'mobiles', frequently bears a close resemblance in style to that of American artist Richard Powers. Lewis produced covers in a variety of styles, though, with figures being a strong point. He too was swallowed up by the commercial art world, working on cartoons and films, but has recently made a comeback in sf. His *Star Wars* cover for the first issue of *Starburst* is a masterpiece of its kind.

Chesley Bonestell

Before examining some of the artists from the 1950s and 60s, it is expedient at this point to make a slight diversion in order to take a closer look at Chesley Bonestell now aged around 90. An American who worked for a time, from 1922, as a special artist for the *Illustrated London News*, he later worked as an architect and designed the ceiling of the San Francisco Opera House. He then moved into films, and after providing the space backgrounds for the classic *Destination Moon* was given the opportunity to destroy famous buildings even more effectively than had Frank R. Paul – in motion, by special effects in films such as *When Worlds Collide* and *War*

of the Worlds (set in America) made in the early 1950s. In the early 1940s he had been commissioned by *Life* magazine to paint a series of scenes on the satellites of the planet Saturn, showing the ringed world as it would be seen by a camera. Although 'dated' by the information from modern space probes, these remain the finest examples of their type. He also worked on a series of articles on Earth satellites and Moon exploration written by Wernher von Braun, Willy Ley and other experts for *Colliers* magazine in 1950, followed by others, which did an enormous amount to establish the climate for a manned space programme during the next decade or so. Both the *Life* and *Colliers* articles were expanded into book form in the 1950s, the most famous being *The Conquest of Space*.

Oddly enough, Bonestell has always denied being a science fiction artist, even though his covers have graced *Astounding*, *Analog* and dozens of issues of *The Magazine of Fantasy and Science Fiction* (better known as *F&SF*) from 1949 to the present day. This is because, despite their obvious appeal to sf readers, these covers were 'straight' astronomical scenes. (Few people would disagree that the Bonestellian Moon, with its soaring, jagged crags, was a much more exciting place visually than the drab rolling hills visited by Apollo astronauts!) But, as already indicated, it is Bonestell's influence on other cover artists that has had such far-reaching, and not generally-realized effects. Not only did he set a standard of photographic reality for space themes, but time and again his hardware has been 'borrowed', while at worst whole rock formations or compositions have been plagiarized outright.

The overall impact on space-orientated sf covers was much more subtle than this, however. Bonestell's portrayals of the Moon and planets, and of the hardware required to reach them, became archetypal, and until NASA spacecraft changed man's picture of the Solar System in the late 1960s and 1970s, even covers by artists with completely original sf ideas inevitably followed Bonestell's model of the universe.

The 1950s and 1960s: American and British artists

Among the cover artists on the 25 or 30 magazines which sprang up in the 50s on both sides of the Atlantic, a few names stood the test of time and went on to develop a recognizable style which even gained them a following of fans, independent of the contents or writers in the books they illustrated. Some moved into the field of paperbacks, which not only paid better – magazines then averaged $100 for a cover, a meagre $10 for black-and-white interior work – but usually had less stringent directives on content and less hectic deadlines. The cover illustrators – most of them with quite individual styles, and some capable of very varied work outside the space field – who produced the most convincing space images in the 1950s and 60s include: John Pederson; Paul Wenzel; Dember; Jack Coggins; Ken Fagg; McKenna; Ed Valigursky; Ron Cobb; Ed Emshwiller (as 'Emsh'); Mel Hunter and Alex Schomburg.

Bruce Pennington's striking painting (above) inspired by the arid landscape of the world Arrakis in Frank Herbert's *Children of Dune*

A beautiful Bonestell pre-Apollo Moon-landing from the October 1960 *Fantasy and Science Fiction*. Just look at those dramatic, soaring mountains!

A robot miner by Coggins, for *Galaxy* 26. This type of robot, designed for a specific purpose, is much more practicable than the humanoid type

A typically attractive cover by Fagg for *If*. In his interpretation of 'Jupiter Five' by Arthur Clarke the details on the planet could be better, but it is a fine rendering otherwise

Schomberg's remote-controlled 'Prospector' for 'Stay off the Moon' by Raymond F. Jones has all the NASA trappings

Emsh was renowned for his technological type pictures, but equally well known for his self-contained humorous covers for *Galaxy*, such as these alien tourists. Note the similarity in design of the spacecraft to Bonestell's *Across the Space Frontier* in this typical Schomburg astronomical cover on the January 1953 issue of *Startling Stories* (UK)

Bergey's artwork for *Space* is not connected with any story, but is an excellent, almost photographic cover combining space-realism with the sexual attraction of some early pulps

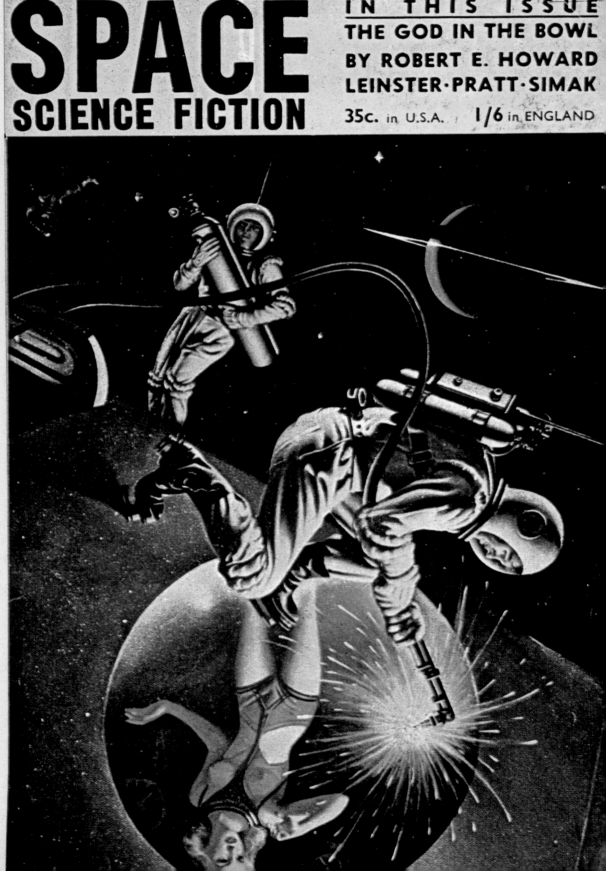

SPACE
Science Fiction

IN THIS ISSUE
THE GOD IN THE BOWL
BY ROBERT E. HOWARD
LEINSTER · PRATT · SIMAK
35c. in U.S.A.   1/6 in ENGLAND

Of these, Mel Hunter perhaps achieved the greatest reputation in the space field, illustrating a factual book, *Nine Planets* by Alan E. Nourse (also a sf writer) and even painting murals in the Transportation and Travel Pavilion at the World's Fair in 1963; even so, astronomical inaccuracies quite often crept into his paintings. Hunter is equally well known for his humorous and sometimes satirical 'robot' series of covers for *F&SF*, in which a gawky, stick-like metal figure eternally wanders a post-nuclear-holocaust Earth, discovering pitiful remnants of civilization. Equally notable as a humorous artist, usually on *Galaxy*, was Ed Emsh. Like Hunter, his covers were usually separate entities, unconnected with the magazine's contents. His human and comic alien characterizations were exceptional and his style realistic.

Jack Coggins also illustrated some factual books, and produced excellent and colourful covers with a free and lively, often almost water-colour (though never wishy-washy) style. Rather similar, and with a vivid imagination, was Ken Fagg; his cover illustration for Arthur C. Clarke's story 'Jupiter Five' on the second issue of *If (Worlds of Science Fiction)* in 1953 is a good example. In the same issue Ed Valigursky, who provided slick and stylish black-and-white halftone illustrations inside front and back covers, appeared to forecast the canyons (though not the craters) of Mars.

While Fagg, Valigursky and McKenna were encouraging public awareness of space travel on *If*, and Pederson, Dember, Coggins, Emsh and others on *Galaxy* and Bonestell and Hunter on *F&SF* were doing likewise, Alex Schomburg had it almost all his own way on the now digest-sized *Amazing* in the 1960s, having done earlier work from around 1950 on *Thrilling Wonder Stories*, *Fantastic Universe* and *Startling Stories*. Schomburg was equally at ease in colour or black-and-white, and at depicting nubile maidens or space hardware. The latter was sometimes Bonestell-inspired, but he produced some really excellent artwork – even if he did sometimes allow his use of the airbrush to create a curiously graduated-blue instead of black space. Schomburg's work reappeared in 1977/78, including his first cover for *Analog*.

Richard Powers' work appeared in the 1950s, when more magazines were appearing every year, usually in the new 'digest' size, but paperback or softcover editions of novels were also introducing a rather different type of cover with less accent on illustrating the contents. Powers' surrealistic forms and almost organic machine-like shapes, which bear little relation to earthly objects, were much copied and greatly influenced the appearance of paperback covers for many years.

As for hardback books, their publishers have always had more constraints placed upon them in the matter of dust-jackets, due to the higher cost of their books. Four-colour printing is quite rare, and two- or three-colour jackets in line rather than half-tone are common. Occasionally this produces little gems of simplification; more often the result is uninteresting. One of the better-known series of sf jackets is the plain bright yellow of Gollancz, with its red and black type-matter.

Several illustrators of the 1950s and 1960s were best known for their black-and-white interiors. These include Don Sibley, a fine figure artist, as was Henry Sharp. With a bolder style and drawings full of action and often humour, Rod Ruth's work first appeared in the late 40s. Herman Vestal's pen and ink evoked many grotesque alien worlds and their populations; so did Gene Fawcette's, but with a highly individual style which sometimes lifted his work out of the run-of-the-mill. Bok, Finlay, Orban and others mentioned earlier were still developing and producing interiors and occasional covers.

There were many other fine artists at work on the proliferating magazines of the 1950s. R. G. Jones, unashamedly commercial, offered beautiful figure-work in a romantic vein; Ebel (the only name by which he appears) painted in a very tight technique subjects which often combined realistic and fantastic elements; Malcolm H. Smith, too, combined a sense of realism with the fantastic. Earle Bergey was a master of the 'traditional' female figure, but could combine this with a really authentic-looking space-hardware background, as proved by his cover for *Space Science Fiction* No. 1. Somewhat less well-known is Albert A. Neutzell who, while professing no interest in sf himself, nonetheless created some fresh and startling imagery before his death in 1969, just before the first Moon landing.

A very surrealistic painting by Ebel for *Space*; as with the picture by Bergey, it combines space-realism with eroticism

Mel Hunter's robot series for the *Magazine of Fantasy and Science Fiction* are now famous, and have been appearing occasionally for more than twenty years. The robot is living on earth after a nuclear holocaust and is seen to be enjoying all the things we enjoyed – riding a sand-buggy, reading sf.

The artist as sf fan

Whether an artist is personally involved in science fiction, whether he even bothers to read it privately (or even professionally sometimes!) is an interesting factor. Quite a few modern illustrators of sf covers are not really 'into' the genre, and it may or may not show in their work. At the other end of the scale, there are those who actually belong to the sub-culture known as 'sf fandom'. They may draw covers or cartoons for the amateur publications known as 'fanzines' totally without charge, of course, whether or not they also paint professionally; design elaborate name-tags for sf convention-goers; or exhibit at those conventions the artwork which adorns paperbacks or magazines.

In America, such an artist is George Barr, whose work is truly deserving of the epithet 'fantastic art' alongside old masters such as Bosch, yet who often produces his miniature masterpieces with ball-point pens. His dragons and aliens are good-humoured and vivacious, and have won him a Hugo (named after Gernsback) – sf fandom's equivalent of an Oscar. So has the sensitive work of Alicia Austin, and the whimsical artistry of Tim Kirk – in fact he has won it twice, the only fan artist to do so. Kirk is probably best known outside the field for his series of paintings based on Tolkien's *Lord of the Rings*.

Among the professional artists whose work can regularly be seen at British sf conventions are Eddie Jones (who also attends US 'cons' along with his American wife, Marsha), Josh Kirby, Edward Blair-Wilkins, David Hardy, George Jones and (more recently) Brian Lewis. Most of these artists adopt the policy of selling their cover artwork to fans, once the publishers have finished with it, at a very reasonable price by auction – pieces fetching from a few pounds to over £100. Most of the best-known US artists mentioned later do the same; some specialize in selling originals, prints and slides.

A dramatic picture (right) of a man/alien symbiosis by British artist Josh Kirby

An exquisite and truly frightening depiction (opposite) by Tim White of 'Revolt in the Year 2000'

Giants of the 1960s: Kelly Freas and Jack Gaughan

In the 1960s two prolific artists began to win many laurels on the sf scene: Frank Kelly Freas and Jack Gaughan. Freas sold his first cover in 1950 to *Weird Tales*, and went on to work for *Astounding* and then *Analog*. The latter magazine consistently uses his covers and interiors, and his approach has undoubtedly helped to shape its visual style. Freas is a meticulous and versatile artist, a supporter of the US space programme (he designed the Skylab I mission badge) whose acrylic paints are as likely to be called upon to lay down an acreage of female flesh as of planetary surface. He is a perfectionist, employing models, photography, visits to observatories or even submarines to obtain the information he requires for authenticity. He also uses any technique that comes to hand to produce the effects or textures needed; pallette knife, pen, crayon, airbrush . . . the results win him a Hugo with almost monotonous regularity, to the chagrin of other deserving professional artists.

Gaughan also does covers and interiors for *Analog*, but is better known for his years with *Galaxy* and its sister-magazine *If*, of which he was at one time art director. Like Freas, he also does a lot of work for paperbacks or pocketbooks. Gaughan's style is freer, and one feels that he relies less on painstaking research than on 'intuition'; some of his thumbnail sketches can take only minutes. Even so, he is extremely versatile and his popularity with editors is understandable since he can produce convincing spacecraft, weird yet believable aliens, swashbuckling sword-and-sorcery characters or semi-abstract, non-representational illustrations.

The 1960s were largely a period of experimentation. As the magazines which had sprung up in the 1950s collapsed and disappeared into oblivion, those remaining tried even harder to maintain their readership (which continued to drop, thanks mainly to the paperbacks, which included short stories in anthology form). Various strange styles of cover were tried and discarded, and even photography was flirted with – as it had been before, briefly, by *Amazing* in 1938 – with disastrous results.

One of the best of the 'new breed' of artists was John Schoenherr, who produced distinctive covers and interiors for *Analog* and for paperbacks. Vaughn Bodé and Gray Morrow both introduced a 'pen-and-wash' technique (looking remarkably similar) to the covers of *Galaxy* and *If*, and have gone on to become successful in the general sf field.

In Britain, with *New Worlds* in decline by the end of the 1960s and featuring virtually pop-art covers by artists such as Malcolm Dean, its 'New Wave' contents now edited by Michael Moorcock, and paperbacks still searching for an individual image, a new magazine appeared in August 1969. *Vision of Tomorrow* was edited by Philip Harbottle. Its first cover is best forgotten, but it had interiors – light pen-sketches – and later two covers by Gerard Quinn, while Eddie Jones produced several covers

Joseph Petagno, an American artist quite new to the scene, achieves some breath-taking effects (opposite) with his semi-surreal approach to astronomical art

Astounding/Analog has consistently used covers by Kelly Freas since the early fifties, and his approach has unquestionably helped to shape the visual style of the magazine

John Schoenherr is another regular cover and interior artist for Analog; his illustrations for *Dune* and *Prophet of Dune* are quite remarkable

and later became its 'Art Consultant' and regular interior artist. It also featured two covers by David Hardy, his first on a purely sf publication. After (though presumably not because of) using some covers by Australian artist Stanley Pitt, the magazine finally faded away in September 1970.

The 1960s culminated with two events which had a great impact on sf art: the film *2001: A Space Odyssey* and the first landing on the Moon. It had been obvious as the decade progressed that space hardware was not developing as the early artists had blithely assumed. (Apart from too-jagged lunar landscapes, pre-NASA space artists inevitably got two things wrong: their Earths were usually cloudless, and they showed long, spectacular rocket flames in space, whereas in fact combustion gases expand in all directions in a vacuum.) Now, not only was a rocket going directly to the Moon, without the benefit of construction in orbit alongside a wheel-shaped space station, but instead of a gleaming, graceful finned shape the landing craft was angular, asymmetrical – in fact, downright ugly. Even the earlier orbital craft, whether Russian or American, were unstreamlined, covered with hatches and odd protuberances and bristling with antennae. *2001* reflected this trend, with the help of artist Robert McCall (who also works for NASA). By 1972 sf book-covers had a new look, especially in Britain. In America, John Berkey was soon painting realistic-looking craft which appear as second- or third-generation NASA vehicles might. Eddie Jones, in England, was much influenced by Berkey, as his work of that period shows. But it was a new artist, Chris Foss, who really changed the face of British paperbacks, starting with Panther books in 1970.

Chris Foss and current British sf art

Foss created space hardware which was not only complex, ungainly and sprinkled with tiny portholes and antennae which indicated its vast scale, but was usually painted in fine, virtually photographic detail. He painted futuristic buildings, robots and barren, arid planets – all the stock-in-trade of sf artists since Paul (but rarely figures), yet as different from 1930s art as Concorde is from a Tiger Moth. Those publishers who did not promptly employ Foss merely suggested that their artists adopt a 'similar style'. The covers need bear no relation to the books' contents as long as they showed a lumpy spaceship; the airbrush became the most overworked – and abused – tool in the studio.

Van Dongen's May 1957 *Astounding* cover illustrates 'Get Out of my Sky' by James Blish, which takes place on an alien world, whose twin planet is about to eclipse the white sun.

Chris Moore (opposite) has a very personal style in hardware.

A distinctively styled picture by British artist Brian Lewis.

Boris Vallejo is one of the leading American artists in the 'fantasy-posing-as-sf' class

David Hardy's 'metal Planet' (opposite)

Andrei Sokolov produces interesting and realistic work, as this *Analog* cover shows

than America's Michael Whelan and Boris Vallejo, and with less success. Chris Achilleos does it better, as does Peter Elson, who signs his work 'P.E.'. Ian Miller has a unique, spidery pen style, David Pelham a stark and deceptively simple airbrush technique. Probably the most successful sf artist working in Britain today is Peter Jones, who has graduated from Foss-type hardware to a very individual style, colourful and clean, with fine figure-work. With the few exceptions noted, the common factor in UK covers today is ultra-realism, and this is in danger of robbing them of all real personality and dynamism.

Fantasy and fact: sf art today

Not to be excluded from an essay on sf art, although he is basically a fantasy artist, is American 'cult figure' Frank Frazetta. Far from selling them at conventions, Frazetta has kept all of his originals, and claims to have turned down offers of over $50,000 for many of them. Another British paper-back artist most at home in the dream-world of fantasy is Patrick Woodroffe. His intricate and beautifully-painted covers can hardly be surpassed for their type, and really rate as art. Roger Dean, best known for his many record sleeves, similarly creates a sort of alternate reality – not strictly photographic, yet with its own inner conviction. Woodroffe's work is well shown in his book *Mythopoeikon*, Dean's in *Views*.

In America, today's leading artists in the fantasy-posing-as-SF class are Michael Whelan and Boris Vallejo ('Boris'), both of whom served their apprenticeship on Marvel-type comics and excel at figures. Steven Fabian and Vincent di Fate have recently come to prominence, although both were working in the late 1960s; so have the Hildebrandt twins, Greg and Tim, thanks to their Tolkien calendar and *Star Wars* poster. Darrell Sweet is a good all-round artist, and 1950s illustrator H. R. Van Dongen has re-appeared recently. Instead of the Foss-type pseudo-technological cover, US space-scene covers are usually astronomically accurate – something which never concerns the Foss School. Writing in *Amazing June 1976*, Gregory Benford includes 'England's David Hardy' with Don Davis and Rick Sternbach as 'most nearly aligned along Bonestell's particular vector' today (he could perhaps have added US artist Don Dixon); all appear regularly on *F&SF*. Hardy's work is collected in *The New Challenge of the Stars*.

Elsewhere in the world sf artists 'do their own thing'. On the continent and particularly in Germany the standard of home-grown art is generally low, and publishers are glad to buy second rights from several British artists (though even so the field is overcrowded). Germany's Helmut Wenske is in Woodroffe's class, if more macabre, and Dutch painter Karel Thole, who now lives in Italy, is possibly the leading exponent of surreal-type sf art today. Behind the Iron Curtain sf art seems still to be going through a somewhat abstract phase, but Andrei Sokolov produces interesting surrealistic and realistic work and has even appeared on *Analog*, while one artist should be the envy of every other in the field: Alexei Leonov, the Soviet cosmonaut.

In 1974 a new magazine appeared in Britain. *Science Fiction Monthly* was strongly art-orientated, large format and unstapled so that its pages could be unfolded to form posters. One of its failings was that it reproduced artwork often larger than it had been painted (originally for paperbacks), so that every brush-stroke and blemish became visible. Until its demise in April 1976, it published interviews with contemporary sf artists, the first issue featuring Bruce Pennington an NEL regular (NEL is New English Library, the publishers of *SFM*.) His cover for No. 1 was the spaceship *Discovery* from *2001* – rather ironically, because Pennington is one artist who never succumbed to the imitation-Foss technological craze, and as a result NEL covers could generally be quickly identified. His work is much more in the fantasy vein, in fact, as his book *Eschatus, 1977* shows; the imagery in this is incredible, but the execution disappointingly loose and unfinished-looking.

British SF art has become rather sterile as the 1970s come to a close. Foss's own covers have become mainly pale parodies of his earlier ones, while he has been out-Fossed by newcomers such as Angus McKie, Tony Roberts, Bob Layzell, Colin Hay and Jim Burns, most of whom have now begun to develop their own styles. Burns in particular has proved an able figure artist. For NEL Tim White has introduced rather Foss-like covers, but is evolving promisingly. Chris Moore has a personal style in hardware, while on the software/fantasy side Bob Fowke and J. Petagno use a less realistic approach

fiction to fact

Patrick Moore

Science fiction writers do not consciously function as oracles for science and technology. Inevitably, when an important part of their subject matter is speculation on future trends, they will be right sometimes. The future may well prove them correct — it will certainly be no surprise to many. Already predictions from the 40s and 50s have proven true.

Illustration by John
Schoenherr (*right*)

19th Century illustration
by Warwick Goble for
H.G. Wells' *The War of
the Worlds*

A spacewalk illustrated by
Mel Hunter, fifteen years
before the real thing, and
remarkable for its
accuracy

'A big greyish, rounded bulk, the size, perhaps of a bear, was rising slowly and painfully out of the cylinder. . . . Two large dark-coloured eyes were regarding me steadfastly . . . There was a mouth under the eyes, the lipless brim of which quivered and panted, and dropped saliva. The body heaved and pulsated convulsively. A lank tentacular appendage gripped the edge of the cylinder, another swayed in the air . . .'

Such was the description of a Martian given by H. G. Wells in his classic novel *The War of the Worlds*, which made its first appearance in 1898 and has remained in print ever since. There can be no science fiction enthusiast who has not read the book, and as a story it is superb, but so far as the Martians were concerned Wells was writing with his tongue very firmly fixed in his cheek – as I know for a certainty, because I once asked him! Even in 1898 it was becoming clear that Mars is not a welcoming kind of place, and Wells, who was after all a qualified scientist, was highly sceptical about creatures of the sort which we now call BEMs or bug eyed monsters. Nevertheless, scientific ideas about Mars in 1898 were still very wide of the mark; so, for that matter, were the ideas which were current only 15 years ago. The same applies to most of the other planets, and to a certain extent to the Moon as well and science fiction writers have had to adapt themselves accordingly.

Early Journeys

Obviously, early science fiction seems very fanciful now – even though much of it was not meant to be taken seriously. Probably the first true Moon-voyage story was the *True History*, written by Lucian of Samosata in the 2nd century AD, in which a ship sailing through the Straits of Gibraltar is caught in a waterspout and hurled up on to the lunar surface. Much later, in the 17th century, came the *Somnium* (or Dream) by Johannes Kepler, one of the greatest astronomers of all time, in whose story the hero is carried to the Moon by demon power. The main difference is that Kepler went on to describe the Moon as he genuinely believed it might be, so that his book was a medley of open fantasy and contemporary science.

Various other modes of travel were proposed at fairly regular intervals, but it may be true to say that the 'modern' era began with Jules Verne, whose *From the Earth to the Moon*, published in 1865, was based firmly upon what was taken to be exact science. Verne's travellers were dispatched Moonward in a hollow projectile fired from the mouth of a huge cannon. The intrepid astronauts were well aware that their journey would be a one-way trip only, though in the event the projectile was diverted by a passing minor satellite and swung back to the Earth. Obviously the space-gun idea will not work, partly because of the shock of departure at escape velocity and partly because of the atmospheric friction, and in addition Verne was wrong in his description of weightlessness; in his story, the crew experienced zero gravity only when their projectile reached the so-called neutral point in which the Earth's pull exactly balanced that of the Moon. But

when allowance is made for these fundamental errors, it is amazing how many of his forecasts came true. The gun was fired from a point not far from Cape Canaveral; the splash-down was not very distant from land-point of Apollo I and the giant telescope on Long's Peak was the fictional forerunner of 200-inch Hale reflector at Palomar. The space-gun theme was naturally copied, and it was even used for the film *The Shape of Things to Come* as recently as the 1930s – to the disgust of members of the British Interplanetary Society, who knew only too well that the rocket was the only practicable solution. However, full circle has now been achieved with Christopher Priest's *The Space Machine 1976* in which a traveller in space and time, marooned on Mars, stows away in one of the Martian guns being used to shoot an invasion force towards the Earth.

Anti-gravity

Although rockets had largely taken over in fiction as well as in fact, anti-gravity was still an important theme, and Wells used it in the form of 'Cavorite' in *The First Men in the Moon*. Another anti-gravity story was Kurd Laszwitz' *Auf Zwei Planeten* (On Two Planets). Laszwitz was Professor of Mathematics at Gotha, and he was one of the first to lay down the principle of the transfer orbit – even though in his novel the discovery was made not by Earthmen, but by the older and wiser Martians. What the Martians did, according to Laszwitz, was to build a complete shell of anti-gravity material. So long as the shell remained open it was subject to gravity in the normal way; but as soon as it was complete its weight vanished, so that it drifted off into an orbit of its own. The builders therefore completed the shell and waited until their own planet had been obliging enough to remove itself from under them. The shell then fell towards the Sun until it reached the orbit of the Earth, and made a straightforward rendezvous. The principle of the transfer orbit is clear enough.

Nobody has yet managed to make anti-gravity material, and it may well be that Wells' Cavorite and Laszwitz' shell are scientific impossibilities. Meanwhile Konstantin Eduardovich Tsiolkovskii had come upon the scene, and his book *Beyond the Planet Earth*, published at the turn of the century, makes fascinating reading. As a story and as a literary effort it can only be described as atrocious, but as a forecast it was decades ahead of its time. For instance, it describes liquid-propellant rockets, step-vehicles, artificial satellites, and true space-stations. Yet he was pessimistic in his time-scale; *Beyond the Planet Earth* is set in AD 2017!

Satellites and space-stations

In 1945, in an article on extra-terrestrial relays, Arthur Clarke predicted the communications satellite; but artificial satellites have loomed large in science fiction for more than 100 years. In *The Begum's Fortune*, Jules Verne described how the evil Professor Schultz fired a shell at the city of Frankville, only to find that the muzzle velocity had been great enough to put the shell into a closed orbit round the Earth (as with *From Earth to the Moon*, of course, air resistance is blithely neglected). Probably the first fictional manned satellite was Edward Everett Hale's 'The Brick Moon', contained in the October 1869 edition of *Atlantic Monthly*. As an aid to measuring longitude, some enterprising scientists decide to provide the Earth with an extra satellite; they build a brick moon two hundred feet across, and launch it by a weird and wonderful arrangement of flywheels. Unfortunately, a slight mishap results

in its being sent 9,000 miles out into space, carrying 37 people with it.

When the Space Age dawned – and this may well be dated from Goddard's experiments made in 1926 – space-stations became more credible. The most popular design was that of the wheel, which could be spun round to simulate gravity in the outer rim. Quoting from Tsiolkovskii's *Beyond the Planet Earth*:

There is nothing to stop us from producing gravity throughout the ship by rotating it, as we have already done once. This gravity can be maintained as long as we like, and costs practically nothing . . . By means of parabolic mirrors [to collect solar energy] we can produce a temperature of up to 5,000 degrees, while the absence of gravity makes it possible to construct mirrors of virtually unlimited size. The high temperature, the chemical and thermal energy of the Sun's rays, makes it possible to carry out all kinds of factory work, such as metal welding, recovering metals from ores, forging, casting, rolling and so forth.

Surely here we have a glimpse of America's Skylab station of 1973–4. Solar power was indeed used, and manufacturing experiments were carried out in a 16-inch diameter sphere exposed to the vacuum of space; welding and casting of metals was accomplished, and valuable information obtained. The main difference, of course, was that no attempt was

The smoothness of space station and ship are now out of vogue in this 1962 painting by Dember

When mobile Mars-rovers are put down on that planet they will not be much different from this prediction by P.E.

made to give Skylab 'artifical gravity' by means of rotation, because earlier experiments – beginning with Yuri Gagarin's epic space-flight in 1961 – had established that weightlessness is not harmful, at least for short periods. This is one reason why present-day designs have abandoned the wheel shape favoured up to a couple of decades ago, and for which elaborate blueprints were drawn up by men such as Wernher von Braun. On the other hand it is still well within the realm of possibility that some form of 'artificial gravity' will be needed for a permanently-manned space-station, and rotation seems to be the only answer, whether the wheel form is retained or not.

Many derogatory things have been said about the pulp magazines, which had their heyday in the 1930s, and most of the criticisms may be justified, but here and there one finds really good space-station designs. Also, most writers were becoming rather cautious about the Moon, simply because so much had been learned about it. It had become abundantly clear that the Moon is both airless and waterless; occasional stories described 'selenites'

Planetary landscape with hindsight

living in underground existence, but the main concentration was upon Lunar Bases of the future. The favourite pattern was the hemispherical dome, kept inflated by the atmospheric pressure inside it, and equipped with an efficient system of airlocks. In fact, this is still widely favoured – and it may turn out to be very near the truth, even though it would be premature to come to any definite conclusions.

The real Space Age began on 4 October 1957, with the launching of Russia's Sputnik I, and at once there developed a new theme in science fiction: the Space Race, with Soviet and American scientists locked in deadly rivalry. There were numerous stories in which rival settlements were set up, so that conflict ensued – generally with disastrous results. This was understandable in the early days of practical space research, with the Soviets apparently well in the lead, but far fewer stories of this type are written now, mainly because the so-called Space Race has proved to be largely a myth. More impressive were the accounts of lunar exploration, notably Arthur Clarke's *A Fall of Moondust* and *Earthlight*. Generally speaking, fictional predictions of what the Moon would be like were fairly accurate, and Neil Armstrong's initial description of the scene when he stepped out on to the Sea of Tranquillity in July 1969 had been foreshadowed many times in sf stories. Of course there were discrepancies; the lunar mountains were much less jagged than had been expected, and the black daytime sky was not star-studded, because of the glare from surrounding rocks. Otherwise there were no surprises. With the planets, things were very different.

Mars

Mars has always been the favourite world of the story-tellers, inasmuch as it is in some ways not too unlike the Earth, and until fairly recently there seemed no reason to doubt that it could support life. In 1902 a handsome prize was offered in France to the first person to establish contact with an extrater-restrial civilization – Mars being specifically ex-cluded as being too easy! It was widely supposed that the famous Martian canals were artifical waterways, and the astronomer Percival Lowell even wrote, in 1909: 'That Mars is inhabited by beings of some sort or another is as certain as it is uncertain what those beings may be.' A list of all the fictional Martians would require a book the size of an encyclopaedia. Almost always they were hostile creatures, generally horrific; Wells had many imitators, though none had his skill.

Few attempts were made to depict the Martians as being similar to ourselves; it was already known that the atmosphere there is painfully thin and oxygen-poor. Ray Bradbury's *Silver Locusts* is a notable exception, however. Human colonists live and play among the ruins of a great Martian civilization, the remnants of which are gentle, *sometimes* humanoid creatures. In A. E. van Vogt's 'Enchanted Village' a marooned Earthman learns to survive in the ruins of

long dead Mars, and gradually metamorphoses into a Martian himself. Sometimes entirely alien beings were described; in Olaf Stapledon's *Last and First Men* the Martians were 'cloudlets', with a swarm of individuals making up a single group-mind. The more sober stories dealt with future voyages to Mars, frequently with what appeared at the time to be authentic backgrounds. Arthur Clarke's *The Sands of Mars* was of this type; again we have hemispherical domes and self-supporting colonies, though an extra twist is introduced by converting the larger of the two midget satellites, Phobos, into a dwarf sun.

Where virtually all the authors went wrong – through no fault of their own – was in describing Mars as a world with a gently undulating landscape, devoid of any sharp relief. The truth is very different. The close-range pictures sent back by Mariner and the two Viking probes have shown that the surface is crater-scarred, with deep valleys and towering volcanoes; one of these volcanoes, Olympus Mons, rises to a height of 15 miles above the general level of the surface, so that it far surpasses any mountains on Earth. Although the 'new' face of Mars is now prompting more 'realistic' sf stories (William Walling's 'Nix Olympica'), in some respects Mars has lost its fictional allure. The canals do not exist in any form; they were nothing more than tricks of the eyes, and we are certain that there can be

no life there apart, just possibly, from primitive single-celled organisms of microscopic size. It may even be that henceforth there will be no more Martians in science fiction.

Venus has been a great disappointment. It too had been a favourite haunt for creatures of all kinds, and with considerable reason, inasmuch as until 1962 there was real prospect of finding marine life there. It was thought quite likely that Venus was largely ocean-covered, so that it would be similar to the Earth in Coal Forest days. No Earth-based telescopes could penetrate the thick, cloudy atmosphere, and even the surface temperature was unknown; writers such as C. S. Lewis in *Perelandra*, could say more or less what they liked. Alas, space-probes have shown that the heat is intolerable, that the atmospheric pressure is crushing, and that the clouds in the carbon-dioxide atmosphere contain quantities of sulphuric acid. In its way, Venus is probably the most hostile of all the planets in the Solar System, and travel there seems to be out of the question, so that fiction writers are robbed of yet another formerly promising venue.

Martian desert by David Hardy

Mercury

Everybody was wrong, too, about the innermost planet Mercury, which is not a great deal larger than the Moon, and which lacks any appreciable atmosphere. The error involved the axial rotation, which was assumed to be of the captured synchronous variety, making Mercury keep the same face permanently turned toward the Sun. Between the zone of everlasting day and the zone of everlasting night there was thought to be a 'twilight zone' over which the Sun would rise and set, always keeping close to the horizon, and this was used to advantage by Isaac Asimov in one of his superb *Robot* stories; but we now know that the rotation is not of this kind, so that there is no region of reasonably equable temperature. Astronomers, as well as novelists, were mistaken. One might even say the astronomers misled the writers, albeit through no fault of their own.

Minor planets, or asteroids, have come in for their share of attention; Arthur Clarke has a story ('Icarus Ascending') about a scientist stranded on Icarus, which moves closer in to the Sun than Mercury and which must at times be red-hot. The astronaut has to 'move round', keeping on the night-side of the rotating asteroid to avoid being scorched up. No doubt Icarus really is like this; but most of the asteroids keep within that part of the Solar System which lies between the paths of Mars and Jupiter, and stories about them are concerned largely with mining valuable materials from them. Whether this will be possible at any time in the future is a matter for debate, but it now seems more likely that the asteroids are barren rock of no commercial interest. Beyond lie the giant planets, of which Jupiter and Saturn are the largest; their gaseous surfaces preclude landings there, although this has not stopped writers in the past from speculating, notably James Blish, who, in his story 'Bridge', has a team of technicians fighting the relentlessly cold and storm-swept surface of Jupiter in an attempt to build a bridge out of Ice IV. The satellite systems are of real interest, however, and there are two more Clarke novels which deal with them in entirely different ways. The book of *2001: A Space Odyssey* leads us to Iapetus, the eighth moon of Saturn, through which the astronaut finally plunges into a different dimension. *Imperial Earth*, set in the future, has what may well be an authentic basis, since it concentrates upon Titan, the only satellite in the Solar System known to possess a reasonably dense atmosphere. Titan, which also orbits Saturn, is a potentially invaluable source of propellant, and of all the worlds in the outer part of the Sun's family it is the most likely to be colonized in the future.

A busy day in Earth orbit of the near future. Illustration by Vincent Di Fate

There is an interesting sidelight to this particular novel. Titan has a relatively low surface gravity; would a man born and brought up there be able to adapt to the much stronger pull of Earth? It is possible that a 'Titanian' could survive for only a limited period under terrestrial conditions. For that matter the same applies to Mars, where the surface gravity is only one-third of that of Earth. It may well be that before AD 2000 there will be distinct races of *homo sapiens*, some of which will be permanently exiled from the planet of their ancestors. This is a theme often used in sf, for example Heinlein's *The Moon is a Harsh Mistress* and Samuel Delany's *Triton*, in both of which life on a planetary satellite has become physically and socially changed from that on Earth.

Journeys through time

During the past couple of decades there has, inevitably, been a swing away from inhabited planets in the Solar System, for the excellent reason that space-research methods have shown that our neighbour worlds are hostile to life as we know it. Therefore, writers who concentrate upon authentic backgrounds have been forced to move further afield, and this introduces difficulties at once, because of the immense distances involved. There is not the slightest possibility of sending a rocket to another Solar System in what may be called a reasonable period. Even at the velocity of light, such a journey would take years, and a speed which is even remotely practicable the time of travel stretches into centuries. So let us examine a few of the themes which are still popular.

What, for instance, about the 'space ark' in which the original crew-members die at an early stage in the interstellar journey, and only their remote descendants survive to reach their target? This idea has been used often enough, but certain examples stand out – Clifford Simak's 'Target Generation', Brian Aldiss's *Nonstop*, Robert Heinlein's *Orphans of the Sky* and Harry Harrison's *Captive Universe*. In all the stories the original purpose of the trip has been forgotten, and the ship has become the Universe. Often the discovery of the ship's log causes some consternation. Another popular idea is that of the 'deep freeze', in which the astronauts are put into a state of suspended animation throughout most of the voyage, for example James White's *The Dream Millennium* and A. E. van Vogt's 'Far Centaurus'. There is some scientific backing for this scheme, but whether the human frame would endure such treatment is more than questionable. Some authors have evaded the issue by the simple expedient of 'instantaneous transfer' by some unexplained process; one is reminded of the stories by Edgar Rice Burroughs, of Tarzan fame, whose hero suddenly finds that he has left Earth behind and has arrived elsewhere, in this particular case, Mars, but the principles are the same. And in Hamilton's *The Star Kings*, there is a mental transfer between an Earthman and a man living on a planet orbiting a star.

Slightly less fantastic is the idea of the time-warp, which has been the theme of countless science fiction novels and short stories. Time, after all, is something

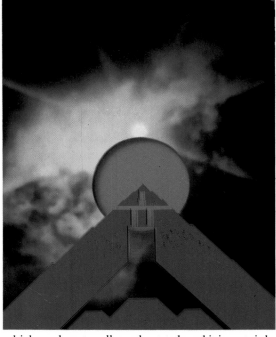

Illustration by Jim Jackson – 'The Mysterious Unknown'

which we do not really understand, and it is certainly not as simple as used to be thought. Wells' *Time Machine* may be incredible, but it has now been established that the time-dilation effect postulated by Einstein in his theory of relativity is genuine, even though the details remain obscure. If it were possible to move a space-craft at something like 99 per cent of the speed of light, the travellers' time-scale would be altered relative to that of Earth – and if time travel is ever to be achieved, it must surely be in this fashion, though the journey, being one way only, would not be encouraging. But the problem remains for space travellers, as shown in Poul Anderson's *The Long Way Home*, that a long mission in space, at close to the speed of light, would mean returning some several thousand years in the future. Anderson's heroes find adventure and intrigue, but other stories have shown the difficulty in psychological adaptation to a new society, conscious of the dead past being one's own past.

Exceeding the velocity of light, and moving in what is loosely termed hyperspace, is another theme. Most writers are content to accelerate their ships to incredible speed (warp factor, light factor – there is endless jargon) and never mind the relativity. But Poul Anderson in *Tau Zero* has a ship accelerating uncontrollably to so near the actual speed of light that as its mass increases according to Einstein's principle, so the occasional 'shudder' passing through the ship is just another Galaxy being nudged out of the way. George R. R. Martin ingeniously suggests in his story 'FTA' that in hyperdrive ships might travel very much *slower* than light, and all the fuss will have been for nothing. Cordwainer Smith, during his brief writing career, was more content to accelerate his space travellers slowly and leisurely on great 'photon catching' sails, gathering the emissions of sunlight. Other writers have played with this idea, and Larry Niven has invented the 'Ramscoop', a drive that feeds off interstellar hydrogen.

A certain amount of respectability has been

Mining the asteroids. Illustrated by Jack Coggins

Landscape on Ganymede *Worlds of Tomorrow*

bestowed on 'space warps' by the recent revelations about Black Holes. Both John Taylor, in his book *Black Holes*, and Adrian Berry in *The Iron Sun* have proposed that Black Holes might be used for trans-galactic space travel, and only infrequently had science fiction been there before them. Broadly speaking, a Black Hole is formed when a very massive star collapses on itself, becoming so small and so dense that not even light can escape from it; the old star is surrounded by a region of space which is, to all intents and purposes, cut off from the rest of the universe – material can enter it, but can never leave in the conventional manner, because the escape velocity has become greater than the speed of light. As yet we have no final proof that Black Holes really exist, but they seem very probable, and provide endless scope for the ingenious author. Would a space-craft plunging into a Black Hole emerge into a different universe or would it be able to materialize in a different part of our own?

What of matter transmission? This, again, remains for the moment an invention of science fiction. The film *The Fly* gruesomely indicates a problem that may arise here, when a man is transmitted with a fly in the transmission chamber, and the two emerge fused. Australian writer Jack Wodhams had some fun with this in his story 'Whosawotsa?' where young couples deliberately travel together through a similar matter transmitter and emerge fused in various compromising positions. Fortunately the process is reversible. Lloyd Biggle's Jan Darzek, in *All the Colours of Darkness*, investigates the disappearance of people who have been transmitted and never arrived. They have, it seems, tuned into an alien transmitter system. The inevitable happens. We cannot yet transmit matter instantaneously, but when we can a lot of the problems will have been worked out in sf.

However, our only real hope of contacting extra-terrestrials, in our present state of technology, is by radio. Attempts have been made, the most celebrated of which was Project Ozma of 1960, when a 'listening watch' was maintained on two relatively nearby stars which are not too unlike the Sun. (Incidentally, rhythmical signals were obtained almost at once, though to the intense disappointment of the researchers they proved to be due to Earth-based military transmissions.) Many stories have been written about messages from deep space, notably Fred Hoyle's *A for Andromeda* and Chloe Zerwick and Harrison Brown's *The Cassiopaeia Affair*. In Hoyle's book the signals give instructions for building a computer, the computer tells them how to build a machine which will create the alien out of Earth's raw materials. Other stories, less ambitious, concentrate on the search for alien messages, such as John Brunner's *Listen, the Stars!* There is in fact no reason to doubt that messages are being sent; we have done so ourselves. But whether they can reach the Earth, and whether we could interpret them even if they did is another matter.

Alien visitors

Last, but by no means least, there are the themes in which the Earth is itself visited by beings from afar. In Arthur Clarke's *Rendezvous with Rama*, an apparently innocent asteroid entering the Solar System proves to be a space-craft, and in Andrew Stephenson's *Nightwatch* a similar arrival proves to be part of an intergalactic public transport. There is a link here, even if a tenuous one, with our own Pioneer 10, the vehicle which by-passed Jupiter in 1973 and is now on its way out of the Solar System altogether, carrying a plaque which will – it is hoped – serve to identify its planet of origin if it is ever found by another civilization. The chances of this may be slight and diminishing all the time, but it is a measure of our changed attitude that it was thought worth while to include the plaque at all.

No Rama has been found, and I for one place no faith in the various flying saucer reports which have made almost constant headlines since the term was first coined in 1949. But we must be honest, and say that even if a visitation from another race is unlikely, it is not impossible. One day it may happen – and may happen, too, in much the way that some of our 20th-century science fiction writers have predicted.

We have come a long way since the time of Jules Verne, when even the Moon seemed impossibly remote; with concepts such as Black Holes, we are even starting to emulate Lewis Carroll's White Queen, who made a habit of believing at least six impossible things before breakfast. The science fiction of yesterday has become the science fact of today, and we cannot tell what lies ahead.

Poul Anderson's novel *The Long Way Home*, illustrated by Kelly Freas, explores the effect on space travellers of arriving back on earth thousands of years after they had left it

A Chris Foss space station of the future (*left*)

Science fiction predicts travel across the Universe in a number of ways, including the use of a 'Stargate', which connects two parts of the *Galaxy*. Illustrated by Kelly Freas

outer limits

Michael Ashley

The study, application and ideas of science fiction have crossed every sea, territory and barrier. Such is the fascination and following in sf that virtually every country has developed its own sub-culture. Some writers have become universal prophets, others have been contained within their frontiers.

EDDIE JONES 77

To English-speaking nations, the United States has become so much the focal point of the development of science fiction that it is easy to forget it exists and prospers elsewhere in the world.

After all, one of the founding fathers of science fiction was the Frenchman Jules Verne 1828–1905. His work, initially serialized in weekly periodicals like *Magasin d'Education et de Recreation*, has been translated into numerous languages and has often awakened interest in sf and scientific potential. Novels like *Twenty Thousand Leagues Under the Sea 1870*, *From the Earth to The Moon 1865* and *Journey to the Centre of the Earth 1864*, are not only cornerstones in the foundation of science fiction, but acknowledged classics of literature.

So much does Verne typify the dawn of science fiction that his reputation has overshadowed those of his countrymen. He was not the first to dabble in the fictional possibilities of science – but he was the first to popularize it as a valid form of fiction.

The noted swordsman Cyrano de Bergerac 1619–55, was responsible for the satirical adventures *A Voyage to the Moon 1650*, and *A Voyage to the Sun 1662*, in which he was the first to postulate the idea of rocket propulsion as a means of leaving the Earth. (And when the rockets fail the intrepid hero is drawn to the Moon by that orb's attraction on the bone marrow with which the hero had smeared himself as a protection against bruises!)

The French politician Sebastian Mercier, 1740–1814, produced a popular future utopia in *L'An 2440 1770*, one of the earliest works to accept *scientific* progress and a great encouragement to other writers to look to the future, in their fiction, as a means of expressing their political and social hopes. At the opposite extreme was *Le Dernier*

Homme 1805, by the renegade priest Jean-Baptiste de Grainville, 1746–1805. After completing his bleak forecast of a disaster-ridden future de Grainville drowned himself in the Somme.

Presaging Verne in the marvellous invention game was the romantic poet Théophile Gautier, 1811–72. In his remarkable novel *Les Deux Etoiles 1848*, he details an attempt to rescue Napoleon from St Helena by submarine in 1821! It was immensely popular, inspiring a number of imitations, and almost certainly influencing the young Verne 20 years before he invented his immortal *Nautilus* and the notorious Captain Nemo.

Two of Verne's contemporaries deserve far more recognition. Paschall Grousset, 1845–1909, better known by his alias André Laurie, wrote several scientific adventures which often alternated with Verne's in the magazines. One of the best was *The Conquest of the Moon 1888*, with the moon being drawn to the Earth by giant magnets. J. H. Rosny *aîné* was the name adopted by Honoré Boëx 1856–1940, when he ceased collaborating with his younger brother Justin. Honoré went on to produce an astonishing output including many science fiction works such as 'Les Xipehuz' *1887*, an absorbing account of an alien life-form on Earth in prehistory, and *La Force Mystérieuse 1914*, one of the earliest works to deal with a form of anti-matter. Unaccountably his only novel to see an English edition was *The Giant Cat 1920*, which the American publishers McBride issued in 1924 in an attempt to capitalize on the Edgar Rice Burroughs boom. Retitled *Quest of the Dawn Man* for the paperback edition, the novel explores the interrelationships between various forms of prehistoric man.

Thanks to Damon Knight several of Rosny's

Two of Jules Verne's contemporaries deserve more recognition; Paschall Grousset, better known as André Laurie, and J-H Rosny *aîné*, the name adopted by Honoré Boex. One of Laurie's best novels was *The Conquest of the Moon*, with the Moon being drawn to earth by giant magnets. Pictures from *Metal Hurlant*

short stories have been translated, whilst Philip José Farmer has retold Rosny's Tarzan-style 1922 novel as *Ironcastle 1976*. In time Rosny may become recognized as one of the true original pioneers of science fiction.

These were not isolated incidents in the development of sf. France alone had many other fictional propheteers like Paul D'Ivoi 1856–1915, Albert Robida, 1848–1926, and Guillaume Apollinaire, 1880–1918. Germany had its own pioneer as early as 1634 with the posthumous publication of the lunar dream *Somnium* by the famous astronomer Johannes Kepler 1571–1630. More important were the works of professor Kurt Lasswitz, 1848–1910, in particular *On Two Planets 1897*. Here Martians visit the Earth in anti-gravity powered spaceships and establish an artificial satellite that orbits the Earth about the poles.

Following Lasswitz came Robert Kraft, 1870–1916, who wrote almost exclusively for the German pulp magazine field. Little of his work is remembered today even though novels like *The New Earth 1910*, where our world faces destruction from hypersonic waves, show much originality. Better known is Kraft's contemporary, Hans Dominik, 1872–1946, an engineer who wrote some thirty books, some science fiction and others popularizing science much like Isaac Asimov does today. His novels however, like *Atlantis 1925*, put as much emphasis on adventure as scientific progress.

Nevertheless, it was in Germany that the first writings appeared that heralded the space race. Two technical works in particular were responsible for this initial impetus, *The Rocket Into Interplanetary Space, 1921*, by Hermann Oberth (a Rumanian by birth and since dubbed 'the Father of Astronautics') and *The Problems of Interplanetary Flight* by Hermann Noordung. These formed the foundation of the new science of astronautics, and were the basis of the later work by Max Valier and Wernher von Braun that led eventually, via the V2, to the first space rockets and the inevitable lunar landings.

Not only did they inspire fact, but fiction as well, including the fledgling German cinema, where Fritz Lang was in the process of producing one of the most important sf films ever made, *Metropolis 1926*. Oberth later served as consultant on Lang's *The Girl in the Moon 1929*, a less successful though no less remarkable film.

The most important effect was in the inspiration these works had on the fiction of Otto Willi Gail, 1896–1956. In *The Shot Into Infinity 1925*, and its sequel *The Stone From the Moon 1926*, Gail scrupulously followed Oberth's theories and included multi-stage rockets, earth satellites, and authentic descriptions of life within a spaceship.

Hugo Gernsback imported these novels and had them translated for his bumper sf magazine *Science Wonder Quarterly* in 1929 and 1930. He was himself a native of Luxembourg, while his literary advisor, the research chemist and bibliophile C. A. Brandt, was German by birth. They were both very aware of the novels being published in Europe and could read them in their original language. Thus Gernsback was able to give American readers a taste of what was appearing abroad.

From Germany came Bruno Burgel with his catastrophe novel *The Cosmic Cloud 1931*, Friedrich Freksa with his novel of an alien invasion of Earth, *Druso 1931*, and Ludwig Anton with his early tale of a journey to Venus, *Interplanetary Bridges 1922*. A most prolific writer was Otfrid von Hanstein, one of the earliest to consider ecology a worthy theme. Novels like *Emperor of the Sahara 1922*, *Electropolis 1927* and *Utopia Island 1931*, deal with the adaptation of deserts and the tropics twinned with a lost world theme. *Between Earth and Moon 1929*, and *In the Year 8000, 1932*, are along more traditional lines.

The French writers were more interested in the catastrophe theme. *The Death of Iron 1931*, by S. S. Held, *The Fall of the Eiffel Tower 1933*, by Conrad de Richter and *The Radio Terror 1933*, by Eugene Thebault all subject the Earth either locally or world-wide to a doom of one form or another.

One of the earliest translations Brandt selected for *Amazing* was the tale of insect invasion, 'The Eggs from Lake Tanganyika', by Curt Siodmak, published in the third issue in July 1926. Siodmak, born 1902, was something of an infant prodigy having had his first story published when he was eight. He came to prominence with the publication of *F.P.1 Does Not Reply 1930*, which suggested the use of aritifical

Illustration by Helmut Wenske, 'Schact'

155

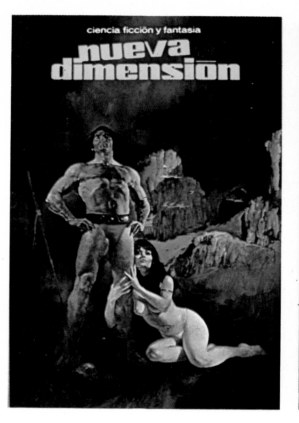

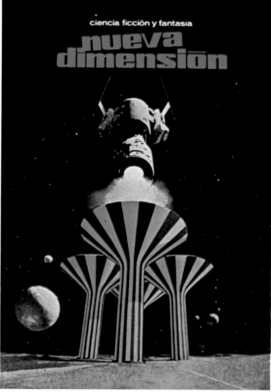

In Spain the emphasis is on translations of Western sf, or stereotyped space opera novels. In fact it is easier for a British writer to sell to Spain than it is for a native countryman. But Sebastian Martinez' *Nueva Dimension* is Spain's own political New Wave magazine, and since 1968 it has stalwartly survived the opposition of the State, although Franco's regime seized at least one issue, and subjected the editor to considerable pressure to cease publication

airports (or floating platforms) constructed in mid-Atlantic for refuelling. The novel was adapted as a film in 1932 (Siodmak collaborating on the screenplay) and was shot simultaneously in German, French and English with three separate sets of actors. The success of the English version, starring Conrad Veidt, resulted in Siodmak heading for Hollywood where he established himself as both a writer and director. As a writer he produced the classic novel of disembodied intelligence in *Donovan's Brain, 1942*, and more recently *Hauser's Memory, 1968*, where a dying man's memory is transplanted into another's mind.

Siodmak is only one of many writers who were born in Europe (and in some cases raised there) but who subsequently moved to the United States and found success. Willy Ley, James H. Schmitz, Algis Budrys, and even Isaac Asimov are all European.

France and Germany were not alone in their development of native science fiction, although English-speaking nations were only aware of translations. As a result much of the potential of non-American or English writers has been suffocated by the language barrier, but at the same time this has allowed these writers to develop sf along their own lines, untarnished by foreign influence. It has, on the other hand, also hidden many true pioneers of sf. The Norwegian dramatist Johann Hermann Wessel, 1742–85, wrote what is believed to be the very first time travel story, *Anno 7603, 1781*. The play was never staged and contains no scientific hardware – the adventurers are transported to the future by a sprite. But it does contain the startling idea, for the time, that in the future the rôles of men and women will be reversed.

Other national pioneers include Denmark's Ludvig Holberg, 1684–1754, whose subterranean ad-venture *Nils Klim 1741*, is a national classic. The Hungarian Mór Jokai, 1825–1904, wrote a number of futuristic stories and fantasies, and more especially the novel *The Coming Century 1874*, wherein Jokai conceived a myriad of new inventions not least an indestructible, malleable plastic and flying war machines. His fellow countryman Frigyes Karinthy, 1888–1938, produced a number of utopian satires, including *Voyage to Faremido 1917*, a sequel to *Gulliver's Travels* in which Karinthy compares men with automatons.

Certainly the second most important European writer after Verne was the Czech playwright Karel Capek 1890–1938. Capek gave the world the word robot in his play *R.U.R, 1921*, but more importantly he showed how well science fiction served as a vehicle for political satire. The first performance of *R.U.R*, just four years after the Russian Revolution, showed only too clearly how man will not be treated like a machine. Capek used several other sf themes in his plays including immortality in *The Makropoulos Secret 1923*, and nuclear power in *Krakatit 1924*.

These powerful works were almost instantly translated but by the mid-1930s the bulk of foreign sf was not being translated into English. When Gernsback ceased publishing sf magazines, the other publications had more than enough material from American writers to bother with foreign works.

From then on foreign sf continued totally uninfluenced by developments in America, with the result that in many countries sf stagnated. This was true even in Australia, where there was no language barrier, but an official import ban on US magazines. Australia's main claim to sf fame in these early days was *Out of the Silence 1919*, by Erle Cox 1873–1950 telling of a revived superwoman who strives to conquer Australia.

The devastation of WWII and in particular the development of the atom bomb gave a world-wide boost to sf writing. Writers, including those behind the Iron Curtain, now began to project the consequences of such developments into the future, some to frighten readers of the hideous potential, others to reassure the public that science was still a useful tool. Thus, throughout the 1950s, country after country saw many writers turning to sf and by the 1960s they were making their work known outside their national boundaries.

Inevitably this development led full circle. Foreign works, inspired to some extent by early American sf, and subsequently influenced by the country's national backgrounds, were translated back into English and in turn promulgated imitations or off-shoots in England and America.

There are three especially important instances of this interface. One comes from non-sf writer Pierre Boulle, noted French author of *Bridge Over the River Kwai*. His 1963 novel *Planet of the Apes* (*Monkey Planet* in the UK) resulted in a highly successful 1967 film, a number of sequels, a television series and paperback novelizations of the films.

Secondly there is the international success accorded the very basic space opera series *Perry Rhodan*. This began in Germany in 1960, the brain-child of writer and translator Walter Ernsting. Having sold the idea, a team of writers, including K. H. Scheer, Kurt Mahr and Ernsting himself (writing as Clark Dalton) set about plotting the adventures, and after phenomenal early sales the series became a regular *weekly* novel. English translations first appeared in America in 1969 and Britain in 1974, but with over 700 novels in print, the prospect of the entire series seeing translation is daunting.

Stanislaw Lem

Of greatest importance is the recognition being accorded the Polish writer Stanislaw Lem, born 1921. Lem's first sf work, *The Planet of Death*, appeared in 1951, but he did not achieve English recognition until the translation of his 1961 novel *Solaris* in 1971, prompted by the release of the Russian film adaptation. Over the preceding 20 years Lem had worked as a remarkable individual talent. Although he was aware of sf appearing elsewhere he only noted it where necessary, and instead wrote as he desired. Hitherto Poland had no tradition of science fiction, although it did have a pioneer in Jerzy Zulawski who wrote a lunar trilogy at the turn of the century. Lem was capable of blending philosophy with adventure right from the start, and the maturing of this process is most evident in the episodic volume *The Star Diaries*. This was a collection of stories Lem had been writing since 1954 which chronicle the galactic voyages of Ijon Tichy, a future-day Gulliver. Rather tongue-in-cheek, much in the mould of Robert Sheckley, Lem nevertheless puts forward many themes long taboo in American sf. Much has been made of Harry Harrison's 'The Streets of Ashkelon' *1962* in showing the reaction of alien cultures to Christian doctrine, but in the first of Tichy's adventures, collected as 'The Twenty-Second Voyage', Lem uses just the same plot to

relate how aliens torture a priest to death in the belief that this was the ultimate in a rather terrifying and macabre existence.

Solaris remains his masterpiece. Plotted like a detective story, it is set on a space laboratory orbiting an alien world which has spawned a global entity capable of drawing on the scientists' memories and creating tangible illusions.

Lem's work reflects a development natural to writers in continental Europe but quite alien to early American sf. While writers like Budrys, Disch and Farmer used this approach in the 1960s, it was always evident in the metaphysical fantasies of Franz Kafka, Dino Buzzati and the Argentine writer Jorge Luis Borges.

A most interesting development in sf which parallels that in America, are the writings in the Soviet Union. There has long been a belief that

Illustration for a novel by Kurt Lasswitz, by the Hungarian artist Sandor Leydenfrost

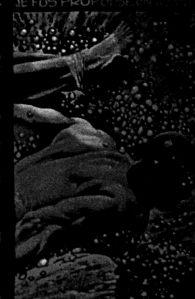

Russia has a long standing tradition of space fiction. For many years in the early 1900s there existed a Russian adventure pulp magazine, *Mirprikusheniya*, that printed not only translations of Jules Verne's work but also space adventures by Russian writers. It was only natural that the 1917 Revolution would influence writers, and one of the earliest was the poet Valery Bryusov, 1873–1924. He highlighted the oppression of the workers in 'The Republic of the Southern Cross' which envisaged a community of millions of workers at the South Pole.

Most revealing was the novel *We* by Eugene Zamiatin, 1884–1937. Written in 1920 it was banned in Russia and has never been published in that country. It first saw print in Paris in 1924. Zamiatin, who had welcomed the revolution, soon realized it was not the answer, and seeing freedom dwindling he wrote *We* as a warning. It tells of a thousand-year old autocracy and portrays a grim and frightening future. It clearly parallels, and possibly even inspired, Orwell's *1984*. Zamiatin was forced to ask Stalin for his release from Russia, and he spent the rest of his life in France.

A contemporary of Zamiatin's also found his work banned, though for a different reason. Mikhail Bulgakov, 1891–1940, was first and foremost a playwright but was equally adept at prose. One tale, 'The Fatal Eggs', has never been published in Russia. Written in the early 1930s it would have seemed quite at home in a concurrent issue of *Wonder Stories*. A quaint story, it dealt with an electric ray that rapidly increased both the size and rate of reproduction of organisms, at the same time imbuing them with total hatred of any other form of life. (It bears comparison with 'Spawn of the Ray' by Maurice Duclos from the February 1938 *Amazing*.) Throughout the story Bulgakov maintains that one cannot rely on the authorities for accurate information, least of all the press, who only print the news in a slanted way to produce the result they want.

The real growth in Russian sf began in the 1950s, spearheaded by the well known Russian sf writer Ivan Yefremov, born 1907. Yefremov started writing in the 1940s and a collection of his stories was published in England as *A Meeting Over Tuscarora* in 1946. These tales, like early American sf, placed more emphasis on scientific advance than on social implications, which is not so surprising considering the fate of Zamiatin of which Yefremov would have been only too aware in his youth. It was in 1957 that Yefremov produced his classic, *Andromeda*, which foresaw an ideal Communist commonwealth thousands of years in the future. The Russian authorities were initially suspicious of the novel, but it was finally published and sold over a million copies, with an English edition in 1959.

Hot on the trail of Yefremov were the brothers Arkadi and Boris Strugatski. Arkadi, born 1925, is the elder of the two and was initially a translator. He sometimes writes alone, but their best work has been in collaboration. Their first success came with *Hard to Be a God 1964*, which the authorities tried to suppress but which was nevertheless published in Siberia. The novel is a first class portrayal of a medieval feudal society on a distant planet to which an agent is sent from Earth to discover why the

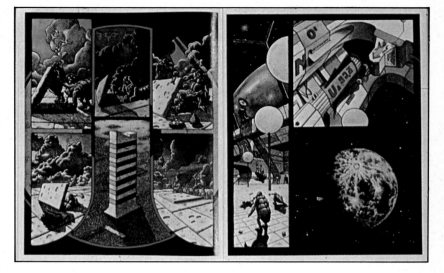

society is retrogressing. They followed this with a more amusing fantasy *Monday Was Saturday* about The Scientific Research Institute for Witchcraft and Enchantment, but thereafter they returned to more politically based novels such as *The Snail on the Slope 1966*, and *The Fairy Tale of the Troika 1968*. By 1970 the Strugatskis had been blacklisted as a result of the anti-Soviet content of their fiction. Yet their work continues to be published and they rate as Russia's most popular writers.

Whereas many American sf writers are young (in their twenties and thirties) the majority of Russian writers are middle-aged and over. Furthermore nearly all the Russian writers are qualified scientists. This includes the younger Strugatski brother, Boris, born 1933, an astronomer and mathematician, which makes Arkadi Strugatski something of an anomaly. Anatoly Dneprov, born 1919, for instance, is the alias of the physicist A. P. Mitskevich.

The strength of Russian sf relies on the accuracy and talent of the translator, and this is frequently the failing of many of the shorter stories. Starting in 1961, a number of anthologies of Russian short sf began appearing in Britain and America, starting with *Soviet Science Fiction*. *More Soviet Science Fiction 1963*, was of special value since it printed Ivan Yefremov's noted human-meets-alien short novel *The Heart of the Serpent*. Richard Dixon subsequently edited a volume of seven stories, *Destination: Amalthea 1963*, with the title taken from the Strugatskis' story. Of particular importance however, not only for their selection but for their superior translations, are those edited and translated by Mirra Ginsburg. These include *Last Door to Aiya 1968*, *The Ultimate Threshold 1970*, and a number of novels including a new translation of Zamiatin's *We*, in 1972.

Two other editors have opened American eyes to the amount of sf being written outside the English language. First the Yugoslav Professor Darko Suvin with *Other Worlds, Other Seas 1970*, which presented stories from the Iron Curtain countries with special preference given to the works of Lem. Then in 1974 came *View From Another Shore* by the German Franz Rottensteiner, which looked at the work of all the European countries, including fiction from Italy, and more especially from

The real growth in Russian sf began in the 1950s, led by Ivan Yefremov (Efremov); close behind him came the Strugatski brothers, Arkadi and Boris, whose best known work *Hard to be a God*, a collaboration, was suppressed by the authorities, although it was published in Siberia. According to SMOLOSKYP, The Organisation for Defense of Human Rights in the Ukraine, after Efremov's death 'guests from the KGB paid a visit to his widow, conducted a ruthless search, seized many valuable manuscripts.' A six-volume edition of his works was then cancelled, although after complaints by other science fiction writers a three-volume edition was permitted; but Efremov's major works, *Time of the Bull, Spare the Razor* and *Thais of Athens* were deleted from the edition

Part of a cartoon spread from the French fantasy comic *Metal Hurlant*, erotic, surreal, nothing short of a New Wave comic

Outrageous French spaceships from the imaginative comic – *Metal Hurlant*.

Montanari, Roberta Rambelli, Vittorio Curtoni and Lino Aldani struggle for recognition.

This applies to Spain and Germany where the emphasis is on translations or sterotyped space opera novels. In fact it is easier for a British writer to place a new novel with one of these publishers.

This is not the case in Romania or Hungary, where writers Adrian Rogoz and Peter Kúczka have established themselves in publishing houses and are encouraging works from fellow writers.

There is scarcely a European country that does not possess at least one sf writer of importance. Belgium, the home of Jacques Sternberg, born 1923, and the late Jean Ray, 1887–1964, now has the talents of Eddy Bertin, born 1944. Sweden can boast the indefatigable Sam Lundwall, born 1940, who, not satisfied with being an accomplished translator and editor, writer and recording artist, is also a first rate researcher. He was the author of the popular *Science Fiction: What It's All About 1971*, which revealed to Americans that Europe had as much a stake in the history and development of sf as America. His novels include *Alice's World, 1971*, where many thousands of years in the future mankind returns to a deserted Earth, and the controversial *2018 AD*.

Lundwall is not alone amongst the Scandinavians. Fellow Swede Sture Loennerstrand has been writing fantasy since 1935 though did not have a story published until 1942. Since then he has maintained a steady output including the prize-winning novel *The Spacehound 1954*. The Swedish cosmologist Hannes Alfvén, writing as Olof Johannesson, produced a future history for computers with *The Tale of the Big Computer 1966*, showing how man and machine will become first interdependent but finally the machine will dominate. Norway's Axel Jensen won an award for his exceedingly downbeat view of the future, *Epp 1966*. Denmark, thanks to the efforts of enthusiasts like Jannick Storm, Niels Søndergaard and Carsten Sciøler is experiencing an upsurge in science fiction with fans rapidly becoming professionals.

However, few writers make a name for themselves outside their country. From Germany only Herbert Franke has established a reputation in America for his perceptive novels like *The Orchid Cage 1961*, and *The Mind Net 1963*. On the whole, French writers have fared better. René Barjavel, born 1911, established himself with a now very dated novel *Ashes, Ashes 1943*. Clearly influenced by the War, the adventure is set in France in AD 2052, when an unaccountable series of catastrophes strike Paris leading to eventual global doom. Since then Barjavel has matured and with *The Ice People 1968*, telling of a woman revived from a long-dead Antarctic civilization, and *The Immortals 1973*, has written sf of a challenging standard.

Much the same applies to Jean Bruller, born 1902, who writes under the alias Vercors, a name he employed when working with the French Resistance. *Borderline 1952*, stands as the definitive

Czechoslovakia's Josef Nesvadba, regarded by many as one of the most polished and accomplished European sf writers.

For all its science fiction activity Italy has produced hardly any talented writers. This is largely due to the fact that Italy's largest sf publishers, Mondadori, fail to recognize the existence of any writers in their country and print only translations of US and UK novels. Thus Italy has had to wait until fans established themselves in the 1950s and then in the 1960s were able to start their own publishing ventures and begin nurturing new talent. This was boosted to some extent by the organization, in 1963, of the Trieste SF Film Festival, which has since become an annual event. Here films from all over the world were given a screening, including minor masterpieces from the Iron Curtain countries. Thereafter writers ceased concentrating on basic space opera and began exploring other avenues of sf. Ugo Malaguti showed great promise from his earliest work, *The System of Welfare 1963*, which took a cynical view of the future of society. Nevertheless outlets are few and authors like Gianni

novel on the theme of the Missing Link and a definition of humanity.

Once a firm home market was established in France with the magazine *Fiction* and later periodicals, new writers were able to test their skills. Thus writers like Charles Henneberg, 1899–1956, and his wife Nathalie, Claude Veillot, Pierre Barbet and Susanne Malaval were encouraged and now rank amongst the leading French writers. The two most important are Gerard Klein, born 1937, and Michel Jeury, born 1934. Jeury has yet to receive due recognition outside his own country, but Klein has already had several novels published in America starting with *The Day Before Tomorrow 1967*, and including the seeming parody but quite original *The Mote in Time's Eye 1965*, a real space-time extravaganza. Most modern French sf however is heavily influenced by American sf, which has been readily available in French translation since WWII, and because French writers are not as parochial as the English and are quite capable of reading American sf in the original English.

Science fiction is by no means restricted to Europe. Australia does not suffer translation problems, and its authors have regularly submitted direct to British and American magazines ever since Alan Connell appeared in *Wonder Stories* in the mid-1930s. The 1950s saw many stories from Frank Bryning, and the 1960s brought an upsurge of talent like John Baxter, Lee Harding, Damien Broderick, Wynne Whiteford and the irrepressible Jack Wodhams. But their fiction reflects all the trappings of traditional sf and cannot be viewed as foreign.

South America has its own Sam Lundwall in the shape of the Argentinian Hector Raul Pessina, although his fan activities far outclass any of his professional work. South America's most prominent writer is the Chilean Hugo Correa. Around the globe in India is Sridhar Rao, and especially, Satyajit Ray. Ray is not only a film director but also a writer of juvenile sf novels, and although India sees mostly reprint sf, there is a small but thriving community of fans and writers.

Perhaps the most explosive new country in the sf domain, a definite rising sun, is Japan. On the accepted literary scene is Kobe Abe, born 1924, whose *Inter Ice-Age 4, 1959*, is another example of the catastrophe novel. It's a theme that reoccurs in Japan's biggest selling sf work, *Japan Sinks, 1973*, by Sakyo Komatsu, born 1931, which has sold over two million copies. An English translation in 1975 apparently drastically reduced the original by a third. Komatsu has written over 20 sf books and is regarded as the Japanese Heinlein. The Japanese Bradbury on the other hand is Shin'ichi Hoshi, born 1926, noted for his short tales and poetic fables. Koichi Yamana, born 1939, is Japan's own prophet of the 'New Wave', and there are nearly a score more professional sf writers. Japan became notorious for its many 'monster-horror' films like *Godzilla 1956*, and it is almost certain this has jaded much overseas opinion of Japanese sf, which on the contrary can be both inventive and original.

What is unfortunate is that while most English sf receives foreign translations, little foreign sf reaches English editions, and that which does loses much in the translation. The British and Americans may think they write and read all that is best in sf, but the truth is they miss much that is good, whereas the many foreign readers who can read English, have the best of both worlds!

Perhaps one day, when we all speak a universal language, we will all be able to enjoy the fruits of international sf. One such universal language that was propounded in 1887 was Esperanto. Whilst it never gained much ground it did gain a footing in a number of countries, and a few sf stories have been published in Esperanto. In America there was J. U. Giesy's 'In 2112', whilst more recently in Holland, J. L. Mahe contributed 'They Still Jump' to the Esperanto magazine *Monda Kultura*.

Clearly sf transcends all boundaries.

Beautiful and sensitive European artwork in the magazine, *Metal Hurlant*. Shapely and seductive figures feature in many stories.

new wave

Christopher Priest

The New Wave movement in science fiction was part of the much larger social revolution in the 1960s. It was a rebellion against the accepted idioms of the sf category, and can be seen as the single most important development in science fiction.

David Pelham's cover for
J.G. Ballard's *The Four
Dimensional Nightmare*

influence was pernicious, and it persists today: the modern paperback book, with its brightly coloured artwork and its sf label, is a direct marketing descendant of the pulp magazines. In fact, nearly all of the so-called classics of science fiction first appeared in the magazines.

There is much mention elsewhere in this book of the pulp magazines and their effect on science fiction, but so far as an understanding of the later New Wave is concerned it is enough to describe their *literary* influence.

The writers who contributed to the magazines were, in one way or another, derivative of each other. They read each other's work, they borrowed ideas from each other, and they were all working for the same few editors who controlled the magazines. (One frequently hears of the debt owed to doctrinaire editors like John W. Campbell, editor of *Astounding* for 34 years.)

To write science fiction at this time was to write in the American way. The main markets for stories were in America, and those that were not – for example, the British magazines that existed from time to time – were so thoroughly influenced by the American model that they were indistinguishable from the real thing.

As a consequence, an orthodox idiom emerged: there was always a strong sense of narrative, the central character was normally a white male, female characters – if any – were almost invariably depicted as beautiful or dumb or delicate, or all three, and there was usually a clearly identifiable, but uncontroversial, threat or problem.

As for style, science fiction was written in plain, businesslike prose, although there were always a few writers who preferred a sort of pseudo-romantic lyricism.

Science fiction, the literature that pretended to look forwards, was in fact the one form of fiction that dwelt in the past, because the orthodoxies established in the past suited no one better than it suited its writers.

By the end of the 1950s, science fiction was becoming set in its ways. Most of the best-known writers were past their youthful peak, most of the 'novels' appearing in book form were magazine stories hastily joined together or expanded beyond their natural length, most of these were at least five or ten years old (and some were even older than that), and what newly written work there was seemed stale, derivative and repetitive.

Science fiction had become middle-aged as well as middle-class, and was redolent of middle-America and its ideals.

In the 1960s, man was travelling in space, computer technology was advancing so fast no one could keep pace, pollution and radioactive fall-out and runaway industrialism were constant concerns; the world was becoming the sort of place the science fiction writers of the 'Golden Age' had dreamed of as the new utopia.

In addition, the 1960s were when the postwar 'bulge' in Western birth-rate came of age: there were millions of new young adults about, seeking to make the world their own. The 1960s were the decade of The Beatles and The Rolling Stones, of Marcuse

The 'New Wave' movement was an attempt to find a fresh approach to the writing of science fiction. It was, in fact, the first new approach to style and content since the creation of the science fiction category in 1926, and although it was partly a rebellion against the accepted idioms of the category, it is much better understood as being a child of its age; the New Wave was a part of the much larger social revolution of the 1960s.

Although individual examples of New Wave science fiction can seem trite, obscure and self-indulgent, the movement as a whole can now be seen as the single most important development of the science fiction genre.

To understand any kind of revolution, one must first examine the established system that was to be overthrown. To understand the Russian Revolution, for instance, one has first to learn about the Tsars; to understand the New Wave, one must first recognize the influence of the American pulp-writing idiom.

For 35 years from 1926, the genre magazines were at the centre of science fiction publishing. Their

and Guevara and McLuhan, of the Maharishi and Haight-Ashbury and psychedelic rock and drug-culture, of Biafra and Vietnam and Czechoslovakia, of John F. Kennedy and Martin Luther King, of the mini-skirt and student protest.

There was a new generation of science fiction readers, and although the power-fantasies and speculative notions of the old science fiction tapped a positive response in the inquiring minds of those who found it, there was a lack of immediacy that was all too apparent.

Soon there was to be a change in science fiction, and it found that immediacy.

Michael Moorcock

Michael Moorcock became editor of the British science fiction magazine *New Worlds* at the beginning of 1964. Prior to this, the magazine had been edited by Ted Carnell for 17 years, and the change came when there was a change in ownership of the magazine, and its companion title *Science Fantasy*. Moorcock's name was virtually unknown to the *New Worlds* readership, although for some years he had been a prolific and popular contributor to *Science Fantasy*, with his series of novellas about the albino warrior Elric. (Carnell, a distinguished editor, moved on to create the *New Writings in SF* series for Corgi Books, and he enjoyed considerable success with it until his death in 1972.)

Moorcock's policy with *New Worlds* was at first cautious. In several of his early editorials he spoke of the shortcomings of the sf idiom, and the need to find writing truer to the age, but he maintained he would continue to publish the best examples of traditional sf he could find. He was true to his word, and during the first three years of his editorship he published good new work by many writers who could not by any stretch of the imagination be called New Wave: Arthur Clarke, E. C. Tubb, Bob Shaw, Joseph Green, Sydney J. Bounds, Harry Harrison, Mack Reynolds, and many others.

However, Moorcock's finger was on the pulse of the 1960s. In the first of several polemical editorials (*New Worlds* 148, *March 1965*), he wrote:

> We need more writers who reflect the pragmatic mood of today, who use images apt for today, who employ symbols gathered from the world of today, who use sophisticated writing techniques that can match the other techniques of today, who employ characters fitted for the society of today. Like all good writing, good sf must relate primarily to the time in which it is written; a writer must write primarily for his own generation. He must not seek to emulate his predecessors in their own territory, neither must he write for a posterity which will anyway not remember him unless he is true to himself and his own age. He can learn from his predecessors, but he should not imitate them.

In spite of the Old Testament resonance of some of this, the magazine's contributors evidently took it – and many similar editorials that followed – to heart, because afterwards there was a transformation in the published stories.

Moorcock had two unique qualities as an editor.

Firstly, he was the opposite of doctrinaire, and could respond to individual merit in a writer's work. He would spend many hours of painstaking work with promising writers, and get them to give of their best. Secondly, he was immensely loyal, both to the writers he discovered and to the writers he already admired, and this in turn inspired a feeling of loyalty in the writers towards *New Worlds*.

Amongst the many writers Moorcock either discovered or encouraged were the following, all of whom were published frequently in *New Worlds*:

Barrington Bayley (who had contributed to the Carnell *New Worlds*, but who did some of his best work for Moorcock); Hilary Bailey (some years later she became editor of *New Worlds Quarterly*); Langdon R. Jones; George Collyn; Thom Keyes; Charles Platt (who later became the designer of *New Worlds*, and, eventually, coeditor first with Moorcock then with Hilary Bailey); Richard Gordon; David I. Masson (most of whose weird and remarkable stories can be found in *The Caltraps of Time*); Terry Pratchett; Bill Butler (the American poet and bookseller, who died tragically in 1977); Peter Tate; Michael Butterworth; David Redd; and John Sladek.

There were more, and we shall come to these later, but between them these writers were the 'New Wave' in Britain at the time. Very few of them were in contact with each other, and in all probability each would deny that his or her own work had anything to do with a literary movement, however labelled. What *can* be safely said of them is that their names were unknown to the wider science fiction public, and that each, with Moorcock's positive encouragement, was finding a singular voice.

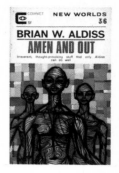

Cover by Keith Roberts for number 165 of the Compact *New Worlds*, 1966

Cover for number 9 of the Hilary Bailey *New Worlds*, which took over from the large format version after number 201

Science Fantasy, edited by Kyril Bonfiglioli rapidly developed into a literate and charmingly eccentric magazine with an atmosphere all its own. This cover is by Keith Roberts

Moorcock was as successful, though in a different way, with the more established authors. In particular, the two British writers J. G. Ballard and Brian Aldiss, both of who produced some of their most extraordinary work for him.

Both men had been frequent contributors to the Carnell *New Worlds*, and both were, and remain, loyal to Carnell's early encouragement, but it was Moorcock who provided the environment in which their talents could best develop. Both Aldiss and Ballard had been lured to the markets across the Atlantic, but with Moorcock's intelligent support they were lured back again to the home magazines. The first Moorcock issue (*New Worlds 142, May-June 1964*), for instance, contained a new story by Aldiss, a long article by Ballard about William Burroughs, as well as the first instalment of a new Ballard serial, *Equinox* (later published in book-form as *The Crystal World*).

After that, hardly an issue appeared without either a contribution from either or both, or without some mention of their work or influence. For example, in *New Worlds 167, October 1966*, Moorcock wrote an editorial called *Ballard: the Voice*, in which he analyzed the writer's work and outlook, and at the end of which he described, possibly for the first time in print, the sort of literary ambience of *New Worlds*:

> In this country there now exists, centred around this magazine, a group of writers and critics who understand and enthusiastically support the work Ballard is doing. This does not mean that they intend to follow Ballard – his is his own direction – but that they realize the need Ballard is fulfilling, and hope, in the future, to play some part in fulfilling that need themselves. . . . The need has been with us for fifty years. It could take another ten to produce a large body of work which can meet this need. But we are now at last marshalling our forces. Watch this space.

None of the readers could have known at this time, but a second great change was soon to overtake *New Worlds*, and Moorcock's editorial contained a hint as to what it might be.

In this first phase of Moorcock's influence – which was for a period of roughly two or three years – the essence of *New Worlds* was therefore contained in a few words. Namely: encouragement, enthusiasm, polemic, and – most important of all – mutual loyalty.

SF Impulse

At the same time as Moorcock had taken over *New Worlds*, the editorship of *Science Fantasy* had passed to an Oxford art-dealer named Kyril Bonfiglioli. At first the two magazines appeared on a bi-monthly basis, alternating with each other, but after a few issues both titles went on to a monthly schedule.

The character of *Science Fantasy* was quite different from *New Worlds*. Bonfiglioli lacked the crusading zeal of Moorcock; his policy was to seek stories he considered good in his own terms. For this reason, *Science Fantasy* rapidly developed into a literate and quite charmingly eccentric magazine, with an atmosphere all its own. In comparison, *New Worlds* was a rowdy-house of revolutionary fervour. Even so, *Science Fantasy* (or *SF Impulse*, as it was retitled in 1966) played its part in the development of the New Wave.

Entropy-on-sea, an illustration by Pauline Jones

Bonfiglioli's best discovery amongst the new writers was certainly Keith Roberts, who became a frequent and much admired contributor. Roberts' early work, on which Bonfiglioli appeared to have a virtual monopoly, revealed an astonishing diversity of range and style. In a paradoxical way, Roberts is a writer who reveals much of interest about the New Wave, because nearly all his work is that of the well-made story, with a soundly conventional narrative, and yet he is identified by many with the sort of 'new' science fiction being written at the time. *SF Impulse* published two of Roberts' early novels in serial form: *The Furies* and *Pavane*. It was not long before Roberts was selling regularly to Carnell's *New Writings*, and later to *New Worlds*, and of course since then has become a well known novelist.

Other writers closely associated with Bonfiglioli's magazine were Johnny Byrne, Alistair Bevan (a pseudonym of Keith Roberts), Thomas Disch, Chris Boyce, Pippin Graham, A. K. Jorgennson, Christopher Priest, Thom Keyes, Philip Wordley and Josephine Saxton. He also published several stories by well established authors like Poul Anderson, J. G. Ballard, Brian Aldiss, James Blish, John Brunner, D. G. Compton, Harry Harrison, Jack Vance and Richard Wilson.

Bonfiglioli edited the magazine for the first two years, and the last few issues were edited by Keith Roberts and Harry Harrison – although Roberts was associated with the magazine in an editorial capacity for much of its existence.

American Exceptions

So far it has seemed that the New Wave was a uniquely British phenomenon, but this is not entirely true. If we accept that the New Wave was a product of the social revolution of the 1960s, then it must follow that it appeared elsewhere, and certainly in the States.

This of course it did, but the social climate in Britain in the early part of the decade was more turbulent than in America, at least as far as the new independence of the young. (John Lennon of The Beatles has spoken of the group's reaction to the audiences on their first American tour; the British audiences were already growing their hair long and wearing casual clothes, while the Americans were still in crew-cuts, Bermuda shorts and braces on the teeth.)

Also, in the sf world, Michael Moorcock was making a positive effort to introduce change. The American magazines, more thoroughly steeped in the traditions of the past, were resistant to change. There were, however, at least two exceptions to this, and they were going on, in a quiet way, at the same time as *New Worlds* was more loudly proclaiming its message. The first of these exceptions is, on the face of it, the more surprising.

Amazing Stories was the original sf pulp magazine, created by Hugo Gernsback in 1926. Its history is not, on the whole, a glorious one, and even as recently as 1952 *Amazing Stories* was still being published as a pulp magazine.

However, in 1953 it changed its format to digest-size, and the fiction tended to be more sober, even

An illustration by Joe Petagno for Mervyn Peake's 'The Inner Landscape'

though the idiom was firmly traditional. Towards the end of the 1950s, Cele Goldsmith (later, Cele G. Lalli) became the editor of *Amazing Stories*, and its companion magazine *Fantastic*.

Goldsmith's influence was at first barely perceptible. The appearance of the magazine changed little, and many of the usual contributors continued to appear. There were no polemical editorials, and there was no trumpeting of any need for revolution.

Even so, it was clear that Cele Goldsmith was receptive to new and younger writers, and those with no apparent links with the traditions of sf.

In 1962, she began publishing a large number of short stories by J. G. Ballard (including 'Thirteen to Centaurus', 'Passport to Eternity', 'The Sherrington Theory' – later retitled 'The Reptile Enclosure' – and two or three stories from the *Vermilion Sands* series), as well as work from Brian Aldiss. In the same year she published the first stories by two previously unknown writers: Thomas Disch and Roger Zelazny.

Disch and Zelazny became frequent contributors to *Amazing Stories* and *Fantastic*, and although they were both eventually to move on to a wider audience and great recognition, the early encouragement she gave them is to Cele Goldsmith's eternal credit.

The two magazines changed ownership in 1965 and with the change came a drastic and conservative policy of reprinting very old stories, but before Cele Goldsmith left she published a large volume of interesting material, including Roger Zelazny's serial *He Who Shapes* (later titled, in book-form, *The Dream Master*), and work by Norman Spinrad, Harlan Ellison, David R. Bunch and Philip Dick.

And perhaps the quietest coup of all: in 1962 *Fantastic* published 'April in Paris', the first of several contributions from Ursula Le Guin.

Frederik Pohl and IF

The second American exception to the rule was *If* magazine, edited by Frederik Pohl.

If was always slightly overshadowed by its more famous companion magazine, *Galaxy*, but in the early 1960s Pohl introduced a policy of publishing a new writer in every issue. Once again, as in the case of *Amazing Stories*, there was no clarion call for a

Cele Goldsmith took over as editor of *Amazing Stories* in the late 1950s, and published much of the early work of J.G. Ballard, Thomas Disch, Roger Zelazny and Harlan Ellison, work which was often outside the traditional sf idiom

Peter Jones painting for Colin Kapp's *The Wizard of Anharitte*

new movement in science fiction, but Pohl was probably acknowledging the fact that any kind of literature will grow stale without a constant influx of new talent.

The 'Ifirstory' (the sort of neologism the sf world seems to thrive on) attracted a great deal of attention in its day, and the quality of stories was generally high. In retrospect, most of these writers were inspired by the science fiction of the past, and thus were as firmly rooted in the traditional idiom as the established writers alongside whom they were being published.

But there are three worth singling out. Gary Jennings and Bruce McAllister both had style and voice of their own, but, sadly, neither has produced much since. And the third? A young writer, so deeply entrenched in the traditional idiom that not even the glibbest debater could argue that he was of the New Wave, but one who has gone on to build a huge audience of his own: Larry Niven.

F&SF and Ace Books

Before returning to Britain and New Worlds, it is worth mentioning one more American magazine, and one publisher.

The Magazine of Fantasy and Science Fiction (or *F&SF* as it is affectionately known) has been a sort of New Wave of its own ever since its inception in 1949. Although it has had a number of different editors in its time, the flavour of the magazine has remained remarkably constant. It has always shown a preference for the well written story (or 'literary', as some would have it), and any one issue will reveal a wide range of different styles and approaches. It is not above publishing unabashed space adventure, nor is it beneath publishing obscure or intellectually ambitious fantasies.

Many of the writers whom we can now describe as 'New Wave' soon discovered that *F&SF* was a natural home for their work. Roger Zelazny, for instance, served his apprenticeship with Cele Goldsmith as already described, but perhaps his best known story from the early days is 'A Rose for Ecclesiastes', which appeared in *F&SF* in November 1963. His early novel *. . . And Call Me Conrad* (later, *This Immortal*) was serialized in *F&SF* in 1965.

In the world of sf publishing, one can never take anything for granted. Ace Books were renowned for their large and popular list of exciting, colourful and undemanding space operas. Reading one Ace Book felt very much like reading another, and although Donald Wollheim – the editor controlling the list – often published stories expanded or rewritten from earlier magazine publication, some of the titles were written especially for him.

In 1962, one such new novel slipped almost unnoticed on to the drugstore stands. It was called *The Jewels of Aptor*, and was written by Samuel Delany. Although this story was superficially of the space adventure type, the novel was remarkable for a dense, baroque style, which has since become recognizably Delany's own; the first edition was shortened before publication, but the full text was published some years later.

The magazine of *Fantasy and Science Fiction* has been a sort of New Wave of its own ever since its inception in 1949. Cover by James Roth

The Jewels of Aptor was followed in 1963 by the first volume in an ambitious trilogy, *Captives of the Flame*, and the other titles, *The Towers of Toron* and *City of a Thousand Suns*, came soon afterwards. Few people had ever heard of Delany, and the books were slow to build a reputation. As the novels became read and talked about, however, and more people sought them out, it was realized that Delany was a major new talent. More novels for Ace followed, and in 1966 *Babel-17* was published, and won the Nebula Award for the best sf novel of that year.

Ace also published Ursula Le Guin's early novels: *Rocannon's World*, 1966, *Planet of Exile*, 1966, *City of Illusions*, 1967, and the prize winning and influential *The Left Hand of Darkness*, 1969.

By 1966, Michael Moorcock's aggressive editorial policy was showing results. *New Worlds* was now a well printed, attractively laid out monthly paperback, and contained, in one issue after the other, new fiction of the highest quality. Many of the contributors had been unknowns only two years earlier; now they were publishing regularly, and gaining recognition. The two *New Worlds* stalwarts, Ballard and Aldiss, were producing some of their most advanced and sophisticated fiction. Moorcock himself, then not well known as a science fiction writer, was contributing some of his most intriguing work: 'Behold, the Man' (an iconoclastic and sensational new look at the Crucifixion myth), the first Jerry Cornelius episodes, of which more later, and a novel called *The Wrecks of Time*, published under the pseudonym James Colvin.

Best of all, *New Worlds* was at last attracting writers of a like mind from America. Zelazny, Disch, Sladek and Delany became contributors to the magazine, and the last three moved to London where, presumably, the cultural ambience suited them better.

And there was another visitor, who had flown to London in 1965: Judith Merril, the American writer, critic and anthologist.

Today, anthologies of the best sf stories of the

year are legion, but it is true to say that Judith Merril started it all. For 11 years she published a series called *The Year's Best SF*, and throughout the books one preoccupation clearly emerged: she was concerned with good writing, with individual voice, with enlargement of the sf idiom. Her books did not merely draw on the established sf magazines; she selected from *Harper's*, and *The New York Times*, and *Playboy*, and *The Socialist Call*, and anywhere else she could find speculative writing.

What drew her to London was the fact that something that had once been just a science fiction magazine, and a rather pale imitation of the American model at that, had become a dynamic literary force in its own right. The science fiction she admired was concentrated in one place, and most of the writers for it were concentrated in one country. What was more, behind the actual fiction there was a great deal of theory and concern, expressed not just by Moorcock, but by the many guest-editorial writers and critics in *New Worlds*.

In 1966, Merril was firmly established as a part of the British science fiction world. In a series of articles for *F&SF* she described what was happening in Britain, and gave sympathetic, if not always favourable, reviews to a number of British writers.

Behind the scenes, Judith Merril was imposing form to what, until then, had been formless.

She went through the *New Worlds* files, and contacted all the writers. She was interested in them, in their work. She treated them all, however new or undeveloped, with a great and flattering seriousness. Sf writers, accustomed to being neglected, at best, or dismissed, at worst, by the world of general literature, suddenly discovered there was someone who could talk to them on their own terms as serious writers. For the first time, the phrase 'New Wave' was being used, and if there was a measure of self-consciousness in it, at least it was being used in a non-pejorative sense.

It was the first hint of how the New Wave would be understood in America.

What in effect Judith Merril did was to see the British New Wave as a movement, a 'school' of writers, so to speak. She brought writers together, discovered common concerns, saw their work as having certain themes or obsessions in common.

All this was heady stuff, and it was not without some justice. Although writers live and work independently of each other, they are nevertheless part of the same cultural environment. Britain in the 1960s was a stimulating place in which to live; change, a quality that strikes through to the sensibilities of speculative writers, was racing through the country. It was inevitable that there would be underlying similarities.

The testament to Judith Merril's sojourn in Britain is an anthology, wincingly entitled *England Swings SF* (published in 1968 in the States; a slightly shorter version was published Panther in Britain in 1972, and called *The Space-Time Journal*).

England Swings SF is a phenomenal book, in the pure sense of the word. Littered with quotes and jottings of the time, and lyrics from *Sergeant Pepper*, and biographical notes by Merril and autobiographical notes by the authors, and the whole set out in a sort of crazy-paving arrangement of typography, the book is one interpretation of what was happening at the time. Not every included author would agree with Judith Merril's conclusions, but it remains that *England Swings SF* is an approximation of the science fiction Zeitgeist of the 1960s.

Meanwhile, *New Worlds* and *SF Impulse* were in trouble. *SF Impulse* was combined with *New Worlds* (although in name only; the flavour remained exclusively that of *New Worlds*), and beset by distribution difficulties and rising costs, the future was uncertain. Brian Aldiss put it to the Arts Council of Great Britain that the continued existence of *New Worlds* was a matter that concerned more than a handful of science fiction fans, and with the support of many writers and critics from outside the genre, his submission was accepted. A new publisher was found, but the arrangement did not last long; eventually Moorcock became publisher as well as editor, and sunk a large amount of his own money into the magazine.

David Pelham's cover for Michael Moorcock's *A Cure for Cancer*, the second Jerry Cornelius novel

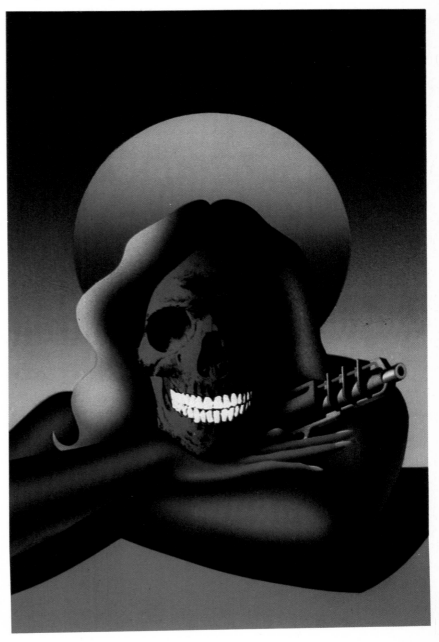

Cover for Keith Robert's *The Chalk Giants*, which appeared segmentally in *New Worlds*

The American Controversy

In America, the emergence of a 'New Wave' of writers had occurred differently, but it had occurred nonetheless. There was no equivalent of *New Worlds*, and by the time the phrase 'New Wave' had been coined, there was an identifiable 'type' of story which the phrase described.

The definition of the New Wave 'type' is this: The writing would be obscure to one degree or another. There would be experiments with the actual prose: with grammar, with viewpoint, with typography. There would be reference to all sorts of eclectic sources: philosophy, rock music, newspaper articles, medicine, politics, automobile specifications, etc. There would be a 'down-beat' or tragic resolution to many stories, if any resolution at all. There would frequently be explicit descriptions of sexual activity, and obscenities were freely used.

This is an analysis of published work, not an approach to understanding the process behind it, but never mind. Because the *type* of writing could be labelled, New Wave, in the American sense, became an idiom. In other words, New Wave became a subcategory of writing inside the category of sf.

The words 'New Wave' became a rallying-call for those who approved, and a term of contempt for those who did not.

In American fan circles, a long and relatively bitter dispute broke out, and several writers joined in. Those writers who worked in the traditional sf idiom, and those fans who admired their work, appeared to feel threatened. Those writers who were attracted to the freedoms of the New Wave, and the fans who admired *them*, argued that a broadening of science fiction could only be for the good. This argument, both sides of it, missed the point.

The purpose of the New Wave, if indeed it can be said to have a purpose, was to release writers and readers from the preconceptions of the pulp magazine idiom. The American argument was about a *product*: a 'type' of story with an invented label. The *process*, which Moorcock and others had been encouraging writers to explore, was to find an individual approach to writing speculative fiction . . . and this process could only be understood by each writer in *his own* terms.

For example: the traditional idiom of science fiction speculates about technology, about man's aspirations, about the future, about inventiveness, and so forth. Is it not possible that similar speculation can be made, in fictional form, about other aspects of man's experience? Why can science fiction not explore the inner world of emotion, of neurosis, of sexual desire, of boredom? Can it not describe transitory experiences like drug-trips, or the appreciation of music, or defecation, or the act of writing itself?

No one ever urged these particular topics on writers, but it was this sort of subject or personal vision with which many writers were concerned.

The American controversy therefore centred on the wrong area. They were not saying: should we or should we not rethink our ideas about sf? They actually said: is it a *good* or a *bad* thing that the New Wave should exist?

As a consequence of this, the phrase 'New Wave' became stigmatized, and no one saw the advantage of being associated with it. The sound of good writers denying that they were New Wave was deafening.

Even so, the process of dynamic social change was moving through America – accelerated, in all probability, by the Kennedy assassination in 1963, and the Vietnam war which was escalating – and writers were responding to it.

Whether the label was accepted or not, a type of writing *was* emerging that owed little to traditional sf. Mention has already been made of Disch, Delany, Le Guin and others, and although the work of these writers was a long way from being obscure or experimental, it nevertheless had great individuality. These authors were firmly associated with the American New Wave of the time.

Editors appeared who were sympathetic to such writers. Damon Knight created the series of anthologies called *Orbit*, the first of which was published in 1966. Although the contents of the first volume were relatively traditional, it included stories by Kate Wilhelm, Thomas Disch and Keith Roberts. In later editions, the emphasis was more firmly on the New Wave, and Knight published writers like Gardner R. Dozois, Gene Wolfe,

Graham Charnock, R. A. Lafferty, Edward Bryant, Carol Emshwiller, Jack M. Dann, Geo. Alec Effinger, James Sallis, Doris Piserchia, Ursula Le Guin, Brian Aldiss and Kate Wilhelm.

In 1967, Harlan Ellison published a mammoth anthology entitled *Dangerous Visions*. Once again, this was not labelled or promoted as New Wave, but its intent was of the same order. The editorial rationale was to allow writers to take on themes or subjects which would, in all probability, be unacceptable to the sf magazines. Many of the stories are conventional, though some indeed deal with subjects – like incest or homosexuality – which had once been forbidden in the narrow world of sf, though not in the world of general literature. *Dangerous Visions* published some excellent stories, but its influence on the field was not a literary one, except incidentally. By its commercial success it established that it was possible for publishers to bring out books containing new, untried stories. It was not the first – *Orbit* preceded *Dangerous Visions* by a year, and the British series *New Writings in SF* had been prospering since 1964 – but it made so much noise it produced imitators.

Samuel Delany and Marilyn Hacker published the first edition of *Quark/* in 1970. Again, this was labelled speculative fiction rather than New Wave, but the intent was clearly similar to that of *New Worlds*. With poetry and graphics as well as short stories, *Quark/* was uncompromisingly New Wave, and its loss was felt when it was discontinued after a few editions.

The first issue of the Arts Council – sponsored *New Worlds* appeared in July 1967. Its appearance had been transformed; instead of being a paperback book, it was now printed in the conventional format of magazines, with a liberal use of artwork, photography and graphics. In its day, it was distinctly different from most sf magazines that had preceded it. Indeed, the fact that *New Worlds* had once been a conventional science fiction magazine was well disguised.

The cover illustration was M. C. Escher's lithograph 'Relativity', and inside there was a rather garbled description of Escher's work. The unsigned leading article made no mention of sf at all, but there were knowing references to Kafka, Lawrence, *Anna Karenina* and Vietnam, and although there was fiction by recognized sf authors (Masson, Zelazny, Disch, Ballard) the pretence was maintained that *New Worlds* had turned overnight into a proper literary magazine.

This first issue set the tone for some time to come, and although the preening and self-consciousness relaxed later, there was an aura of intellectual snobbishness and complacency that many readers found disappointing.

It was as if the crusades of the past had achieved their ends: the Holy City had been taken and the infidels crushed. While *New Worlds* had railed against the traditional idiom it had been an abrasive and stimulating magazine; now science fiction was dead – indeed, it was as if it had never existed – and *New Worlds* was in an intellectual vacuum.

The magazine continued on a more or less monthly basis until the beginning of 1971, and for all this time Moorcock was associated with it, but the named editors varied enormously, especially towards the end. Editors from one issue to the next included James Sallis, Langdon R. Jones, Graham Hall, Graham Charnock and Charles Platt; under the new and more liberal arrangement with Moorcock as publisher, *New Worlds* was loosely organized as a cooperative venture. Unfortunately, this showed in the magazine's sense of direction; its purpose now seemed vague.

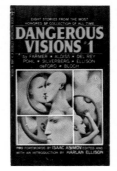

Harlan Ellison published *Dangerous Visions* in 1967; the rationale of the collection was to allow the writers to take on themes and subjects that would be unacceptable to most sf magazines

An emotive illustration by Bruce Pennington

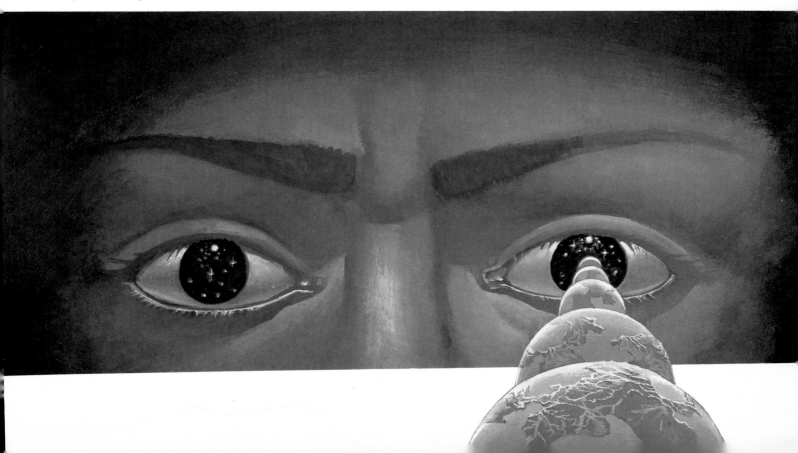

Blocking out the roar of the rocketships? An unintentionally symbolic painting

The quality of the actual fiction was erratic. Although the short stories were often self-defeatingly introspective and unapproachable, the longer works were more successful. A listing of the novels alone reads like a survey of the most memorable works of the late 1960s.

Camp Concentration by Thomas Disch was the first serial as such; this symbolic and philosophical novel about the enhancement of human intelligence by use of a drug derived from the syphilis virus was probably the best single work *New Worlds* published in this period. At the same time as the serialization of this novel, *New Worlds* was publishing some of the stories by Brian Aldiss that eventually became *Barefoot in the Head*. Aldiss' *An Age* (later retitled *Cryptozoic!*) was serialized. A long extract was published from John Brunner's *Stand on Zanzibar*. Norman Spinrad's *Bug Jack Barron* – a realistic and cynical novel about manipulation by the media – provided *New Worlds* with a famous controversy; because of some explicit language in Spinrad's novel, two major British distributors refused to handle the magazine, and a Question was asked in Parliament about why public money was subsidizing 'pornography'. Michael Moorcock's Jerry Cornelius novel, *A Cure for Cancer*, was also run as a serial.

Jerry Cornelius, perhaps the most famous of Moorcock's fictional creations, and hero or anti-hero of four of his novels, became the ideographic protagonist of *New Worlds*. In Cornelius was represented the laid-back *New Worlds* response to the 1960s. The character, who at different times and in different places could be all things to all men, was 'borrowed' by several other writers, including Norman Spinrad, Brian Aldiss and M. John Harrison, who wrote Jerry Cornelius adventures of their own.

Some of the individual short stories were excellent. *New Worlds* published the award-winning 'Time Considered as a Helix of Semi-Precious Stones' by Samuel Delany, and 'A Boy and His Dog' by Harlan Ellison. There were two new writers issues, which introduced, amongst others, Robert Holdstock, Barry Bowes, Graham Charnock, M. John Harrison and Marek Obtulowicz. Other regular contributors included John Sladek, Dr Christopher Evans, J. G. Ballard, Pamela Zoline, Michael Butterworth, Langdon R. Jones, Hilary Bailey, Giles Gordon, James Sallis, Harvey Jacobs, Leo Zorin, Ian Watson, Chris Lockesley, and the poets George Macbeth and D. M. Thomas.

The last issue of *New Worlds* in magazine format (No. 201, *March 1971*) was published for subscribers only, and was dedicated to 'that Kindly Conqueress Queen: Good Taste'. It contained only one story, a delightfully sentimental comedy called 'Feathers From the Wings of an Angel' by Thomas Disch.

Now that the New Wave, as a positive and aggressive movement, is no longer with us, it is possible to try to assess its worth.

There were undoubtedly some excellent stories and novels written as a result of enlightened editorial encouragement. New writers were brought to print, when in another time they might not have been; established authors were encouraged to expand and experiment with their art.

At the same time, it is true to say that much of the New Wave was unsuccessful.

This was not because the work was obscure or difficult, but because obscure and difficult writing can too easily be used to disguise a poverty of imagination or skill. The New Wave quickly developed a vocabulary of clichés, in particular the use of 'experimental' typography to fill space, and an elliptical form of storytelling in which the burden of maintaining continuity was passed from the author to the reader.

In addition, there was always a danger, often realized, that the New Wave itself would become a writing idiom, so that young or inexperienced writers would see obscurity and experimentation as ends in themselves.

One can also ask: where are the New Wave writers today?

Authors' names have been scattered throughout this article, because in their day they were, in a sense, representative of what was going on. But how many have shown staying power, how many have become authors in their own right?

Six names dominated the New Wave, three British and three American. They were: Aldiss, Ballard, Moorcock, Disch, Delany and Zelazny.

Aldiss and Ballard were already well known before the New Wave as such got under way. They were formed writers, and the New Wave period brought forth perhaps some of their best and most controversial work, but the suspicion has to remain

that they were going this way already.

Moorcock, like no other writer of the time, applied the message of his editorials to his own writing and became the better for it. This perhaps tells us no more than that all literary polemic is basically autobiographical.

Disch, Delany and Zelazny, although first published during the New Wave period, do not seem to be products of a literary movement; each writer clearly has a unique talent, one which would have found acceptance within the established idiom, though probably, at first, for the wrong reasons. (Delany is a case in point. His first eight novels were successfully published by an American paperback house renowned for juvenile space-opera.)

All of these writers are today going their own way, and each is successful on his own terms.

Of the others, Ursula Le Guin, M. John Harrison, Keith Roberts, Ian Watson and Robert Holdstock have become novelists in their own right, but of these only Harrison was closely identified with the spirit of the New Wave movement. Peter Tate and Hilary Bailey have published novels; David Masson's stories have been collected. Michael Butterworth has written novels in collaboration with Moorcock, and *Space 1999* novelizations.

But as for the rest, many of whom seemed genuinely promising and talented at the time . . . what? Was theirs a talent that could only be brought to bloom by certain editorial green fingers, and one that withered away when the hothouse was demolished?

It is wrong to particularize writers; the benefit of the New Wave lies elsewhere.

What Moorcock and the other advocates of the New Wave achieved was a release from the dependence on the orthodox idioms of the pulp magazines. These were themselves an abstraction originally: *Amazing Stories* and the other pulps had extracted a type of story from general fiction (the type epitomized, in those days, by the work of H. G. Wells and Jules Verne) and made a commercial virtue of it. The rest followed from there, with imitation piling upon imitation, and the genre inventing unwritten rules for itself, and becoming ever more closed about itself and hostile to the outside world.

The New Wave was an attempt to restore a sense of perspective to speculative fiction.

In this it was a success. Today many novels are being published under the sf label which, ten years ago, would have seemed impossibly avant garde. *Crash* by J. G. Ballard and *Dhalgren* by Samuel Delany are two excellent examples.

But is this enough? The idiom of traditional science fiction remains untouched; the ghetto mentality still exists. The New Wave movement lost its momentum in the late 1960s, became a sub-category within the sf category, and the rebellion was quelled by being absorbed into the system.

The motives behind the New Wave remain as valid today as they were in 1964, when Moorcock took over *New Worlds*. The idiom of science fiction is no less strong; now it is simply broader in its scope. How much longer need the idiom continue? That will probably be the next revolution.

The Final Programme was the first of Moorcock's Jerry Cornelius novels

Bruce Pennington's cover painting for Christopher Priest's novel *Indoctrinaire*

yesterday today

Malcolm Edwards

The horizons of science fiction broadened enormously in the 1970s.
At the one extreme *Star Wars*, and the continuing and flourishing
pulp component of sf ; at the other extreme young writers are
bringing a heightened literary awareness to the field of
imaginative and speculative fiction. Commercially and
intellectually sf is growing alarmingly fast.

and tomorrow

Recent advertisements for the Science Fiction Book Club in the USA offer two books with the warning 'explicit scenes and language may be offensive to some' – a formulation devised at the time of *Dangerous Visions*, the book which became the cornerstone of the Old Wave/New Wave controversy in America in the 1960s. The intention was presumably to protect those who wished to preserve the traditional purity of science fiction, who believed that the outspokenness of some 1960s writers constituted a threat to their precious bodily fluids. Yet the two novels so labelled in 1977 are *The Ophiuchi Hotline* by John Varley and *Mindbridge* by Joe Haldeman: respectively the first and the second novels by young writers each of whom has been labelled the 'new Heinlein' by some of his admirers, each of whom is said to embody many of the traditional virtues of sf – strong plotting, solid extrapolation, good storytelling.

Clearly, sf has changed considerably in the last decade. The change has been beneficial – indeed, necessary if sf is to claim serious attention as adult literature. Restrictions, largely the product of commercial magazine requirements (and of editors reared on those requirements), have been lifted; it would now seem ridiculous to group together writers who have in common only their disinclination to conform to the transitional, straitjacketed requirements of pulp sf, under such a specious label as 'New Wave'.

Dismantling the 'New Wave'

Those writers once closely associated with the New Wave – one thinks at once of Aldiss, Ballard, Delany, Disch, Ellison, Moorcock, Spinrad and Zelazny – now seem as disparate as any group of writers could be. In the 1960s the names of Delany and Zelazny in particular were closely linked, almost as though they were two manifestations of a single larger entity. Now their works have nothing apparently in common. Roger Zelazny has become notably less ambitious, alternating slices of his immense fantasy epic, the *Amber* series *(Nine Princes in Amber, The Guns of Avalon, Sign of the Unicorn, The Hand of Oberon)*, with quite conventionally-told sf adventures *(Today We Choose Faces, To Die in Italbar, Doorways in the Sand)*. The closest he has come, in the 1970s, to the writer he promised to be in the mid-1960s, is his imaginative, Jack Vance-influenced fantasy, *Jack of Shadows 1971*.

Samuel Delany, by contrast, has been nothing if not ambitious, producing after years in gestation the immense *Dhalgren*, which may claim the dubious distinction of being the longest sf novel ever published. His obsession with minute exactitude of description (which accounts, in part, for the book's length) is here carried to almost surreal extremes; *Dhalgren* is a novel which makes intense demands on the reader. It has nevertheless become something of an instant cult classic since its publication in 1975, selling over half a million copies.

Brian Aldiss and J. G. Ballard both had well established individual reputations before the New Wave briefly claimed them as part of a movement. This was always misleading, in Aldiss's case

particularly: for example, the greatly-undervalued *Report on Probability A* was written long before Moorcock's *New Worlds* came on the scene; what arose in the late 1960s was a climate in which it could be published. Aldiss continued in the 1970s to be one of the least predictable of sf writers, restlessly exploring new territory in each novel, refusing to be shackled by the traditional reader's expectation that an author's next book should be much like his last. Little of his recent work is readily classifiable as science fiction. It includes the second novel of his *Hand-Reared Boy* sequence, *A Soldier Erect 1971*, in many respects his best novel to date, outspoken, funny, and thoroughly convincing in its evocation of soldiering in the Far East during WW II; *Frankenstein Unbound 1973*, a sort of literary by-product of his sf history, *Billion Year Spree*, creating a fantasy world in which a modern American can travel back in time and meet not only Mary Shelley, but also the characters of her seminal novel; and *The Malacia Tapestry 1976*, an anachronistic historical fantasy, set in an imaginary city-state somewhere in the Balkans. What informs all these novels is Aldiss's imaginative exuberance and *joie de vivre* (qualities which become a rather overstrained jollity in his 1974 *The Eighty-Minute Hour*), though there are also tinges of an underlying darker version.

J.G. Ballard: the alienation king

Ballard, who might be said to have become the Messiah of the New Wave in Britain, as Moorcock was its Prophet, returned to comparatively conventional novels (which still, however, conveyed the familiar Ballardian obsessions). The 'condensed novels' and other experiments of the 1960s were put behind him, while his psychosexual fantasy *Crash 1973* seemed to exorcize his fixation with car accidents. *Concrete Island 1974* neatly and convincingly inverted the Robinson Crusoe story, writing of a man marooned on a traffic island surrounded by motorways. *High-Rise 1975* was clearly a return to the territory of Ballard's early psychological disaster novels; in this instance the breakdown of society is confined to a single large apartment block where the services fail. In Ballard's recent novels it is no longer necessary for the whole world to experience a disaster, as in *The Drowned World*, *The Drought*, etc; the occurrence can now be confined to a single person, or a single tower block, while the rest of the world carries on oblivious and indifferent.

In one sense this can be taken to mean that Ballard is no longer writing sf. However, that would suppose a very mechanistic definition of sf, one couched entirely in terms of externalities. Ballard, like Aldiss (and, as we shall see, like Disch, Moorcock and others), no longer writes fiction which would be recognizable as science fiction to, say, readers of *Astounding Science Fiction* in the 1940s (as Ballard's earlier works, however heretical, *were* recognizable). Without being drawn into attempting a general definition of sf (a singularly futile pursuit, as has been amply shown by the many writers who have tried), one can look at this basically in two ways: either these writers have abandoned sf and are now writing other things (whatever those things may be),

or they have instead widened the horizons of sf, given us a less restrictive view of what sf is and what it can do.

The latter approach is surely the more satisfactory, especially if science fiction is viewed as being something more than just another category of commercial fiction, analogous to the western or the romance. In novels like *High-Rise* we see a refinement of Ballard's long-recorded insistence that *inner* space rather than outer space is the most fruitful subject matter for sf. Another factor in Ballard's writing which has been more widely recognized in recent years is his wit (something which Aldiss had pointed out many years ago, to general lack of response). This is a further result of his adoption of more personalized disasters: no one could miss the inherent irony of the situations outlined in *The Concrete Island* and *High-Rise*. His attitude towards sf seems to have mellowed over the years: whereas in the 1960s he wrote scathing reviews for the *Guardian*, he now writes an informed and appreciative column for the *New Statesman*.

Disch, Spinrad, Ellison and Moorcock similarly went their individual ways in the 1970s. Thomas Disch wrote *334*, a very accomplished novel set in an overcrowded New York of the early 21st century (the title refers to the single apartment block in which all the chief characters reside, although the affinities to *High-Rise* end there). Disch also enjoyed considerable success with a delicious parody of the

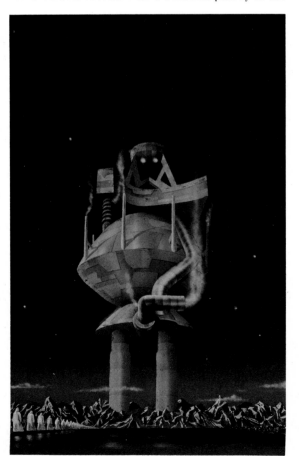

Painting by Colin Hay for John Sladek's *The Steam Driven Boy*

Victorian gothic romance, *Clara Reeve*, published under the pseudonym 'Leonie Hargrave'.

Spinrad, too, had a commercial success outside sf, with a Hollywood bestseller, *Passing Through the Flames*; but he has also established himself as a fine and imaginative sf writer, closer to the mainstream of the genre than his New Wave compatriots, with such stories as 'The Lost Continent' and 'Riding the Torch'. *The Iron Dream 1972* is one of the oddest and best sf novels of the 1970s, a genuine *tour de force* creating the science fiction novel Adolf Hitler might have written if the Nazi Party had failed and he had emigrated to the USA and become a pulp writer! Apart from presenting Hitler's novel (*Lord of the Swastika*, what else?), *The Iron Dream* is also, in the introductions and commentaries which accompany Hitler's work, one of the few notable explorations of the difficult, but rewarding, subject of parallel worlds and alternative histories. Until the 1970s, sf had produced just three worthwhile novels on this subject – Ward Moore's *Bring the Jubilee*, Philip Dick's *The Man in the High Castle* and Keith Roberts's *Pavane*. Now we have three more: *The Iron Dream*, Harry Harrison's exuberant *A Transatlantic Tunnel, Hurrah!* and Kingsley Amis's long-awaited first sf novel, *The Alteration*.

Michael Moorcock has continued to enjoy enormous popular success with his numerous sword-and-sorcery novels, in which, with the passing of time, the various series and characters have begun to intersect with one another, until they now allegedly form a single vast cycle that also encompasses virtually all his other work. It is difficult to tell whether or not this is meant at all seriously, or whether it is a subtle marketing gambit (read one Moorcock book and – in order to finish the series – you've got to read them all). In 1977 he finally published the last volume of his Jerry Cornelius tetralogy, *The Condition of Muzak*. This is probably his best novel to date, ambitious, densely-written and accomplished, far removed (in achievement if not intent) from the first Cornelius novel, *The Final Programme*. The tetralogy provides a good index of Moorcock's development as a writer over the decade it has taken to complete – a factor, one suspects, which has made it harder for him to finish satisfactorily. Moorcock's more serious work has also included the delicate, ironic and decadent fantasies of the 'Dancers at the End of Time' – sf as Max Beerbohm might have written it.

Moorcock has frequently disavowed any interest in sf, and said that he doesn't think of himself as an sf writer in any sense and doesn't like sf; Harlan Ellison similarly, but more strenuously, has striven to have the label removed from his work. There is some irony in this, because Ellison's stories have continued to collect sf awards at regular intervals in the 1970s; only Fritz Leiber has won more. His collection *Deathbird Stories 1975* contains many of his best stories, including the two Hugo winners 'The Deathbird' and 'Adrift Just Off the Islets of Langerhans: Latitude 38° 54′ N, Longitude 77° 00′ 13″ W'. Ellison is a restlessly energetic writer, initiating projects in all directions. He followed up his monumental *Dangerous Visions* anthology with a doubly-huge successor *Again, Dangerous Visions*

1972, which like its predecessor contained award-winning stories and novels (Ursula Le Guin's *The Word for World is Forest* and Joanna Russ's 'When it Changed') but did not attract the same intensity of interest, perhaps because blockbusting anthologies which aim to smash down ghetto walls and trample on taboos are, by their very nature, unrepeatable experiences. A third book in the series, *The Last Dangerous Visions*, has been promised since the second volume appeared (it was to have followed six months later). In 1973 the American fanzine *The Alien Critic* published a letter from Ellison outlining the contents of the book, which then stood at nearly 450,000 words of fiction (*Dhalgren* would look puny by comparison) plus an estimated 100,000 or more words of introductions. Since then the book has continued, reportedly, to grow and has continued not to appear, gaining a reputation as science fiction's very own *Flying Dutchman* (or Harlan Ellison's personal albatross).

Ellison has also gained a reputation for excoriating criticism of science fiction fans and their shortcomings. If he has been their scourge, their ogre, in the 1970s, has been the unlikely figure of Barry Malzberg. Malzberg has managed to attract to himself, seemingly, all the oppobrium which in the 1960s was parcelled out among a number of renegade writers. His 'crime' has been to write very prolifically books which are not very easy to read (in the sf world you can do one or the other, but not both!). It is true that there are repetitive elements in Malzberg's books – the assassination of John F. Kennedy and the NASA space programme, to name the two most obvious – but at his best, in novels like *Beyond Apollo 1972* and *The Men Inside 1973*,

Malzberg shows an original vision, sustained with paranoid intensity. His novel *Herovit's World 1973*, about the disintegrating mind of a hack science fiction writer, is both funny and penetrating.

Lately, Malzberg has been making a somewhat ostentatious farewell to sf, declaring in a magazine article that he will no longer write sf, then popping up a little later in another magazine to say the same thing, in case some people hadn't noticed . . . and so on. His announcements carry something of the same air of finality as Frank Sinatra's retirements, but there is no reason to doubt that he means what he says. He is not the only writer to declare himself fed up with sf, with the lack of perception of many of the most vociferous critics within the field and the neglect of good writing. Another case, and in many ways, as Malzberg would readily admit, a more interesting and disturbing one, is that of the novelist Robert Silverberg.

It is possible, looking back over sf in the 1970s, to single out two dominant figures, uniquely part of this period and pervasively influential within it. This is not to say that there are no other writers of comparable stature, but for one reason or another nobody else casts quite such a giant shadow as Ursula Le Guin and Robert Silverberg. Of the two, Silverberg is perhaps the less obvious choice. His work is the subject of some critical dispute; he is accused of being a cold, remote writer, too facile by half; it is alleged that his many years of prolific hack writing have made writing fatally too easy and straightforward for him.

There are elements of truth in these charges. On the other hand, and weighing powerfully against the criticisms, there is the astonishing range, grasp and

Barry Malzberg's *Beyond Apollo*, a very controversial novel, deals with the first flight to Venus, and the insanity it induces in the Captain of the vessel

The illustration for Robert Silverberg's *Those Who Watch*, in which a UFO crashes on earth and the humanoid crew are aided, and ultimately loved, by their human helpers

The amazing painting for Jack Vance's *The Anome*

sheer *amount* of his work. The only sf precedents, in terms of quantity *and* quality, are Robert Heinlein in the period 1939–1941 and Philip Dick around 1964–1966. Yet Heinlein was not so prolific, nor was his work, outstanding though it was by the then-prevailing standards of pulp sf, of comparable literary standard; while Dick, superb as his novels of that period were (they include *Martian Time-Slip, Dr Bloodmoney, The Penultimate Truth* and *The Three Stigmata of Palmer Eldritch* plus half a dozen others) did not show the same range as Silverberg: he was obsessively, brilliantly, returning to the same preoccupations.

Silverberg first marked himself as a serious sf writer of note with the publication in 1967 of his novel *Thorns* and his long story (later expanded into a novel) 'Hawksbill Station'. *Thorns* was a jagged, barbed piece of work, establishing themes of pain and alienation which were to become familiar Silverberg territory; 'Hawksbill Station' was the first of a number of stories re-examining the idea of time travel. His work continued to develop in the late 1960s, most notably in two brilliantly accomplished short stories, 'Passengers' and 'Sundance'; his fecundity was already remarkable but his artistry, for the most part, was still suspect. He was indeed a little too facile, a little too glib, entertaining and well-wrought though novels like *The Masks of Time, Nightwings* and *To Live Again* undoubtedly were.

In 1970–1972 he hit his stride, publishing no less than eight novels, all of them worthy of serious attention: *Downward to the Earth 1970, Tower of Glass 1970, A Time of Changes 1971, The World Inside 1971, Son of Man 1971, The Second Trip* serialized in 1971, *Dying Inside 1972* and *The Book of Skulls 1972*. He also produced such short stories as the Nebula Award winning 'Good News from the Vatican' *1971* and 'When We Went to See the End of the World' *1972*. Even the least successful of them have many things to be said in their favour: *The World Inside*, for instance, is entirely too diagrammatic to succeed as a novel, yet it presents a telling scenario of a world come to terms with unlimited population growth; while *A Time of Changes*, in most respects a thoroughly traditional excursion into Jack Vance territory, conjuring up a colourfully odd human society on another world, is at least a compellingly readable work which (perhaps because of its greater conventionality) won Silverberg another Nebula – the only major sf award any of his novels have received.

The Second Trip is worth also singling out, if only because it is Silverberg's 'forgotten' novel. Appearing amidst many other Silverberg titles it was entirely missed by the critics (H. W. Hall's massive *Science Fiction Book Review Index* does not record a single review in any major sf publication) and has not been reprinted. Yet it is one of Silverberg's most compelling novels, despite some moral ambiguity in the treatment, telling of two personalities battling for control of a single body in a future where persistent major criminals have their minds erased and new personalities built in their place.

The Book of Skulls and *Dying Inside* are Silverberg's best novels to date; both gave rise to arguments about whether or not he was still writing sf – arguments in some cases which made it appear that this was more important than whether or not

the work of a number of others writers – most evidently Gregory Benford (in his short stories) and Barry Malzberg in the USA, and Robert Holdstock in Britain. The otherwise great disparities between these writers are further testimony to Silverberg's range.

Ursula Le Guin's career began quietly, uninsistently, so that it came as some surprise when she emerged as a mature, skilled writer with *A Wizard of Earthsea 1968* and *The Left Hand of Darkness 1969*. Since those twin successes her popularity and stature have grown and grown, until she has (no doubt reluctantly) become a kind of touchstone, a symbol of sf's potential quality. Not only does the sf community recognize how good she is, everyone else recognizes it too. In fact the 1970s have not been especially productive for her (although she has never, admittedly, been a prolific writer). In 1971 and 1972 she published the concluding volumes of her Earthsea trilogy, *The Tombs of Atuan* and *The Farthest Shore*. Ostensibly children's books, the Earthsea novels, like all the best children's literature, are equally satisfying to adults. *The Farthest Shore*, in particular, is as accomplished a fantasy novel as has been published for many years, and not at all the light reading one might expect from a book intended for children; 1972 also saw the publication of her short novel *The Word for World is Forest*, an indictment of imperialist exploitation which also creates a fascinating alien culture in which dreaming – seen as an equally valid reality as waking – plays an important part.

Her major work of the 1970s, though, is *The Dispossessed 1974*. Subtitled 'an ambiguous utopia', this long novel attempts to create and give life to a society based on anarchist principles (as outlined by Paul Goodman, Kropotkin and others), and to contrast it with other societies more familiar to us. This is a delicate and difficult undertaking, full of fatal pitfalls for any writer with a tendency to moralize; Le Guin manages to evade almost all of these nimbly, largely because she does not attempt to gloss over the potential frailties of her 'utopia'. Most importantly of all, though, it is not a tract: it is a novel about very real people. Moreover one of them, Shevek, is a theoretical physicist, and the theoretical physics we see him working at is some of the most convincing extrapolated science in any sf novel. Small wonder, then, that *The Dispossessed* (like *The Left Hand of Darkness* before it) carried off both the Hugo and the Nebula Awards.

Although it is a facile generalization to make, Le Guin also exemplifies another phenomenon largely of the 1970s – a major woman sf writer. It is not difficult to see why the 'boys' own' ethos of the pulp magazines attracted few women writers, and those who were present often had suitably ambiguous names (Leigh Brackett, C. L. Moore). Now that situation no longer exists, it was to be expected that more women would be attracted by the potential of the sf medium. They include such names as Anne McCaffrey, Marta Randall, Pamela Sargent and Josephine Saxton. Kate Wilhelm has established a

they were any good. *The Book of Skulls*, about a quartet of college students in search of a means of immortality which may or may not be genuine, is the more doubtful case, but only in the very rigid terms we rejected earlier. *Dying Inside*, however, is a classic exploration of a major sf notion – what the experience of telepathy would be like, particularly for a lone telepath in our society. The fact that it takes much of the form of a straightforward New York Jewish novel about loss of potency (with the diminution of telepathic ability substituting for the male menopause) does not make it any the less effective. Both novels are powerfully written and convincingly characterized; both are literary, yet immensely readable. Both are very good sf novels which are also very good novels.

Silverberg's later work has not quite matched these heights, although *The Stochastic Man 1975*, in some ways similar to *Dying Inside*, with precognition replacing telepathy, comes close. His only other novel since 1972 is *Shadrach in the Furnace 1976*, his longest book to date, which while satisfying is not, by Silverberg's own standards, outstanding. He has also produced a number of fine short stories and novellas, most notably 'Schwartz Between the Galaxies', *1973* and 'Born With the Dead' *1974*; these have been collected into several books.

Shadrach in the Furnace is avowedly Silverberg's last work of fiction; he claims now to have retired completely from any sort of fiction writing. One hopes he will eventually recant: although he has had a long career he is still a comparatively young man, and his best work should still be ahead of him. Already, though, his influence can be seen in some of

formidable reputation for her many stylish stories in *Orbit*, while Joanna Russ contributed one of the most convincing of all telepathy novels – the one which perhaps goes farthest in attempting to show what the experience of telepathy might be like – *And Chaos Died 1970*. Her later work was more polemical, culminating in *The Female Man 1975*, possibly the first overtly feminist sf novel.

Dwindling magazines and doomed anthologies

Traditionally, the sf magazine has been the initial outlet for short stories, which may later be re-used in collections or anthologies; throughout the 1970s the magazines continued much as before. *Worlds of If* was merged with *Galaxy* after each had enjoyed a quarter of a century of independent existence, otherwise the long-established magazines all survived – *Amazing, Analog, F&SF, Fantastic*. New efforts came and – sadly – went: *Cosmos, Science Fiction Monthly, Vertex* and *Vortex*. Still, by the end of 1977 two new titles – *Galileo* and *Isaac Asimov's Science Fiction Magazine* – each had a foothold.

Painting by Tony Roberts

A different approach was the anthology of all-new stories; a few had been attempted previously, but not until the 1960s, with Ted Carnell's *New Writings in SF* and Damon Knight's *Orbit*, did the idea really catch hold. By 1971, the number of competing series had greatly proliferated: there was Terry Carr's *Universe*, Samuel Delany and Marilyn Hacker's *Quark/*, Harry Harrison's *Nova*, Robert Hoskins's *Infinity*, Silverberg's *New Dimensions* and Moorcock's *New Worlds Quarterly* (the magazine *New Worlds* reincarnated in paperback form). It was persuasively argued that the sf magazines were now out of date (none of them except *Analog* could be said to be flourishing) and that the anthology series, widely distributed in paperback, would take their place.

But it did not happen. For whatever reason – perhaps because they were in competition with other anthologs rather than with the magazines, and their line-ups of untried stories, often by new and little-known writers, were not sufficiently appealing – the anthology series did not prosper. Of the eight listed above, only *Universe* and *New Dimensions* survived to the end of 1977, and they had both had to change publishers to keep going. True, other series appeared to replace those that died, such as Judy-Lynn Del Rey's *Stellar* and Peter Weston's *Andromeda* – but others still, like David Gerrold's *Emphasis*, died almost before they had been born.

As well as the series of original anthologies, there were innumerable single volumes. Some of these had rationales behind them; more often, though, they were just one more set of previously unpublished stories. With nothing particular to commend them, it is not surprising that most of them sold poorly. The worst culprit in this boom was the editor Roger Elwood, who at one time claimed contracts for over 70 different anthologies. One consequence of the boom in anthologies was that for a while the market for sf writers was greatly widened, which was a help to less-established writers. However, although a few writers have come into prominence largely, in the first instance, for their work in various of the anthology series – Gene Wolfe and Kate Wilhelm in *Orbit*, Gardner Dozois in *Orbit* and *New Dimensions*, Barrington Bayley in *New Worlds Quarterly* – nobody has emerged with any distinctiveness from the Elwood anthologies.

It is surprising that so few sf anthologies – and virtually no original anthologies – have tried to define and examine current themes of particular interest. Most reprint anthologies are built around notions – *Great Science Fiction About Corn Flakes* – rather than themes. There were exceptions, such as Roger Elwood and Virginia Kidd's anthology of ecological sf, *Saving Worlds*, and Stephen Goldin's collection of stories about aliens, *The Alien Condition*, both of which appeared in 1973.

Although the range of sf at any moment is quite wide, there are inevitably at different times themes which seem particularly to occupy the minds of sf writers. In the early 1970s, ecology – man in relation to his environment – was an obvious example. No better example could be given of the way sf, for all that it may be set in the future, actually reflects the concerns and attitudes of the period in which it is written. With pollution destroying river and sea life, and widespread use of insecticides disrupting the ecological balance on land, how were we to survive famine, particularly with the population still growing unchecked? What Dave Kyle might have termed the 'food and weather milleniums' (*sic*) were upon us; how would we cope?

Sf writers diligently applied themselves to these and other questions. The greatest compendium of likely disaster was John Brunner's *The Sheep Look Up 1972*, which presented very nearly the worst of all possible worlds. It also tended to the shrilly polemical, as did many stories of this theme. Two telling stories to emerge from this period were Silverberg's darkly ironic 'When We Went to See the End of the World' and Spinrad's powerful evocation of a decayed future America, 'The Lost Continent'.

Astronomical theories and possible worlds

New developments and speculations in astronomical and cosmological subjects have always been a fruitful and central area for sf writers. If there is a difference in approach in the 1970s it is perhaps that they are no longer the exclusive preserve of the hardcore sf writers. Some of the most original and fascinating stories along these lines have been written by authors notably lacking in scientific bias. One fine example is Christopher Priest's *Inverted World 1974*, which presents a world shaped like an inverted hyperbola, stretching to infinity at its axes. Another, even stranger book is John Crowley's first novel, *The Deep 1975*. One of the most extraordinary first novels in modern sf, *The Deep* is a highly-formalized fantasy, by James Branch Cabell out of *Macbeth*, set in a strange world which its inhabitants believe to be in the shape of a saucer on top of a pillar, at the base of which – in the Deep – is curled the monster Leviathan. A third story worthy of mention is 'The Pit' by D. West, from the *Gollancz/Sunday Times Best SF Stories*, where the characters' cosmological theory is that they live in a world which is a bubble of air in a universe which otherwise is solid rock. In each of these stories, the thrust of the narrative is the gradual revelation of the true, as opposed to the perceived, situation; in none of them is the answer simple or predictable.

Black holes are a fine example of an astronomical theory widely extrapolated into science fiction. Before Black Holes became popular other large, collapsing stars had featured in several stories, such as Larry Niven's 'Neutron Star' and Poul Anderson's 'Kyrie'. Niven won his first Hugo Award for 'Neutron Star' and later collected another for 'The Hole Man', a story which described quantum Black Holes (a theoretical prediction which we now know would be unstable, so swiftly can science leave sf behind). Other stories which feature Black Holes include Ian Watson's 'The Event Horizon' and Frederik Pohl's *Gateway*, while the possibility that they might provide a means of faster than light travel has begun to be exploited in a number of works, including Joe Haldeman's *The Forever War*.

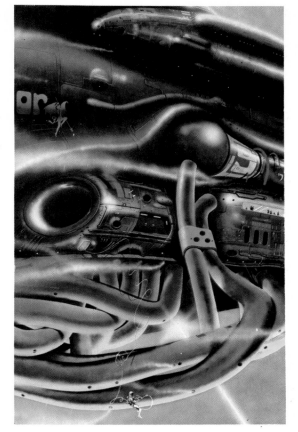

Niven won another Hugo for *Ringworld 1970*, a novel based on the Dyson Sphere concept. The scientist Freeman Dyson has suggested that very advanced technological civilizations would increase their living space, and make maximum use of their main energy source, their sun, by breaking up the large outer planets of their solar systems and using the matter to build a shell round their suns. Niven's Ringworld is a less ambitious project, though still grandiose enough: a world in the shape of giant hoop, girdling its sun. The problem with Niven's novel is that, having created this huge artifact, he was unable to think of very much to do with it; somehow, for all that his characters wander around on it, being duly impressed, its size is never properly conveyed to the reader.

By contrast, Bob Shaw's *Orbitsville 1975* not only goes a step further than Niven in tackling the concept of an entire Dyson sphere, but also manages to devise a story which makes the concept come alive. In the last decade, since the publication of his first novel, *The Two-Timers*, in 1968, Shaw has become one of the most reliable and enjoyable sf writers, thoroughly expert and utterly unpretentious. His work is a happy marriage of careful, logical extrapolation (which always yields unexpected, yet inevitable twists) and convincing characterization. He is now the author of a dozen novels, among the best of which are *Other Days, Other Eyes 1972*, in which he develops the concept of 'slow glass' – glass which greatly retards the passage of light – first introduced in his short story 'Light of Other Days', and *A Wreath of Stars 1976*, which introduces the startling notion of an invisible anti-neutrino world occupying the same space as Earth.

Painting by Joe Petagno

Clones and aliens

Cloning, the artificial production from a single sexually-born individual of one or more genetically identical 'twins', has been another popular (and at times almost pervasive) subject of 1970s sf. At least two popularly successful novels not published as sf have taken cloning as their subject: *Joshua, Son of None* by Nancy Freedman and *The Boys from Brazil* by Ira Levin. Ben Bova's *The Multiple Man* is another book aimed at the same wide audience. The impact of these books depends partly on surprising the reader with the mere concept of clones; the 'purer' sf treatments hinge more on the psychological and metaphorical implications, using the idea of cloning as a method of examining the nature of identity. Stories written on or around the subject include, among many others, *Clone* by Richard Cowper, *Imperial Earth* by Arthur Clarke, 'Nine Lives' by Ursula Le Guin and *Cloned Lives* by Pamela Sargent. The two most satisfying treatments, however, are Kate Wilhelm's *Where Late The Sweet Birds Sang 1976* and Gene Wolfe's *The Fifth Head of Cerberus 1972*. Wilhelm's novel, a Hugo Award winner, argues that clones, lacking individuality, would ultimately (and fatally) lack both creativity and adaptability. It is a quiet, and very well written novel, whose weakness is that its arguments are stated rather than convincingly dramatized: Wilhelm sets herself an immensely difficult task in attempting to create a society of clones, and doesn't quite bring it off.

A still more subtle approach, which uses cloning (in its title segment) as one aspect of a more general examination of identity is, *The Fifth Head of Cerberus*, undoubtedly one of the most complex, engrossing and rewarding sf books of the 1970s. Wolfe is a very careful and precise writer, who never spells things out more than he absolutely needs to, and in some of his stories this results in a maddening (but perfectly-wrought) obliquity. In his best work, which also includes 'The Island of Dr Death', its Nebula Award winning sequel 'The Death of Dr Island', and 'The Hero as Werwolf', he has shown himself to be among the very best modern sf writers.

The setting of *The Fifth Head of Cerberus* is a distant twin-planet system, where French settlers have established a fascinating, decadent society. On one of the worlds an intelligent alien species is said to exist (though officially they are extinct), capable of changing their shape and passing for human. The novel thus confronts (in a thoroughly unclichéd manner) one of the great enduring themes of sf, and one which has been revitalized in the 1970s: the nature of the alien and, by induction, the nature of man on the planet Earth.

The growing influence in sf of the 'soft' sciences – anthropology, psychology, sociology – has been particularly evident in the way authors have treated aliens. This does not mean that they create an alien species simply by transposing some little-known terrestrial culture to another planet (as may have been the case in the 1950s in, for example, the sf stories of anthropologist Chad Oliver); it means, rather, a wider understanding of the variety of human life which enables writers to create non-human beings which are something more than liberal Americans (or illiberal Russians) with exotic physiology. This can be seen especially in the work of such writers as Michael Bishop, Robert Holdstock, Ursula Le Guin and Ian Watson.

Even Isaac Asimov, who very rarely introduced alien species into his early work (largely to avoid either having to pander to or clash with John W. Campbell's xenophobia), developed a complex alien society in *The Gods Themselves 1972*. One of the most ambitious attempts to render a truly alien civilization is contained within *The Mote in God's Eye 1974*, by Larry Niven and Jerry Pournelle. Unfortunately, the novel in which it is embedded wastes hundreds of pages on imperial space navy adventures which would deter all but the most hardy readers. (It is, in fact, Horatio Hornblower in space, translated so faithfully that one almost expects each space ship to have a man lying in the bows, dangling a long chain to determine how many fathoms they are above the nearest planet.)

We have seen how those writers who in the 1960s were identified with the New Wave have asserted their individuality and largely prospered in the 1970s. What of the more traditional writers who had already established their reputations before the decade began? How have they fared?

Clifford Simak is one writer who has faded very noticeably. A leading figure in the late 1940s and early 1950s, he reestablished himself strongly in the

1960s with such novels as the Hugo winning *Way Station 1963*. However, from about 1968 his novels have become much more lightweight: they are gentle, often pleasantly nostalgic, recyclings of familiar Simakian tropes, and instantly forgettable. Poul Anderson began the decade strongly, publishing his best novel for some years in *Tau Zero 1970*, a taut extrapolation in the best tradition of hard core sf. He followed by carrying off the double of Hugo and Nebula awards two years running with his stories 'The Queen of Air and Darkness' and 'Goat Song' *1972*. Thereafter he has gone unaccountably into decline (at least temporarily), retreading familiar ground in his stories and rarely attacking any idea with the verve which makes him, at his best, one of sf's most potent storytellers.

Alfred Bester and Theodore Sturgeon, both of whom had been largely absent from sf for many years, both returned. Bester's novel *Extro 1975* was arresting in parts, confusing in others, an uneasy mixture of bravura effects and outright self-indulgence; it was as though Bester, trying to recapture the manic extravagance of his earlier successes, could not quite remember how the trick was done. His authentic touch was more evident in his story 'The Four Hour Fugue', which forms the basis of his forthcoming novel *Golem-100*. Sturgeon, sad to say, seemed even more out of touch: despite winning Hugo and Nebula Awards for 'Slow Sculpture' *1970*, his come-back made little impact. Other authors who returned, after shorter periods of general absence, included Algis Budrys, Frederik Pohl and Robert Sheckley. Sheckley had published a few short stories, which demonstrated a darker irony than was apparent in his earlier work; *Options 1975* was his first novel since 1968. It was another self-indulgent piece of work, full of crazy and authentically Sheckleyan scenes, but with a ramshackle, thoroughly stoned narrative structure. Budrys, on

the other hand, returned in triumph: his novel *Michaelmas 1977* was published to one of the most enthusiastic critical receptions ever afforded an sf novel. In this and other stories, Budrys has begun to map out a future world which includes very advanced techniques in holography and computer technology.

It is Pohl, though, who has made the greatest impact. Following a period of low productivity and indifferent success – his work in the 1960s seemed to prove only how much he missed his dead collaborator, C. M. Kornbluth – he has powerfully re-established his reputation. Ironically, while in published speeches and articles he has been scornful of those 'experimental' writing techniques classed as New Wave, for example the Dos Passos montage technique adopted by John Brunner in *Stand on Zanzibar*, he has shown no hesitation in embracing them himself when the occasion demands. Stories like 'The Gold at the Starbow's End' and 'We Purchased People' demonstrated his new potency, which bloomed fully in his novels *Man Plus 1976* and *Gateway 1977*. *Man Plus* is a plausible, realistic novel of biological engineering: a human is surgically adapted for life on Mars. Unusually, it gives consideration to the likely psychological effect on the volunteer thus transformed into a monster. *Gateway* is better still: again the focus is psychological, this time in an imaginative story of a highly dangerous method of space exploration using the leftover spaceships of a long-vanished alien species. *Gateway* is a long, richly detailed novel, its complex background effectively conveyed with the help of those very techniques Pohl decried in Brunner's novel. Happily, sf writers do not always practice what they preach.

Brunner himself has had an indifferent time in the 1970s. His most ambitious novel, *The Sheep Look Up*, attempted to give the same detailed exposition of the environmental crisis as *Stand on Zanzibar* had attempted for the population problem. It is a scaring piece of work, as Brunner obviously intended it to be, but unfortunately the polemic tends to unbalance the novel. His other major work, *The Shock-Wave Rider*, was inspired by Alvin Toffler's *Future Shock*. The rest of his 1970s novels are highly competent, commercial sf, extremely professional, but apparently written without his heart in them.

Two writers who maintained and even added to their high reputations were Philip Dick and Fritz Leiber. Dick, who was to the 1960s what Silverberg has been to the 1970s, has been much less prolific, but has produced two novels to rank among his best: *Flow My Tears, The Policeman Said 1973* and *A Scanner Darkly 1977*. Dick is now less prodigal with his invention, and his work has a darker, more bitter tone. The obsession with the nature of reality, and our inadequate perception of it, is still basic to his work; the disorienting perceptual shifts still surprise and delight, but the setting is more identifiably the present day, and Dick's anger and distress over elements of American society are communicated powerfully. The resultant novels are less intellectually stimulating than some of his previous work, but compensate for that with a great increase in emotional substance. As a novel, *A Scanner Darkly*

Illustration by David Bergen for *Babel 17* by Samuel R. Delany

Painting by Peter Goodfellow for Brunner's *The Sheep Look Up*

has flaws, but it is a deeply felt, deeply personal book. The extrapolation of the drug culture into the future, with the development of a drug so devastating that the narcotics agent/hero (himself ruined by it) is no longer capable of realizing that the junkie he is trailing is himself, is harrowing, compassionate and effective.

Leiber, whose first story was published in 1939, the year which also gave sf Asimov, Heinlein, Sturgeon and Van Vogt, has survived the passage of time better than anyone. His career has had its reverses, but his work has never stagnated; he has never fallen into repeating himself. Moreover, he has developed into the best stylist of his generation. His sword-and-sorcery saga, featuring the characters Fafhrd and the Gray Mouser, is completely unrivalled in that subgenre, while his sf remains quirky and original. He is now the most honoured writer in sf, with a total of six Hugo and three Nebula awards to his credit (two of each in the 1970s).

Many other writers have produced worthwhile stories, and it is impossible to give many of them more than a passing mention in the compass of this essay. They include Frank Herbert, who followed the disappointment of *Dune Messiah* with a much stronger conclusion to his trilogy in *Children of Dune 1976*, a difficult, mystical novel, but one which recaptured much of the original power of *Dune*. He also produced the excellent *Hellstrom's Hive 1973*, in which genetic engineering techniques are used to build a secret human colony on beehive lines. His *The Dosadi Experiment 1977* is another immensely complex book, very demanding on the reader, but ultimately rewarding, not least in its presentation of a great variety of convincing alien species. Wilson Tucker does not write much, but *The Year of the Quiet Sun 1970* is an excellent time-travel novel which deservedly won a retrospective John W. Campbell Memorial Award in 1976. Harry Harrison's *A Transatlantic Tunnel, Hurrah!* is an enjoyable exploration of the parallel worlds concept, written with typical verve, while *Skyfall 1976* was his contribution to a successful subgenre of the 1970s (both in and out of sf), the catastrophe novel. Jack Vance was as uncompromisingly individual as ever; *The Anome 1971* contains one of the most intricate and satisfying of the many peculiar societies he has devised.

Among British writers, D. G. Compton at one time seemed likely to establish himself as a leading figure: *The Continuous Katherine Mortenhoe 1974* was a fine novel of character which also developed an intriguing sf notion (of a TV reporter whose eyes *are* his camera). It followed several earlier successes. However, he has since fallen silent. Keith Roberts wrote what is likely to prove one of the most enduring sf novels of the 1960s in *Pavane*. His major work since then has been *The Chalk Giants 1974*, a tortuous, demanding, intermittently brilliant story cycle, ranging forward in time from a basic post-holocaust setting, its theme an exploration of guilt. Richard Cowper has advanced considerably since the 1960s. Some of his novels are basically slight and frivolous, but the best of them, in particular *The Twilight of Briareus 1974*, combine a concern for writing a good novel, with genuine characters and well-wrought prose, with the ability to develop a striking speculative notion. Like Compton, Cowper has no roots in the American (or British) pulp tradition which infuses so much sf, even today; if he is writing in any tradition it is that of Wells, Wyndham, Christopher. His stories, collected in *The Custodians 1976* have brought him deservedly (if belatedly) into prominence in the USA.

What happened to the supergiants?

The three giants of sf – Issac Asimov, Arthur Clarke and Robert Heinlein – became superstars in the 1970s. Asimov appeared in TV commercials; Clarke lectured American congressional committees; Heinlein's infrequent public appearance had a mystique reminiscent of Greta Garbo. As writers, though, they have not been particularly active. Asimov did publish *The Gods Themselves* in 1972, his first authentic sf novel for 15 years; it duly won both Hugo and Nebula Awards, as did his latest robot story, 'The Bicentennial Man' *1976*. However, his sf stories were only very occasional diversions from his steady, prolific output of non-fiction books on innumerable subjects. Heinlein's two novels, *I Will Fear No Evil 1970* and *Time Enough for Love 1973* were both very long and sold well; most critics, however, found them flaccid and verbose.

Clarke was rather more successful. His novel *Rendezvous With Rama 1973*, which also swept the awards, was his first since the huge success of *2001: A Space Odyssey*. Though the novel creaked in places, Clarke demonstrated his unique lucidity in describing Rama, a gigantic alien spacecraft which enters the Solar System. Of all sf writers, Clarke most genuinely evokes the 'sense of wonder' beloved of old sf fans. Much of the same quality is apparent in 'A Meeting With Medusa' *1971*, where strange life-forms are encountered in Jupiter's atmosphere. It was not so evident, however, in *Imperial Earth 1975*, although Clarke himself considers the novel his *magnum opus*.

Cover from Harry Harrison's *Skyfall*, a novel firmly in the tradition of the disaster novel – an orbiting spaceship, with a nuclear pile, begins to fall back to earth out of control; extrapolation of its decaying orbit shows it will strike an area of high population. Illustration by Tony Roberts

Asimov, Clarke and Heinlein all personify the growing commercial strength of sf – a phenomenon which has developed enormously in the wake of films like *2001* and cult novels such as *Dune* and *Stranger in a Strange Land*. Sf novels such as *Imperial Earth* and *Children of Dune* now feature prominently in bestseller lists, and draw from publishers advances which would have seemed fantastic in the 1960s.

On TV and in the cinema, sf subjects (although often not identified) as such are presented with increasing frequency. The best known TV programme is still *Star Trek* which maintains a fanatical following even though the programme was scrapped years ago. It is difficult to see just why this should be so: the programme itself is standard US series-fare, translated into space, its values as conventional as its storylines.

As the years have gone by, the *Star Trek* cult has grown in strength, despite the absence of new programmes. Conventions of *Star Trek* fans attracted five-figure attendances in the USA, dwarfing the largest science fiction conventions. Minor *Star Trek* performers developed whole new careers, making lucrative personal appearances at such jamborees. The spin-off industry was comparatively slow to develop, although books based on the series sold steadily; it really took off with the runaway success of *Star Trek Blueprints*, a set of engineering diagrams of the USS Enterprise and its equipment. Other equally arcane bestsellers followed. The logical consequence of this would have been a revival of the programme, but here there was a major stumbling block in the refusal of Leonard Nimoy to return to the key role of Mr Spock. He was fed up with the type-casting (his autobiography was emphatically titled *I Am Not Spock*) and insisted he had hung up his pointed ears for good. A cartoon series was attempted, but proved embarrassingly poor.

At the time *Star Trek* appeared the only alternatives were a variety of children's programmes, so it was welcome despite its clichés. Now, in contrast, one can find an sf series almost every day of the week, most of them dreadful, it's true: *The Six Million Dollar Man*, *The Bionic Woman*, *The Gemini Man*, *The Invisible Man*, *The Man from Atlantis*, *Fantastic Journey*, *Space 1999*, *The Survivors*, *1990*, *Blake's Seven*, *Holmes and Yo-Yo*. None of these exhibit a fraction of the imagination and charisma of the increasingly-adult *Dr Who*.

In 1977, however a cult even bigger than that boldly followed by the 'Trekkies' emerged. *Star Wars* had arrived.

There had been hugely successful sf films before *Star Wars* – notably *2001* and *A Clockwork Orange* – but nothing to compare with its runaway popularity. The scale of *Star Wars'* success almost defies explanation. It is certainly an enormously enjoyable film: an old-fashioned pulp sf adventure told with great pace and visual panache, taking in its stride special effects that previous sf films (*2001*, for instance) had dwelt on at length in an effort to impress. The mere fact that an out-and-out sf film could be so popular is the clearest indication one could have of the extent to which science fiction and its imagery have become an integral part of our society and culture, particularly youth culture.

This can be seen in numerous ways, many of them very trivial. It shows in TV advertisements for safety razors which draw on the imagery of *2001*; it shows in the way sf elements have become commonplace in TV thriller series; it shows, above all, in rock music – perhaps the most powerful communicating medium of popular culture. Whereas in the 1960s a group like Jefferson Airplane were unusual, and a trifle eccentric, in their use of sf imagery, such adaptation is commonplace. The most popular exponents include such groups as Hawkwind, Pink Floyd and Yes. Album covers feature designs adapted from old sf magazines; posters advertising a new Queen album, featuring a Kelly Freas robot from a 1953 issue of *Astounding Science Fiction*, can be seen on hoardings everywhere as this is written.

Allied to this is the explosion in popularity of posters and lavishly illustrated books of sf and fantasy art. The fantastic dream landscapes of Roger Dean adorned the covers of records by Yes and other groups; a book based on these, *Views*, proved a runaway bestseller. Similar volumes followed, featuring the painting of Patrick Woodroffe and Bruce Pennington, both well known for their sf paperback covers. The dominant figure in British sf illustration in the 1970s, however, was Chris Foss, whose intricately-designed, knobbly spaceships inspired a host of imitators, and whose selling-power was intimately connected with the great popularity of the space operas of E. E. Smith, on whose books Foss's covers first made an impact. Similarly, in

A Bob Layzell space craft passing close to an exploding body in the depths of space

The futuristic and the
rural enchantingly
combined in an
illustration for *Venus
Plus X*

have with Graham Greene. And yet, because of commercial categorization, there is a link. Le Guin's books appear in paperback with just the same packaging as E. E. Smith's, although the disparity in their content could hardly be greater. One hopes that the reader fired with enthusiasm by *Star Wars* (or by *Gray Lensman*) and looking for more of the same will sooner or later hit upon Le Guin or Silverberg or Ballard or Dick, and see how great the potential of sf truly is. It is painful for a distinctive and individual writer to be lumped, willy-nilly, into a category; to have their books treated like competing brands of washing powder in a supermarket. The one possible consolation is that in this way they may keep touch with a popular audience in a way many more acceptedly serious writers cannot.

The rising stars

Who, then, are the prominent new writers of the 1970s? Three or four years ago the prospects, in America at least, looked bleak. The new star, by his own proclamation, was David Gerrold, who shared some of Harlan Ellison's talent for self-promotion. His novels, the most competent of which were *When Harlie Was One 1972* and *The Man Who Folded Himself 1973* were slick, professional, and forgettable. In their time they were much touted for awards. Other acclaimed new stars included Gardner Dozois, Geo. Alec Effinger, Ed Bryant and Gordon Eklund – sincere writers all, but all seemingly lacking a little in vitality. Each of them has produced good work, although none of them has lived up to his early promise. Eklund's greatest success was the episodic novel *If The Stars are Gods 1977*, written in collaboration with Gregory Benford: it told of man's discovery of life elsewhere in the solar system, and beyond. The title segment, first published as a separate story, won a Nebula Award. Benford has quietly established himself as a noteworthy writer, although his output is sparse. By profession he is a theoretical physicist, and his work combines informed and absorbing speculation with a stylistic concern unusual in hardcore sf writers. His novel *In The Ocean of Night 1977* – about mankind's first encounter with alien intelligence – has been widely acclaimed.

Since then, a new and more rewarding generation has appeared. It includes Michael Bishop, who has not yet made an entirely convincing transition from short stories to novels, but who has produced some highly original sf on anthropological themes: 'Death and Designation Among the Asadi' *1973*, *A Funeral for the Eyes of Fire 1975*, *Stolen Faces 1977*. There is George R. R. Martin, a romantic somewhat in the Poul Anderson tradition, but very much his own man, writing traditional sf about modern characters. Aliens also play a large part in his work, as in his Hugo-winning 'A Song for Lya' *1975*. His first novel, *Dying of the Light 1977*, contains some of the most potent action writing in recent sf. There is James Tiptree Jr, a mysterious man who in 1977 was revealed as being a woman, 'his' real name being Alice Sheldon. Her work is tough, original, colourful, sometimes sentimental; in a real sense she is to the 1970s what Delany and Zelazny were to the

America, the most successful and most imitated figure was the fantasy artist Frank Frazetta. A profile of Frazetta in the *Sunday Telegraph Magazine* suggested he was 'the most successful commercial artist alive today' – an extravagant claim, but one which the reported total sales of his posters (some 6½ million) would tend to corroborate. Just as some of E. E. Smith's popularity in Britain can be attributed to the selling-power of Foss's covers, so can Frazetta claim some of the credit for launching the even more successful Robert E. Howard revival in the USA.

The question which arises from this is, what bearing does the commercial success of sf have on its increasing artistic respectability, if any? In a sense it is irrelevant. *Star Wars* has no more to do with the work of Ursula Le Guin than the James Bond films

1960s. The story which really shot her into prominence was 'And I Awoke And Found Me Here On The Cold Hill's Side' *1972*, which provided an extremely startling notion of the psychological effect of man's contact with aliens, namely that it would be dominated by ungovernable sexual attraction. Since then a number of Tiptree stories have won awards: 'The Girl Who Was Plugged In' *1973*, 'Love is the Plan, the Plan is Death' *1973*, 'Houston, Houston, Do You Read?' *1976*. Her first novel, *Up The Walls of the World 1978*, is as extravagantly inventive as might have been expected, featuring a very strange and original alien species. Vonda N. McIntyre is clearly much influenced by Ursula Le Guin, but is rapidly developing a distinctive and powerful voice. Her first novel, *The Exile Waiting 1975*, was derivative in its elements, but colourful and fluent. Her second, *Dreamsnake 1978* is set on the same desolate future Earth and based on her Nebula Award winning story 'Of Mist, and Grass, and Sand' *1973*. It signals the arrival of a considerable talent.

So we come back to the two American writers mentioned at the beginning of this article, Joe Haldeman and John Varley. Haldeman's *The Forever War 1975* realistically tackles the mechanics of an interstellar war. It has been widely compared with Heinlein's *Starship Troopers*, but Haldeman's book is grimmer and more realistic. A veteran of Vietnam, he has a thoroughly unromantic view of war. *The Forever War* showed a powerful grasp of narrative technique and instantly established itself as the definitive sf treatment of its theme (inevitably it won both Hugo and Nebula awards). It was a hard debut to follow, but Haldeman managed respectably with *Mindbridge 1976*, although the novel was almost *too* technically assured. Using all kinds of incidental paraphernalia, in the manner of Brunner and Dos Passos, its narrative became virtually diagrammatic. Haldeman writes tough – the opening sentence of *Mindbridge*, 'Denver pissed him off', is a classic example – which is a posture that could become wearing. Thus far, though, he was established his reputation more quickly and surely than any other writer for years. Varley has not yet reached the same stage. His stories so far have a common background, and it is, blessedly, a *complex* background: a future in which many social and technological changes have occurred, which the characters take entirely for granted. His first novel, *The Ophiuchi Hotline 1977* is confident debut.

Among British writers, as we have seen, Bob Shaw has come into prominence. So too has Michael Coney, whose first novel did not appear until 1972, but whose total of books already runs into double figures. There are repetitive elements in his novels, for example, settings on alien planets which closely resemble Cornish fishing villages, but his best work shows an admirable ability to work out thoroughly and entertainingly the implications of his ideas. *Mirror Image 1972* and *Hello Summer, Goodbye 1975* are his best novels to date.

The three major young British writers are M. John Harrison, Christopher Priest and Ian Watson. Harrison is the least prolific, and he has so far failed to capitalize on his impressive first novel, *The Committed Men 1971* – very much a 1970s post-catastrophe novel, with echoes of Ballard and Wyndham, but not a derivative book. His best stories, exemplified by the superb 'Running Down' *1975*, about a man who is a walking vortex of entropy, contain writing of a power few contemporary sf writers could hope to match.

Priest came into prominence with *Fugue for a Darkening Island 1972*, an admirably terse and cleverly structured novel of a Britain torn apart by racial tensions. This was followed by the conceptually striking *Inverted World* and an accurate (if slightly overlong) recreation of the Wellsian scientific romance in *The Space Machine 1976*. 'An Infinite Summer' *1976* is a beautifully balanced and poignant time story, while *A Dream of Wessex 1977* is easily his most accomplished novel to date. Its basic idea – of a project in which a group of people participate in a shared dream to create a construct of the future – is arresting and the story built around it is thoroughly satisfying: a complex, controlled narrative structure, which proceeds by logical steps to unexpected destinations.

Ian Watson is in some respects the most interesting, in others the most infuriating of the trio. His work fairly overflows with ideas, to the extent where at times he is almost impossible to follow; he is probably the most intellectually demanding writer in modern English-language sf. *The Embedding 1973*, *The Jonah Kit 1975*, *The Martian Inca 1977* and *Alien Embassy 1977* are full of fascinating concepts, not always fully worked into novels. However, his control is improving with each book, and if he can retain his fecundity of invention his future seems very bright.

Behind these three are a number of similarly promising writers. Robert Holdstock has produced two novels, *Eye Among the Blind 1976* and *Earthwind 1977* which show considerable originality and skill; his preoccupation with alien cultures is unusual, and refreshing, in an English writer. Garry Kilworth's first novel *In Solitary 1977*, though excessively compressed – a fear of excess fat carried to anorexic extremes – is a thoughtful and original variant on the theme of Earth conquered by aliens. Other writers are beginning to make their mark including Charles Partington, Don West, Dave Langford, Andrew Stephenson and Barrington Bayley.

The 1970s have thus far been a fruitful decade for sf. The field has diversified to the point where to describe it any longer as a genre, while a convenient shorthand, is hopelessly inadequate. Sf, if the term means anything, is a form of contemporary metaphor, a literary device for examining our world and our lives from another perspective. It is a significant form of the contemporary novel: not a substitute for it, nor a poor relation of it, but an integral part of it. Its species of imaginative metaphor is one which has been attracting more intelligent readers and more serious and dedicated writers in the 1970s. Looking back on a decade which has already produced such diverse works as *Frankenstein Unbound*, *Crash*, *334*, *The Iron Dream*, *The Condition of Muzak*, *The Book of Skulls*, *The Deep*, *The Fifth Head of Cerberus*, *Michaelmas*, *Gateway*, *A Scanner Darkly*, *The Dispossessed*, *The Forever War*, *A Dream of Wessex* and *The Embedding* who could say otherwise?

contents

There is an enormous collector's market for the memorabilia of science fiction, the old magazines, the yellowed manuscripts, the faded artwork, the long forgotten novel, or the new first edition. To the uncommitted observer, though the value of certain books is obvious, it is often incomprehensible that cash should change hands for such an accumulation of musty, outdated and 'childish' comics, books, and youthful experiments in amateur printing. To the committed insider it is payment to share in the glory of sf's past, a transitory joining of the soul to a time when Sense of Wonder was evoked from garish front cover to Charles Atlas back cover, when science fiction was unpretentious but was undeniably bad, when it was written for its entertainment value, and was undeniably fun.

The collectors market can be divided into three areas – the true memorabilia, including artwork; the science fiction book; and the science fiction magazine.

A number of collectors, among them the re-nowned Forrest J. Ackerman, have accumulated vast museums of film posters, props, models and outfits from a wide variety of sf and fantasy films. The collector's market for this sort of memorabilia is small, but intensely visited where the interest is felt. Interest in such ephemera, these days, is confined to the fringe groups, the Trekkies, the Doctor Who fans and, presumably, the Star Wars fans. At Star Trek conventions, replicas of many gadgets, gim-micks and so on can be obtained and not surprisingly the offer of any of the real 'McCoy' causes consider-able ecstasy. A recent collection of Starship Enter-prise Blueprints became a bestseller. Prior to these sf fringe groups the dominating cults were the fol-lowers of Lovecraft and Shaver, but memorabilia of the writers involved in these movements no longer noticeably change hands. The belief that iron nails from H. P. Lovecraft's coffin can be bought for $500 is not true. It is far less.

Manuscripts

The two items of memorabilia that unfailingly attract interest are manuscripts – top copy original, preferably copy-edited – and fanzines. Once again it is the manuscripts of H. P. Lovecraft that are most eagerly sought, as well as the original scripts by Robert E. Howard, especially those featuring that muscle-brained mercenary, Conan. Fantasy manu-scripts, as with books and magazines, are the more fiercely collected, probably because they are rarer, or only now becoming truly appreciated. Nonetheless, the original, or even a copy, of the manuscript of any significant novel, or recent novel, enjoys the dubious distinction of becoming a collector's item.

At a convention in England, in 1975, a manuscript copy of Bob Shaw's *Orbitsville* fetched £20 ($40). A copy of Christopher Priest's *The Space Machine* fetched much the same. Both these novels were newly published. The value of any Hugo Award Winning Novel, especially one by Robert Heinlein, would be far greater, and there are many classic novels that never received awards, and their manu-scripts, if they came onto the market, would be valuable indeed.

Fanzines by young fans who later became well known writers also are collector's items. A fanzine is, an amateur magazine, usually mimeographed, featuring articles and fiction, and many writers have produced them in their younger days. Notables in this connection are Ray Bradbury, who produced an excellent fanzine *Futuria Fantasia* between 1939 and 1940, Robert Silverberg, who produced his fanzine *Spaceship* in the early 1950s, when Harlan Ellison was greeting the world with his fanzine *Dimensions*. Copies of Bob Shaw and Walt Willis' *Hyphen* are easier to find, and still well worth the finding. You will be lucky to find the fanzine version of *New Worlds* (called *Nova Terrae*) edited by Ted Carnell in the late 1930s, but it is quite possible to obtain Christopher Priest's *Con*.

The price of a rare book reflects the demand for that book, of course, but until a really large collection is sold off it is hard to get a good idea of how the value of books has risen; the asking prices varies wildly and widely. When P. Schuyler Miller died in 1975 his collection was put up for auction; Miller had, for several decades, been the book reviewer of *Astounding/Analog*, and he had nearly every first edition of an American book there was. The auction occurred in 1977 and was perhaps the most complete sf collection sold in years.

First editions

The rare hardbacks are almost invariably the first editions, preferably signed, and there are many of them. For example Ursula Le Guin's *Wizard of Earthsea*, the first of her immensely popular so-called juvenile fantasy series, was first published by a small west coast publisher called Parnassus Press. The print run was small, and it is now almost impossible to find a copy of it; when it does surface it can fetch upwards of $100. It is usually books of stature that become collector's items and a glance through the section on Awards will indicate quite clearly which first editions to watch for, for example Walter Miller's *A Canticle for Liebowitz*, Tolkien's *Lord of the Rings*, the Putnam first edition of Heinlein's *Stranger in a Strange Land*, Bester's *The Demolished Man*. Richard Adam's *Watership Down* was originally turned down by nearly every major publisher in London, and the first edition, a very amateurish looking book from Rex Collings, is now a very valuable item. The 1967 Doubleday first edition of Harlan Ellison's mammoth collection *Dangerous Visions* now sells for $150, though the second volume, *Again Dangerous Visions* is not rare at all, the print run having been far larger. This happens with other books too, notably Frank Herbert's enormously popular *Dune* series. The original book, *Dune*, after being serialized in *Analog* in eight parts (two separate novels, *Dune World* and *Prophet of Dune*) was published by Chilton Press in 1965, in a small edition of 2–3,000. It was an immediate collector's item and cult book, and received both Hugo and Nebula Awards. The second volume, *Dune Messiah*, was published by Putnam in enormous numbers in 1968 – so many that copies were ultimately remaindered. When Putnam came to print the third volume, *Children of Dune*, they had learned the wrong lesson; they underprinted and the book was a collector's item before it was even published. It is, like *Dune*, very rare indeed.

Old books

Ever popular among young readers, it is perhaps fitting that the original edition of E. E. 'Doc' Smith's *History of Civilization* should have become a much sought item; in six leather-bound volumes, it is unlikely that editions of this work will appear anywhere but Sotheby's. Other very old books, the sort that surface in secondhand bookshops and jumble sales, include Christopher Blair's 'The Cheetah Girl'. Privately published in the 1920s, it ran to an edition of 20 copies. This long short story should have appeared in the *Purple Sapphire*, a current anthology of fantasy fiction, but was considered too risqué. A very rare book, first published by Milwaukee Fictioneers, is Stanley Weinbaum's *Dawn of Flame*. And finally H. P. Lovecraft's *The Shunned House*, printed by W. Paul Cook in 1928, became a collector's item so quickly that a large number of forgeries have appeared. Cook printed a 200 copy edition but left the sheets uncollated – soon after, R. H. Barlow bound up and sold 12 at $2.00 each.

Unusual books by well known science fiction writers also are in demand, such as the first edition of James Blish's masterpiece on the life of Roger Bacon, *Doctor Mirabilis*, and notably Philip Dick's non-sf novel *Confessions of a Crap Artist*: published three years ago, in a 500 copy edition, it sold out instantly. And each year the North Boston Science Fiction Convention publishes a Guest of Honour Book, an original piece of work, or collection, by the Guest of Honour; in particular, look out for Isaac Asimov's collection *Have you seen these?* in 1974, and L. Sprague de Camp's *Scribblings* in 1972.

Perhaps the rarest first edition of all is Roger Zelazny's *Nine Princes in Amber* (Doubleday, *1968*). Copies of this hardcover book were in the warehouse awaiting distribution, alongside a pile of Zelazny's previous book, the very obscure *Creatures of Light and Darkness* which not unsurprisingly had sold very poorly. A decision was taken to cut the losses on *Creatures*, and to Doubleday at this time this meant just one thing: pulp the book. The memo, it seems, was slightly ambiguous: Pulp Zelazny! Before the mistake was spotted every Roger Zelazny book in the warehouse had become cardboard boxes, including the eagerly awaited *Nine Princes*. All that remain of that first edition are a few review copies. Find one and retire rich.

The value of the paperback collector's market is gradually increasing, but is still largely under-estimated; first editions are more commonly hardback, the smaller print run helping to increase the rarity of the item. In the 1960s and 1970s, however, the number of books that have made their first appearance in paperback has enormously increased. There are now many extremely rare paperback first editions, the early Ace Doubles being a prime example. These were two books in one, usually by the same author. Each book had its own cover and preliminary pages: having read book one to approximately the middle of the volume, turn book upside down and there, before you, is the second book. Start again. Notable collector's items here are Jack Vance's *Big Planet/Slaves of the Klau*, Leight Brackett's *Swords of Rhiannon*/Howard's *Conan the Conqueror*, Philip José Farmer's *Celestial Blueprint/Cache from Outer Space*, Harlan Ellison's *Man with Nine Lives/A Touch of Infinity*. Other rare paperbacks are Philip Dick's *Doctor Bloodmoney* (Ace) and *Cosmic Puppeteers* (an Ace Double with André Norton's *Sargasso of Space*), and the Berkeley editions of J. G. Ballard's story collections *The Voice of Time* and *The Impossible Man*.

Another paperback, made rare because of the scarcity of copies, is *The Gas*, a piece of sf pornography written by Charles Platt for Ophelia Press. The story, of an experimental gas that leaks into the English countryside and afflicts every man, woman and child with an insatiable sex drive, smacks of an adolescent joke, but the book is passionately sought after. Erotic sf of a far superior variety, more convincingly rooted in the sf idiom, are the first editions from Essex House of Philip José Farmer's books *Image of the Beast 1968* and *Blown 1969*; the third volume, *A Feast Unknown 1969* and Hank Stine's *Season of the Witch 1968* are less rare.

Magazines

Magazines, though, attract the most attention among collectors and fans, and are constantly in demand. Although copies of most sf magazines can be obtained relatively easily through specialist book dealers, the magazine field – as a unified whole – is a collector's item. There are few complete sf magazine collections and many collectors who aspire to owning one. The rarity of magazines varies, according to age, print run, condition (some pulps were printed on such awful paper that now only mint condition copies can even be opened, let alone read) and the presence of early stories by now great names. Single issues can be very rare, especially the first and last issues which often shared a common fate: smaller print runs. Valuable first issues are *Astounding*, *Amazing*, *Weird Tales* and most particularly *Beyond*, a magazine that ran to ten issues, all of which are real collector's items. *Unknown* is similarly valuable, but it is the second and third issues that are the rarest, the first issue appearing on the collector's market more frequently.

Lester del Rey's *Fantasy Stories* is another very rare magazine, appearing in the early 1950s. But it is regrettably true to say that most of the pulp magazines are now a rarity, or at least an expensive commodity. Only ten years ago it was quite possible to pick up copies of *Thrilling Wonder*, *Planet Stories*,

Startling Stories, Marvel and all the rest with ease; now they are pricey, and seldom seen in mint condition. The reason? Books that popularize the pulps, science fiction, and especially science fiction artwork; that great wave of popular books that has been the best thing to happen to sf booksellers.

British magazines, and British reprints of American pulps, are easier to obtain, although even now the original British magazines of the 1940s and 1950s are becoming scarce. Perhaps the rarest magazine of all is the *first* edition of *New Worlds* (21), of which only one copy is known to exist; the plates were reset with different fictional material before the edition was distributed; all copies were pulped. All the fiction ignored in the subsequent second edition of No. 21 appeared later in other issues.

The last issue of *New Worlds*, No. 201, is also a rare item. Falling sales and waning support forced Moorcock to abandon the magazine format of *New Worlds* and adapt it into an original anthology. The last issue was a subscribers issue only, and there were painfully few subscribers. It featured Thomas Disch's story, 'Feathers from the Wings of an Angel', plus an index of the previous 29 issues of *New Worlds*.

You will also possess a rare item if you own the *Astounding, Amazing, Galaxy* or any other magazine with the first story by any well-known writer, in particular Asimov (*Amazing, March 1939*) A. E. Van Vogt (*Astounding, December 1939*), Sheckley (*Imagination, May 1952*) Silverberg (*Nebula, February 1954*), Aldiss (*Science Fantasy, July 1954*) and many others. The value of these magazines is relative – though they may not be rare, they are worth more to the collector of science fiction than to the collector of science fiction magazines.

Fandom

Science Fiction Fandom

There is a famous acronym in fandom – fiawol: fandom is a way of life. This expresses the amount of involvement experienced by many fans in such activities as publishing 'fanzines', attending sf conventions and corresponding with people almost anywhere in the world about almost anything, united by the common interest of their literary tastes. There are several thousand fans throughout the world, although only several hundred who are as involved as this. Many well-known sf writers were once active fans (Robert Silverberg, Harlan Ellison, for example); many still are (Bob Shaw for example). Many sf writers attend conventions, local meetings, or write for various fanzines on the same unpaid basis as fans – for their own, and others' pleasure. This interaction between an informal group of 'fans' (or devotees) and a literary – or any other – 'genre' is probably unique to sf, in extent if not in kind.

Fanzines

These are amateur magazines – amateur in the true sense, produced by fans for other fans. There have been many hundreds of different fanzines over the years, ranging from the unreadable and the illiterate, to the compulsively readable and often savagely critical of the sf literary form. Many fanzines have become semi-professional, even professional magazines as their voice, and the views of their contributers, won acclaim: *Algol, Science Fiction Review, Speculation, Vector*; even *New Worlds* was once a fanzine.

The true fanzine, however, remains unpretentious, unconcerned with the merits of professional presentation. An issue can be written and produced by one person, or several; can emerge once a month, once a year, or even once every five years; they can be two pages long, or a hundred pages long. They are frequently duplicated (mimeographed) and often produced by offset litho. The veneer of professionalism thus produced usually indicates a dissatisfaction with the crude, honest dedication of the 'true-fan'.

Fanzines are normally only sent to those who show interest in them. Although the interest can sometimes take the form of a small amount of money, it is more commonly expressed in a letter of comment, an exchange of fanzines, a review, or a verbal comment – anything, in fact, which extends the complex lines of communication that are the core of sf fandom. There is a great sense of personal achievement in publishing fanzines. They are produced for fun, and for friendship, they draw on the shared dreams of readers, and the unrecognized validity of science fiction in a decade of general literary self-indulgence. Themselves indulgent, fanzines nonetheless can focus attention on the freshness of vision of the science fiction field. There are many types of fanzine, but a few formats dominate this sub-literature. Firstly the critical and serious magazine, which draws directly from science fiction, and is about science fiction – examples here abound: *Vector*, the magazine of the British Science Fiction Association, Geoff Rippington's *SF Arena*, Richard Geis' *SF Review*, Bruce Gillespie's *SF Commentary* (Aus), Robert Jackson's *Maya*. Secondly, the fanzine of more general interest: Victoria Vayne's *Simulaarum*, Kevin Smith and Dave Langford's *Drilkjis*, Pat Charnock's *Wrinkled Shrew*. Thirdly the humorous magazine, often what is known as a 'personalzine', for example, Dave Langford's *Twll Ddu*, Leroy Kettle's *True Rat*, Terry Hughes' *Mota*, Brian Wegenheim's *The Pickersgill Papers*. Fourthly the fiction fanzines, never very good, but never better than The Oxford University SF Group's magazine *Sphinx*, Rob Holdstock's *Macrocosm*, David Taylor's *Nebula*.

One thing is certain: if science fiction ceased to exist, fanzines and fandom would continue.

Fringe Cults

Aside from the central core of science fiction fandom, a number of fringe fandoms have taken shape, many of them forming the status of 'cults'. They frequently hinge upon the writings or beliefs of an individual, and the four most often associated with science fiction (much to the dismay of sf purists) are the Cthulhu Mythos, the Shaver Phenomenon, Dianetics, and the UFO/Flying Saucer followers.

The Cthulhu Mythos

The Cthulhu Mythos was a term invented after Lovecraft's death to describe those dozen or so stories written by H.P. Lovecraft which fit within a common background and setting. This centres upon a race of supernatural beings, the Ancient Ones, who once held supremacy over the Earth. A more benign race of Elder Gods succeeded in banishing this evil race from the Earth and keeping them at bay, but occasional dabblings by ignorant mortals allow the Ancient Ones to breach the restraints and return to Earth. Lovecraft never set out to write a special series about these gods, which revel in such names as Cthulhu, Yog-Sothoth and Nyarlathotep, and consequently many followers argue over stories that belong to the series and those that do not. One important early piece was 'The Nameless City' *1921* which introduced the mad Arab Abdul Alhazred who had penned that hideous ancient tome *The Necronomicon*. *The Necronomicon* became a standard prop in all later Cthulhu stories, and many readers believed it actually existed. For a joke Manly Wade Wellman once called into a musty old bookstore and asked the proprietress if she had a copy. To his shock she said she had somewhere, if only she could find it. Alas, she couldn't.

'The Call of Cthulhu', which was published in *Weird Tales* for February 1928, was the first proper story in the cycle, and one wherein Lovecraft introduced and interlinked most of the major concepts. It was however more a sequence of events than a story narrative, but with his next two tales – both long stories by Lovecraft's standards – 'The Dunwich Horror' and 'The Whisperer in Darkness', Lovecraft settled down to relating a solid story. They rank amongst his best.

'The Whisperer in Darkness' appeared in the August 1931 *Weird Tales*, by which time many of Lovecraft's friends and fellow writers had incorporated elements of the Cthulhu background, and in turn Lovecraft had acknowledged this in 'The Whisperer . . .'. The most important contributors to the flowering Mythos were Frank Belknap Long (1903–), Clark Ashton Smith (1893–1961) and Robert E. Howard (1906–36) who introduced many new concepts and ideas. Lovecraft also included elements into the stories he was rewriting for aspiring authors like Zealia Bishop and Hazel Heald, so that by the time of Lovecraft's death in 1937, there was a considerable volume of work in existence hinging upon Lovecraft's basic concept. August Derleth, Robert Bloch, Henry Kuttner and others all added to the Mythos, none more so than Derleth who began to bring out Lovecraft's work in book form after establishing his Arkham House publishing venture.

Derleth completed a number of Lovecraft's story fragments, and wrote his own 'Trail of Cthulhu' series in the 1940s. In later years he encouraged other writers to add to the Mythos, and this expanded when Lovecraft's work became more readily available in paperback in the early 1960s. A new generation of writers – foremost J. Ramsey Campbell, Brian Lumley and Gary Myers – brought the Mythos into the 1970s, especially Lumley who rationalized many of the more erratic elements in scientific terms. Even Colin Wilson experimented with some of the ideas in his novel *The Philosopher's Stone 1971*.

The following for the Cthulhu stories has grown dramatically in recent years with a number of anthologies devoted to inspired fiction, and many amateur publications acting as forums for the devotees. The following bibliography is a basic guide to the core of the Mythos.

H. P. Lovecraft

The Call of the Cthulhu (1928)
The Dunwich Horror (1929)
The Whisperer in Darkness (1931)
The Shadow Over Innsmouth (1936)
At The Mountains of Madness (1936)
The Dreams in the Witch-House (1933)
The Thing on the Doorstep (1937)
The Shadow Out of Time (1936)
The Haunter of the Dark (1936)

August Derleth

The Mask of Cthulhu (Arkham House, 1958)
The Trail of Cthulhu (Arkham House, 1962)

Anthologies

Tales of the Cthulhu Mythos, edited by August Derleth (Arkham House, 1969)
The Spawn of Cthulhu, edited by Lin Carter (Ballantine, 1971)
The Disciples of Cthulhu, edited by E.P. Berglund (DAW Books, 1976)

The Shaver Phenomenon

By way of theme the Shaver concept has elements in common with the Cthulhu Mythos. In his stories, Richard S. Shaver (1907–75), told how the Earth had once been the abode of two mighty races, the Titans and the Atlans. At length these beings began to suffer from harmful radiation emitted by the Sun, and though they took refuge in caverns under the Earth, they realized Earth was no longer safe. And so they abandoned the Earth to the inferior mortals.

Some of these humans discovered the underground caverns, complete with the advanced machinery of the 'gods', and learned how to make them work. But the machines released harmful rays which made the humans degenerate zombies, or 'deros' in Shaver's terminology. Turning these rays onto the Earth's surface they were able to influence the thoughts of humans into committing all the evil in the world.

The essential difference however was that Lovecraft treated all his work as fiction, and its expansion with his friends was often treated as an in-joke. In Shaver's case he believed in all he wrote, and the Shaver stories were published as fact in fictional form in the pages of *Amazing Stories* starting with '''I Remember Lemuria!''' in the June 1945 issue. Science fiction purists took an instant dislike to the Shaver sensationalism, and particularly the editor Raymond Palmer who was apparently milking the 'lunatic fringe' for all it was worth. But Shaver was genuine in his own beliefs, and maintained this to his death. In a letter written to Mike Ashley in September 1975 he said:

'I wrote to spread the understanding of the nature of evil as a magnetic phenomenon about which something could be done by magnetic manipulation. Yet the sf fans never seemed to get the point because of mind-control from dero sources, I believe. I think the whole mass-mind of the fans and the general populace is obscured in this essential area ... the error caused by disintegrant energy flows in the ion-flows along the neurons and connecting tissue and visualization-screens in the mind. At that time I imagined that sf fans were interested in real science and were tinkerers at heart who would construct a device to alter the evil drive we see working out in world wars. Yet the fans only saw the stim and the sex orgy and the sensationalism in the *Amazing* magazine set-up, never what I wanted them to see and absorb ... the nature of evil and how to do something about it with magnetic control devices which alter the flow of thought into a better pattern than the 'norm' ...'

The effects of the Shaver Mystery stories were far-reaching. Initially they alienated the core of sf fandom, who Palmer only partly placated by introducing a special department to review fan publications, 'The Clubhouse'. More important they attracted to *Amazing* readers interested in the inexplicable events in the world, and the inevitable clutch of readers who had visited the dero-caves. It fired in Palmer an added interest in the occult. Originally he too had been sceptical about Shaver, but after visiting the man at his home, was rapidly converted. The subsequent sensationalism in *Amazing* was not solely a result of Palmer trying to boost circulation. It was a genuine interest, fired by an astonishing reader response. Palmer realized *Amazing* was not the place for discussing the occult, and so he pseudonymously established his own publishing company and issued a quarterly magazine titled *Fate*, with the first issue dated Spring 1948. It was an instant success, and attracted contributions from most of the leading authorities on the occult,

including Vincent H. Gaddis (1913–), the man who invented the term 'the Bermuda Triangle'.

Richard Shaver was never content with Palmer's handling of his material. He reported once: 'Palmer to this day appears to espouse the spiritualistic cause, more or less, and this attitude colors my work since so many ascribe my work to Palmer.'

Although Shaver continued to write straight action space opera for Palmer until the mid-1950s, and the occasional 'Mystery' story, the work was shunned by most sf readers. Nevertheless Shaver continued his investigations, and he began to fabricate an entire picture of prehistoric Earth, envisioning many of the ideas later used by writers like Erich von Däniken. No magazine (outside Palmer's) would touch Shaver's material, and so he published booklets himself. The whole history of the Earth, he claimed, was written in the rocks. Rocks and stones were the original books of the elder world, and by careful study of the images and patterns embedded within their worn and eroded surfaces, one can painstakingly build up a picture of life and events in the times before the global Deluge (the Biblical Flood), which Shaver maintained was caused by the Moon coming too close to the Earth. Earth was saved when the Moon was repulsed by magnetic opposition at the North Pole.

Not only did Shaver photograph many scenes of the Elder days from the rock books, but he began to understand their language, the original tongue of Earth or 'Space pidgin, brought to Earth by the first space ships.'

Shaver was totally convinced of his beliefs. To those who could not see pictures in the rocks, or understand the original language, this was all the fault of mental blockage brought about by the dero mind-rays. In some ways Shaver had us all beaten. If the world is subject to mass hypnotism, how can any one of us possibly prove otherwise?

The UFO Enigma

The ideas of flying saucers fitted exactly into Shaver's own theories. He maintained that our Moon was hollow and that the saucers came from an alien base there.

Sightings of flying saucers exist from the ancient past, and recent researches have managed to bring any number of visions into the UFO mythology. However, the real rise in UFO interest came just after the Second World War with the information that Governments were suppressing the real facts.

The important date for the sightings was 24 June 1947, when Kenneth Arnold had sighted a mysterious chain of nine saucer-like objects, whilst flying his own plane. His attempts to find out the facts met shut-doors whenever he tried, so he turned to Raymond Palmer who promoted the affair in the first issue of *Fate*. Eventually Arnold and Palmer would publish the full story as *The Coming of the Saucers 1952*. By then a number of books on the saucers had appeared, including *The Flying Saucers are Real 1950* by Donald Keyhoe, *The Riddle of the Flying Saucers 1950* by Gerald Heard, and *Behind the Flying Saucers 1950* by Frank Scully. Subsequently George Adamski added his famous volume *The Flying Saucers Have Landed 1953*, which included his admission that he had met and conversed with a Venusian. By the time of Gray Barker's *They Knew Too Much About Flying Saucers 1956* a large UFO cult had come into existence, and Barker's book looks in depth at their own lives.

The sf magazines soon latched on to the UFO boom. *Fantasy Stories* for November 1950 revealed the so-called inside story of the fate of Major Vernon Piper who had disappeared in March 1950 whilst investigating saucer sightings. Willy Ley contributed an article to the first issue of *Galaxy* called 'Flying Saucers: Friend, Foe or Fantasy?' where he weighed up the pros and cons. But it was Palmer who made the most of the sightings. Many pages of *Other Worlds* were devoted to stories about UFOs, including 'I Flew in a Flying Saucer' ghost-written by Palmer from the experiences of an anonymous captain. *Fate* and his other occult magazine *Mystic* frequently fed a hungry readership. In the end *Other Worlds* metamorphosed into *Flying Saucers* in 1957. That year saw a UFO boom, with a bonanza in sightings, and two other sf magazines, *Amazing Stories* and *Fantastic Universe* devoting many pages to UFO facts and fiction.

Thereafter sf and UFOlogy veered apart, although to this day the general readership will connect 'sci-fi and flying saucers' in one breath.

Dianetics

During the 1940s science fiction was beginning to dabble more and more with the powers of the mind. John W. Campbell encouraged such fiction, and with classics like A.E. van Vogt's *Slan* as an end-product, there was good reason for investigating the field further. As ever, though, people can go too far; and in this case it was the worst mistake Campbell ever made.

In 1950 sf and adventure writer L. Ron Hubbard (1911–) submitted an article to Campbell, 'Dianetics: The Evolution of a Science' which he rushed into the May 1950 issue. At the same time the New York publishers of Hermitage House launched Hubbard's *Dianetics: The Modern Science of Mental Health*. They caused a sensation, although the sf fraternity were sceptical. The Shaver Mystery was all too fresh in their minds, and the idea that Campbell was now promoting a quick course in mental freedom had all the makings of another hoax.

Hubbard's basic premise was that the mind was split into the active and aware Analytical Mind, and the more subconscious Reactive Mind. The Reactive Mind often erratically feeds false information to the Analytical Mind, resulting in wrong, often fateful decisions. (Here were shades of Shaver's deros at work!) However by a process dubbed auditing, the Reactive Mind could be erased, just like a computer's memory banks, resulting in an individual becoming a 'clear'. The 'clears' are mentally superior because of their immediate and exact ability to think, plan and diagnose without a befuddled mind.

Although sf fandom shied away from Hubbard, until then one of the more popular sf writers, he acquired a major following. Hubbard established a Dianetics Foundation, which included A.E. van Vogt as an 'auditor'. Although established science called Hubbard a charlatan, his following grew. The Foundation ran into a number of legal and financial problems by the mid-1950s, but Hubbard achieved a quick transformation and invented a religion – Scientology. This way he dodged paying taxes, and his funds and following grew! But Scientology, currently banned in Britain, although it has its roots in dianetics, has changed drastically over the last twenty years and has no connection at all with science fiction.

pseudonyms

Writers have many different reasons for using a pseudonym. Some may feel they are flooding the market with too much work and the pseudonym is a protection against over-exposure. Others may wish to separate different parts of their work for reasons of convenience, or because of conflicting interests; some may not wish to be associated with the more commercially orientated elements of their work. A few writers use a pseudonym for all their work and never use their real name, for example William Tenn (in reality, Philip Klass), Cordwainer Smith (Paul Linebarger), Stuart Gordon (Richard Gordon) and Richard Cowper (John Middleton Murry). Where the author's real name would mean little to the general reader these pseudonyms have not been included in the list; nor have pseudonyms which appeared perhaps once in an obscure magazine, nor little-known pseudonyms of little-known writers.

Instead this is a selected list of interesting or important pen-names of the more popular writers.

William Atheling Jr JAMES BLISH was a famous critic in fanzines of the fifties and sixties and even reviewed novels by James Blish. Atheling was as respected for his criticism as James Blish was to become for his fiction. His essays have been collected under the titles *The Issue at Hand* and *More Issues at Hand*.

Richard Avery EDMUND COOPER is the author of *The Expendable* series of novels. Cooper probably reaches a wider audience with his occasional reviews in the *Sunday Times*.

Bill Barclay MICHAEL MOORCOCK wrote two sf novels for Compact Books in the sixties: *Somewhere*

MICHAEL MOORCOCK

in the Night and *Printer's Devil*. The first of these went some way towards forming the basis for Moorcock's novel *The Chinese Agent*. (See also Edward P. Bradbury and James Colvin.)

Alistair Bevan KEITH ROBERTS wrote several short stories for the magazines *Science Fantasy* and *SF Impulse*. At the same time, as Keith Roberts, he was writing his famous Anita stories, and *Pavane* for the same magazines.

Edward P. Bradbury MICHAEL MOORCOCK wrote *Warriors of Mars*, *Blades of Mars* and *Barbarians of Mars* for Compact Books which published *New Worlds*, the magazine Moorcock was editing at this time. These books have since been reissued as *City of the Beast*, *Lord of the Spiders*, and *Masters of the Pit*. Moorcock partially supported the magazine by his novel writing. (See also Bill Barclay and James Colvin.)

James Colvin MICHAEL MOORCOCK was the main book reviewer for *New Worlds* under the editorship of Moorcock himself for some years, and also wrote *The Wrecks of Time* and several short stories, some of which were collected as *The Deep Fix*. James Colvin was the victim of a fake obituary in *New Worlds* 197 written by Charles Platt but published under the pseudonym William Barclay. (See also Bill Barclay and Edward P. Bradbury.)

Cecil Corwin CYRIL M. KORNBLUTH was one of the many pseudonyms used by Kornbluth, and certainly the most famous, in magazines during the forties and fifties. A selection of his early pseudonymous stories has been edited by James Blish under the title *Thirteen O'clock*. Kornbluth killed off his pseudonym in the well-known story 'MS Found in a Chinese Fortune Cookie' which had Cecil Corwin as the unfortunate protagonist. (See also Cyril Judd.)

ROGER ZELANZY

ISAAC ASIMOV

Hank Dempsey HARRY HARRISON wrote a series of stories about an organisation called CWACC, most of which appeared in *Analog*. The reason for the pseudonym was that the series was 'slightly inimical towards the more stuffy aspects of the medical profession' (quoted from *SF Impulse*). Harry Harrison was, for a number of years, a correspondent of a medical newspaper and this prevented a conflict of interests. He also wrote as Felix Boyd.

Harrison Denmark ROGER ZELAZNY was a name used in Zelazny's early days in *Amazing* and *Fantastic*. Many thought the name was an alias for Harry Harrison, who at the time was living in Denmark, but Harrison wrote to *Amazing*, fervently denying it.

Paul French ISAAC ASIMOV published six juvenile novels about David 'Lucky' Starr between 1952 and 1958. Asimov used a pseudonym because the original idea was to supply a serial hero for TV and he was afraid the TV people might ruin the stories to the detriment of his reputation. The books have been recently rereleased under Asimov's true name.

Bron Fane ROBERT LIONEL FANTHORPE was one of the many pseudonyms used by Fanthorpe for the British Badger Books novels and their magazines *Supernatural Stories* and *Out of This World*. Fanthorpe was something of a writing phenomenon – at least in terms of quantity – and wrote most of Badger Book's output for some years. His other pseudonyms include Lee Barton, Lionel Roberts, Neil Thanet, Trebor Thorpe and Pel Torro which are all partial anagrams of his own name. Some of the novels under one of Badger Books' house-names, John Muller, were also by Fanthorpe.

Charles Grey E.C. TUBB. Tubb is the most prolific user of pseudonyms having had novels and stories appearing under 58 in all. Some of these names are house-names, covering for a variety of writers (e.g. King Lang, Gill Hunt, Roy Sheldon). Tubb's Grey alias was solely his own and acquired a big following in the early 1950s. He also used the names Douglas West, George Holt and Alan Guthrie.

Volsted Gridban was one of the mainstays of the *Vargo Statten* SF magazine in the fifties. There were 17 novels written under this name, 12 by John Russell Fearn and 5 by Ted Tubb.

HARRY HARRISON

Tak Hallus STEPHEN ROBINETT wrote several stories and a novel. *Stargate* for *Analog* in the 1970s before reverting to his real name. He is one of America's best new writers.

John Beynon Harris JOHN WYNDHAM was more correctly the real name and John Wyndham the pseudonym. Christened John Wyndham Parkes Lucas Beynon Harris he had plenty of names to choose from and in fact used them all. He began writing in the thirties as John Benyon Harris, then turned to John Beynon, once used Wyndham Parkes, became John Wyndham and finally, with the publication of *The Outward Urge*, as John Wyndham and Lucas Parkes together. The latter name was added as an imaginary scientific adviser.

Cyril Judd CYRIL M. KORNBLUTH and JUDITH MERRIL wrote three novels in the 50s of which *Gunner Cade* is the most famous and memorable.

Gregory Kern mostly E.C. TUBB is the author of the 'Cap' Kennedy novels which are very popular in the United States.

Calvin M. Knox ROBERT SILVERBERG was the most frequently used of Silverberg's pseudonyms. It was suggested by magazine editor Robert Lowndes when Judith Merril told Silverberg he would never sell books under a Jewish name. Silverberg inserted the 'M', however, claiming it stood for Moses! (See Robert Randall.)

Darrel T. Langart RANDALL GARRETT was used as a pseudonym in the early sixties in *Astounding* because editor John Campbell felt he was publishing too many of Garrett's stories. Garrett used the not over-devious pseudonym to sell to Campbell without him knowing. He also used the names David

JUDITH MERRIL

RANDALL GARRETT

LESTER DEL REY

ROBERT HEINLEIN

Gordon and Walter Bupp. (See also Mark Phillips and Robert Randall.)

Rene Lafayette L. RON HUBBARD wrote a famous series of stories about Ole Doc Methusalah for *Astounding* in the forties, while at the same time writing a number of stories and serials under his own name. Hubbard was later to become better known as the founder of Dianetics and thence Scientology.

Edson McCann LESTER DEL REY and FREDERIK POHL won a $6500 prize awarded by *Galaxy* and the publishers Simon and Schuster for the novel *Preferred Risk*. H.L. Gold, the editor of *Galaxy*, asked Pohl to write a novel when he realized the competition was not the success he had hoped. Pohl asked del Rey to help him and the result won, but was not very good.

Anson MacDonald ROBERT HEINLEIN was used as a pseudonym in the forties in *Astounding* to distinguish Heinlein's output that did not fall into his 'Future History' series from that which did. Heinlein also used the names Caleb Saunders and Lyle Monroe.

K.M. O'Donnell BARRY MALZBERG wrote several short stories and some novels in the late sixties and early seventies and although there was some interchange between the two names at one point, O'Donnell has been dropped and Malzberg's sf since then has been under his own name. He says he has now stopped writing sf under any name.

Lawrence O'Donnell HENRY KUTTNER and/or C.L. MOORE was one of the many pseudonyms of Kuttner's and one of two famous ones used by the great husband and wife writing team. It is hard to say which one wrote which story but they influenced each other even if they did not collaborate. Their famous novel under the O'Donnell name was *Fury* – now published as being by Henry Kuttner. Kuttner also wrote under the names C.H. Liddell, Keith Hammond and many others. So great was the number of his pseudonyms, and so varied his styles, that when Jack Vance, a great writer himself, first started, many people thought this was another Kuttner alias and this fact appeared in many books at the time. (See Lewis Padgett.)

Finn O'Donnevan ROBERT SHECKLEY was a name used to publish some ten stories, mostly in *Galaxy* in the fifties, at a time when Sheckley was writing many stories for that magazine under his own name.

JOHN W. CAMPBELL JNR

PHILIP JOSÉ FARMER

JOHN BRUNNER

C. L. MOORE

Lewis Padgett HENRY KUTTNER and/or C.L. MOORE is the other pseudonym used by these writers and is justly their most famous one, under which they wrote many superb stories and two short novels, *Tomorrow and Tomorrow* and *The Far Reality*. The name was derived from Kuttner's mother's maiden name (Lewis) and Moore's grandmother's maiden name (Padgett).

Mark Phillips RANDALL GARRETT and LAURENCE JANIFER – used for three serials in *Astounding*

between 1959 and 1961 about Kenneth Malone, an FBI agent a little out of the ordinary. (See Darrel Langart and Robert Randall.)

Robert Randall ROBERT SILVERBERG and RANDALL GARRETT – several stories and one novel, *The Dawning Light*, appeared in *Astounding* and other magazines in the late fifties.

LAURENCE JANIFER   POUL ANDERSON

Winston P. Sanders POUL ANDERSON had several stories published in the late fifties and early sixties, mostly in *Astounding/Analog*. Anderson also wrote under the name Michael Karageorge.

Vargo Statten JOHN RUSSELL FEARN had a science fiction magazine named after him in Britain in the fifties. The magazine was filled with pseudonymous writers. Fearn was an extremely prolific author under many names and in many fields. Interest in his work managed to produce a new British science fiction magazine in the early seventies (*Vision of Tomorrow*). Charles Platt was greatly influenced by his writing.

Don A. Stuart JOHN W. CAMPBELL JR – used by Campbell to distinguish his more serious fiction from his equally successful intergalactic melodramas. The name came, quite simply, from his wife's maiden name, Dona Stuart.

Kilgore Trout was a creation of Kurt Vonnegut and has appeared in several of his novels, notably *God Bless You, Mr Rosewater* and *Breakfast of Champions*. One of the novels Trout was credited with writing was *Venus on the Half Shell*. Philip José Farmer, under the Trout pseudonym, turned the imaginary novel into unreadable reality.

Keith Woodcott JOHN BRUNNER – pseudonym used for three short stories and a novel, *Crack of Doom*, in *New Worlds* and *Science Fantasy* in the fifties and sixties. The surname was chosen by the editor, Ted Carnell, out of a telephone directory. Other pseudonyms of Brunner's include Trevor Staines and John Loxmith (used for his first published magazine story in *Astounding* in 1953).

Tully Zetford KENNETH BULMER wrote the Hook series of novels in 1974 and 1975. They were not as successful as his Dray Prescot novels and only lasted four books.

Throughout the world there are many awards for Science Fiction and Fantasy. On the whole they are presented to the 'best' novel of the year, although the two awards most famous in sf, the Hugo and the Nebula, are awarded in all categories of fiction, including Art and Dramatic presentation (although at the time of writing the Science Fiction Writers of America have voted that the Nebula will no longer be awarded for sf film).

This selective look at awards concentrates on awards for novels, and does not include any references to science fiction in the cinema.

Prix Jules Verne

Awarded by the French publishers Hachette Library from 1927 to 1933 for the best original story, the winner receiving Fr. 5000. It was revived in 1958 by Hachette and Gallimard and ran until 1963, during which time the following awards were presented: in 1958, to Serge Martel for *L'Adieu Aux Astres*, 1959 to Daniel Drode for *Surface de la Planete*, 1960 to Albert Higon for *La Machine du Pouvoir*, 1961 to Jerome Seriel for *Le Sub-espace*, 1962 to Philippe Curval for *Le Ressac de L'Espace*, and 1963 to Vladimir Volkoff for *Metro Pour L'Enfer*.

World Fantasy Awards

Awarded by a panel of judges and presented at the annual World Fantasy Convention. In 1975 the award for the best novel went to Patricia McKillip, for *The Forgotten Beasts of Eld*; a Life Award was presented to Robert Bloch. In 1976 the award for the best novel went to Richard Matheson for *Bid Time Return*, and the Life Award to Fritz Leiber.

Prix Apollo

Originated in France by Jacques Sadoul in 1971 to commemorate Apollo XI, it is annually awarded to the best sf novel published in France by a jury of 11 distinguished non-sf writers, critics, journalists and one scientist. The books so far favoured are: 1972, *Isle of the Dead* (Roger Zelazny), 1973, *Stand on Zanzibar* (John Brunner), 1974, *The Iron Dream* (Norman Spinrad), 1975 *The Embedding* (Ian Watson), 1976 *Nightwings* (Robert Silverberg) and 1977 *Cette Chère Humanité* (Philippe Curval).

John W. Campbell Memorial Award

Presented each spring by a small panel of critics and writers for the best novel of the previous year: 1973, to Barry Malzberg for *Beyond Apollo*; 1974 tied between Arthur Clarke's *Rendezvous with Rama* and Robert Merle's *Malevil*; 1975 to Philip Dick for *Flow My Tears the Policeman Said*; 1976 to Wilson Tucker for *The Year of the Quiet Sun*, published 1971 (the judges decided that no novel published in 1975 came up to the standard required, forcing both

Silverberg's *The Stochastic Man*, and Shaw's *Orbitsville* into the position of 'runners up'); 1977 to Kingsley Amis for *The Alteration*.

Pilgrim Award

Presented by the Science Fiction Research Association to individuals who have advanced the scholarly understanding of sf by their academic effort in the field. The award is named after J.O. Bailey's pioneering work *Pilgrims Through Space and Time*. The award has gone to: J.O. Bailey (1970), Marjorie Nicholson (1971), Julius Kagarlitski (1972), Jack Williamson (1973), I.F. Clarke (1974), Damon Knight (1975).

The International Fantasy Award

Presented by an international panel of judges for the best sf novel and non-fiction book of science-fictional interest of the year; the non-fiction category was dropped after 1953. In 1951 it was awarded to *Earth Abides*, by George R. Stewart, and to Willy Ley and Chesley Bonestell for *The Conquest of Space*; in 1952 to *Fancies and Goodnights* by John Collier, and to Arthur Clarke for *The Exploration of Space*; in 1953 to *City* by Clifford Simak, and to Willy Ley and L. Sprague de Camp for *Lands Beyond*; in 1954 to *More Than Human* by Theodore Sturgeon; in 1955 to *A Mirror For Observers* by Edgar Pangborn; in 1957 (there was no award in 1956) to *Lord of the Rings* by J.R.R. Tolkien.

The John W. Campbell Award

Presented annually at the World Science Fiction Convention and decided by popular vote. It is an award for the best new writer. The year stated is that in which the convention was held. In 1973 to Jerry Pournelle; in 1974 to Spider Robinson and Lisa Tuttle; in 1975 to P.J. Plauger; in 1976 to Tom Reamy; in 1977 to C.J. Cherryh.

The Nebula Awards

Presented annually by the Science Fiction Writers of America, the members of which nominate and vote for works in a large number of categories. Recently the award for Dramatic Presentation has been dropped, to the concern of many members. The voting system has also caused internal controversy, and many writers have made it clear that they do not wish even to be considered for a Nebula. Below are listed the winning novels in each year, and a selection of the winning shorter fiction. A selection from the novel 'runners up' is also given, since this illustrates the basic unfairness of any award system that considers only a single novel to have won. The dates are the year of American publication.

NOVELS: *Dune* Frank Herbert, (1965); *Babel 17* Samuel Delany, and *Flowers for Algernon* Daniel

Keyes (1966 tied); *The Einstein Intersection* Samuel Delany (1967); *Rite of Passage* Alexei Panshin (1968); *The Left Hand of Darkness* Ursula Le Guin (1969); *Ringworld* Larry Niven (1970); *A Time of Changes* Robert Silverberg (1971); *The Gods Themselves* Isaac Asimov (1972); *Rendezvous with Rama* Arthur Clarke (1973); *The Dispossessed* Ursula Le Guin (1974); *The Forever War* Joe Haldeman (1975); *Man Plus* Frederik Pohl (1976)

RUNNERS UP: Only a selection is included here, but they give an idea of the immensely high standard of the sf novel, and of the difficulty in selecting a clear winner: *Dr Bloodmoney*, Philip Dick; *The Genocides*, Thomas Disch; *The Three Stigmata of Palmer Eldritch*, Philip Dick; *Nova Express*, Burroughs; *The Moon is a Harsh Mistress*, Robert Heinlein; *Thorns*, Robert Silverberg; *Black Easter*, James Blish; *Do Androids Dream of Electric Sheep*, Philip Dick; *Past Master*, R.A. Lafferty; *Stand on Zanzibar*, John Brunner; *Bug Jack Barron*, Norman Spinrad; *Slaughterhouse 5*, Kurt Vonnegut; *The Year of the Quiet Sun*, Wilson Tucker; *The Steel Crocodile*, D.G. Compton; *The Byworlder*, Poul Anderson; *What Entropy Means to Me*, George Alec Effinger; *The Book of Skulls*, Robert Silverberg; *Dying Inside*, Robert Silverberg; *Time Enough for Love*, Robert Heinlein; *Gravity's Rainbow*, Thomas Pynchon; *Flow My Tears the Policeman Said*, Philip Dick; *334*, Thomas M. Disch

SHORTER FICTION: the following is a selection of award-winning fiction of short story to novella length: *He who Shapes*, Roger Zelazny (1965); *The Saliva Tree*, Brian Aldiss (1965); *The Last Castle*, Jack Vance (1966); *Behold the Man*, Michael Moorcock (1967); *Aye and Gomorrah*, Samuel Delany (1967); *Dragon Rider*, Anne McCaffrey (1968); *Time considered as a Helix of Semi-Precious Stones*, Samuel Delany (1969); *Passengers*, Robert Silverberg - (1969); *Ill met in Lankhmar*, Fritz Leiber (1970); *The Missing Man*, Katherine MacLean (1971); *When it Changed*, Joanna Russ (1972); *Of Mist, and Grass, and Sand*, Vonda N. McIntyre (1973); *Born with the Dead*, Robert Silverberg (1974); *San Diego Lightfoot Sue*, Tom Reamy (1975); *The Bicentennial Man*, Isaac Asimov (1976); *A Crowd of Shadows*, Charles L. Grant (1976).

GRAND MASTER AWARD: presented for 'lifetime achievement in science fiction writing': in 1974 to Robert Heinlein; in 1976 to Clifford Simak.

The Hugo Awards

More correctly called the Science Fiction Achievement Awards, although the nickname 'Hugo' is invariably used. The nickname is, of course, from Hugo Gernsback, editor of the first English language sf magazine, *Amazing Stories*. The awards are presented annually at the World Science Fiction Convention and are decided by popular vote. Over the years the categories have changed, for example with the introduction of an award for Dramatic Presentation, and the distinction between a novelette and a novella. The award began in 1953 at the Philadelphia World Convention. The dates given are the years of the convention.

NOVELS: *The Demolished Man*, Alfred Bester (1953);

no award (1954); *They'd Rather Be Right*, Mark Clifton and Frank Riley (1955); *Double Star*, Robert Heinlein (1956); no award (1957); *The Big Time*, Fritz Leiber (1958); *A Case of Conscience*, James Blish (1959); *Starship Troopers*, Robert Heinlein (1960); *A Canticle for Leibowitz*, Walter Miller (1961); *Stranger in a Strange Land*, Robert Heinlein (1962); *The Man in the High Castle*, Philip Dick (1963); *Here Gather the Stars (Way Station)*, Clifford Simak (1964); *The Wanderer*, Fritz Leiber (1965); *And Call me Conrad*, Roger Zelazny tied with *Dune* Frank Herbert (1966); *The Moon is a Harsh Mistress*, Robert Heinlein (1967); *Lord of Light*, Roger Zelazny (1968); *Stand on Zanzibar*, John Brunner (1969); *The Left Hand of Darkness*, Ursula Le Guin (1970); *Ringworld*, Larry Niven (1971); *To Your Scattered Bodies Go*, Philip José Farmer (1972); *The Gods Themselves*, Isaac Asimov (1973); *Rendezvous with Rama*, Arthur Clarke (1974); *The Dispossessed*, Ursula Le Guin (1975); *The Forever War*, Joe Haldeman (1976); *Where Late the Sweet Birds sang*, Kate Wilhelm (1977).

OTHER CATEGORIES: The Hugo, on occasion, has been awarded in many areas of sf and fandom, categories often being created to honour a specific person or work. A sampling follows:

In 1953 Forrest J. Ackerman was awarded the Hugo for being the Fan Personality of the year; and in 1959 to Walter Willis for being the outstanding 'actifan' of the year. In 1967 the categories of Best Fan Artist and best Fan Writer were introduced, and among the latter who were subsequently honoured were: Alexei Panshin, Ted White (now editor of *Amazing*), Harry Warner, Bob Tucker, Richard Geis, Terry Carr and Susan Wood.

In 1956 Robert Silverberg was awarded a Hugo as 'the most promising New Author'. This award has not been made since.

Special committee Hugo Awards have occasionally been made: in 1960 to Hugo Gernsback as 'The Father of Magazine Science Fiction'; in 1963 to P. Schuyler Miller for the best book reviews (in *Astounding/Analog*) and to Isaac Asimov for 'adding the science to science fiction' in his articles in *The Magazine of Fantasy and SF*; in 1974 to Chesley Bonestell for his remarkable contributions in the area of art; in 1975 to Donald Wollheim and Walt Lee for their contributions to sf. In 1966 an award was presented for the Best All-Time Series. It went to Isaac Asimov for *Foundation*.

The Dramatic Presentation Awards have gone to a variety of media-trips: *The Twilight Zone* (1960, '61 and '62), *Dr. Strangelove* (1965), episodes of *Star Trek* (1967 and '68), *2001: A Space Odyssey* (1969); *TV coverage of Apollo XI* (1970), *A Clockwork Orange* (1972), *Slaughterhouse 5* (1973), *Sleeper* (1974), *Young Frankenstein* (1975).

The Hugo Award for the best magazine has gone to *Astounding/Analog* (six awards), *Magazine of Fantasy and Science Fiction* (nine awards), *Worlds of If* (three awards), *Galaxy* (one award), *New Worlds* (one award). This category was replaced in 1973 with an award for the best professional editor, which Ben Bova of *Analog* took five times running. Best Professional Artist has been Frank Kelly Freas (ten awards), Ed Emshwiller (five awards), Jack Gaughan (three awards), Hannes Bok (one award), Leo and Diane Dillon (one award), John Schoenherr (one award), Roy Krenkel (one award), Frank Frazetta (one award) and Rick Sternbach (one award).

SHORT STORIES: Among the many shorter works of fiction that have received the Hugo are: *The Star*, Arthur Clarke (1956); *Flowers for Algernon*, Daniel Keyes (1960); *The Hothouse* series, Brian Aldiss (1962); *Neutron Star*, Larry Niven (1967); *Weyr Search*, Anne McCaffrey (1968); *Nightwings*, Robert Silverberg (1969); *Slow Sculpture*, Theodore Sturgeon (1971); *The Word for World is Forest*, Ursula Le Guin (1973); *The Girl Who Was Plugged In*, James Tiptree Jr (1974); *The Deathbird*, Harlan Ellison (1974); *A Song for Lya*, George R. Martin (1975); *Catch that Zeppelin*, Fritz Leiber (1976); *The Bicentennial Man*, Isaac Asimov (1977)

The Australian Science Fiction Achievement Awards

More familiarly known as The Ditmar Awards, a nickname derived from Ditmar 'Dick' Jenssen who was involved in their conception. The awards are presented annually at the Australian National sf convention, and are decided by popular vote. Awards are given for the Best Australian Fiction of the year, the Best International Fiction of the year, the best Australian Fanzine, and in 1969 was awarded to Brian Aldiss as the Best Contemporary

author, in 1970 to *Vision of Tomorrow* as the best professional magazine, and in 1973 to a hilariously bad fannish film entitled 'Aussiefan', directed by John Litchen; this received the award for Dramatic Presentation. *Best Australian Fiction: False Fatherland*, A. Bertram Candler (1969); *Dancing Gerontius*, Lee Harding (1970); *The Bitter Pill*, A. Bertram Chandler (1971); *Fallen Spacemen*, Lee Harding (1972); *Let it Ring*, John Foyster (1973); no award (1974, 1975); *The Big Black Mark*, A. Bertram Chandler (1976); *Walkers on the Sky*, David Lake (1977)

Best International Fiction: Camp Concentration, Thomas Disch (1969); *Cosmicomics*, Italo Calvino (1970); no award (1971); *Ringworld*, Larry Niven (1972); *The Gods Themselves*, Isaac Asimov (1973); no award (1974); *Protector*, Larry Niven (1975); *The Forever War*, Joe Haldeman (1976); *The Space Machine*, Christopher Priest (1977)

The British Science Fiction Association Award

This is for the best novel by a British writer and is awarded at the Easter Convention. The award has variously been decided by popular vote and by BSFA committee decision. In 1974 it was awarded to *Rendezvous with Rama*, Arthur Clarke; in 1975 to *Inverted World*, Christopher Priest; in 1976 to *Orbitsville*, Bob Shaw; in 1977 to *Brontomek*, Michael Coney.

magazines

The following list is selective in that it concentrates on those magazines that are predominantly science fiction rather than fantasy or horror. Certain borderline cases are included where of importance. Contents are designated thus:

SF = Science Fiction; Fy = Fantasy; H = Horror Symbols are listed in order of predominance and are preceded by the number of issues published, e.g. 5 SFFyH means this magazine is mostly science fiction with some fantasy and occasional horror story.

Country	Title	Dates	Number of Issues	Contents
North America	A. Merritt's Fantasy Magazine	Dec 1949–Oct 1950	5	FySFH
	Adventures Futuristes, Les	March–Sept 1949	10	SF
	Air Wonder Stories	July 1929–May 1930	11	SF
	Algol	Nov 1973–current	10 (winter 78)	SF
	Amazing Detective Tales (see Scientific Detective Monthly)			
	Amazing Stories	April 1926–current	485 (Jan 78)	SF
	Amazing Stories Annual	Summer 1927	1	
	Amazing Stories Quarterly	Winter 1928–Fall 1934	22	SF
	Analog (see Astounding Stories)			
	Arkham Collector, The	Summer 1967–Summer 1971	10	HFySF

Country	Title	Dates	Number of Issues	Contents
North America	Arkham Sampler	Winter 1948–Autumn 1949	8	HSFFy
	Astonishing Stories	Feb 1940–April 1943	16	SF
	Astounding Stories/SF (retitled Analog from Feb 1960)	Jan 1930–current	573 (Aug 78)	SF
	Astounding SF/Stories Yearbook	Summer–Fall 1970	2	SF
	Avon Fantasy Reader	Feb 1947–Winter 1952	18	FySFH
	Avon Science Fiction Reader	Spring 1951–Winter 1952	3	FySF
	Avon SF & Fantasy Reader	Jan–April 1953	2	SFFyH
	Beyond Fantasy Fiction	July 1953–Spring 1955	10	FySFH
	Beyond Infinity	Nov–Dec 1967	1	SFFy
	Bizarre Fantasy Tales	Fall 1970–March 1971	2	HFy
	Bizarre Mystery Magazine	Oct 1965–Jan 1966	3	HSF
	Captain Future	Winter 1940–Spring 1944	17	SF
	Captain Hazzard	May 1938	1	SFFy
	Captain Zero	Nov 1949–March 1950	3	SFFy
	Comet	Dec 1940–July 1941	5	SF
	Cosmic Stories/SF	March–July 1941	3	SF
	Cosmos SF & Fantasy	Sept 1953–July 1954	4	SFFy
	Cosmos SF & Fantasy	May 1977–Nov 1977		SFFy
	Coven 13 (continued as Witchcraft & Sorcery)	Sept 1969–March 1970	4	FyHSF
	Dream World	Feb–Aug 1957	3	FySF
	Dynamic SF	Dec 1952–Jan 1954	6	SF
	Dynamic Science Stories	Feb–April 1939	2	SF
	Eerie Tales	July 1941	1	FySF
	Eternity SF	July 1972–current	4	SF
	Famous Fantastic Mysteries	Sept 1939–June 1953	81	FySFH
	Famous SF	Winter 1966–Spring 1969	9	SF
	Fanciful Tales	Fall 1936	1	FySFH
	Fantastic (Stories)	Summer 1952–current	195 (June 77)	FySFH
	Fantastic Adventures	May 1939–March 1953	129	SFFy
	Fantastic Adventures Yearbook	Spring 1970	1	FySF
	Fantastic Novels	July 1940–April 1941 March 1948–June 1951	5 20	FySF
	Fantastic SF	Aug–Dec 1952	2	SF
	Fantastic Story Magazine/ Quarterly	Spring 1950–Spring 1955	23	SF
	Fantastic Universe	June/July 1953–March 1960	69	SFFy
	Fantasy Book	Summer 1947–Winter 1951	8	SFFy
	Fantasy Fiction/Stories	May–Dec 1950	2	HFySF
	Fantasy Fiction Magazine	Feb/March–Nov 1953	4	FySFH
	Fear	May–July 1960	2	HSFFy
	Flash Gordon Strange Adventure Magazine	Dec 1936	1	SFFy
	Frank Reade Library	Sept 1892–Aug 1898	191	SF

Country	Title	Dates	No. of Issues	Contents
North America	Frank Reade Weekly	Oct 1902–Aug 1904	96	SF
	Forgotten Fantasy	Oct 1970–June 1971	5	FyHSF
	Future Fiction/SF	Nov 1939–July 1943 May 1950–April 1960	17 48	
	Galaxy SF/Magazine	Oct 1950–current	238 (July 77)	SF
	Galileo	Sept 1976–current	7 (March 78)	SF
	Gamma	Spring 1963–Sept 1965	5	SFFyH
	Great SF (retitled Science Fiction Greats from Winter 1969)	Winter 1965–Spring 1971	21	SF
	Haunt of Horror	June–August 1977	2	HFySF
	If (also known as Worlds of If though not official title)	March 1952–Dec 1974	175	SFFy
	Imagination	Oct 1950–Oct 1958	63	SFFy
	Imaginative Tales (retitled Space Travel July–Nov 1958)	Sept 1954–Nov 1958	26	SF
	Infinity SF	Nov 1955–Nov 1958	20	SF
	International SF	Nov 1967–June 1968	2	SFFy
	I. Asimov's SF Magazine	Spring 1977–current	7 (May 78)	SF
	Magazine of Fantasy & Science Fiction (usually known as F & SF)	Fall 1949–current	317 (Oct 77)	SFFyH
	Magazine of Horror	Aug 1963–April 1971	36	HFySF
	Magic Carpet (see Oriental Stories)			
	Marvel (Science) Stories/Tales/SF	Aug 1938–April 1941 Nov 1950–May 1952	9 6	SFH
	Marvel Tales	May 1934–Summer 1935	5	SFFy
	Miracle Science and Fantasy	April/May–June/July 1931	2	SFFy
	The Most Thrilling SF Ever Told (retitled Thrilling SF from Spring 1971)	Summer 1966–July 1975	42	SF
	The Mysterious Traveller Magazine (predominantly a mystery/crime magazine)	Nov 1951–Fall 1952	5	HFySF
	Mystic (retitled Search and continued with non-fiction)	Nov 1953–July 1956	16	FyHSF
	Odyssey SF	Spring–Summer 1976	2	SFFy
	Orbit SF	Summer 1953–Nov/Dec 1954	5	SF
	Oriental Stories (retitled Magic Carpet from Jan 1933)	Oct 1930–Jan 1934	14	FyHSF
	The Original Science Fiction Stories (see Science Fiction)			
	Other Worlds Science Stories (retitled Flying Saucers in June 1957 and continued with non-fiction)	Nov 1949–July 1953 May 1955–Oct 1957	31 14	SFFy
	Out of this World Adventures	July–Dec 1950	2	SFFy
	Planet Stories	Winter 1939–Summer 1955	71	SFFy
	Rocket Stories	April–Sept 1953	3	SF
	Satellite SF	Oct 1956–May 1959	18	SFFy
	Saturn SF and Fantasy (retitled Saturn Web Detective and later Web Terror Stories)	March 1957–March 1958	5	SFFy

Country	Title	Dates	No. of Issues	Contents
North America	Science Fantasy (Yearbook)	Summer 1970–Spring 1971	4	SFFy
	Science Fiction (Stories)	March 1939–Sept 1941 Winter 1953–May 1960	12 38	SF
	Science Fiction (Canadian edition)	Oct 1941–June 1942	6	SFFy
	Science Fiction Adventures	Nov 1952–May 1954	9	SF
	Science Fiction Adventures	Dec 1956–June 1958	12	SF
	Science Fiction (Adventure Classics)	Summer 1967–Nov 1974	30	SF
	Science Fiction Digest	Spring–Summer 1954	2	SFFy
	Science Fiction Plus	March–Dec 1953	7	SF
	Science Fiction Quarterly	Summer 1940–Spring 1943 May 1951–Feb 1958	10 28	SFFy
	Science Fiction Yearbook	1967–1971	5	SF
	Science Stories	Oct 1953–April 1954	4	SFFy
	Science Wonder Quarterly (see Wonder Stories Quarterly)			
	Science Wonder Stories (see Wonder Stories)			
	Scientific Detective Monthly (retitled Amazing Detective Tales in June 1930. Sold by Gernsback to Wallace Bamber who continued title as straight detective)	Jan–Oct 1930	10	SF
	Space Adventures	Winter 1970–Summer 1971	6	SF
	Space SF	May 1952–Sept 1953	8	SF
	Space SF Magazine	Spring–Aug 1957	2	SF
	Space Stories	Oct 1952–June 1953	5	SF
	Space Travel (see Imaginative Tales)			
	Spaceway	Dec 1953–June 1955 Jan 1969–June 1970	4	SF
	Star SF (only magazine issue of *Star* paperback anthology series)	Jan 1958	1	SF
	Stardust	March–Nov 1940	5	SFFy
	Startling Mystery Stories	Summer 1966–March 1971	18	HFySF
	Startling Stories	Jan 1939–Fall 1955	99	SF
	Stirring Science Stories (half the magazine called Stirring Fantasy Fiction)	Feb 1941–March 1942	4	SFFy
	Strange Fantasy	Spring 1969–Fall 1970	6	FySF
	Strange Stories	Feb 1939–Feb 1941	13	FyHSF
	Strange Tales	Sept 1931–Jan 1933	7	HFySF
	The Strangest Stories Ever Told	Summer 1970	1	HFySF
	Super Science Fiction	Dec 1956–Oct 1959	18	SFH
	Super Science Stories	March 1940–May 1943 Jan 1949–Aug 1951	16 15	SF
	Super Science Stories (Canadian edition) (retitled Super Science and Fantastic Stories from Dec 1944)	Aug 1942–Dec 1945	21	SFFy

Country	Title	Dates	No. of Issues	Contents
North America	Suspense	Spring 1951–Winter 1952	4	FyHSF
	Tales of Magic and Mystery	Dec 1927–April 1928	5	FyHSF
	Tales of the Frightened	Spring–August 1957	2	HFySF
	Ten Story Fantasy	Spring 1951	1	SFFy(n)
	The Thrill Book	March–Oct 1919	16	FyHSF
	Thrilling SF (see The Most Thrilling SF Ever Told)			
	Thrilling Wonder Stories (see of Wonder Stories)			
	Tops in Science Fiction	Spring–Fall 1953	2	SFFy
	Two Complete Science Adventure Books	Winter 1950–Spring 1954	11	SF
	Treasury of Great SF Stories (title became Great SF Stories with third issue)	1964–1966	3	SF
	Uncanny Tales (Canadian) (not to be confused with the US terror pulp Uncanny Tales)	Nov 1940–Sept 1943	21	SFFy
	Unearth	Winter 1977–current	6	SF
	Universe SF	June 1953–March 1955	10	SFFy
	Unknown (Worlds) (titled Unknown until Oct 1941 issue)	March 1939–Oct 1943	39	FyHSF
	Unusual Stories	March 1934–Winter 1935	3	FySF
	Vanguard SF	June 1958	1	SF
	Venture SF	Jan 1957–July 1958 May 1969–Aug 1970	10 6	SF
	Vertex	April 1973–Aug 1975	16	SF
	Vortex SF	(Summer)–(Fall) 1953	2	SFFy
	Weird Mystery	Fall 1970–Summer 1971	4	FySF
	Weird Tales	March 1923–Sept 1954 Summer 1973–Summer 1974	279 4	HFySF
	Weird Terror Tales	Winter 1969–Fall 1970	3	HFySF
	Whispers	July 1973–current	10	HFySF
	The Witch's Tales	Nov–Dec 1936	2	FySFH
	Wonder Stories (titled Science Wonder Stories up till May 1930; retitled Thrilling Wonder Stories from Aug 1936. Two pulp reprint selections appeared in 1957 and 1963)	June 1929–April 1936 Aug 1936–Winter 1955	78	SF
	Wonder Stories Quarterly (retitled) Science Wonder Quarterly)	Fall 1929–Winter 1933	14	SF
	Wonder Story Annual	1950–1953	4	SF
United Kingdom	Alien Worlds	Summer 1966	1	SFHFy
	Amazing Adventures see Strange Adventures			
	Amazing Science Stories (reprinted from the Australian *Thrills Inc.*)	(March)–(April) 1951	2	SF
	Authentic SF Monthly (see Science Fiction Fortnightly.)			

Country	Title	Dates	No. of Issues	Contents
United Kingdom	British SF Magazine (see Vargo Statten SF Magazine)			
	British Space Fiction Magazine (see Vargo Statten SF Magazine)			
	Cosmic Science Stories (reprint of Sept 1949 US Super Science Stories abridged)	(Summer) 1950	1	SF
	Fantasy	(Summer) 1938–(Summer) 1939	3	SF
	Fantasy	Dec 1946–Aug 1947	3	SF
	Fantasy Tales	Summer–current	2	FyHSF
	Futuristic Science Stories	(Summer) 1950–(Summer) 1954	16	SF
	Futuristic Stories	1946–1947	2	SF
	Impulse (see Science Fantasy)			
	Nebula	Autumn 1952–June 1959	41	SF
	New Worlds	(Summer) 1946–current	211	SF
	Other Times	Nov 1975–Feb 1976	2	FySF
	Outlands	Winter 1946	1	FySFH
	Science Fantasy (retitled Impulse from March 1966)	Summer 1950–Feb 1966 March 1966 –Feb 1967	81 12	SFFyH SFFy
	Science Fiction Aventures	March 1958–May 1963	32	SF
	S.F. Digest	Summer 1976	1	SF
	Science Fiction Fortnightly (retitled Authentic SF Monthly)	Jan 1951–Oct 1957	85	SF
	Science Fiction Library	1960	3	SF
	Science Fiction Monthly	Feb 1974–May 1976	28	SF
	Scoops	Feb 1934–June 1934	20	SF
	Space Fact & Fiction	(March)–(Oct) 1954	8	SF
	Strange Adventures (first issue also titled Amazing Adventures)	1946–1947	2	SF
	Tales of Tomorrow	(Autumn) 1950–(Summer) 1954	11	SF
	Tales of Wonder	(Winter) 1937–Spring 1942	16	SF
	Vargo Statten SF Magazine (retitled British SF Magazine from issue 6, and British Space Fiction Magazine from June 1955)	Jan 1954–(Feb) 1956	19	SF
	Venture (fiction reprinted from US Venture and F & SF)	Sept 1963–Dec 1965	28	SFFy
	Vision of Tomorrow	Aug 1969–Sept 1970	12	SF
	Vortex	Jan–May 1977	5	SFFy
	Wonders of the Spaceways	(Winter) 1951–(Spring) 1954	10	SF
	Worlds of Fantasy	(Summer) 1954	14	SF
	Worlds of the Universe	(Winter) 1953	1	SF
	Yankee SF (sf issues of Swan Yankee Magazine)	1941–1942	3	SF

Country	Title	Dates	No. of Issues	Contents
United Kingdom	Worlds Beyond	Dec 1950–Feb 1951	3	SFFy
	Worlds of Fantasy	(Sept) 1968–Spring 1971	4	FySFH
	Worlds of If (see If)			
	Worlds of Tomorrow	April 1963–May 1967 (Summer) 1970–Spring 1971	23 3 3	SF
Argentina	Hombres del Futuro	Late 1940s	3	SF
	Geminis	June–July 1965	2	SF
	Mas Alla	June 1953–June 1957	48	SF
	Minotauro (Spanish edition of US F & SF)	mid-1960s	10	SFFy
	Narraciones Terrorificas	1939–1950	72	SFFyH
	Pistas del Espacio	June 1957–1959	14	SF
	La Revista de Ciencia Ficcion y Fantasia	Oct 1976 – Feb 1977	3	SF
	Urania	Oct–Dec 1953	2	SF
Australia	American SF Magazine	May/June 1952–Sept 1955	41	SF
	F & SF	Nov 1954–July 1958	14	SFFy
	Fantasy Fiction	1949–1951	6	FySF
	Future SF	July 1953–March 1955 April 1967	6 1	SF SF
	Popular SF	July 1953–March 1955	6	SF
		April 1967	1	SF
	Science Fiction Monthly	Aug 1955–Jan 1957	18	SF
	Scientific Thriller	Nov 1948–May 1952	43	SFFy
	Selected SF	May–Sept 1955	5	SF
	Thrills Incorporated	March 1950–June 1952	23	SFFy
	Void	Fall 1975–current	5	SFFy
Austria	Star-Utopia	1957–1958	10	SF
	Uranus	1957–1958	10	SF
Belgium	Anticipations (published in French)	Sept 1945–May 1946	14	SF
	Apollo	May 1972–Nov 1973	20	SFH
	Atlanta	Jan 1966–Dec 1967	12	SF
	Trifid	May 1973–April 1974	4	SFFy
	Utopia	June 1961–May 1963	24	SFFy
Brazil	Galaxia 2000	1968	1	SFFy
Denmark	Manadens Bedste Science-Fiction (Title translates as The Best SF of the Month)	Sept 1975–April 1977	16	SF
	Planetmagasinet	Jan–June 1958	6	SF
	Proxima	Oct 1974–current	12 (Oct 77)	SF
	Science Fiction Magasinet	June 1977–current	7	SF
Finland	Aikamme	Aug–Dec 1958	5	SF
France	Argon	April–Oct 1975	7	SFFy
	Chroniques Terriennes	1975	1	SF

Country	Title	Dates	No. of Issues	Contents
France	Conquêtes	August 1939	2	SF
	Fiction	Oct 1953–current	287 (Oct 77)	SFFy
	Galaxie	Nov 1953–April 1959 May 1964–Aug 1977	65 158	SF
	Horizon 3000	Fall 1976	1	SF
	Nova	Feb 1977	1	SF
	Piranha	March 1977–current	5	FySF
	Satellite	Jan 1958–June 1962	43	SFFy
	Science Fiction Magazine	1953	1	SF
	Science-Fiction Magazine	Nov 1976–May 1977	7	SF
	Spirale	June 1975–Oct 1976	6	SF
	Univers	June 1975–current	11	SF
Germany	Comet	May 1977–current	3	SF
	Galaxis	March 1958–July 1959	15	SF
	Kapitan Mors	1908–1914	180 +	SFAdv
	Ullstein 2000	1971–current(?)		SF
	Utopia-Magazin	May 1955–August 1959	26	SF
Hungary	Galaktika	Fall 1972–current	27	SF
Italy	Altair	Oct 1976–May 1977	8	SFFy
	Au dela du Ciel	March 1958–Feb 1961	40	SFFy
	Cosmic	June 1957–May 1958	3	SF
	Cosmo	Nov 1961–April 1965	89	SF
	Fantascienza Sovietica	Sept 1966–June 1967	7	SF
	Futuro	March 1963–Nov 1964	8	SF
	Galassia (two earlier magazines called Galassia existed in 1953 and 1957)	Jan 1961–current	229	SF
	Galaxy	June 1958–March 1964	72	SF
	Gamma	Oct 1965–March 1968	27	SF
	I Capolavori di Urania	March–Oct 1967	8	SF
	I Romanzi del Cosmo	June 1957–May 1967	202	SF
	I Romanzi di Urania (retitled Urania from Issue 152)	Oct 1952–current	nearly 700	
	Nova	May 1967–current		SF
	Oltre il Cielo	Sept 1957–Feb 1970	154	SF
	Robot	April 1976–current	21	SF
	Scienza Fantastica	April 1952–March 1953	7	SFFy
	Urania (see I Romanzi di Urania)			
	Urania (original companion to above)	Nov 1952–Dec 1953	14	
Japan	Hoseki (title means jewel)	(Summer) 1956	1	SF
	Kiso–Tengai (title means fantastic)	Jan–Oct 1974 April 1976–current	10 21	FySFH SF
	Seiun (title means nebula)	Jan 1955	1	SFFy
	SF Magazine	Feb 1960–current	226 (Sept 77)	SFFy
Mexico	Ciencia y Fantasia (Mexican edition of US F & SF)	Sept 1956–Dec 1957	14	SFFy

Country	Title	Dates	No. of Issues	Contents
Mexico	Los Cuentos Fantasticos	July 1948–May 1953	44	SFFy
	Enigmas (Mexican edition of US Startling Stories)	Aug 1955–May 1958	16	SF
	Fantasias del Futuro	Sept 1958	1	SF
Netherlands	Essef (retitled Orbit after first issue)	Jan 1977–current	4	SF
	Fantasie En Wetenschap	Dec 1948–March 1949	4	SFFy
	Galaxis	Oct 1966–Feb 1967	5	SF
	Morgen	Sept 1971–Nov 1972	5	SFFy
		May 1975	1	
	Orbit (see Essef)			
	Planeet	Jan 1953	1	SF
Norway	Science Fiction Magasinet (title changed to Nova in Spring 1973)	Jan 1971–current		SF
	Tempo-Magasinet	Nov 1953–March 1954	5	SF
Romania	Collectia Povestiri	June 1955–Oct 1969	373	SF
Spain	Anticipacion	Oct 1966–April 1967	7	SF
	Fantastica	1948	19	SFFy
	Neuva Dimension	Jan 1968–current		SFFy
Sweden	Galaxy	Sept 1958–July 1960	19	SF
	Häpna	March 1954–Jan 1966	137	SF
		Winter–Autumn 1969	4	
	Hugin	April 1916–Dec 1920	82	SFFy
	Jules Verne Magasinet	Oct 1940–Feb 1947	332	FySF
		May 1969–current		
Turkey	Antares	March 1974–Spring 1975	6	SFFy
	X-Bilinmeyen	April 1976–current		SF
Yugoslavia	Galaksija	April 1972–current		SF
	Kosmoplov	March 1969–May 1970	23	SF

Films

Title	Date	Director	Country
Aelita	1924	Yakov Protazanov	Russia
Airship Destroyer The, (aka Battle in the Clouds, Aerial Torpedo, Aerial Warfare)	1909	Walter Booth	Great Britain
Andromeda Strain, The	1971	Robert Wise	United States
Animal Farm	1954	John Halls and Joy Batchelor	Great Britain
At the Earth's Core	1976	Kevin Connor	Great Britain
Barbarella	1967	Roger Vadim	France/Italy
Battle for the Planet of the Apes	1973	J. Lee Thompson	United States

Title	Date	Director	Country
Bed Sitting Room, The	1969	Richard Lester	Great Britain
Beast from 20,000 Fathoms, The	1953	Eugene Lourie	United States
Beginning of the End, The	1957	Bert I. Gordon	United States
Beneath the Planet of the Apes	1970	Ted Post	United States
Blob, The	1958	Irvin S. Yeaworth	United States
Boy and His Dog, A	1975	L.Q. Jones	United States
Brick Bradford (serial)	1947	Spencer Bennet and Thomas Carr	United States
Buck Rogers (serial)	1939	Ford Beebe and Saul A. Goodkind	United States
Bug	1975	Jeannot Szwarc	United States
Captain Nemo and the Underwater City	1969	James Hill	Great Britain
Cars That Ate Paris, The	1974	Peter Weir	Australia
Charly	1968	Ralph Nelson	United States
Chosen Survivors	1974	Sutton Roley	United States
Clockwork Orange, A	1971	Stanley Kubrick	Great Britain
Close Encounters of the Third Kind	1977	Steven Spielberg	United States
Conquest of Space, The	1955	Byron Haskin	United States
Conquest of the Planet of the Apes	1972	J. Lee Thompson	United States
Crack in the World	1965	Andrew Marton	United States
Crazy Ray, The/Paris Qui Dort	1923	Rene Clair	France
Creature From The Black Lagoon, The	1954	Jack Arnold	United States
Damned, The	1961	Joseph Losey	Great Britain
Day Mars Invaded the Earth, The	1963	Maury Dexter	United States
Day the Earth Caught Fire, The	1961	Val Guest	Great Britain
Day The Earth Stood Still, The	1951	Robert Wise	United States
Death Race 2000	1975	Paul Bartel	United States
Demon Seed	1976	Donald Cammell	United States
Destination Moon	1950	Irving Pichel	United States
Dr Strangelove: or, How I Learned to Stop Worrying and Love The Bomb	1963	Stanley Kubrick	Great Britain
Doppelgänger/Journey to the Far Side of the Sun	1969	Robert Parrish	Great Britain
Duel	1971	Steven Spielberg	United States
Empire of the Ants	1977	Bert I. Gordon	United States
Escape from the Planet of the Apes	1971	Don Taylor	United States
Fahrenheit 451	1965	François Truffaut	Great Britain
Fantastic Planet	1973	Rene Laloux	France/Czechoslovakia
Fantastic Voyage	1966	Richard Fleischer	United States
Fin du Monde, La	1931	Abel Gance	France
Final Programme, The	1973	Robert Fuest	Great Britain
First Men in the Moon	1964	Nathan Juran	Great Britain
Flash Gordon (serial)		Frederick Stephani	United States

Title	Date	Director	Country
Flash Gordon Conquers the Universe (serial)	1940	Ford Beebe and Ray Ray Taylor	United States
Flash Gordon's Trip to Mars (serial)	1938	Ford Beebe and Robert F. Hill	United States
Food of the Gods	1976	Bert I. Gordon	United States
Forbidden Planet	1976	Fred M. Wilcox	United States
Forbin Project, The	1969	Joseph Sargent	United States
Four-Sided Triangle, The	1953	Terence Fisher	Great Britain
F.P.I. Does Not Answer	1932	Karl Hartl	Germany
Die Frau im Mond/Woman in the Moon	1929	Fritz Lang	Germany
Futureworld	1976	Richard T. Heffron	United States
Giant Spider Invasion, The	1975	Bill Rebane	United States
Godzilla	1955	Inoshiro Honda	Japan
Green Slime, The	1968	Kinji Fukasaku	United States/Japan
Himmelskibbet/A Trip to Mars/Sky Ship	1917	Holger-Madsen	Denmark
Homunculus (serial)	1916	Otto Rippert	Germany
Horror Express/Panico en el Transiberianio	1972	Eugenio Martin	Spain/Great Britain
Human Duplicators, The	1964	Hugo Grimaldi	United States
I Married a Monster from Outer Space	1958	Gene Fowler Jr	United States
Ikarie XB 1/Voyage to the End of the Universe	1963	Jindrich Polak	Czechoslovakia
Illustrated Man, The	1968	Jack Smight	United States
Incredible Shrinking Man, The	1957	Jack Arnold	United States
Invaders From Mars	1953	William Cameron Menzies	United States
Invasion	1966	Alan Bridges	Great Britain
Invasion of the Body Snatchers	1956	Don Siegel	United States
Invisible Man, The	1933	James Whale	United States
Invisible Ray, The	1936	Lambert Hillyer	United States
Island of Doctor Moreau, The	1976	Don Taylor	United States
Island of Lost Souls, The	1932	Erle C. Kenton	United States
It Came from Outer Space	1953	Jack Arnold	United States
It's Alive	1974	Larry Cohen	United States
Just Imagine	1930	David Butler	United States
King Kong Escapes	1967	Inoshiro Honda	Japan
Kronos	1957	Kurt Neumann	United States
Land That Time Forgot, The	1974	Kevin Connor	Great Britain
Last Man on Earth, The	1963	Sidney Salkow and Ubaldo Ragona	Italy/United States
Living Dead at the Manchester Morgue, The	1974	Jorge Grau	Spain/Italy
Logan's Run	1976	Michael Anderson	United States
Lost World, The	1925	Harry Hoyt	United States
Lost World, The	1960	Irwin Allen	United States
Man's Genesis	1911	D.W. Griffith	United States

Title	Date	Director	Country
Man with the X-Ray Eyes, The	1963	Roger Corman	United States
Man Who Fell To Earth, The	1976	Nicolas Roeg	Great Britain
Marooned	1969	John Sturges	United States
Meteor	1978	Ronald Neame	United States
Metropolis	1926	Fritz Lang	Germany
Mind of Mr. Soames, The	1970	Alan Cooke	Great Britain
Moon Pilot	1961	James Neilson	United States
Moon Zero Two	1969	Roy Ward Baker	Great Britain
Mysterians, The	1957	Inoshiro Honda	Japan
Night of the Lepus	1972	William F. Claxton	United States
Night of the Living Dead, The	1968	George A. Romero	United States
No Blade of Grass	1970	Cornel Wilde	Great Britain
1984	1956	Michael Anderson	Great Britain
Nothing but the Night	1972	Peter Sasdy	Great Britain
Omega Man, The	1971	Boris Sagal	United States
On the Beach	1959	Stanley Kramer	United States
One Hundred Years After	1911		France
Panic in Year Zero	1962	Ray Milland	United States
Peace Game, The/Gladiators, The	1969	Peter Watkins	Sweden
People that time Forgot, The	1977	Kevin Connor	Great Britain
Phantom Empire (serial)	1935	Otto Brower and B. Reeves Eason	United States
Phase IV	1973	Saul Bass	Great Britain
Planet of the Apes	1968	Franklin J. Schaffner	United States
Power, The	1967	Byron Haskin	United States
Project X	1967	William Castle	United States
Projectionist, The	1968	Harry Hurwitz	United States
Punishment Park	1970	Peter Watkins	United States
Purple Monster Strikes, The (serial)	1945	Spencer Bennet and Fred Brannon	
Quatermass and The Pit/Five Million Years to Earth	1967	Roy Ward Baker	Great Britain
Quatermass Experiment, The	1955	Val Guest	Great Britain
Quatermass II	1957	Val Guest	Great Britain
Queen of Outer Space	1958	Edward Bernds	United States
Rabid	1976	David Cronenberg	Canada
Reluctant Astronaut, The	1966	Edward J. Mongagne	United States
Robinson Crusoe on Mars	1964	Byron Haskin	United States
Rocketship XM	1950	Kurt Neumann	United States
Rollerball	1975	Norman Jewison	United States
Santa Claus Conquers the Martians	1964	Nicholas Webster	United States
Sausage Machine, The/Charcuterie Mechanique	1897	Lumiére Brothers	France
Silent Running	1972	Douglas Trumbull	United States
Slaughterhouse-5	1972	George Roy Hill	United States
Sleeper	1973	Woody Allen	United States

Title	Date	Director	Country
Solaris	1972	Andrei Tarkovsky	Russia
Soylent Green	1973	Richard Fleischer	United States
Space Children, The	1957	Jack Arnold	United States
Spaceways	1953	Terence Fisher	Great Britain
Star Wars	1977	George Lucas	United States
Superman (serial)	1948	Spencer Bennet and Thomas Carr	
Tenth Victim, The/La Decima Vittima/La Dixieme Victime	1965	Elio Petri	Italy/France
Terminal Man, The	1973	Michael Hodges	United States
Them	1953	Gordon Douglas	United States
Thing from Another World, The	1951	Christian Nyby	United States
Things to Come	1936	William Cameron Menzies	Great Britain
This Island Earth	1954	Joseph Newman	United States
THX 1138	1969	George Lucas	United States
Time Machine, The	1960	George Pal	United States
Trip To The Moon, A/Le Voyage Dans La Lune	1902	Georges Méliès	France
Trollenberg Terror, The/Crawling Eye, The	1958	Quentin Lawrence	Great Britain
Twenty Million Miles to Earth	1957	Nathan Juran	United States
Twenty Thousand Leagues under the Sea	1907	Georges Méliès	France
Twenty Thousand Leagues under the Sea	1916	Stuart Paton	United States
Twenty Thousand Leagues under the Sea	1954	Richard Fleischer	United States
2001: A Space Odyssey	1968	Stanley Kubrick	Great Britain
Undersea Kingdom (serial)	1936	B. Reeves Eason and Joseph Kane	United States
Ultimate Warrior, The	1975	Robert Clouse	United States
Unearthly Stranger	1963	John Krish	Great Britain
Unidentified Flying Objects	1956	Winston Jones	United States
Visit to a Small Planet	1959	Norman Taurog	United States
Voyage to the Bottom of the Sea	1961	Irwin Allen	United States
Voyage to the Planet of Prehistoric Women	1968	Peter Bogdanovich	United States
War Game, The	1965	Peter Watkins	Great Britain
War of the Worlds	1953	Byron Haskin	United States
Way . . . Way Out	1966	Gordon Douglas	United States
Westworld	1973	Michael Crichton	United States
When Worlds Collide	1951	Rudolph Maté	United States
Wild in the Streets	1963	Barry Shear	United States
World, the Flesh and the Devil, The	1958	Ranald MacDougall	United States
World Without End	1956	Edward Bernds	United States
Zardoz	1973	John Boorman	Great Britain
Zero Population Growth	1971	Michael Campus	United States

Note: The above films are only a representative sample of the broad spectrum of science fiction films, in which are included both key *genre* films and less notable examples.

conventions

These are annual gatherings of fans. Mostly conventions involve showing SF films, having discussions about various aspects of SF and fandom, drinking and talking through the night, buying and selling magazines and books and generally socializing either within, or regardless of, the confines of an official convention programme. The conventions are held at hotels and are run by volunteer groups of fans who sometimes bid against each other for the dubious privilege of organizing them, and sometimes inherit their roles from friends from the previous year.

Conventions are held in most countries where there are fans. Britain has four regularly: Eastercons, of which there have been 28 since the war besides a handful of wartime and prewar conventions, attract up to 500 people every year; Novacons, held in November with an attendance of about 300; Silicons, held during August bank holiday with about 50 fans; and a small purely socialcon held in January or February. These last two have minimal or no programming. In America, besides the World Conventions, there are many regional cons: the Westercons on the West Coast draw over a thousand people as do the Boskones (on the East coast) sometimes.

The Philcons in Philadelphia have been going since 1936, longer than any other American convention. There are conventions throughout Europe: the Eurocons are held in different countries every year; Wiencons held in Vienna; Beneluxcons held alternate years in Belgium and Holland; and many more. Australia has had 16 national conventions (and has hosted one Worldcon) and numerous regional cons.

Worldcons

For almost 20 years from 1939 the Worldcons were totally an American affair, but the rules were changed eventually so that one year out of four or five the convention could be held outside the United States but during the intermediate years it was held in either East, West or Mid-America. The Worldcons are thus only a little more global than the American 'World' series in baseball – out of 36 Worldcons so far 32 have been held in the United States. However, they are the biggest SF conventions in the world – the 1974 convention attracted over 4400 people. In addition the most famous SF award, the Hugo, is voted for and presented at Worldcons.

Year	Convention	Location	Guest of Honour	Attendance
1939	Nycon 1	New York	Frank R. Paul	200
1940	Chicon 1	Chicago	Edward E. Smith Ph.D.	128
1941	Devention	Denver	Robert Heinlein	90
1946	Pacificon 1	Los Angeles	A.E. van Vogt and E. Mayne Hull	130
1947	Philcon 1	Philadelphia	John W. Campbell Jr	200
1948	Torcon 1	Toronto	Robert Bloch and Bob Tucker	200
1949	Cinvention	Cincinnati	Lloyd A. Eshbach and Ted Carnell	190
1950	Norwescon	Portland	Anthony Boucher	400
1951	Nolacon	New Orleans	Fritz Leiber	190
1952	Chicon 11	Chicago	Hugo Gernsback	370
1953	Philcon 11	Philadelphia	Willy Ley	750
1954	SF Con	San Francisco	John W. Campbell Jr	700
1955	Clevention	Cleveland	Isaac Asimov	380
1956	Newyorcon	New York	Arthur Clarke	850
1957	Loncon 1	London	John W. Campbell Jr	268
1958	Solacon	Los Angeles	Richard Matheson	322
1959	Detention	Detroit	Poul Anderson and John Berry	371

Year	Convention	Location	Guest of Honour	Attendance
1960	Pittcon	Pittsburgh	James Blish	568
1961	Seacon	Seattle	Robert Heinlein	300
1962	Chicon III	Chicago	Theodore Sturgeon	950
1963	Discon I	Washington DC	Murray Leinster	800
1964	Pacificon II	Oakland	Edmond Hamilton and Leigh Brackett and Forrest J. Ackerman	523
1965	Loncon II	London	Brian Aldiss	350
1966	Tricon	Cleveland	L. Sprague de Camp	850
1967	Nycon III	New York	Lester del Rey and Bob Tucker	1500
1968	Baycon	Oakland	Philip Jose Farmer and Walt Daugherty	1430
1969	St Louiscon	St Louis	Jack Gaughan and Eddie Jones	1534
1970	Heicon	Heidelberg	Robert Silverberg and E.C. Tubb and Herbert W. Franke	620
1971	Noreascon	Boston	Clifford Simak and Harry Warner Jr	1600
1972	Lacon	Los Angeles	Fred Pohl and Buck and Juanita Coulson	2007
1973	Torcon II	Toronto	Robert Bloch and William Rotsler	2900
1974	Discon II	Washington DC	Roger Zelazny and Jay Kay Klein	4435
1975	Aussiecon	Melbourne	Ursula Le Guin and Susan Wood and Mike Glicksohn and Donald Tuck	606
1976	Midamericon	Kansas City	Robert Heinlein	2800
1977	Suncon	Miami Beach	Jack Williamson	2050
1978	Iguanacon	Phoenix	Harlan Ellison and Bill Bowers	
1979	SeaCon	Brighton	Fritz Leiber and Brian Aldiss	

authors

Robert Holdstock

Robert Holdstock was born in Kent, in 1948, surrounded by gorse, pebbles and a very bleak stretch of the Romney Marsh. He read Applied Zoology and Parasitology at the University College of North Wales, Bangor, and in 1970 moved to London to obtain a Master's degree in Medical Zoology and then take up research in immunology. He has been reading and writing science fiction since he was nine years old; his first sf story was published in *New Worlds* and he has had work in *New Writings in SF, Science Fiction Monthly, Stopwatch, Andromeda, Vortex,* and *Supernova.* He sold his first novel, *Eye Among the Blind,* in 1975 and took the opportunity to turn freelance. He now lives and works in a converted Mill house in Hertford, England; his two most recent novels are *Earthwind 1977* and *The Necromancer 1978.*

Chris Morgan

An economics graduate and former industrial executive, Chris Morgan relinquished a lucrative, self-important and soul destroying cultural desert of big business to become a full time writer of and about science fiction. He has written reviews for *Vector* and *Foundation, the review of science fiction,* and has published several science fiction short stories. His interests include natural history, the arts and the expansion of his collection of speculative fiction books. He now lives in Dorset, England.

Harry Harrison

Harry Harrison was born in Connecticut in 1925. He studied art in New York, breaking only to serve in the US army as a machine-gun instructor during World War II. He was a commercial illustrator for a while, then art director and editor of various magazines. When he began writing he also began travelling, and has lived in Mexico, England, Italy, Denmark, Spain and California. He now lives in Ireland. He is well known for his *Deathworld* novels and for his *Stainless Steel Rat* stories; other memorable works include *Make Room, Make Room! 1966,* a very powerful novel about overpopulation at the end of this century, which inspired a film; *Captive Universe 1969, In Our Hands the Stars 1970,* and a host of very funny sf novels, including, *Bill the Galactic Hero 1965, The Technicolour Time Machine 1967, A Transatlantic Tunnel, Hurrah! 1972* and *Star Smashers of the Galaxy Rangers 1973.* He has edited numerous anthologies, including *Nova,* and with Brian Aldiss *The Years Best SF* (from *1968*) and *The Astounding-Analog Reader.*

Malcolm Edwards

Malcolm Edwards was born in London in 1949. He read Social Anthropology at Cambridge, England, then moved back to London to work in a library, and then as sf editor at Victor Gollancz. He is now the administrator of the Science Fiction Foundation at the North East London Polytechnic. He has been seriously involved with science fiction for seven years; he was editor of *Vector*, the journal of the British Science Fiction Association, for two years, and now is editor of *Foundation, the review of Science Fiction*. He has written sf criticism and reviews for a number of magazines.

Michael Ashley

Michael Ashley was born in Middlesex in 1948. He soon became interested in science fiction by way of BBC Radio series *Journey Into Space* and the adventures of 'Captain Condor' in the *Lion* comic. He began research to locate stories his father had told him about. In 1965 he became an active fan writing articles and stories for most of the leading fanzines in UK and US. He married in 1972 and began editing sf and horror anthologies in 1973; he has to date compiled ten books including a five-volume *History of the Science Fiction Magazine* and a two-volume *Best of British SF*. Others include *Weird Legacies*, *SF Choice 77* and *Souls in Metal*. Also compiled a *Who's Who in Horror and Fantasy Fiction*. He has contributed to *Science Fiction Monthly* and *The International SF Yearbook* and is currently working on *The Seven Wonders of the World*.

Christopher Priest

Christopher Priest was born in Cheshire in 1943 and spent his childhood in the north of England. After leaving school he moved to London where he spent nine years discovering that he and the accountancy profession were not made for each other. He started writing in 1963 and became a full-time writer in 1968, publishing stories in *Science Fantasy*, *New Worlds*, *New Writings in SF*, *Galaxy*, *Amazing Stories*, and *Quark*. His first novel, *Indoctrinaire*, was published in 1970, followed by *Fugue for a Darkening Island 1972*. He won the British Science Fiction award for his third novel, *Inverted World 1974* and was nominated for a Hugo. His two most recent novels are *The Space Machine 1976* and *A Dream of Wessex 1977*. He has published two volumes of stories, *Real Time World 1974* and *An Infinite Summer 1978*. He lives and works in Harrow and is a part time teacher of science fiction appreciation at London University.

Brian Stableford

Brian Stableford was born in Shipley, Yorkshire, in 1948. He has degrees in biology and sociology, and is currently lecturing in the sociology department of the University of Reading, where he is working on both a D.Phil thesis on The Sociology of Science Fiction, and a history of Witchcraft. His published books include *Cradle of the Sun 1969*, *The Blind Worm 1970*, *The Days of Glory 1971*, *In the Kingdom of the Beasts 1971*, *Day of Wrath 1971*, *To Challenge Chaos 1972*, *Halcyon Drift 1972*, *Rhapsody in Black 1973*, *Promised Land 1974*, *The Paradise Game 1974*, *Swan Song 1975*, *The Face of Heaven 1976*, *The Mind Riders 1976*, *Critical Threshold 1977*. He has written a non-fiction book, *The Mysteries of Modern Science 1977* and is currently working on a novel called *The Walking Shadow*.

Douglas Hill

Douglas Hill, author, journalist and publishing consultant, has been reviewing science fiction (pseudonymously) over fifteen years for the weekly newspaper *Tribune,* of which he is now literary editor. He has also written sf for adults and children, has acted as sf adviser for several leading publishers, and the fifth anthology he has edited in the sf/fantasy fields was published in early 1978. Outside sf he has written more than two dozen non-fiction books on such subjects as North American history, English history, popular folklore and literary biography. At present he is working on two separate sf adventure series for younger readers.

Patrick Moore

Patrick Moore was born in 1923 in Middlesex, England. He served as an officer in the Royal Air Force during the Second World War, flying as a navigator. From 1965–68 he lived in Northern Ireland and was the Director of the Armagh Planetarium. He is a regular television broadcaster and writer of science fiction novels. He now lives in Southern England and has his own private observatory – a 15-inch reflector being the main telescope. He is a member of the International Astronomical Union, and a Fellow of the Royal Astronomical Society. In 1967 he was awarded the Order of the British Empire (OBE). He is currently Vice-President of the British Astronomical Association.

Alan Frank

Alan Frank was raised and educated in East Africa. He read science at the University of Cape Town, South Africa and Medicine at Cambridge, England. A longtime science fiction buff, his first radio play was broadcast when he was only 16. Since then, he has written and broadcast sf regularly. Although he wasted 16 years in advertising in Europe and the Caribbean, he has had the distinction of visiting the moon four times – albeit on film sets. He is a prolific writer of science fiction in the cinema as well as having a regular film review column. He was an erstwhile jury member at the 3rd Festival of Fantastic Films (1976) held in Belgium. He is married with two children and lives besides the river Thames, London.

David Hardy

David Hardy was born in Birmingham, England in 1936. He first began to paint his planetary landscapes in the 1950s and from here progressed to produce drawings for television programmes, roughs for stage productions, record sleeves, book jackets and factual stories for comics. He is strongly motivated to produce anything which would help project to the public an accurate picture of space and space travel. In 1972, he produced thirty six paintings for his major co-authored title, *Challenge of the Stars.* His work is now in demand in fields far removed from astronomy and space research, and he is especially popular with modern rock musicians. His work has an international following with originals decorating the walls of authorities such as Arthur Clarke, Carl Sagan, Isaac Asimov, the Smithsonian Institution, Washington D.C. and the Marshall Space Flight Center, Alabama.

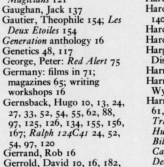
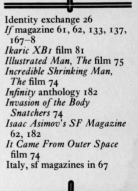

ACKNOWLEDGMENTS

The publishers would like to thank the following individuals and organizations for supplying material and information for use in this book:
Greg Pickersgill, Susan Anne Raven, David Langford, Sheila Holdstock, F. G. Smallmount, Viv Croot, Dot Houghton.
Transparencies from: Granada Publishing Ltd., Hutchinson Publishing Group Ltd., Penguin Books Ltd., Sphere Books Ltd., Transworld Publishers Ltd.
Magazines and books from the collections of: Michael Ashley, John Baxter, Malcolm Edwards, John Eggling, Robert Holdstock, Roger Peyton, Gerry Webb, Peter Weston.

The following are thanked for their kind permission to reproduce the illustrations in the book:
Academy *Space Cruiser 1977* 81; Chris Achilleos 45, 115; Aubrey Company/Paul N. Lazarus III/AIP *Futureworld 1976* 80 below; David Bergen 24 above and below left, 49, (Ace Books) 185; Berkley Publishing Corporation 171 above; Alex Brown 198 centre and 217 below, 218 centre left; Sarah Brown Agency (Peter Elson) 94 above, 188 (Fred Gambino) 98 above; Mike Carter 219 centre right; Columbia Pictures Industries *Close Encounters of The Third Kind 1977* 68-69, 84; Cooper-Bridgeman Library 124; Eagle-Lion *Destination Moon 1950* 73 above; East Kent Gazette 218 centre right; Ediciones Dronte 156 left and right; Dean Ellis (Ace Books) 44 below left; Peter Elson 76, 142-143, 145 below; Mary Evans Picture Library 20, 21 left, 22 below, 23 below, 24 below right, 25, 27, 88 above right; Vincent di Fate case, (Pyramid Books) 148; Virgil Finlay © Beverly C. Finlay 17; Folio (Mervyn) 1, 12, (Joe Petagno) 136-137, 184, (Ean Taylor) 102 below; Chris Foss 2-3, 32 above, 48 above, 89, 96, 100, 103, 150; Frank Kelly Freas 8-9, 97 above, 127, 137 above right, (Analog 1972) 122-123; Jack Gaughan (Pyramid Books) 102 above; Goodtimes/Gladiole *The Final Programme 1973* 79 above; David Hardy 109 below, 147; Hung-Art/Sandor Leidenfrost 157; James Jackson 149 above; Eddie Jones 128-129, 152-153; Pauline Jones 166 below; Peter Jones – Solar Wind Ltd. 44 above right, 86-87, 94-95, 116-117, 168 above,

170; Josh Kirby 111 below right, 134; J. K. Klein 6-7, 197, 198-199; Lancer Books 34 above; Brian Lewis – Linden Artists Ltd. 139 below; Mike Little 165 below; London Film Productions *Things to Come 1936* 74; Mansell Collection 21 right, 22 above, 125 above, (Wm Collins, Sons & Co. Ltd.) 23 above; Mayflower Books 173 above; Metro-Goldwyn-Mayer *No Blade of Grass 1970* 77, *Soylent Green 1973* 80 above; Charles Moll (Pocket Books) 179 above; Chris Moore 28-29, 46-47, 138; New English Library (Bruce Pennington) 131 above, 173 below, (Tim White) 99 below, 135, 179 below; Paramount Pictures Corp. *Star Trek 1978* 85; Pearsons Magazine/ Warwick Goble 144 centre left; David Pelham 164, 169; Joe Petagno 34 below, 35, 108 above, 162-163, 167 above;Howard Purcell 14 above left; Tony Roberts endpapers, 186 below left; David Roe 174-175; John Schoenherr 41 below, 137 below right, 144 above right; Szafran (Signet Books – New American Library) 108 centre; Twentieth Century Fox *Star Wars 1977* 82, 83; U.F.A. *Metropolis 1926* 70; Universal *Flash Gordon* 73 below; Boris Vallejo 113, 119, 140 above; Warner Bros. *The Ultimate Warrior 1975* 79 above; Warner Bros./Polaris *A Clockwork Orange 1971* 78; Helmut Wenske 155; Patrick Woodruffe cover art for 'Waldo' by Robert Heinlein, published by Pan Books 101; Young Artists (Jim Burns) 15, 33, 38, 172, 180-181, 183, (Peter Goodfellow) 106, 177, 186 above right, (Colin Hay) 43 below, 92, 121, 178, (Bob Layzell) 31, 36, 40, 90, 110 above, 187, (Angus McKie) 16, 30, 91, 146, (Tony Roberts) 11, 182.

Also the following commissioned artists for supplying original art work:
Joe Petagno 6-7, 104-105; Malcolm Pointer 50-51, 190-191 and all line illustrations in the text.

Thanks are given to the following publishers for the use of their magazines:
Robert J. Abramson & Associates Inc./Galaxy Publishing Corporation, Condé Nast Publications Inc., Jean-Pierre Dionnet, Hamilton & Co. (Stafford), Love Romances Publishing Co., Mercury Press, Nova Publications, Popular Publications, Scion Ltd., Standard Magazine Inc., Street and Smith Publications Inc., Sol Cohen of Ultimate Publications, Universal – Tandem Publishing Co. Ltd.